EUROPEAN PAGANISM

EUROPEAN PAGANISM

The realities of cult from antiquity to the
Middle Ages

Ken Dowden

London and New York

First published 2000
by Routledge
11 New Fetter Lane, London EC4P 4EE

Simultaneously published in the USA and Canada
by Routledge
29 West 35th Street, New York, NY 10001

Routledge is an imprint of the Taylor & Francis Group

Typeset in Garamond by J&L Composition Ltd, Filey, North Yorkshire
Printed and bound in Great Britain by
St Edmundsbury Press, Bury St Edmunds, Suffolk

British Library Cataloguing in Publication Data
A catalogue record for this book is available from the British Library

Library of Congress Cataloguing in Publication Data
Dowden, Ken, 1950–
European paganism : the realities of cult from antiquity to the
Middle Ages / Ken Dowden.
p. cm.
Includes bibliographical references and indexes.
1. Europe—Religion. 2. Paganism—Europe—History. I. Title.
BL689.D68   1999
200′.94–dc21   99–28007
CIP

ISBN 0–415–12034–9

CONTENTS

CONTENTS

CONTENTS

ILLUSTRATIONS

ACKNOWLEDGEMENTS

The following is a list of sources and acknowledgements for permission to reproduce figures:

The principal sources for most line artwork included in the text are: J. von Falke, *Hellas und Rom: Eine Kulturgeschichte des klassischen Altertums* (Stuttgart n.d. [1878–80]); J. Scherr, *Zwei Jahrtausende deutschen Lebens kulturgeschichtlich geschildert* (Stuttgart n.d. [1876–8]); and W. Zimmermann, *Illustrierte Geschichte des deutschen Volkes*, vol. 1, Stuttgart 1873.

Figure 2.2 is from *Temples and Sanctuaries of Ancient Greece: A Companion Guide*, courtesy of Thames and Hudson, 1973, p.161.
The source for Figure 7.2 is the frontispiece of Antoine Chrysostome Quatremère de Quincy, *Le Jupiter olympien ou l'art de la sculpture antique* (Paris 1814), courtesy of the Getty Research Institute, Research Library. The source for Figure 7.5 is O. Henne am Rhyn, *Kulturgeschichte des deutschen Volkes*, vol. 1 (Berlin 1892), p.20.

Thanks are due to Dr Terry Slater, School of Geography, the University of Birmingham for the use of photos in Figures 6.1 and 12.1, also to Richard Stoneman for the use of the photo in Figure 2.3 and James Dowden for Figure 2.1.

FOREWORD

I was once invited to write forty pages on European paganism to a very tight deadline. This book has grown out of that experience in data-compression. I have always believed that smaller areas were best understood in larger contexts and in many ways the whole question of paganism in Europe requires the largest of views. The largest of views, however, takes more room and more time than one would ever imagine, and what started in the mind's eye as a short book giving a good representative sample of the range of pagan phenomena has grown into a larger book which still seems to leave so much out. I would like a lifetime to write the real, encyclopaedic version of this book. But it might stretch to a volume or two . . .

My aim was not to write a history of pagan Europe – that has been done with real commitment by Jones and Pennick (1995) – nor to write a history of the decline and fall of paganism to Christianity, which is just as well as Fletcher has now written a glorious book (1997) on just that subject. Rather, I wanted to show paganism in action, see what it looked and felt like, let the reader see the evidence and listen to the authors, even boring old Caesarius of Arles and grumpy Maximus of Turin.

There are clear problems of evidence and it is truer in this field than in others that it is the privileging of evidence and even its actual existence that drives writing on the subject. I did not want to be evidenced into a corner by treating each European culture separately – Greeks, Romans, Celts, Germans, Slavs, Balts. In few cases does anything like a representative range of evidence exist. The result could so easily be a patchy and inconsequential discussion of routine topics: Druids, ossuaries, lakes and gods of whom only their name is known for Celts; grand Wagnerian mythology for north Germans, with a bow to Tacitus for the south. Rather, I decided that topic by topic was the best way and most illuminating way. There are questions to be asked about springs and groves and time and temples and priests. They are interesting questions which can be illustrated from across the range of cultures, however thin the information from a particular culture.

As I have tried to focus on living paganism and the witness of the written word, I have been less interested but not uninterested in the deductions to be made from archaeology. I have cited archaeological material where it helps the picture under discussion but not gone back to prehistory. This has also dictated the time period that I have allowed. Wherever there is a written account of some aspect of paganism, I have wanted to be able to include it. That has taken me from the beginnings of historical Greek civilisation to the end of European paganism in fifteenth-century Lithuania and on to some survivals. I have also had to make a choice: I could, and perhaps should, have done more to research recent archaeology, but I think that however unfashionably elderly some of my bibliography and many of my authors may be, there was a greater danger that their achievement and interest should be forgotten and lost. English-language readers have in a real sense not had access to this material and might never. Herodotos would understand.

I am a classicist by training, profession and mentality. I have not dealt with neopaganism at all, because, in a stern classical way, I am unconvinced of the security of the alleged links between ancient paganism and modern. I may tend to take Greek and Roman things for granted, but in a way I have tried to repress them. Thus Greek and Roman material is in principle used in those areas which are comparable with other European paganisms and not elsewhere. Thus I have made no room for mystery religions (Mithras, Isis ...) or for philosophy and mysticism (Plato, Stoics, Pythagoreans, Orphics, Plotinus, Iamblichos and theurgy). I should probably have made room for oracles, but, I'm sorry, I haven't. And emperor cult has no parallel outside the old Roman Empire. On the other hand, classicists themselves should find here a wealth of evidence which may at times cast interesting light on their home cultures.

I am also a European, one who deplored the insularity of British politics and culture in the 1980s and early 1990s. But there is nothing mystical about Europe. It is a convenient area to think with, but a fuller and yet more impossible book could be written about the pagan phenomena I have isolated if one looked across the whole world – though it might tend to the inconsequentiality of Frazer, darting across the globe to cite yet another stultifying custom. Occasionally, if inadequately, I have allowed myself out to see the Near East or India. Nevertheless, there is some sense in restricting one's attention to Europe if there is significance in the Indo-European hypothesis, certainly one of eighteenth- and nineteenth-century scholarship's finest achievements. The core of languages from Welsh to Sanskrit originates in a language once spoken, perhaps around 3500 BC, perhaps just north of the Black Sea. Though our Heisenbergian age has tried to sacrifice this hypothesis to the great god of Ambivalence, anyone who actually understands historical linguistics will realise that it is fundamentally unshaken and that it has cultural

xiv

implications, even if the age has long since gone when we could envisage offensively Aryan warriors sweeping away earlier populations. (Some reflection is occasioned by the discovery of a current inhabitant of Cheddar sharing the mitochondrial DNA of a man of millennia earlier.) Language and religion are both cultural manifestations and there is no obvious reason why one should move without the other. Both balance innovation with conservatism, migrants with substratum. In the pagan cultures which we examine there is at least some sense that we are looking at offshoots of a single culture, however refreshed by local encounters and population mixture. In that sense, however limited (and it is not shared by Basques, Hungarians, Finns or Estonians), there is some prospect of coherence in Europe. That this is so becomes chillingly clear in the last chapter.

It is certainly exhilarating, branching out into the whole of European culture. In so doing one quickly finds where the high standards prevail among authors. The Germans in particular have made some contributions of startling quality. I have been indebted to de Vries's account of German religion (1956) and to so much of the commentaries in the huge *Monumenta Germaniae historica*, but above all I have been overwhelmed by the stupendous erudition of Jacob Grimm (1875; 'Jacob Grimms meisterhaftes Monumentalwerk', Jente 1921: iii) and I hope I have learnt from his way of briefly dealing with fascinating topics and copiously showing the real evidence. Grimm started from the concept of 'god'. That is the one thing I have felt unable to do. In particular, I do not feel that the trivial discussions of lists of gods, which so often pass for the section on 'religion' in books on this or that culture, are at all satisfactory. Cult is what matters. If gods are to be handled, they are a very complicated ideological problem and need quite separate discussion, just as mythology does – cult and story-book rarely belong together and have only been forced together in order to deliver pseudo-bibles for non-credal cultures. So under 'gods' I have handled only a few themes which seemed to demand attention. I have made no attempt to list the gods of Europe.

The Christian authors seem important to me because it was they who had to confront paganism, even in its tired and degenerate folksy forms. We need to hear what they say and to understand the limitations of their vision. They were at times tiresome and self-righteous, unscientific and lacking in human understanding, but of most of them it must be said that they were men (rarely women) of principle. They also were the agents of the urban civilisation to which we are the heirs. They created the new Europe, in many ways repressive and regrettable, but history was against the pagans and that is why we have difficulty even understanding what they were and what they did. I hope that this book for all its shortcomings and omissions will give readers access to much more information and a much fuller view than they ever had before.

I particularly thank Jan Bremmer and Ronald Hutton, scholars of formidable erudition in their different fields who have been particularly generous with information, guidance and encouragement. Colleagues in various disciplines at Birmingham and around the country have graciously suffered inquisitions about such things as oak trees and Old High German orthography. Library staff, even in these curious times when any book written before 1980 is obsolete, have been helpful beyond the call of duty, particularly in the University of Birmingham and at the splendid Oxford libraries, as various as paganism itself. It may seem sycophantic to praise one's publisher, but I cannot pass over Richard Stoneman who has, as ever, been unfailingly helpful, constructive, imaginative and supportive, despite my repeated delays. And a final word of thanks to family – to Jayne for always finding another *oppidum* to march around, to Sophie for her magical control of her father's moods, and to James for insistent cross-examination and alarmingly well-informed suggestions for further study.

Birmingham,
All Souls' Day 1998

HOW TO USE THIS BOOK

There is a lot of chronology and geography in this book. To help with chronology, I have included a time-chart on pp. xx–xxi. For geography, there would be no solution short of a map of Europe. I have therefore tried to give a sense of the location of often rather obscure places so that the reader may more or less locate the place from easily obtainable good road atlases and within limits from the in principle ideal, but in practice rather thin, route-planning CD-ROMs. In the case of France I have usually specified the département and in other countries the nearest equivalent. I have also specified nearby towns you may hope to find in the index of an atlas.

The book is full of quotations, largely from ancient and medieval writers, sometimes from modern. My aim has been to show, as near as I can, at first hand the actual evidence for statements about pagan religions. I intend the book to have the virtues of a sourcebook without damaging its readability. The quoted texts, often referred to in footnotes in other books, are not always easy to find, much less to find in English. I have therefore included at the end of this book, within the bibliography, a section listing where you can find texts and translations of particular authors and also giving some basic details, mainly dates, for the many Christian writers. Translation is an area where I hope this book will be useful. The age has long since gone when, in the manner of Grimm, evidence could be heaped together with formidable erudition in whatever language. My undergraduate students, to whom I owe much, are some of the cleverest people of their generation in Britain, but French is a trial for them and other languages are usually off the map. An important function of this book, therefore, is to make accessible what has been written in Greek and Latin and other ancient languages and above all the material brought forward in modern works in the variety of languages that you may see in the bibliography. I have tried to keep as exactly as I can to the content of the original even if that leaves the translation rather wooden.

The algebra of the footnotes is required to record where evidence has been found and who said what where. There can be few things more maddening to writers or readers than not being able to recall or discover the evidence for some interesting point. Given the variety of sources for the information in this book and the variety of interests that will lead readers to it, it is more than usually necessary to be meticulous about documentation. The algebra, however off-putting, can be decoded fairly simply. Author plus year (e.g., Leite de Vasconcellos 1905: ii.266) means that there is an entry in the bibliography which will tell you exactly which book is at issue; ii.266 means 'volume two, page 266'. The first part of the bibliography should help you find references to ancient and medieval authors, though in the nature of things you may well need a good university library to find them. When the reference is of the form 'Pausanias 8.7.2' it means that this is in the Greek author Pausanias (see bibliography, section 1) and comes from 'book 8, chapter 7, section 2'. If the work is a single-book work, e.g. 'Maximus of Turin, *Sermon* 63.1', then chapter (or in this case, sermon) number 63, section 1 is indicated. Numbering is usually the same no matter what edition you use, but there are exceptions and I have tried to make clear in the bibliography which edition I was using. A final bibliographical point: for some collections of texts, encyclopaedias and so on, I have used abbreviations, e.g. *PL* or *LPG*, which I have decoded at the top of the bibliography.

Where I am not sure what a passage means or whether it makes any sense at all, I have put (?) in the text. Where I am offering an explanation or comment during a translation, it is in square brackets: [i.e. Thursday]. Where I am presenting the meaning of a word quoted e.g. in Latin, or the actual Latin for the word so translated, it is in round parentheses: (*luxuria*); I also use parentheses to fill out the sense of a sentence: 'they did not dare to cut (the groves)'.

Quotations often bear on more than the point currently at issue. Should I repeat quotations? But that is so wasteful. Should I cite only those parts which bear on the current issue? But it is not always possible to detach only that part and even where possible it destroys our perception of the character of the source by fragmentation and means that one is forever setting the same passage in context. In the end I have chosen to let passages run on, so that the reader may indeed gauge their character, and to pick them up again later when they are needed, with a 'see also' cross-reference.

An asterisk is used: (a) in the case of individual words, to indicate that this word is hypothetical and is not directly evidenced, like, for instance, all Indo-European words (*treyes*, 'three') or the Germanic god *Tiwaz; (b) in the case of books and articles, to indicate that I have been unable to consult this work, e.g. *J.-G. Bulliot, 'Le culte des eaux sur les plateaux éduens', *Mémoires lus à la Sorbonne*, 1868. I have consulted all that are not so marked.

< . . . > Use of these angle brackets in an old text means that the editor of the text (or myself) does not believe that the text makes sense as it stands, that there is something missing and that the text contained within the angle brackets should be added. Our manuscripts are nearly always copies rather than the author's original, and a number of errors are usually made in the copying process.

Notes on navigation

- Where the whole word 'Chapter' is used, it refers to a chapter *in this book of mine*, e.g. 'Helmold 2.108 (Chapter 7)' means: 'turn to Chapter 7 of this book and you find this passage discussed or quoted'. Otherwise I use 'ch.'
- Where the text says '(above)' or '(below)', this indicates earlier or later *in the same chapter*.

Notes on languages

OHG is *Old High German*, the ancestor of modern ('New High') German (rather than of Low German – Dutch, the dialects of North Germany that border on Dutch, English too).

MHG is *Middle High German*, the stage in-between OHG and Modern High German.

OE is *Old English* or 'Anglo-Saxon', the ancestor of today's English.

ON is *Old Norse*, the ancestor of the Scandinavian languages.

AUTHORS AND EVENTS: A TIME-CHART

	Authors	Roman Empire/Holy Roman Empire	'Barbarians'/outside the Empire
100s BC	Writers on Spain: Asklepiades of Myrlea, ?Sosthenes of Knidos; 90s? Poseidonios in Gaul; 70s? Metrodoros of Skepsis; 50s Caesar in Gaul	101 Cimbri and Teutones invade Italy	106 Servilius Caepio raids the lake at Toulouse
99–1 BC	55–AD? Timagenes in Rome		
47	Varro's *Human and Divine Antiquities*; 30 Diodoros' *History*		
AD 1–99	18 Strabo, *Geography*; 50s Pliny the elder, *Wars with Germany*; 70s Pliny the elder, *Natural History*; 98 Tacitus, *Germania*		9 Quinctilius Varus killed with his legions in the Teutoburgerwald
100–299	160s? Pausanias, *Guide to Greece*; 258 † Cyprian	c. 225 dedication to Mars Thingsus	
300s	382 † Ulfila; 380 † Zeno of Verona; 397 † Martin of Tours; 397 † Ambrose	303–11 the Great Persecution; 312 Constantine Emperor; 353 sacrifices banned; 360–2 Julian the Apostate; c. 375? Chrocus destroys the temple of Mercury at the Puy de Dôme; 385 execution of Priscillian; 389 sacrifices banned	376 Goths cross Danube
400s	c. 420 † Maximus of Turin; c. 420 † Sulpicius Severus; 430 † Augustine (of Hippo)	416 pagans excluded from public service; 438 the *Theodosian code*; 451 further decree against paganism on your property	449 arrival of pagan 'Anglo-Saxons' in Britain; 461? † Patrick; 496? Clovis appeals to the God of Clothilde
500s	543 Caesarius of Arles; 551 Jordanes on the Goths; 573 Martin of Braga on pagans; c. 594 Gregory of Tours; c. 600 Venantius Fortunatus	511–695 Merovingian church councils	560 last Feast of Tara (Ireland); 596 Gregory sends Augustine; 597 conversion of Ethelbert

	Authors	Roman Empire/Holy Roman Empire	'Barbarians'/outside the Empire
600s	604 Gregory I, the Great		605 † Augustine 627 Edwin baptised at York
700s	731 Bede's *History* 750/780? *Indiculus superstitionum*	742 Laws of Carloman	Conversion of Frisians 754 † Boniface Conversion of Saxons: c. 780 Irminsul chopped down
800s	801 Nennius on Britons 840 † Einhard 856 † Hrabanus Maurus of Mainz 865 Rudolph of Fulda 882 † Hinkmar of Reims	814 † Charlemagne Arrival of pagan Normans in France	Arrival of pagan 'Danes' in Britain 864 conversion of Bulgaria 869 † Cyril
900s	990s Aelfric *On False Gods*	911 Normans converted	962–92 Poland becomes Christian 988 Russia decides for (Orthodox) Christianity 997 Hungary Christian
1000s	c. 1000: the *Dindshenchas* 1010 Burchard of Worms, *Decrees* 1015 Dudo of St Quentin 1018 Thietmar of Merseburg 1075 Adam of Bremen		1000 Iceland Christian 1035 † Canute 1050–1150 Denmark and Norway become Christian
1100s	(oldest Irish manuscripts) 1118 the (Russian) *Primary Chronicle* 1175 Helmold of Bosau		1128 Pomerania Christian 1169 Rügen taken
1200s	1208 Saxo Grammaticus on Danes		1236 Hungary reincorporates pagans 1226–83 Teutonic Knights take Prussia Lithuania a pagan state 1251 Mindaugas a Christian of sorts
1300 +	1326 Peter of Duisberg on Prussians 1442 † Michael Junge on Prussians 1480 Jan Dlugosz on Poles 1551 Johann Maletius on Balts 1630s/40s Paul Einhorn on Prussians		1414 Samogitia becomes Christian

Notes: † death of
? date not certain

1

APPROACHING PAGANISM

What is 'paganism'? Where did it exist in Europe and by what stages did it disappear? What do authors tell us about European paganism in its hey-day? These are the questions which this introductory chapter addresses. We shall look later at the stylised views that Christian authors have of dying paganism, in Chapter 8.

PAGANS, SO PRIMITIVE

Shortly before the Second World War, the editor of a translation of medieval books of penance began his introduction with the observation that these documents 'were employed in administering a religious disci-pline to our forefathers during their transition from paganism to Chris-tianity and from barbarism to civilization'.[1] Thus our forefathers had ready to hand convenient repressive codes, as hallmarks of their transition to civilisation, which told them how many days penance they must do if, due to overeating and overdrinking, they vomited up the holy wafer and, worse, failed to throw it on the fire (or, even worse again, a dog ate it), or if they committed acts of bestiality or sodomy or masturbated 'with their own hand or someone else's', or burnt down a church, or, catastrophically, saved a soul from Hell that didn't deserve to be saved, or found a cow that had fallen from a rock and wondered whether it was pious to eat it (answer: only if it has shed blood), or sought healing at springs, trees, stones or crossroads. We all have our ideas of what constitutes civilisation and it is perhaps best to be clear at the outset that there is no uniform evolution of civilisation such that barbarity and paganism go hand in hand. To most classicists it will seem that the pagan Greek and Roman civilisations, for all their terrible errors, were at least as 'civilised' as much of the Christian Middle Ages and if it does not seem so, they had better learn another discipline.

Or take this:

> In religion the savage is he who (while often in certain moods, conscious of a far higher moral faith) believes also in ancestral ghosts or spirits of woods and wells that were never ancestral; prays frequently by dint of magic; and sometimes adores inanimate objects, or even appeals to the beasts as supernatural protectors.
>
> Lang 1913: i.34 n.1

From this single sentence we can recognise Andrew Lang's *Myth, ritual and religion* as a product of the Victorian age, confidently rehearsing and implying views which would cause offence in our own age. Yet we should be careful that we do not ourselves slip into this type of view when thinking about our ancestors. Ancient Europeans were not at some primitive stage of intelligence because they practised pagan rites or focused their worship at stones and trees, nor were they superstitious slaves to ghosts, spirits and ancestors. Superstition is in the eye, and religious code, of the beholder. It is not a puzzle that these ancient peoples failed to be Christian and we should abandon the Christianocentric supposition that 'in certain moods' they sensed a 'far higher moral faith', viz. Christianity. It is true that in most modern religions, religious codes of conduct have taken the character of morals, but it is certainly not a necessary feature of religion as such to supply morals to a population – and without religion we are not therefore immoral.

Finally, it may indeed be characteristic of many modern religions, notably Christianity, to promote 'faith' to the extent that nowadays to be a religion is to be a 'faith', preferably a 'living faith'; but students of ancient religion are well aware that paganism did not promote 'faith'. Of course, ancient pagans believed certain things without adequate evidence, but whether they believed 'in' them (a peculiar piece of jargon which we derive from New Testament Greek)[2] is another question. Paganism was not credal, but a matter of observing systems of ritual. Ritual too is a language, one which involvingly defines the place of man in the world. It is no worse than credal or theological language in achieving that objective and in some ways escapes more easily the danger of asserting something which needs to be verified or died for. Paganism can accept the beliefs and practices of others much more readily than more ideological religions. The persecution of the Christians by the Romans was not a matter of crusade or *jihad* and was caused by an unusual and special conflict in views of ritual and society.

'Pagan*ism*' is a misnomer. With its Latin first element (*paganus*, a 'villager') and Greek second (*-ism*, as though it were a system of belief), it is an impossible contradiction. The only pagans who held to systems of belief were, contingently, philosophers who happened also to be pagans and philosophised religion as they philosophised everything else. It was, however, characteristic of philosophy under the Roman Empire that it was drawn increasingly into the description and articulation of religion – the catalyst for the incorporation of theology *within* Christianity. *Paganismus*, a singular religious environment, is a word invented by the fourth-century Christians so that they can talk about 'it' in the same breath that they talk about Christianity and Judaism.[3]

Until the advent of neopaganism, paganism had always been a derogatory term denoting any non-Christian religion. As it is derogatory, it would be accurate but insulting to call the religious practices of Hindus 'pagan'. Because, however, our ancestors find no shelter under a multi-cultural umbrella, are protected by no legislation, will never have to be confronted face to face, and are remote enough to be gratuitously insulted, we have the freedom to call them 'pagans' and mentally to demean their cultures. Thus overwhelmingly 'paganism' refers intolerantly to the pre-Christian religious practices of Europe and that is what it was originally designed for. A *paganus* is a 'villager'; why this should come to mean 'pagan' is not clear. Zahn suggested in 1899 that it extended the sense 'local people, non-combatants' in reference to the 'soldiers' who fight the good fight in the metaphorical army of Christ.[4] More usually, the 'villager' has been seen as a backward country person, a yokel, who is still engaged in the rustic error of paganism. This would then go back to the difficulty which Christianity experienced in advancing from the towns of the Roman Empire into the countryside. The problem is that the word *pagani* applies as much to townspeople as to rural people. To solve this problem, Chuvin (1990: 9) has proposed returning to an earlier interpretation that they 'are quite simply "people of the place," town or country, who preserved their local customs, whereas the *alieni*, the "people from elsewhere," were increasingly Christian'. Be that as it may, paganism did in fact last longest in the countryside and *rustici* ('country-people, rustics') becomes a term interchangeable with *pagani*.[5]

English, and the Germanic languages, have another word, 'heathen', which we owe to the Goth Ulfila (on whom more below). He used the word *háithnô* at Mark 7.26 to translate the Greek word *Hellenis*, 'Greek (female)' in the extended sense of non-Jew ('Gentile' in the Revised English Bible).[6] It looks from the perspective of the other Germanic languages as though it is their equivalent of the Latin *paganus* or *rusticus* and refers once again to those who live at a distance from perceived centres of culture: these inhabit open, rough land, *heaths* in fact. As a matter of fact, the word 'heath' does not turn up in Gothic, but, to be brutal, there is nothing else it can come from. Before it was taken up for use by Christians, I suspect this was a term of comparative civilisation, such as Goths conceived it, and denoted 'someone who lives in wild places'.[7]

Modern 'pagans' are naturally convinced that there is a continuity between ancient pagans and themselves, something which I doubt but am not particularly concerned to dispute.[8] Nor am I qualified to analyse spiritual conditions in late twentieth/early twenty-first-century liberal Europe. One cannot fail, however, to notice a problem of deracination and of disgust with certain aspects of the development of material culture and with established institutions that find it so hard to recognise sea-changes. Thus 'ecology', 'environment' and 'green' have become first buzzwords, then commonplace; and above all urban dwellers have increasingly felt a deep sympathy with the unpolluted landscape and its 'endangered' creatures. A special place is held in this recovery of a Golden Age by the term 'Celtic', a vector to the quasi-primeval inhabitants of the land (so very 'old'), their ancient songs and strange myths, and their mysterious magical powers in a revered landscape. This is a modern mythology, and like all myths works so well because it is not true.[9]

CHRISTIAN ENDING

Roman government

If paganism is simply the negative of Christianity, it follows that the history of the end of paganism is the history of the rise of Christianity. Thus the end of the pagan period is a matter of Christian rulers and councils and bishops stamping out the last vestiges of pagan practice. This naturally happened at different times in different parts of Europe: the arrival of Christianity, and with it the demise of paganism, is part of a wave of culture slowly sweeping across the continent. Barbarian kings may be viewed as signing up for membership of the European Union and entering into profitable communication with great powers by the act of adopting Christianity. One tale, however mythic, may stand as an icon of this religio-cultural influence, the story of how Vladimir, Prince of Rus', the embryonic Russia, convoked a council of boyars in 986/7 in order to decide which religion they should sign up for of those that were being pressed upon them – the Judaism of the Khazars,[10] the Islam of the Bulgars,[11] the Roman Christianity of the Germans, or the Greek orthodoxy of the Byzantines. It is reminiscent of choices offered to Third World

Figure 1.1 Nero and the Christians, an enduring image

countries during the Cold War and the interpretations of Marxism and of western democracy that resulted.

Popular culture hears much of how 'the Romans' persecuted the Christians, fed them to lions and so on, but in fact the Roman Empire was the vehicle by which Christianity conquered Europe. The Great

Persecution of Diocletian in 303–11 (in fact more of others who were driving his policy by then) was the last in the west: in 312 Constantine seized Rome and became its first Christian Emperor. Against all cynicism, there can be no doubt that Constantine, within his own understanding of it, was committed to Christianity and concerned to harmonise and harness it in the interests of the Empire. This was decisive, despite the reversion to paganism of the Emperor Julian ('the Apostate') in 360–3, despite some futile resistance by the tiny, if temporarily indulged, conservative establishment in the city of Rome under Symmachus (*praefectus urbi*, i.e. mayor, 384–5), and despite occasional relapses or concessions to paganism in the wake of the demoralisation caused by barbarian depredations of great urban centres (Trier 406, Rome 410, Bordeaux 414).[12]

Repression of pagans was more sustained than the persecutions of Christians had been. Almost every set of Emperors established their Christian credentials by issuing pompous, repetitive and not therefore wholly effective edicts.[13] In 341–2 sacrifices were banned, but temple buildings outside the walls of Rome were to be left to be the focus of plays and spectacles. In 346 sacrifices were banned on pain of death and temples closed. In 353–8 nocturnal sacrifices, then any sacrifices and any adoration of statues, were banned on pain of death and the temples were closed. In 381–5 sacrifices, day or night, were forbidden and so was divination. Emperors were particularly worried about divination, in whose efficacy they clearly believed: in a standard Roman sacrifice, you inspected the liver and entrails of the sacrificed animal for *signs* (banned 385) and traitors might look for signs of *when the Emperor might die*. Temples, however, might now be opened for meetings: statues were to be considered as mere art, museum stuff – too highbrow a view to last long. At the end of the century, in 389–92, pagan holidays were turned into workdays, sacrifices and visiting temples or sanctuaries at all were banned, as was 'raising eyes to statues', on pain of a hefty fine; even household cult was proscribed. Nor did it matter what class you belonged to. Sacrifices to inspect entrails were treason. And you should not decorate trees with fillets or make turf altars on pain of forfeiting your land and house. Even to connive at sacrifices, as public officials might, meant a fine. This was the period when the great sanctuary and temple of Sarapis at Alexandria, that centre of pilgrimage and devotion, was besieged and sacked.

While the Emperors Arcadius and Honorius were routinely banning sacrifice and entry to shrines and temples in 395, Alaric and his Goths sacked the sanctuary of Eleusis, a day's procession from Athens, where the Mysteries had offered pagans their highest form of religious experience, so they said. Christians built a small church next to the ruins of the great Telesterion and buried their dead in its once holy precinct.[14] Priests now had their historic privileges withdrawn, the state support that no-one seems to have noticed before 396; this specifically included the 'hierophants' who displayed the holies to the *mystai* at Eleusis – so that was it for pagan mystic experience. A little later, in 407, we find temple income being diverted to soldiers, a more urgent need, and in 415 confiscation of sacred places and funds for religious bodies, like the Dendrophoroi – the 'Tree-bearers' who on 22 March each year bore the felled pine tree in a funeral cortège through the streets of Rome for the goddess Cybele and her consort Attis, ever dying young.[15]

As we see from their edicts, the Roman Emperors did not have the firm control of policy and its implementation that modern governments suppose they have. It was not the case that the Emperors decided for Christianity and the population of the whole Empire was suddenly automatically Christian. Though the Church had a new authority to back its cultural revolution, the hard work of conversion and the destruction of first urban, then rural culture remained. The sermons of Zeno of Verona (d. 380) focused on hard work in a world where 'sacrifices in urban temples were regularly practised, *parentalia*, mainly domestic rites for the dead, were still being celebrated and *haruspices*, those experts in the symbolic meaning of the warm innards of sacrificial animals, were still consulted; the official pagan calendar was still being observed' (Lizzi 1990: 162). Christianity had been hitherto very much an urban phenomenon, where in any case official policy mattered more and bishops were generally efficient organisers and campaigners; the more difficult problem was the conversion of the countryside, often owned by powerful urban dwellers. In the sermons of both Zeno and, thirty to forty years later, Maximus of Turin we see a concern that landowners should do something to roll back paganism on their estates and stop in effect conniving at rural paganism centred on the *fana*, buildings too humble to be called temples.

> At this point, Christians, you must ask whether your sacrifice can be accepted if you know every clod, pebble and furrow on neighbouring properties, but are uniquely ignorant of the *fana* that smoke everywhere on your estates – which, if one were to tell the truth, you are cunningly maintaining through an act of pretence. It doesn't take much to prove it. Daily you are conducting actions to prevent people from taking away your [legal] right to temples (*ius templorum*).
>
> Zeno of Verona, *Sermon* 1.25.10

> Apart from a few devout people, there is practically no-one whose lands are unpolluted by idols, practically no estate which can be considered free from the cult of demons. Everywhere the Christian eye is struck, everywhere the most devout mind is

lashed; wherever you turn you see altars of the devil or the profane divinations of the pagans or the heads of cattle fixed to doorways . . . Moreover, whatever master knowingly accepts this sort of gift from his rustics, which he knows is brought to him by polluted hands, what joy will he derive from their possession, whose first-fruits he suspects were tasted by demons before they were tasted by the master? Let us therefore take care equally for ourselves and for our people. And since holy Quadrigesima is upon us, let us call pagans to Christianity and those in preparation (*catechumini*) to baptism!

Maximus of Turin (probably), Sermon 91.2

It would fit this attack on rural paganism if, as Lizzi thinks, the edict of 392 prescribed the same fines for *landowners* conniving at paganism as for the actual performers of the sacrifice.[16]

While Zeno was active in Verona, in the Touraine and its environs St Martin (*c.* 315–97) was confronting active paganism with its sacred trees and festivals, though perhaps other factors than the bravado of St Martin – for instance, recession and the failure of state support – hastened the decline of the Gaulish sanctuaries.[17] Martin's work was not in any case the end of the story. Fifth-century decrees in Rome proceeded to ban pagans from employment in the army, bureaucracy or legal system (416) and continued to declare penalties for paganism more generally.[18]

The laissez-faire attitude of landowners to their property continued sufficiently for a repeat decree in 451 and even, if one can believe him, into the time of Caesarius at Arles (d. 542):

So Christians should neither make vows at trees nor worship at springs if they wish through God's grace to be freed from eternal punishment. Accordingly, anyone who has trees or altars or any sort of *fana* on his land or in his villa or next to his villa where wretched men are accustomed to make any vows – if he does not destroy them and chop them down, he will be without doubt implicated in those sacrileges which take place there.

Caesarius, Sermon 54.5

Germanic invaders

One might have thought that the migration of barbarian tribes into the Western Empire, which brought about its 'Fall', would have stopped Christianity in its tracks and returned Europe to paganism, but that is far from the truth. Despite their military strength, the invading peoples

Figure 1.2 The Goths crossing the Alps into Italy

displayed cultural weakness in the face of urban civilisation and the lights of Empire were not switched off overnight.

If we watch the Goths crossing the Danube into the Empire in 376, we can see that, though they are by no means universally Christian, there is among them already a substantial Christian community with its very own Gothic bishop, Ulfila (*c.* 311–82). Ulfila was no pathfinding missionary, either, despite what is often said of him; if anything, he was a Moses, as

9

the Emperor Constantius II called him.[19] There had already been a Christian infiltration, a seepage from the Empire, before they crossed into it. Perhaps it began with Christian slaves. The most lasting Gothic kingdom was in Spain, where Euric, king of the Visigoths ('Western Goths'), had by 484 conquered the whole peninsula, except for Galicia, which remained under the control of the Suebi (Swabians). In addition he ruled a substantial part of southern and central France.[20] This did nothing to undermine Christianity, except for Ulfila's legacy – the thinking man's Gothic Arianism, which lasted till the 580s.[21] Arianism, if it helps, is the heresy of denying the consubstantiality of Father and Son.

Barbarians did not sweep aside former inhabitants or their systems of government and administration: new overlords stepped in above existing structures and institutions. The last of the Roman philosophers, Boethius, was consul in Rome in the impossibly late year of 510 and was a Christian who wrote on Catholic doctrine. If he was executed in 524 by the Ostrogothic ('East Gothic') king Theoderic it was not for being a Christian: Theoderic and his Ostrogoths had long been Christian, if, of course, Arians.

The Goths had Christianised early. More commonly, conversion of invading peoples was somewhat slower: 'Although most of the Germanic peoples were pagan when they entered the Roman world, nearly all were converted to the faith within a generation or two of their arrival' (Todd 1992: 123). In 507 the Visigoths were heavily defeated at Vouillé near Poitiers by the (Germanic) Franks under Clovis who were now so to dominate France that they lent their name to it. But Clovis's wife, the Burgundian Clothilde, was a devout Christian and worked on her husband till finally, in an echo, probably not coincidental, of Constantine at the battle of the Milvian bridge (the defining moment at which he defeated his pagan adversary Maxentius and the Roman Empire became Christian), Clovis is said in his battle against the Alemans in 496 to have called upon 'Clothilde's god'. St Clothilde later retired to a monastery at Tours and her grandson would be St Cloud.

Characteristically, the one part of the Iberian peninsula not under Gothic control turns out to be the one with some evidence for pagan practice. Martin of Braga (*c.* 515–80) was fortunate still to find a certain amount of paganism surviving in Galicia among the Swabian peasants.[22] Nevertheless, in western Spain and Portugal Christian progress had in any case been slowed down by schism. A contemporary of Martin of Tours, Priscillian (*c.* 340–85), had in his enthusiasm embraced what appeared to be heretical, almost Manichaean, views. Martin of Tours perhaps sympathised with his activism and opposed his execution in vain; despite his death, and maybe, as Sulpicius Severus thought, because of it, Priscillian's brand of Christianity was an important vehicle of independent sentiment for almost two centuries.[23]

Figure 1.3 Clovis calls on the god of Clothilde

Beyond the Roman pale

So, the public paganism of Greece and Rome and of the Celts of Spain, France and Britain had gone; only local customs remained. The paganism of the German tribes that immigrated into the Western Empire, excluding Britain, had now also gone. The surviving pagans were the peoples that lay beyond the historical Roman Empire and, in due course, beyond Charlemagne's Holy Roman Empire.

These peoples include the invaders of Britain, the 'Angles, Saxons and Jutes', whose 'conversion' is associated with St Augustine of Canterbury (sent in 596; d. *c.* 605) and others in the seventh century as chronicled in Bede's *Ecclesiastical history* of 731. Back on the continent of Europe, the Frisians were slowly and waveringly converted by St Willibrord (archbishop of the Frisians 695) and Boniface in the years following 719 (murdered 754).[24] The Saxons were forcibly converted by the Frank Charlemagne (see Figure 1.4, p. 13): in a terrible atrocity he massacred 4500 of them in 782 in a grove at Sachsenhain ('Saxon-grove') bei Verden, as well as chopping down the revered pillar Irminsul (see Chapter 7). Revolts of the Saxons over the following century typically involved the ritual of return to paganism. The north Germans, that is, the Scandinavians, took longer. In northern France the Normans (Norsemen) arrived pagan after Charlemagne's death in 814 but were obliged to convert, if rather shallowly, in 911. Meanwhile, their invasion of Britain and the establishment of the Danelaw in the 860s reintroduced paganism, and Christianity only recovered sole control with its adoption by Canute (1016–35). In Denmark and Norway Christianity made progress, sometimes brutally imposed, from the mid-tenth century to the mid-eleventh under such Christian heroes as Olaf Tryggvesson (ruled 995–1000) and St Olaf (ruled 1015–28) – and the colony of Iceland was bribed into Christianity in 1000. The Swedes followed rather later, from the 1020s to the 1120s, and there remained some vigour in their paganism, centred on the great temple at Uppsala.

East of the Saxons were the Slavonic, Baltic and Finnic peoples. Several fell to Christianity in the later tenth century. Poland was converted in the period 962–92, the Czech bishopric of Prague dates from 973, and the official date for the conversion of the Hungarians is 997 – though due to the reincorporation of a pagan enclave in 1236, paganism survived longer than one might expect.

Poland was, however, something of a Catholic island amid the west Slavs. It was harder, and took longer, to convert the Wends ('Sorbs' in their own language). Some of them lived between Poland and the Baltic in the region of Pomerania, now part of Poland, and the aristocracy there only adopted Christianity in 1128. To the west in Brandenburg, Slavs and some Saxons were still actively pagan in the middle of the century. The key success was that of King Waldemar of Denmark (1131–82), who in 1169 took the island of Rügen with its major sanctuary of the god Svantovit which we shall meet later in this book.

East of the Wends and Poles are the various Baltic peoples, a group affiliated to, but far from identical with, the Slavonic – the Prussians to the west around Gdansk and Kaliningrad (note: Prussians were *not* Germans), and the Latvians (or Letts) and Lithuanians to the east. Prussia was conquered in a long and brutal war with the Teutonic Knights, operating from their base at Riga, the modern capital of Latvia, between around 1226 and 1283. Lithuania developed a state paganism during the thirteenth century under King Mindaugas, who became a nominal Christian in 1251, and pursued an exemplary policy of religious tolerance; one area, Samogitia, did not become Christian until 1414. This late conversion, together with a persistent oral tradition, means that even today we can learn something of European paganism from Latvian folksong, the *dainas*.

Beyond the Balts lie a considerable variety of (non-Indo-European) Finno-Ugric peoples – the better known include the Estonians, the Finns and the Lapps. Even today, according to Jones and Pennick (1995: 178), they are not all converted (perhaps their lands were less worth stealing) and the attempted conversion of Lapland between 1389 and 1603 resulted in a sort of compromise between paganism and Christianity.

Figure 1.4 Charlemagne's method of converting the Saxons

Beyond the Byzantine pale

The (Greek) Eastern Roman Empire survived, however vestigially, until the capture of Constantinople in 1453. This survival, and the fact that so much of the military opposition came from Turks already ideologically committed to Islam, meant that there was less impetus to rolling back paganism than there was in the Latin west, though in the end the (Turkic) Bulgars and the Russians attempted subscription to Byzantine civilisation and imperialism through conversion.

Slavs in Pannonia, the area reaching north from Zagreb well into Hungary, were probably converted early, around 700. But the great mass of Slav conversion, in a swathe of territory reaching from Croatia in the north down to Bulgaria in the south had to wait for the ninth century.[25] This was when Cyril and Methodius were at work. St Cyril in particular is well known for his invention of the Glagolitic alphabet, later modified to create the 'Cyrillic' alphabet: this Greek-based script was used to translate scriptures into an early form of Bulgarian known as Old Church Slavonic, repeating at a distance of 500 years the Gothic feat of Ulfila. So, for instance, the Bulgarians, after a false start with the

Figure 1.5 Ulfila translating the Bible into Gothic

conversion of King Kurt in 613, became Christian in 864 thanks to Cyril. Cyril's brother Methodius lived longer but was affected by conflict with Germanic bishops in Moravia (part of the Czech Republic) and even today a dividing line can be seen in Europe between the Latin-alphabet west, e.g. Poland and Croatia, and the Cyrillic east, e.g. Russia, Bulgaria and Serbia. Russia would not fall to Christianity, as we have seen, till a century later when Prince Vladimir decided on it as a deliberate act of policy.

EVIDENCE

Latin and other languages

There is no beginning of paganism. It has no founder, no holy book that, once written, defined it. Before Christianity by definition all societies were pagan. The only alternative would have been atheism, a lack of religion altogether. It is an interesting fact of human history that there is no evidence for atheist societies, something which encourages the view that religion is in origin a dimension of society. My interest in this book, however, is in paganism in action, in visible human history, rather than in the archaeology of paganism. I have focused on paganism as it emerges into history, not on its prehistory. This means that I have privileged the written record. Who then are the authors and what is their language?

First, Greek. Greek is the language of Greece itself, of Greek Asia Minor (the western coast of Turkey), of the Greek colonies, of the eastern Mediterranean following on the conquests of Alexander the Great, and ultimately of the eastern half of the Roman Empire, which survived, transmuted, to become the Byzantine Empire. Second, Latin. Latin is the language of Rome, Italy and the civilised west, progressively from the time of the Emperors. Inscriptions are written in Latin, scarcely ever in Gaulish and never in Brythonic (proto-Welsh), because inscriptions are an instrument of civilisation.[26] Greek and Roman writers, however, have their own way of viewing barbarian pagan practice, which we will look at in the next section.

Latin is also, as a result of the Roman Empire, the language of the Catholic Church (as Greek is of the Greek Orthodox Church) and of intellectuals throughout the Middle Ages and indeed through the Renaissance and beyond. Most of the Christian authors and law codes that I cite are written in this common, civilised language. Christian authors write with 'attitude' and to a large extent in clichés. It will be important as this book progresses to develop a feel for this 'attitude'.

Italian, French, Occitan (the language group of southern France), Catalan, Spanish, Galician and Portuguese are in origin mutated forms of Latin, the *Romance* languages, so called because their speakers speak *Roman*, not German and not quite Latin. They started to emerge as languages identifiably different from Latin around the time of Charlemagne, but they are not used to record the information we require. Latin was. Even German laws, where paganism is an issue, were on the whole written in Latin, because they are only written once German nations have entered the Latin-Christian cultural ambit. That is what makes the following law so utterly startling:

> Whoever has broken into a shrine and removed any of the sacred
> objects, is led to the sea and, on the sand which the incoming tide

covers, his ears are chopped off and he is castrated and sacrificed
to the gods whose temples he has violated.

> *Law of the Frisians*, Additio, titulus xi (*MG Leges* 3.696 f.)

Someone, misreading the politics of AD 802, appended this traditional law
to an otherwise very Christian set, as after all Charlemagne had dictated,
specifying civilised penalties, mainly fines. How was it that no-one
noticed?[27] More satisfactorily Roman, and helpfully explicit, is a law of
the Merovingian king Carloman:

> We have decreed that in accordance with the canons each and
> every bishop shall take trouble in his parish, with the assistance
> of the Count who is the defender of the Church, that the people
> of God shall not perform pagan acts but shall cast aside and
> reject all the foul features of paganism, such as sacrifices for the
> dead, lot-casters or diviners, amulets (*phylacteria*) and auguries,
> incantations, sacrificial victims which foolish men sacrifice in the
> pagan way next to churches in the name of the holy martyrs or
> confessors, provoking God and his saints to anger, or those
> sacrilegious fires which they call *nied fyr* ('need fire')[28] – in sum
> all these practices of the pagans, whatever they are, should be
> energetically prohibited by them.

> Capitulary of Carloman, *MG Leges* 1.17 (AD 742)

Similarly, Germanic authors, such as Bede or Adam of Bremen, are
writing for an educated audience and write therefore in Latin.

There is no Celtic writing contemporary with Celtic paganism: we are
not going to discover a *Lost books of the Druids*, apart from the forged
Barddas of 'Iolo Morgannwg' (1747–1826).[29] The resources, however, of
traditional literature may contain relics of paganism which we can use to
add colour to our picture, though next to nothing on cult.[30] The Welsh
Mabinogion regrettably contains little of substance for our purposes and
will not be cited in this book.[31] Old Irish literature is a little more useful.
Its oldest manuscripts, however, only go back to the twelfth century, long
after the end of paganism; the texts are of limited usefulness and it is
largely wishful thinking to suppose that much material earlier than the
early Middle Ages has survived in this tradition: they may preserve some
useful social detail, for instance testifying to the existence of druids and
prophets, but considerably less on pagan religious attitudes.[32] In the
Germanic languages the most notable evidence comes from the Norse
Eddas and sagas, all however dating, at least in the form we have them,
from Christian times. The reason, we suppose, that these poems and
sagas, Celtic and Norse, contain such pagan elements as they do is
because they represent the oral literature, which was characteristic of

these pagan cultures. In Gaul, quite apart from the class of *wateis* (bards), we hear of the association of druids with the preservation of sacred traditions:

> [Trainee druids] are said to learn by heart a large number of verses. As a result, some of them spend twenty years learning. Nor do they consider it right to set this material down in writing, though they use the Greek alphabet for most other purposes, for public and private records . . .
>
> The Gauls assert that they all descend from Father Dis [the Latin name of the god of the Underworld] and they say that this is handed down by the Druids.
>
> Caesar, Gallic war 6.14.3 and 6.18.1

And though they lack the druid class, the south Germans too had such traditions:

> They celebrate in ancient songs, which is the only mode of memory and of annals that they have, how the god Tuisto was born from the earth. To him they ascribe a son Mannus [evidently 'Man'], the originator and founder of their nation, and to Mannus three sons from whose names those next to the Ocean are called Ingaevones, those in the middle Herminones and the others Istaevones. Certain of them, using the licence that goes with antiquity, allege that more eponyms of the nation were born of the god – Marsi, Gambrivii, Suebi – and that these are genuine ancient names.
>
> Tacitus, Germania 2.2–3

It is therefore tempting to think that a continuous oral tradition links, say, Old Irish literature with scenes out of Caesar. But we should remember, in using this evidence, that we conform to the romantic picture propagated by the brothers Grimm, that oral tradition perpetuates ancient myth, whereas there is a danger that supposedly oral works are better at conjuring up an impression of antiquity than its details.[33] We learn staggeringly little of the Bronze Age from Homer and maybe just as little of the Iron Age, certainly of its religion, from Irish literature. In fact, the oral tradition, and its last degenerate descendant, folklore, are frustrating and often unreliable sources. Folklore in particular is a surprisingly inventive medium. Nor can we be sure that Celtic culture was sufficiently uniform for Irish and Gaulish to be unhesitatingly merged.

Even among the Slavs, many of whom in the north remained pagan until the twelfth century, there are no pagan texts.[34] Indeed, pagan societies, with the (formidable) exceptions of Greece and Rome, are particularly accursed in never being literate at the point at which they are still pagan. In Europe there is a clear reason: the transition to a cultural type characterised by writing was made through subscription to the dominant model, that of Roman, and Greek, Christianity. So it is that our evidence for local pagan practices very often comes through their denunciation in Latin, the voice of the culture that destroyed them. A different but particularly poignant case is that of Gaul, where the native culture was developing its own distinctive urbanism, based on very substantial *oppida*, whose ruins should be trodden before dismissive statements are made, and a literacy was beginning using the Greek alphabet to write Gaulish, but only at the point at which it came under Roman control. So it was that Latin culture, powerfully developed already, crushed this embryonic literacy, ousted the druidic class and ritualised the subscription of Gaulish leaders to Roman power through the vehicle of the Emperor cult.

Greek and Roman windows on barbarian culture

If we want to know about ancient Celts, the best known are those of Gaul, and we should turn to the best ancient authority on Gaul, the *Histories* of Poseidonios (*c.* 135–51 BC). Doubtless we would – if they had survived. However, later authors liberally helped themselves to his information, at times to the point of plagiarism, and so we may read instead, for instance, Diodoros of Sicily's *History* (of *c.* 30 BC) and Strabo's *Geography* (books 3–6 date from around AD 18). Book 23 of Poseidonios' *Histories* dealt with the Celts. From tatters of it we learn of a Celtic custom of duelling at a feast for the best portion (*FGH* 87F16)[35] and of the bards that were kept in the entourage of the prominent in order to sing their praises (F17). Book 30 dealt with Germans, a people maybe newly invented by Poseidonios himself;[36] certainly he described their habit of eating roast joints with milk and drinking, barbarously, undiluted wine (F22). So far Poseidonios might seem unduly interested in food, an impression which results from his being quoted by Athenaios, whose large surviving *Deipnosophists* ('Sophists at a dinner-party') is an anthology of ancient culture determined by how much of it one can eat. In fact Poseidonios had travelled for himself in Gaul and was well acquainted with the culture from personal observation. In a particularly engaging passage he mentioned the habit of Gauls of his day of nailing the heads of their dead enemies to their doorposts: 'I saw this sight everywhere. At first I found it revolting,[37] but afterwards I bore it calmly as I got used to it' (Poseidonios, reconstructed from *FGH* 87F55 (Strabo 4.4.5)). So it looks as though he got beyond the Greek comfort of the Languedoc and Provence, though scholars debate how far.[38] Other fragments which it is harder to place in his output tell us about religion. For instance, he talks

Figure 1.6 Priestesses and human sacrifice among the Cimbri

about the Cimbri, a tribe who despite their apparently Celtic name are said to be German[39] and who are best known for their invasion of Italy in 101 BC. Here, he seems to have mentioned 'grey-haired divining priestesses dressed in white, with buckled cloaks of flax and a brass belt, but bare-foot':

19

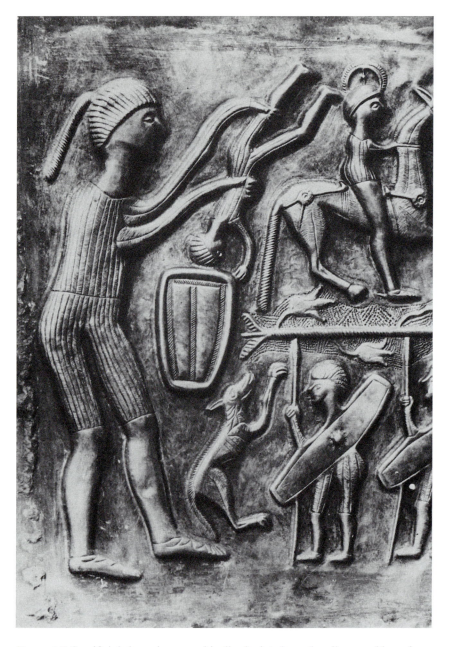

Figure 1.7 Sacrificial drowning, graphically depicted on the silver cauldron from Gundestrup (see p. 21). Photo: The National Museum of Denmark

sword in hand, they used to meet the prisoners in the camp and, putting garlands on them, lead them to a bronze vessel of about 20 amphoras' capacity. And they had steps which the priestess climbed so that from that height she could cut the throat of each one as he was held aloft. From the flow of blood into the vessel, they performed a certain divination, whilst other priestesses, splitting them open and examining the entrails, proclaimed victory for their own people.

Poseidonios, FGH 87F31 (Strabo 7.2.3)

This twenty-measure vessel is authentic and its use is illustrated on the first-century BC Gundestrup cauldron, where a giant godlike figure dangles a human head first into such a vessel.[40] A similar barrel (*cupa*, cf. our word 'cooper') appears among the Suebi at Bregenz (Austria) around AD 611, holding twenty-six measures of ale and used for sacrifices to Wodan, which would suggest human sacrifice; St Columban caused its metal rings to give way.[41] In another passage Poseidonios tells us about the Gauls and their sacred treasure at Toulouse. This was deemed by some writers, characteristically of their Greek-is-best culture, to have been the very same treasure which the invading Gauls had taken from Delphi back in 279, not, however, by the careful Poseidonios. In any case, it was now sacrilegiously taken by the Roman consul Servilius Caepio in 106 – and misappropriated:

The valuables found at Toulouse weighed around 15,000 talents [*c.* 388,000 kg], some of it stored in enclosures, some in sacred lakes, not made into anything, but simply unworked gold and silver . . . the land [of Gaul] is rich in gold[42] and all over the Celtic land there were treasuries, given that the people are superstitious and do not have expensive lifestyles. In particular, lakes provided them with inviolable places and they dropped weights of silver or even gold into them . . . In Toulouse the shrine too was holy, much revered by the people in the vicinity, and it had a lot of valuables for this reason, as many made offerings and no-one dared to lay hands on it.

Poseidonios, FGH 87F33 (Strabo 4.1.13)

In a final passage (F116), whose existence we must deduce from suspicious similarity between later authors, Poseidonios presented three classes of person concerned with the sacred or with tradition in Gaulish society – bards, druids and *wateis* – all three of them Gaulish words. We shall return to this passage in Chapter 12.

Were there other Greek writers on western and northern Europe? Poseidonios' older contemporary, Metrodoros of Skepsis (killed 71 BC) wrote on the characteristics and produce of lands, mentioning the River Po and also Germany and the Baltic 'island'.[43] Poseidonios' younger contemporary Timagenes of Alexandria, who was brought to Rome a prisoner in 55 BC and bought by Faustus Sulla, son of the brutal dictator, lived to write history under – and be extremely rude to – Augustus. He evidently gave a very thorough account, perhaps in a *Galatika* ('On Gaul' F13) of the various alleged origins, largely mythic, of the Gaulish people and he seems to have developed the bards–druids–*wateis* trinity in various ways, notably to view praise-poets (bards) as a step in the general evolution of music (*FGH* 88F2, F10). He also discussed the fate of the shrine-robber Servilius Caepio, in particular how his daughters were reduced to prostitution and he died in disgrace (F11). But it is evident that Spain,[44] Gaul and Germany were badly neglected by Greek writers, despite the colossal amount of papyrus expended on other areas of the Greek or Roman world, whose very tatters occupy thousands of pages in Jacoby's collection of the *Fragmente der griechischen Historiker*.

> All the areas that are barbarian, out of the way, minor, scattered – on these the [Greek] handbooks are neither reliable nor numerous. All things distant from Greeks increase their ignorance. Now, the Roman authors imitate the Greeks, but do not get very far: what they report they translate out of the Greeks and they do not contribute much of a spirit of scientific enquiry on their own account. So, whenever the Greeks leave a gap, the rest do not have much to fill it with, especially as the biggest names tend to be Greek.

These withering comments are those of Strabo (3.4.19).[45]

Gaul was of course conquered by Julius Caesar, one of the most intelligent and literate Romans of his day. He has also left us a work, the *Gallic war* of the 50s BC, which pauses briefly in the sixth book to tell us about the customs and religion of the Gauls. Nothing perhaps better illustrates the unscientific standards of antiquity and the value of Strabos' remarks than this passage. One cannot be sure that it contains any original or authentic observations by Caesar himself. It may well be that every detail is out of Poseidonios. Indeed, as de Vries (1961: 18) acutely speculates, Caesar must have read up about Gaul before he set out, in Poseidonios and maybe others. This mentality is well exemplified by a passage of Vitruvius, a Roman writer on architecture who had served Caesar as an engineer:

> Of these matters there are some which I have observed for myself, others which I have found written in Greek books. The following are the authors of these books: Theophrastos, Timaios,

22

Poseidonios, Hegesias, Herodotos, Aristides, Metrodoros. They wrote with great attention, and infinite pains, to the effect that the characteristics of areas, the quality of the water, the nature of regions as a result of the inclination of the heavens [i.e. the climate] are so distributed.

Vitruvius, *On architecture* 8.3.27 (Poseidonios, *FGH* 87T13)

To this one must add a Victorian confidence in their own culture, for which Greeks too were to blame, distinguishing the world into Greeks and 'barbarians' – 'blah-blahs', because you can't understand what they say. It is amusing but characteristic when Plutarch, talking of an instance of human sacrifice by Romans in the 220s BC, expresses surprise because the Romans aren't really barbarians. Thus, surviving from antiquity there are no books about Gaul other than Caesar's, one broad-brush book about Germany, Tacitus' *Germania*, and no books about Britain or Spain. Druids occasionally catch the eye, because they are distinctive, are thought wrongly to correspond to a Platonic mirage of 'philosophers in power' and practise human sacrifice.

Not only are Greek and Roman writers uninterested in nations below their cultural *niveau*; even when they describe features of their civilisation, they filter those features through a mask constructed by their own culture, to an extent much greater even than we do now. Druids can be philosophers or priests or both. Foreign nations worship this god above all, and these other gods with their Greco-Roman names: so Gauls worship Mercury above all, and also Apollo, Mars, Jupiter and Minerva; Germans also worship Mercury above all, and also Hercules and Mars (Chapter 11). We can neither correlate these statements with such other evidence as we have, nor learn anything of substance from these translations into Roman, the so-called *interpretatio romana*. Why is Mercury the favoured god of the Gauls? We have little idea. Because he is the god of merchants? Do merchants spend their time on mountaintops, then? And why is Wodan made out to be the equivalent of Mercury (*mercredi* – *Wednesday*)? These are the products of historical accidents and tell us nothing essential: perhaps Poseidonios' source first met 'Mercury' as a traveller's god in a little shrine in the vicinity of Narbonne and then was stuck with the name; perhaps, once 'Mercury' ends up on every hilltop in Gaul, the Wodan of a Wodansberg has to be a Mercury too. This is then reinforced by the numerous points of comparison between Lug (Mercury) and Wodan.[46]

In imperial times Pliny the elder wrote a major twenty-book work on *Wars with Germany*. It is lost, but Pliny's prodigious research energy must have produced a work which incorporated all Greek knowledge to date and which was doubtless of great use to Tacitus in his little monograph *On the origin and situation of the Germans*, which we call the *Germania* for short – a book which has been described as 'in parts astonishingly well informed in the areas of religion and, scarcely to be separated from it, law'.[47] Origins reflect Timagenes' approach to the Gauls, situation the geography of Poseidonios or Strabo, miniaturism the urbane manner of Caesar. It is not clear, however, that any of this writing actually increased the information stock about Germany, though Pliny's military service there might have helped, assuming he had a 'spirit of scientific enquiry'. Perhaps, indeed, he, almost uniquely among Romans, may have had this spirit, judging by the younger Pliny's account: as Vesuvius disgorged a large black cloud like a compressed tree, 'being a very learned man, he thought it was important and that he should take a closer look' (*Letters* 6.16.7). The following morning, bravely leading others to safety from the eruption, he had a heart attack and died.

And that is simply it. For the remainder of the Empire, no-one wrote at any length on Gaul, Spain or Germany. At first sight the pages of references to Gaulish culture that Burnand lists (1996: 4–6) may seem impressive, but individually they deliver rather little and cumulatively they report only very patchily on Gaulish religion. It is arguable that it is beyond the evidence to write a comprehensive book on Gaulish religion, though, for instance, Brunaux (1996) has written what is possible on 'the Gaulish religions' and Duval (1976) has done what he can with 'the gods of Gaul'. That is one reason why this book looks at individual phenomena of paganism in Europe rather than dealing exhaustively with a culture at a time. The first phenomenon we will look at is place.

2

DIVIDING THE LANDSCAPE

If paganism is largely not a matter of belief, then it speaks the language of actions, the language of ritual. Like the language of words, ritual recedes beyond sight into the prehistoric past. It is characteristic of religious ritual to be laden with rules for the time and place at which it will occur. This chapter deals with place. Doubtless, some religious rituals may be performed instantly in any place if circumstances demand it – for instance, an urgent personal prayer or a vow. Most, however, are performed in the place that is 'religiously correct', in Latin *fas*, and it is no accident that Latin ritual often takes place in a *fasnom, or, as they actually pronounced it, *fānum* ('shrine').[1] How is a place to be identified as *fas*? Why is it there and not somewhere else? What features of the landscape invite ritual? How is the sacred place to be positioned relative to the settlement?[2] What power is felt in a feature like a sacred stone such that it magnetically attracts ritual?

LOCATION

Focus and area

I start by making a fundamental distinction which will also serve to structure succeeding chapters. Religious place consists of two distinct elements: *at* and *within*, or, to give them a noun each, *focus* and *area*. So, a ritual is, for instance, performed *at* an altar *within* a sanctuary. The focus is obligatory, for without it there is no place for ritual; the word *focus* itself is in origin the Latin word for the hearth-fire, the geographical and psychological centre of the family, its home and its land, and the appropriate place for rituals of family solidarity. The area is optional. The area is designated as sacred and contrasted with the normal, profane, human territory. The boundary of such an area may well be specially marked, for instance, with a wall, if it is not otherwise evident. The area may correspondingly have restricted rights of entry and in any case it conditions your approach to the focus. The ideal pairing of central focus and area with perimeter shows up very clearly how the sacred site is not only (sometimes, not even) a thing in nature but an ideological mould imposed on an inert world. To mark the site is to format its disk.

The interaction of focus and area may be compared to a stone thrown into a pond. The area may in effect be the ripples proceeding from the stone – the area is sacred because of the focus it contains. But alternatively, it may be the pond that is identifiable and the position of the stone that is arbitrary within it. So the sacrality of a grove may rest in the identifiable wood or forest, rather than on the altar placed, doubtless conveniently, within it: 'In the nearby groves were the barbarian altars at which they had slaughtered tribunes and centurions of the first rank' (Tacitus, *Annals* 1.61).

Buildings cloud this picture. If we take the model of the family, then its land is the area specially associated with the family and its special character is marked by concepts such as privacy and trespass. The built house is apparently focal from outside, but becomes, once you enter, an area, if a more powerful one marked by concepts such as 'breaking and entering' or burglary. It is then, within the ancient house, the hearth that is the irreducible focus (perhaps the television today). Transferring this model to the sacred, we immediately become aware that the function of sacred buildings varies, with a particularly sharp division between Greco-Roman paganism and modern Christianity. To take a 'typical' English rural church: you enter the sacred area, which is walled off, through a lych-gate. To call it a sacred area is perhaps a slight exaggeration: it would be disrespectful, maybe, to perform some particularly profane act there, but the disrespect would largely be to the dead who are buried there and who account for the excellent growth of those yew trees. The church itself has a more firmly marked sacred character and within it you can advance to a central crucifix and to an altar. But the 'typical' Greek sanctuary has a much stronger sense of sacrality from the outset: the moment you crossed its boundary you were unambiguously on holy ground. Yes, there was the temple and the historic statue of the god within, but the altar, a pagan focus later borrowed by Christianity, was *outside* the temple and in front of it. The building is an accessory, if a mighty one of which wealthy states might be proud: 'the holiness of the site is a prerequisite for the building of a house of God' (Nilsson 1955: 74). These things, however, develop. Greek temples may have an *abaton* (a no-entry), all the more holy because more restricted, and there are signs that even Italian groves might have a similarly restricted area.[3] In Rome there was special concern with the status of the ground on which a temple was built, as a third-century AD lawyer tells us: 'Once a sacred temple has been built, even when the building is destroyed, the place remains sacred' (Aelius Marcianus, *Digest* 1.8.6.3).[4] All the same, modern European Christianity is much more insistent on its buildings. Is it the danger of rain in northern climates? Did pagan rites have to take place outside because of the fire and the filth of real sacrifice on real altars? Or is it that the emphasis on the building and its interior is characteristic of modern religions and of credal religions, as though the interiority of belief required ritual too to assume an interior form?

What determines where religious *areas*, and their modern buildings, are situated? In modern times an entirely new sacred building may perhaps be sited solely with regard to catchment area, ease of access and planning permission, though some care may be taken over its orientation. Even in ancient times, for instance in Gaul, this was often the case in established towns. But many buildings continue a longstanding tradition that the place itself is holy, a continuity which is an important fact of religious history and to which buildings tend to blind us.[5] So the worship of Athene on the Acropolis at Athens, which we today mostly associate with the Parthenon, has a particular sacred geography which privileges the shrine of the primal king Erechtheus, the Erechtheum, which contains the sacred olive-tree of Athene[6] and which is situated where the *megaron*, the focal room of the Mycenaean (Bronze Age) palace, had been.[7] The name of the goddess can be seen from its structure (older form, *A-tha-na*) to antedate the Greek language and the site itself, puzzlingly plural (Athen*s*), may in fact be a locative case of the noun, meaning 'at Athana'. So persistent is the association of worship with place, particularly in a pagan age when other and earlier gods are not automatically dismissed. Similarly, in Gaul around fifteen sites of sanctuaries have been seen by aerial photography to be in the vicinity of Bronze Age tumuli, now levelled.[8]

Paganisms do not on the whole repudiate each other, but Christianity, distinctively, repudiated paganism. This was true, however, only at the dogmatic level or among enthusiasts, as we will discover when we come to the policy of reuse of *fana* and temples as Christian churches and the conversion of sacred sites, ostensibly on pragmatic grounds, to Christian purposes (Chapter 7).

As we turn back the clock and recede deeper into the past, everywhere we see temple buildings, like cities, fading away. 'In cities they shall have shrines (*delubra*); in the countryside they shall have groves and seats of the Lares [gods of the property]' (Cicero, *De legibus* 2.19). If there was an Indo-European homeland, there were no temples there, only landscape. Sacral area must therefore in origin be identified by geography, not buildings. The buildings we have today, where they do represent long-standing religious tradition, continue a geographical sense of sacrality. In this sense 'nature' inevitably underlies the choice of place in which to perform ritual.

Let us envisage for a moment some primeval, hitherto uninhabited landscape, and ask: how is a holy place to be recognised? It may be a place at which an event occurs – lightning strikes, a meteor falls, a significant person dies – but this will be rare. In most cases landscape itself quietly dictates observance and it is the function of myth and oral tradition to devise the event that imbued this place with its special significance. A landmark or determinate point of some sort is required: it would be impossible to identify a focus or an area in a featureless desert. 'If purely and absolutely homogeneous, [space] would be of no use and could not be grasped by the mind' (Durkheim 1915: 11). Sacred place is one recognition, and registration, of anomaly.

It may occur to some readers to wonder whether sun, moon and/or stars are not also factors in determining the location of the sacred place. Generally, they may be factors determining orientation, as we shall see in the case of temples, or even layout, as has been argued for megalithic monuments by A. Thom and, more restrainedly, A. Burl.[9] But they do not generally determine actual location. In this book I deal mainly with literary evidence for paganism, which restricts us to its last period. Time-reckoning was still important (Chapter 10), but in earlier times the position of heavenly bodies may well have had greater impact on sacred structures. I have even heard of a site in southern Spain which was abandoned because the desired configuration of celestial bodies

Figure 2.1 The situation of Delphi. Photo: James Dowden

ceased to be visible from there. This would be a borderline case of determination of site.

Physical features (absolute position)

What features in the landscape invite registration as a sacred focus or area? Working entirely from first principles, we might compose lists such as these:

Category	Focus	Area
Height	peak	hill or mountain
Land/water boundary		shore, island
Water	a spring, well, pool, lake, river	
Rock	a particularly large stone/ rock, or one curiously shaped; a stalagmite or stalactite	cave
Growth	a notable tree	specially fertile land (meadow) wood/forest (grove)

In the case of hills and mountains there is some fluidity between focus and area. A mountain-peak seems in our diagrammatic imaginations an identifiable point, but is less so in reality. Most often when 'peak sanctuaries' are described, what is meant is the *area* of the mountaintop, and the point of worship still needs to be chosen. There are nonetheless occasional examples of peak-focus: on the very top of Mount Lykaios (Arcadia), the cult of Zeus Lykaios heaped up bones and ashes – today thirty metres wide and one and a half metres high.[10] Conversely, hills may seem an area, but are often identifiably separate and therefore do not result from 'ripple'. In this connection, it is noticeable how the Anglo-Saxon *hearg* tended to be on 'high ground' (Chapter 7).

Lakes and rivers, though more extensive than usual foci, are not the area within which participants worship. Nevertheless, their extent means that there must be an additional determining factor, or arbitrary choice, of where precisely worship should take place. Why worship here rather than another five kilometres downstream? For rivers, the identified points tend to be their *source*, where they become aqueous, or *crossing points*, where the land dangerously and as a result of human interference impinges on the aqueous domain. I shall treat sources under 'springs'.

Figure 2.2 The sacred oak at Dodona, a singular tree providing the focus for cult. Note the subordinate role of the sacred building in the 4th and 3rd centuries BC and compare with Figure 2.3. Source: E. Melas, *Temples and sanctuaries of ancient Greece: a companion guide*, Thames and Hudson, 1973, p.161

On lakes, it is less clear what factors other than convenience come into play, though the presence of forest (grove) and mountain may have some influence.

The distinction between a focus and an area matters particularly in the case of trees. 'Grove' is not the collective for 'sacred trees'.[11] Perhaps in a grove, one tree may be more sacred than another and serve as the focus of worship, though I know of no such example. The sacred tree I know is an isolated and unique specimen, otherwise it would not be sacred. Like a cat, it does not team up with others of its kind, but prefers the company of a stone and a spring (below).

These, then, are natural features but people too may add artificial anomalies to the landscape. There is also power where roads meet, at crossroads, or where they surmount or defy the nature of a natural obstacle, at a pass or, as we have seen, at a bridge or ford. Imposing burial mounds mix the natural category of hill with the human category of death. Manmade features quickly become naturalised. So initially a burial mound is a way of marking, and thereby sacralising, the landscape. But later, when the man is long dead, although it may still be recognised

Figure 2.3 The sacred oak, and shrine, at Dodona today. Photo: Richard Stoneman

as artificial, the feature may by its aura of mystery and times past 'become part of the landscape'. Conversely, sometimes, as in Arcadia, a small hill might wrongly be supposed to be a mound.[12]

Relative position

Religious siting is part of a system of co-ordinates. Religious co-ordinates may coincide with others by which we orient our life. But they may also clash, creating a sort of counterpoint or syncopation. So a settlement has its own site and centre to which a religious instance may or may not conform. In relation to a settlement, a feature may be central, close or marginal (distant-peripheral). Cole, studying the shrines of Demeter in Greece, has categorised their locations as 'within the city, just outside, and at the borders of the city's territory' (in Alcock and Osborne 1994: 215). This may not seem to leave much, but it does identify the dynamics of positioning.

Ownership: public and private

Paganism is characteristically public. It involves shared ritual owned by the whole community, even where it is not performed by the whole community. There may be rites particular to citizen women, but they are for all persons of that class, viz. citizen women, in the community.

31

In the case of worship in the home ('household cult'), the internal paganism of the family, which of course assists its bonding, is common to *all* families in the community.

It is therefore more unusual for religious practices to be privately owned. This has, however, been alleged to occur in Anglo-Saxon paganism. The placename Patchway (Sussex) is said to mean 'Pæccel's *wēoh*', the pagan shrine owned by Pæccel, and similarly an estate Cusanweoh in the vicinity of Farnham (Surrey) is thought to imply 'personal ownership'.[13] One almost gets the picture from Wilson's arguments of a small, private enterprise, wayside shrine. But we have no other evidence than these two placenames that a personal operation is at issue and it must be said that the decoding of English placenames is beset with the invention of individuals of a given name to act as eponyms, much as the Greeks invented heroes to account for placenames.[14] In any case the relationship of shrine to these individuals is unclear: (a) 'in personal ownership', (b) 'an individual's responsibility' for the community, or (c) the old *wēoh* that is on Pæccel's land, where Pæccel is in fact a perfectly conventional Christian? If there is any individual enterprise here, which I doubt, it would have to be held to reflect the weak political cohesion among these Germans.

Within more developed societies, as at Greece and Rome, greater privacy and the personalisation of religion becomes possible. A certain flexibility can be found in these paganisms so that a given individual may privilege one or more particular gods in their worship. Traders are important because they are isolated from their societies by travel and must make their own religious decisions; they are exposed to religious practices of other groups and societies and may therefore act as carriers for innovation. So it is clear that a cult of the Greco-Egyptian goddess Isis came to Italy in the first century BC through the activities of traders both Italian and foreign. Within a century Isis had become an available extra choice for individuals that lay beyond the paganism of the state. Among the remains of traditional household worship of Lares and Penates from Pompeii and Herculaneum, overwhelmed and preserved by the eruption of Vesuvius in AD 79, are found statuettes of Isis – quite apart from her substantial temple. In the city of Rome the establishment was concerned largely to prevent religious innovation by groups of individuals – it savagely repressed the cult of Bacchus in 186 BC, repeatedly tried to get the cult of Isis and the Egyptian gods out of Rome, until in the 40s AD they were embraced by the Emperors, and of course attempted from time to time to eliminate Christianity. These are interesting reactions of a conservative state to religious pluralism, or rather additionalism (except for Christianity you didn't deny the old gods to adopt new), which was the result of the development of a more complex society. Greece, on the other hand, so far as we can tell, was not in the business of resisting the waves of new cultures by restricting individual choice. Athenian paganism, to take the only mainland example we know at all well, did indeed regulate worship to ensure that it was done well on behalf of the state, but it did not stop a resident foreigner from setting up his own private shrine of *Mēn*, the Phrygian moon god, which he regulates with all the formality that a state would.

> Xanthos of Lycia [in west Turkey] founded the shrine of Mēn Tyrannos ('the Lord Moon') through the god's choice [i.e. he appeared in a dream to Xanthos] with good fortune and no-one to approach unpurified but let him be purified from garlic and pigs. And no-one is to sacrifice without the permission of the founder and if anyone forces their way the sacrifice is unaccepted by the god. One is to provide the god with what is correct – a right leg, pelt and olive-oil on the altar and a lamp and a libation. And one is purified from a dead body on the tenth day and from menstruation[15] on the seventh, anyone who has killed a man is not even to be in the place, from rape on the fortieth day, from a woman [i.e. from sex] washing head to toe on the same day. Propitious be the god to those who worship him with sincere soul. If anyone has a problem or falls ill or is away from home, let him worship whatever god he devotes himself to. But whosoever interferes, let him pay the penalty to Mēn Tyrannos whom he shall be unable to propitiate: let him surrender head and feet and chest.
>
> Inscription, *SIG* 1042 (Lane 1971: no.12)

Perhaps the greatest irony is that, but for this growing individualising loophole in Greco-Roman paganism, a product of mobility in a pagan empire, it would not have been possible for Christianity to spread. Where later Christianity spread from the Roman world to the barbarians, barbarians actually had (or were supposed) to give up their religion altogether in order to adopt Christianity; there may have been some cases of limited, tolerated Christian communities, like that of Ulfila, but the real business consisted of the tribal king and his oligarchy declaring new religious rules for the society at large. It would have been absurd for Paul and his ilk to expect the states of the Roman world to do this. Christianity could only advance through the vehicle of individual choice. Constantine came later. Once established, however, it required the devolved conditions of the fragmentary societies of the Dark Ages to stamp out any pluralism, something which was only possible with the greatest difficulty under the old Roman Empire.

So paganism may be publicly owned or it may be individually owned, but the latter is very rare and occurs only under special conditions.

POWER

The god in the stone?

Once identified, or felt as different, the place itself is receptive to the psychological perceptions we wish to have of it. It will typically be felt to have some special, innate, religious force and that force may be concentrated in the natural or artificial centre. The rock or stone may be a *baetyl* (from 'beth-el', the 'house of God' in West Semitic), the tree a holy tree. The word *mana* is loosely used in this context.[16] From the tree and the stone, sometimes as a pillar moving towards the condition of the tree, derives the statue or cult-image (being, after all, generally a shaped tree or stone).[17] The Great Goddess among the Semites, Przyluski tells us, becomes assimilated to the sacred stone, the *Asherah*, or to a stone pillar.[18] The stone stands in an ambivalent relationship to the adored, either being what is adored or only representing (or transmitting) it.

What is the relationship of, for example, the tree to the object of worship? It obviously is not worshipped for the brute thing that it is – all that Christians affected to notice: 'there is no *religio*', declared St Martin, 'in a tree stump' (see Chapter 4). Rather, it is a sign mediating between the worshipper and something else.[19] What, then, is that something else which the tree points to? Is the tree a *dwelling-place* of a divinity – a Greek tree-nymph, a hamadryad? Is it the actual body of that hamadryad?[20]

> In most, if not all, of these cases the spirit is viewed as incorporate in the tree; it animates the tree and must suffer and die with it. But, according to another and probably later opinion, the tree is not the body, but merely the abode of the tree-spirit, which can quit it and return to it at pleasure.
>
> Frazer 1911: *Magic art* ii.33

Is it true, as Przyluski claims (1950: 54), that 'Artemis originally had her seat in a tree'?

We should not be too impressed by Greek and Roman poetic anthropomorphism (see Chapter 4). The perception that the tree itself is a vehicle of power logically precedes the creation of a place for it within an anthropomorphic system. First, powerful tree; then, personal gods; then, mopping up the trees by turning them into residences for the personal god.

> Cult worship of trees gives us no excuse to treat them as the dwelling-place of supernatural beings. We have already retracted conclusions of Mannhardt's that had gone too far, when he wanted to interpret popular ideas through divine beings that lived

34

in trees. The yew in Uppsala, the Oak of Jupiter in Geismar [Chapter 4] and the oak at Dodona were not holy because a god had his home in them. They stood only in a particularly close relationship to the gods. The tree was already holy in itself – through the symbolic character of its natural growth.

De Vries 1956: i.351 (my translation)

De Vries is right: if the tree is sacred, that is the fundamental fact, prior to any gods looking for a nice place to live; the spirit is only a way of accommodating the worship of a brute tree into a religious universe now more accustomed to personal divinities. Trees, stones and springs talk a different religious language from gods and nymphs; we must beware the infiltration of personalities and god-language into raw ecology.

Nevertheless, there is a difference between a tree and a stone. A stone may sometimes stand for the god, but it is the tree that is alive. Female divinities in particular are closely associated with the growing tree, as we shall see, and it is possible to put a costume on a post, a tree-trunk, to declare it personal.[21]

Strength in numbers: tree, stone, spring

The commonest markers of a pagan site are, often *in combination*, tree, rock and water – 'the rocks that are the bone of the ground, the waters that give it fertility, and the trees that are its most impressive display' (Przyluski 1950: 60).[22] So these features tend to be fellow-travellers in both pagan and in Christian thought. In a letter to his young friend the Emperor Verus, the orator Fronto expresses his delight at his recovery from illness through a veritable catechism of sources of respect (AD 162), claiming to have given his thanks 'at every hearth, altar, sacred grove, consecrated tree'.[23] And Christians rarely denounced one feature without denouncing the others:

> §23 We call upon pastors as well as priests to take care that, whenever they see persons persist in such foolishness or perform deeds incompatible with the Church at any rocks, trees or springs, the designated places of the pagans, they should with their sacred authority expel them from the Church and not allow people who maintain the practices of the pagans to share the holy altar.
>
> Council of Tours, 18 November 567[24]

> I appeal to you . . . not to go to those diabolical feasts which take place at a shrine (*fanum*) or at springs or at certain trees.
>
> Caesarius, *Sermon* 54.6

These denunciations of springs, stones and trees are frequent in church synods, the writing of the fathers and early law-codes.[25]

This is not just a matter of association of ideas. Throughout paganism, these features are physically found together, reinforcing the sacrality of the holy place, securely identifying and marking it. In Egypt, long back in 2300 BC, Pharaoh Pepi II gave orders that new centres of worship, obviously already possessing altar-stones, should also be marked by the planting of a Syrian fir.[26] Presently in Canaan, the standard equipment of a 'high-place' would be an altar, a stone pillar (*massebah*) and a sacred tree or post.[27] The post is an *asherah*, which is also the name of a goddess, originally the wife of the Ugaritic El or even, as some have thought, of Yahweh himself.[28]

> So the people of Israel feel ashamed . . .
> who say to a block of wood (*asherah*), 'You are our father'
> and cry 'Mother' to a stone.
> > Jeremiah 2.26 f. (Revised English Bible)

Stones, too, were worshipped widely in the Near East and account for names like the Hebrew *Ebenezer* ('Stone-of-help') or the Phoenician *Ebenshamash* ('Stone of the Sun'). Stones star also in some curious Old Testament passages: Yahweh is apparently a stone or a stone marks where patriarchs had met El.[29] An 'altar' is simply a formalisation, a civilisation, of a large stone, just as a statue formalises the pillar-stone or the tree whose form is striven after by the pillar.[30] Greek altars were usually made of stone blocks or, more cheaply, from bricks which were then whitewashed in order, surely, to give the appearance of a monolith.[31]

A similar combination of tree and stone energised Bronze-Age Minoan religious sites, something which we dimly perceive through their depiction on seal-rings. In the iconography of Athenian vases, the combination of altar plus a particular tree is used to suggest the sanctuary of the corresponding god: palm-tree for Leto and the god-children she bore at the sacred palm at Delos, Apollo and Artemis; or laurel for Apollo, and in any case olive for Athene.[32] Pausanias comments on the array of (exotic) palm-trees before the temple of Artemis at Aulis.[33] The sacred topography of Aulis a millennium earlier is nicely gathered in the words which Homer gives to Odysseus as he recalls the mustering of the Trojan expedition:

> And we, around the spring, at the holy altars
> sacrificed perfect hekatombs to the immortals
> beneath the fine plane-tree, whence flowed the glorious water.
> > Homer, *Iliad* 2.305–7

Significant numbers of Welsh wells are close to large rocks (62) or tumuli (14).[34] In other Celtic lands too – Scotland, Ireland, the Isle of Man, Cornwall and Brittany – megaliths are associated with holy wells and springs (Jones 1954: 14 f.) and ritual might embrace both, as where the sick bathed in the spring and then slept on the stone or 'proceeded to a stone circle' (*ibid.* 16). And the combination of tree and stone is characteristic of the inauguration sites of Irish kings.[35]

The most common association of springs and wells is with *trees*. Trees of course grow readily around a spring and indeed they are so deeply rooted in the Welsh imaginaire that it is almost second nature to name a spring after a tree, but all the same there is such an overwhelming amount of evidence that we must conclude that sacred tree and spring or well do indeed form a pair (*ibid.* 8, 15, 19–20). In Ireland, too, 'very frequently a sacred tree overhangs or grows by the sacred fount' (Plummer 1910: i.clii), a principle neatly enshrined in the placename Toberbilly (Old Irish *tobar* 'sacred spring', *bíle* 'sacred tree').[36] Similarly, when St Brendan discovered the fount of a river, 'there was above that fount a tree of amazing height covered in the whitest birds, which so covered the tree that human eyes could scarce make out the whole' (*First Life of St Brendan*, 26 (Plummer 1910: i.113)). This is widely paralleled. We shall see the poet Horace's favourite spring associated with a tree. And in Norse mythology as the end of the world takes shape in the *Völuspá*, the seeress tells:

> An ash I know, hight Yggdrasil [*the world-tree*],
> the mighty tree moist with white dews;
> thence come the floods that fall adown;
> evergreen o'ertops Urth's [*Fate's*] well this tree.
> *Völuspá* §19 (transl. Lee M. Hollander)

The world-tree is the ultimate mythic projection of this sacred tree – and perhaps mountains like Olympus project the sacred stone.[37] At Uppsala there was a mighty tree (see Chapter 4), compared by Chadwick (1899: 75) with the world-tree, and it too had its spring.

It is of course possible – the obvious example is at the hot springs of Bath – to build a temple and other buildings at or over a spring (Hutton 1991: 230). But where there are no buildings, the tree substitutes for the temple and is in fact the only place, short of resting things around the well, where objects may be left and displayed. This seems particularly to happen in the case of healing. 'Crutches were hung on the oak above the Llancarfan well (Glam.), and great oaks grew over Priest's Well (Mon.) and Ffynon Dderw (Carm.)' (Jones 1954: 19). The 'rag-wells' of Wales, Scotland and England fit here: at these wells, pieces of cloth are tied not of course to the well but to the associated tree and are a rather more intense equivalent of Roman 'fillets' (see Chapter 4). Sometimes the rag-well is associated with healing and the cloth with which the wound was bound and then bathed is hung, complete with the illness, in the tree.[38]

With a combination of tree, spring, stone, we cannot miss the pagan sacred place.

3

FOCUS I: SPRING, LAKE, RIVER

Having distinguished a focus of adoration from an area which acts as a sacred environment, we can now look in detail at the nature and uses of springs, stones and trees. These, above all, are the heart of pre-urban paganism and survive with surprising tenacity even when the temple culture has provided the technological replacement. In this chapter we look at those instances of focus where natural water, a force powerfully felt,[1] is taken into the language and culture of religion. Lakes and rivers will be of importance, but it is springs that are most remarkable.

SPRING AND WELL

What a spring is

Look up the Latin for a 'spring' and what do you find? *Fons, fontis,* 3rd declension masculine, 'a flow of water issuing from the ground' (*Oxford Latin dictionary*) – and that is the marvel of it, that this pure, cold liquid should suddenly, and unaccountably, spring from the earth, 'unmuddied, silvery with gleaming waters' (Ovid, *Metamorphoses* 3.407). *Aqua potabile,* too, a 'font of sweet water' (Cicero, *Verrines* 4.118), often with particular paradox bursting, a liquid, from the solid rock.[2] Well might Varro speak of 'living water pouring forth from the ground' (*Lingua latina* 5.123) or Ausonius close a happy poem with an address to a spring in his native Bordeaux:

Hail, spring of unknown origin, sacred, nurturing, perpetual,
Glassy, grey-blue, deep, sonorous, mud-free, dark;
Hail, spirit (*genius*) of the city, drinkable in healing draughts,
Divona, spring which the language of the Celts has added to the
   divi ('gods').[3]

Ausonius, *The order of noble cities* 14.31 f.

Springs are beloved of poets and with delightful, but not inept, roman-
ticism, Leite de Vasconcellos suggested that in this affection poets are
perhaps close to 'men who live in the state of nature' (1905: ii.237).

With his encyclopaedic fascination for what is magical anywhere in the
world, Pliny the elder captures something of the wonder of springs and in
particular their medicinal qualities:

Unstintingly, far and wide in numerous lands waters gush forth –
sometimes cold, sometimes hot, sometimes both, as amongst the
Tarbelli, a people in Aquitaine and, a short distance away, in the
Pyrenees, sometimes lukewarm or with the chill taken off, claiming to help with diseases and bursting out to help, out of all
animals, man alone. They increase the number of the gods under
various names and they found cities, like Puteoli in Campania
['wells', now Pozzuoli], [Aquae, 'waters'] Statiellae in Liguria
[now Acqui Terme between Genoa and Turin], and [Aquae]
Sextiae in the Province of Narbonne [now Aix-en-Provence], but
nowhere more abundantly than in the bay of Baiae [near Poz-
zuoli] or with more kinds of beneficial effect: some with the
efficacy of sulphur, some of alum, some of salt, some of soda,
some of bitumen, some even with an acid or salt mixture. Some
are beneficial from the actual steam and so great is their strength
that they warm baths and even make cold water boil in [earth]
basins.

Pliny the elder, *Natural history* 31.4 f.

A well (Latin, *puteus*) in today's English, except in affected poetic usage,
is something different from a spring – a shaft artificially sunk into the
earth to reach the water table. These manmade wells differ sharply from
the natural miracle of the unbidden spring. So when authors talk of 'wells'
in religious contexts they are generally reverting to affected usage, though
they also think of the pools formed by springs. We can see this in Jones's
account of the 'wells' (*ffynhonnau*) of Wales, whose character he describes
as follows (1954: 1 f.):

most wells are formed in cavities in the ground, usually circular in
shape. The springs . . . feed the well from the bottom of the

cavity, but occasionally flow into the well from a little distance away. The overflow . . . sometimes forms a shallow pool which in certain districts was also considered holy.

The reader should therefore bear in mind that 'well' in these discussions does not usually correspond to the modern English sense and that it is not easy to disentangle when it is the modern well that is being discussed. You should normally assume that it is Jones's spring and pool. This pool is presumably the place where sacred fish live, perhaps fitted with rings,[4] whose behaviour might be scrutinised for divination and which might have special curative properties.[5] Interest in sacred fish, however, tends to be a Near Eastern phenomenon that only starts when you reach the cultures of pre-Greek Asia Minor:[6]

At Myra in Lycia at the spring of Apollo whom they call Curius (*Koureios*, 'of youths'), fish come for divination when called thrice by pipe. If they snap at meat which is thrown in, it is a good sign for enquirers; but if they drive it away with their tails, it is a terrible sign.

Pliny the elder, *Natural history* 32.17

Just so, at the celebrated shrine of the Syrian goddess Atargatis at Hierapolis ('Sacredville', on the Euphrates, east of Antioch), fish were considered especially holy and the sacred fish came to the call of the sacristans.[7]

Prevalence

Anyone looking at paganism in Europe will quickly realise that 'the worship of springs and streams is common to all Indo-European peoples' (de Vries 1956: i.§248)[8] and that 'holy wells are revered all over Europe' (Jones and Pennick 1995: 107). Christian denunciation of pagans, in sermons, treatises, councils and law-codes, has them spending their time worshipping 'at springs or trees'.[9] A sermon in the huge collection indiscriminately attributed to Augustine attacked 'anyone who celebrates Neptunalia [held on 23 July] at the sea or prays where there is a spring or a river rises from its source'.[10] Caesarius of Arles, who collected, used and revamped such sermons and was so influential for the church councils, constantly, if formulaically, denounces practices at springs.[11]

More individually, Martin of Braga (d. 580) described, or constructed, a whole pagan aquatic system:

Apart from this, many of those demons that have been expelled from heaven have their seat in the sea or in rivers or in springs or in woods and in the same way men ignorant of God worship them as gods and offer them sacrifices. They are called: in the sea, Neptune; in rivers, Lamiae; and in springs, Nymphs.

Martin of Braga, *On reforming pagans* 8

Martin's comment on Lamiae is at first sight absurd, as, of course, Lamiae are actually the name of Greek bogeys, but there is a very obscure and little-used Latin word, *lama*, referring to boggy land which reflects a widespread Indo-European word, as in the English word 'loam'. This root appears in a number of Spanish placenames connected with water (possibly from an 'Old European' language) and it may be that, beneath his cliché-ridden exterior, Martin actually knows something about local cult – and that the worship of water powers was a significant part of it.[12] One piece of evidence may even be the nearby River Limia/Limaea, on which more below.[13]

Holy wells and springs are strong survivors. The number in Ireland was estimated in 1895 as over 3000.[14] Jones's study of Welsh wells deals with no less than 1179 across Wales, whose religious character stands out from the large number with saints' names (437),[15] from the offerings made there of pins (53) or rags (10), and from their associations with forms of ritual: chapel or feast (66).[16] Hope (1893), in a book which was little more than a scrappy collection of reports by correspondents, at least showed what a huge resource of English wells existed and a what a rich tradition they had. I think there is no doubt that a systematic study of England would produce a picture comparable to Wales.[17] A particularly acute instance of continuity is supplied by St Anne's well at Buxton where until 1709 it had been 'lined with Roman lead and surrounded with Roman brick and cement' (Hope 1893: 50). In the Anglo-Saxon laws which Archbishop Wulfstan of York ghosted for Canute (King of England, 1016–35), presumably in a Viking context, he defines paganism as follows (and the reader may enjoy some Old English):[18]

Hæðenscipe byð þæt man deofolgyld weorðige, þæt is þæt man weorðige hæðene godas, and sunnan oððe monan, fyr oððe flod, wæterwyllas oððe stanas oððe æniges cynnes wúdutreowa, oððon wiccecræft lufige oððon morðweorc gefremme on ænige wisen oððon on blote oððon fuyrhte, oððon swylcra gedwimera ænig þinge dreoge.

Paganism is when one worships devil-idols, i.e. one worships heathen gods, and sun or moon, fire or running water (rivers),[19] wells (springs) or stones or any kind of wood, or loves witchcraft or accomplishes any murderous deed in any wise, either in sacrifice or divination, or performs any thing out of such mistaken ideas.

Canute, *Laws* II.5.1 (*GA* i.312 f.)

In Germany archaeology can show spring-offerings going back to the Stone Age and the Germans themselves, more recent arrivals, were continually belaboured for their worship of springs, among other features of nature.[20] So the laws of the Lombard king Liutprand made provision in 727 against those 'who worship at a tree, which the rustics call sacred, and at springs'.[21] And Charlemagne's laws include these two passages, the first specific to the repression of the Saxons, the second more general: 'If anyone makes a vow at springs or trees or groves or makes any offering in the manner of the pagans and eats in honour of the demons, if he is a noble let him pay 60s., a freeman 30s., a serf 15s.' (*Capitulary of Paderborn* §21 (*MG LegesII* 1.69) of *c.* 780); 'Also, concerning trees or rocks or springs, where some stupid people do lights or perform other observations, we altogether instruct that this terrible practice, loathsome to God, wherever it is found be removed and eradicated' (*Admonitio generalis* §65 (*MG LegesII* 1.59) of 789). German placenames also testify to 'holy springs': Heilbrunn, Heilbronn, Heilborn and so on (Grimm 1875: i.487). The English equivalent is forms such as Holywell, Halliwell, though one cannot exclude that in certain instances the holiness derives from the use for baptismal purposes in the nearby church.[22] But why was the church near by?

Leite de Vasconcellos refers to a substantial continuing tradition of springs and wells in Portugal which ultimately goes back to pre-Roman times, and there is sufficient evidence for such cult in Spain, too.[23] In Gaul, springs were often *aménagés*, kitted out with specially constructed pools, in temple precincts.[24] In more modern times Bertrand (1897: 198–210) described how springs very widely continued to attract visits for healing, festivals and pilgrimages, and how very numerous they were, including no less than fifty-eight springs of St Martin, who, as he observed (1897: 205), did not deny that miracles occurred at springs, but wished them to be performed in the name of Christ and his saints rather than of pagan demons.

Schachter finds it necessary to deny 'in all likelihood' that '*every* spring' in Greece and presumably Italy was sacred.[25] The fact that it is so hard to deny is very revealing about the overwhelming number of sacred springs in Greece. Often springs were associated with maidens who had perhaps died there and given the spring their name; and from springs would be drawn the water for the bridal bath, that act of washing which marked the end of maidenhood. In Rome we have the blunt statement of Servius, '*nullus enim fons non sacer*', 'there is in fact no spring that is not sacred', and there are numerous references in dedications and literature to such things as the *genius* (spirit), or the power (*numen*), of the spring, the power of the nymphs of the water, the spring powers, the divine springs, the most holy spring.[26] In Rome itself there were many individual revered springs, for instance, the springs of the Camenae (who were later identified with the Greek Muses), from which the Vestal Virgins drew pure water for the temple of Vesta.[27] Springs, like trees, were adorned with stone structures, with altars and with 'fountain-houses' – where the word for 'house', *aedes*, is also an important word for a temple. In addition to the worship devoted to individual springs, there was even a public Festival of the Springs, the Fontinalia, on 13 October when they were plentiful again.[28] On this day flowers were thrown in the springs and their fountain-structures were garlanded. Even as the Roman state became ever more urbanised, a temple was built, in 231 BC, to the god Fons.

Purity and health

The visible purity of spring water, and conversely the association of dank water with disease, readily makes the spring a place of health and healing.[29] Before the age of hygiene, which arrived slowly during Victorian times, bathing was often a medical matter and it figures, for instance, in the practice of Greek medical experts such as Hippocrates and generally in the practice of the Middle Ages.[30] Taken, water refreshes but is also a cure. Working from outside or inside, it is felt to heal, though whether its 'medicinal properties' are actually sufficient to be perceptible or effective may be another question.[31] Pliny the elder (*Natural history* 31.5–12) certainly believed in them and indeed classifies springs by their mineral contents (above) and according to what in particular individual springs cure: sinews, feet, sciatica, dislocations, fractures, constipation, wounds, head, ears, eyes, infertility, stones in the bladder, miscarriage, not to mention 'tertian ague'. Each spring has its own particular effect:

> Next to Rome the Aquae Albulae cure wounds and are cool, but the Cutiliae in Sabine country are so very cold that they penetrate the body with a sort of suction, so that it might seem almost like a bite – very suitable for the stomach, sinews and the whole body.
>
> Pliny the elder, *Natural history* 31.10

Modern descendants can be found at Volvic (near Clermont-Ferrand), Vichy, and at Vergèze (Gard) where the Source Perrier gives delight to European supermarkets, as also at the various spas (German 'Baden') where those who worry about their health may take 'the' cure. Connecting ancient with modern is 'Wiesbaden, city in west central Germany at the southern foot of the Taunus Mountains, on the River Rhine, capital of Hesse, near Frankfurt. Famed for its 26 hot mineral springs and mild climate, Wiesbaden is one of the leading watering places of Europe, and tourism is vital to the local economy.'[32] Pliny knew these springs, presumably from his personal experience of Germany, and held that water from them stayed boiling hot for three days (31.20).

The spring of Sequana (the Seine) answered the prayers of those in ill health: one Rufus left 836 coins with her. You might come from far away to perform such rites, as we can see from the diverse tribal origins of coins found at the spring of Verneuil-sur-Avre (Eure). Various healing divinities were associated with Celtic springs.[33] Among them were gods called 'Mars' or 'Apollo' in Gaul and Britain, typically with a local Celtic title added, like Mars Nodens at Lydney (Gloucestershire), and Sulis Minerva at Bath.[34] Apollo's speciality in Gaul, according to Caesar (*Gallic war* 6.17) was *depellere morbos*, 'to get rid of illnesses'.[35] Maponus ('Youth'), a title of this healing god 'Apollo', has a spring, *Mabonus fons*, still named after him in a cartulary of the abbey of Savigny (Rhône) around 1090.[36]

A special place is occupied by *hot* springs, which placenames often mark. Thermopylai in Greece, Formiae (Latium), Worms in Germany, and most interestingly for ancient religion a whole string of places beginning *Borm-* look as though they reproduce the Indo-European root *$g^w herm$* or *$g^w horm$* ('hot', our 'warm'). The *Borm-* places reach along the coast from Spain to Lombardy and generally correspond to the area once inhabited by the obscure Ligurians, though there are also a few examples rather far north in France and Germany and indeed further afield, particularly a *Bormanon* among the Iazyges in Hungary.[37] The god of such hot (or, perhaps, 'seething') springs has a regular place in discussions of Celtic religion.[38] Apollo Bormo, or simply Bormo or Borvo,[39] is evidently the god of hot springs, whose worship is attested at many spas, *aquae* (Latin), *Aix* (French): Aachen (*Aquae Granni* – the 'Waters of Grannus', Aix-la-Chapelle), Aix-en-Provence, Aix-en-Diois (Drôme), Aix les Bains (Savoie).[40] Two inscriptions to a god Bormanicus from Iberian Celtic devotees were found at Caldas ('hot baths') de Vizella, south of Braga and Guimarães.[41] These both carry the Latin abbreviation VSLM (*votum solvit libens merito*, 'paid the vow gladly and deservedly') and the obvious guess is that a vow had been made that if the cure worked there would be a dedication forthcoming; the inscriptions are therefore the evidence of the efficacy of the cure.

Three hundred and sixty-nine of Jones's Welsh wells are explicitly known as healing wells, though all, as he observes (1954: 10), may once have been. Health-giving wells are also found in Ireland, even in its mythology where those mortally wounded in the second battle of Magtured were nevertheless restored to health by the magic properties of the well looked after by its guardian Dian Cecht, an Irish Asklepios.[42]

What happens at springs and wells

Health and physical cleanness are interrelated with the metaphysical notion of purity and it is purity that is the principal motor of rites at springs or using spring-water. The affected person washes impurity away, something which continues in Christian baptism, whose archetype is a bathing in the River Jordan, and whose practice is typically nominal bathing in a sacred *font*, the Latin word for spring.[43] Water is useful at dangerous moments, particularly moments of transition. Indeed it may be said that impurity makes a transition to purity imperative and that conversely any transition – for instance, between the unmarried state and the married – creates a condition which is to be disposed of, a form of impurity. Greek springs and streams, sweet unsalted water in motion, were the chosen mediums of lustration and purification for statues, for bridal baths, for mother and child after childbirth, and in instances of defilement more generally.[44] It was vital that the water should be flowing and it was the more powerful if collected from a plurality of sources, even 'twice seven'. Sea-water, too, which if unavailable might be manufactured with water and salt, had a special place in purification, perhaps because in its vastness it was unpollutable, at least until modern times.[45]

Prayers would be made at pagan springs and these are reflected in the votive tablets that might crowd round a Greek spring, as we know from an example on the island of Delos.[46] But prayer is worthless without payment and consequently offerings must be made at the spring: for instance, by tossing objects into its waters. This practice has a certain compulsion and survives to our own times in the trivial superstition of wishing wells. A more powerful offering, however, is a sacrifice into the waters of the spring, celebrated in Horace's famous ode to his local spring, composed maybe on the occasion of the Fontinalia:

> Spring of Bandusia, more gleaming than glass,
> deserving sweet wine and flowers too,
> tomorrow you shall be given a kid . . .
> . . . it shall stain your chilly streams
> with red blood . . .
> you too shall become a famous spring
> when I tell of the oak above the hollow
> stones from which your chattering
> waters gush.
>
> Horace, *Odes* 3.13

To us this might seem to pollute the spring, but religious pollution is not a matter of environmental health. To pollute a well, you must dishonour it: you fill it in, or find a dead cat or dog to throw into it.[47] And a spring, like its opposite, a river disgorging into the sea, is something you should not urinate in, according to the antique Greek author Hesiod (*Works and days* 757 f., maybe before 700 BC). There were, however, excesses and 'the mighty spring at Lerna was allowed to become completely polluted by the sacrifices',[48] at least in our sense.

Wells in England have delivered human skulls, some, as Hutton nicely puts it (1991: 230), 'freshly severed'. But it is perhaps important that these instances are artificial wells, fitting into a broader category of offerings laid in foundations and pits. On the other hand, it is a known custom to drink out of a skull as a cure (e.g. for whooping cough!)[49] and a skull might thus be an appropriate ingredient for a health-giving well.

If wells have power for good, they may also have power for ill. The most fascinating details of folk-practice are recounted by Jones (1954: 120–2). In 1820 a fee of five shillings was paid to the guardian for a curse, but of fifteen shillings to lift a curse, showing 'how strong the belief was in the power of the well' (ibid.: 121). The name of the cursee was written on slate (a heavy material so that it might sink), or if on parchment then folded in lead. Pins might be dropped in the well and 'secret words of cursing' uttered. A person seeking to be freed of the curse might walk three times around the well (circumambulation, here as often in a magical context)[50] and take a corresponding slate or lead package away with him. Together with this went more commonplace stuff, such as effigies with pins in them and ritual Bible-reading. All this might seem harmless modern superstition but for the dire effects it had on those who believed in it and but for the discovery of 130 Romano-British lead curse tablets (defixiones) in the spring at Bath.[51] There is a remarkable preoccupation of British curses with property, in contrast with the wider interests of other Greco-Roman curse tablets (Tomlin 1988: 60). They tend to be written to formula – that is how curses work – and it may help to roll out a set of these formulae: I have lost x, stolen, I curse/give/assign x, whoever did x, whether man or woman/boy or girl/free or slave, I complain/ask, your majesty, that you should exact/not allow, satisfy with his blood/not pay back even with his blood, until x, as long as he shall live (ibid.: 60–8).

41. [very damaged]: . . . stolen, that [you may demand] the price for these [and e]xact this by his blood and he[alth] and that of his family and not allow them to [drink or] eat, to sit on the latrine or [to urinate . . . until] he has paid this off.
65. To Minerva, the goddess Sulis, I have given the thief who stole my hooded cloak, whether slave or free, man or woman; may he not redeem this gift except by his blood.
97. Basilia gives to the temple of Mars her silver ring. If slave or free keeps quiet about it this long or knows anything about it, (I ask) that he be fixed in blood and eyes and all his limbs or even have all his intestines eaten away, the person who stole the ring or who was a middleman.

Curse tablets from Bath (Tomlin 1988)[52]

It was a standard trick to give a stolen object to the divinity so that the job of recovering property, and getting revenge, could be passed on to a professional with supernatural powers, to god as bailiff.

In sacred places you may also discover things you cannot elsewhere; so springs may act as oracles. At Patrai (north-western Peloponnese), next to a grove lay a temple of Demeter:

> In front of the temple of Demeter is a spring. On the side facing the temple, there is a drystone wall; on the side facing out, they have made a descent to the spring. Here there is an infallible oracle, not of general application but for people who are ill. They tie a mirror[53] to a string made of fine thread and let it down, measuring to ensure that it does not go too far into the spring but only enough to touch the water with its rim. Then, praying to the goddess and burning incense, they look in the mirror and it shows them the ill person either alive or dead. That is how far this water reveals the truth, but at Kyaneai very close to Lycia [region of south-western Turkey] there is an oracle of Apollo Thyrxis. The water at Kyaneai provides anyone who looks inside into the spring with the opportunity to view absolutely everything that he wants.
>
> Pausanias 7.21.12 f.

This is clearly a very special oracular site. We are, I think, less startled by the oracle at Hysiai (Boiotia, Greece) where 'in ancient times, according to what the Boiotians say, people used to get oracles by drinking from the well' (Pausanias 9.2.1). The spring Kastalia at that most famous oracular site, Delphi (Boiotia), is perhaps also more than just an accessory.

Such a landscape is wonderfully evoked in Vergil's scene where the legendary King Latinus, wondering whether to marry his daughter to Aeneas (father of the Roman race), consults the spring at Tivoli:

> But the king, worried by the portents, goes to the oracle of Faunus
> his fate-speaking father, and consults the groves beneath tall
> Albunea, the greatest of forests, which from its sacred
> spring resounds and darkly breathes out harsh sulphur.
> From here the tribes of Italy and the whole Oenotrian (Italian) land
> seek responses in uncertainty. When the priest has brought gifts here
> and beneath a silent night lain on slaughtered sheep's
> skins spread out and sought sleep,
> he sees many images flitting about in marvellous ways

and hears many voices and enjoys converse with
the gods and speaks to Acheron [the lake of the dead] in the
    depths of hell.
Here on this occasion father Latinus himself, seeking responses,
duly slaughtered a hundred wool-bearing sheep,
and lay resting on the back of these and on the laid-out
fleeces. Suddenly a voice came from deep within the grove . . .

Vergil, Aeneid 7.81–95

This splendid rhapsody is not so distant from real cult: the grove is the
environment and the fount, a special sulphurous one, its focus. The
offering of sheep is made (a hundred is presumably the tariff for a
legendary king) in order to achieve credit and pay for the vision. There
follows 'incubation', the technical term for sleeping at a holy place in the
hope of receiving a vision.[54] In this example there is obvious power in the
ritual of sleeping on the skins of the very animals that were sacrificed.
And the vision generally follows, though in this instance it is replaced by
the powerful motif of the Voice from the Grove, affiliated to the rustling
of leaves which we see at Dodona (Chapter 6). Springs apparently
remained a popular site for gaining oracular information: Pope Gregory
III, at any rate, saw fit in 731 to forbid 'the auguries of springs'.[55]
    Calendar too may matter for springs. Individual Welsh wells were often
to be visited at specific times of the year, usually in spring and summer,
though 'New Year's Water' could be specially powerful.[56]

Saints, the conversion of the aniconic, and heads

As the Greeks developed an increasingly human sense of religion and
mythology, myths about heroes were used to bring brute stones into the
new environment, by associating the stones with heroes in some way. In
the same way the language of saints is used to christianify pagan wells: the
saint wept here, or struck the ground with his staff, or was healed here, or
did penance here.[57] Irish wells often figure in the *Lives* of Irish saints.[58]
Columba terminated pagan worship at a Scottish spring and blessed it
(Adamnan claims, it had made people *ill* before Columba!): now its
healing powers were authorised, a pattern widely repeated and with particular frequency in France.[59] More alarmingly, given the well-known cult
of skulls among the Celts and archaeological discoveries of real specimens, a number of Welsh Christian myths tell of the death of a saint at a
well, particularly by beheading, and a standard type of story tells how a
virgin is chased by a rapist, beheaded by him and a well appears where the
head falls or blood drips.[60] This Welsh theme is not unparalleled: in the
Auvergne St Julian's head too gives a spring its curative properties.[61]
Jones (1954: 39) delightfully suggests that 'the red stain of iron found

at chalybeate wells helped to give rise to these tales', which you may believe if you do not have the stomach for the cult of skulls, amply evidenced in wells.

A strange counterpoint to this Celtic association of well–tree–skull is found in Norse tradition. Odin apparently gained his wisdom, losing his eye for it, at the spring of the giant Mimir. Here the three motifs are associated: the tree of Mimir (maybe Yggdrasil itself), the spring of Mimir (and its evidently oracular wisdom) and Mimir's oracular head.[62] It is perhaps no coincidence that his name recurs in some German and Swedish river-names. The head is perceived as a source of power, recalling how now and again one comes across special care to bury heads (leaving trunks to rot) because that is where the soul is.[63]

OTHER WATER

Lake

Lakes focus peoples, and their worship. The Retharii or Redarii who inhabited Rethra were also known as the Tholenzi, and their site appears to be at the Tollensee; there is also a River Tollense. And it seems too much of a coincidence that there was a tribe, very probably of the Ljutiči, called the Ploni, as well as the Plönersee in the territory of the Ljutiči.[64] These lakes are centres of identity – they are the people of the lake – and Rethra was the focal centre of religion in the territory.

A different focus, at a more marginal location, is found among the Gauls of the Gévaudan (Lozère). At the lake of St Andéol thirty kilometres north-west of Marvejols there still survive remains of a Gaulish temple. Here, a three-day festival was held every year and people from miles around sank their offerings:

There was a mountain in the land of the Gabali [the area Gévaudan, Lozère], called Helanus,[65] with a big lake. Here, at a certain time, a large gathering of rustics, as though they were making offerings to that lake, threw in pieces of cloth, and material for the making of men's clothes. Some gave fleeces of wool, very many cheeses and wax, or bread, and all sorts of things, each one according to their resources, which I consider it would take too long to list. They came with waggons, bringing food and drink, slaughtering animals, and feasting for a period of three days. But on the fourth day, just before they had to go, there would be a storm with mighty thunder and lightning. And so huge a rainstorm would descend, with the force of stones, that scarce any of them thought they would escape. So it happened every year and the foolish people were engulfed by terror. A long time afterwards, a priest from the city [Gabali, the former Anderitum, now Javols, north of Marvejols] who had taken up the bishopric went to the place and preached to the crowd that they should desist from this to avoid being consumed by the anger of heaven, but his preaching had no effect on such basic rusticity. Then, inspired by the Divinity, the priest of God built a basilica in honour of St Hilary of Poitiers [more likely, St Hilary Gabalitanus, of the Gévaudan] at a distance from the shore of the lake, in which he placed his relics, saying to the people, 'Do not, my sons, do not sin before the Lord; [note the manner of Martin of Tours:] there is no religious power in a lake . . .' Then the people, touched to the heart, were converted and, leaving the lake, they took all the things they had been accustomed to throw in the lake and brought them to the basilica.

Gregory of Tours, *On the glory of the confessors* 2

And there were no storms ever again. Astonishingly, annual meetings there appear to have continued until 1868.[66]

As for the terror which the lake inspired in the peasants of the Gévaudan, one of my good friends who come from Lozère told me that it has not disappeared. Peasants do not pass along the shores of the lake without throwing coins into it; and it is not certain that people do not still go there individually on pilgrimage.

Bertrand 1897: 212

We should perhaps envisage similar integrating ceremonies at the revered shrine at Toulouse with its 'enclosures and sacred lakes'. This is where the huge quantity of valuables including unworked silver and gold was looted by the consul Q. Servilius Caepio in 106 BC (see Chapter 1).

River

The *Order of noble cities,* a poem of Ausonius celebrating fourteen cities in the Roman Empire, often makes a point of mentioning and praising their rivers. Indeed, many European cities are rightly proud of the rivers that they stand on, quite apart from any usefulness they have. There is something elemental about rivers altogether:

Now destroyers of sown land and houses in their impetuous course; now fertilisers of the plain when serene and gentle; man lives always among mysterious forces which he will worship or exorcise depending on circumstances.

Leite de Vasconcellos 1905: ii.224 (my translation)[67]

Even this may be too utilitarian a view of these mighty forces. It is therefore no surprise to discover a significant role for them in the various paganisms of Europe. This may indeed go back to Indo-European times, to judge by the existence of such worship in almost every descendant culture, including the Indian and Iranian.[68]

There is also a fascination in the fact that rivers flow: they move, they are alive.[69] Canute's laws which we saw earlier in this chapter identify not only springs but *flod*, water on the move. Likewise a Roman may talk of a *vivum flumen*, the *live* river water that makes it suitable for purifications before sacrifice or generally for rituals of cleansing spaces, 'lustration'; this contrasts with the static and artificial water found in cisterns and pipes.[70] Rivers, then, by their flow, continue the miracle of life which their springs had started. The god Bedy (probably pronounced 'Wedü'), wor-shipped by Macedonians and Thracians, appears to have been a god of water wherever it flowed, in rivers or springs.[71] And Slavs 'also [in addi-tion to the god of lightning, i.e. Perun] worship rivers and nymphs and certain other spirits and they sacrifice to all of these as well. And they perform their divinations at these sacrifices' (Procopius, *Gothic war* (pub-lished *c.* AD 551) 3.14.24). Germans, in this case the Alamans, 'pray to certain trees and streams of rivers and hill-tops and gorges and to these, as though they were performing holy rites, they sacrifice horses and cows and thousands of other things, by decapitation' (Agathias, *Histories* (*c.* AD 580) 1.7 Keydell). Indeed, the catastrophic battle half a millennium earlier in the summer of AD 58 between the Germanic tribes, the Hermunduri and Chatti (Chapter 9), was occasioned by a salt-bearing river which was simultaneously a sacred focus, though we discover little of its nature from Tacitus' attempt (*Annals* 13.57) to get inside the primitive mind: 'an ingrained religious belief that those places were specially close to heaven and that the prayers of mortals were nowhere more closely heard by the gods'. It must be said, however, that the evidence for a German cult of rivers is sparse and that the river-names, largely feminine, do not seem to generate a mythology – Rhine-maidens apart![72]

Very many rivers are known to be connected with cult in the Greco-Roman world and Waser catalogues around 200 of them, many more than just the major ones that do not dry up in the summer.[73] Herakles even wrestled with one, Acheloös, and Homer's Achilles was not to be outdone when at Troy he fought the River Xanthos (that 'men call Skamandros', *Iliad* 20.74). It is a presupposition of the epic that rivers can take human form, that rivers are addressable in the same way that gods are.[74] As Wilamowitz (1931: i.25, my translation) inimitably puts it:

Gods that dwell in their element which is known to man and accessible to him, in tree and bush, spring and meadow, do not

need to assume a form to make man aware of their divinity . . .
But in his thought they become persons.

So the shipwrecked Odysseus, fearing being pounded to death on the
rocks, sees his only hope in the river and does not stop to ask whether
it is divine:

> But when to the mouth of the fair-flowing river
> he came swimming, here then seemed to him the best place,
> smooth of rocks and there was shelter from the wind,
> and he recognised it as it flowed out and prayed in his heart:
> 'Hearken, Lord, whoever you are: I come to you, who receive
>   many prayers,
> trying to escape the sea and the threats of Poseidon . . . '
>
> > Homer, *Odyssey* 5.441–6

In the marvellously hyperbolic imagination of the poet, rivers can even
attend councils:

> Zeus bade Themis call all the gods to assembly
> from the head of Olympos with its many folds; and she going
> everywhere bade them proceed to the house of Zeus.
> And none of the rivers was absent, except Okeanos,
> nor any of the nymphs that inhabit beautiful groves
> and sources of rivers and grassy meadows.
>
> > Homer, *Iliad* 20.4–9

Homer is the foundation for, or at least represents the movement towards,
anthropomorphic sculpture. In the fullness of time, river-gods will become
popular on coins and in sculpture, reclining to assume the position
appropriate for a river (they tend to be rather horizontal) and convenient
for those awkward corners in pediments.[75] Rivers, then, had a further,
geographical, convenience: on coins they reminded you where this wild
western Greek new town actually was. So the coins should not lead us to
conjure up a plethora of river worship in Greece, though it certainly
happened, as we shall now see.[76]

Acheloös is an unusual example, as his worship is widespread – far
beyond any direct connection with the river that bears this name – and he
may in some way act as a focus for the worship of all rivers.[77] Another
well-known river-god is Alpheios, perhaps because he flows past prestigious Olympia. Descent from rivers, as from other gods, is possible (in
the same way the Gaulish king Viridomarus claimed descent from the
Rhine).

The Romans were not quite so interested, except under Greek influence, in river-gods. The Tiber was not worshipped in the old religious calendar of Rome, but he was already saluted in the early second century BC by the father of Latin epic poetry, Ennius:[78] 'and you, Father Tiber, with your holy stream', looking fashionably like a Greek Acheloös or Okeanos.[79] He can be invoked in prayers and has a shrine on the Tiber island in the heart of Rome, whose foundation date and therefore feast date was 8 December.[80] Here he appears also to have been worshipped by the guild of fishermen and divers on 7 June. Vergil, the most Greek of Roman poets, evidently liked this line of Ennius, used it of the Tiber (*Aeneid* 8.72) and, slightly modified, of the 'sacred stream' of Clitumnus (*Georgics* 2.147), but Clitumnus' magic is of course in the spring (see Chapter 6). Other rivers too were worshipped: the Volturnus, whichever river of that name was meant, even had an ancient priesthood, the *flamen Volturnalis*, and a festival, the Volturnalia, on 27 August; and rivers such as the Tiber were included by name in the prayers of the augurs and the litanies of the pontifices.[81]

The paganism which appears most devoted to rivers is that of the Celts. The name of the River Marne originates as *Matrona* ('Mother') and at the source of the Seine, even if it counts as a spring, lay the sanctuary of the goddess *Sequana*.[82] To these goddesses we can add, for instance, the Yonne and Saône. In Britain the Dee, Clyde, Severn and Wharfe, as well as the Braint (Anglesey) and Brent (Middlesex) – both from *Brigantia – and in Ireland the Boyd and Shannon may all be goddesses of this type.[83] Indeed, *Deva* (Dee) is simply Celtic for 'goddess', as Ausonius sensed in his address to the spring Divona in Bordeaux (above).[84] There is another spring Divona, known from a thirteenth-century source, which accounts for Divonne-les-Bains (Ain, on the Swiss border).[85] De Vries (1961: 115) cites river-names from this root in Belgica (north-eastern Gaul) – the Deve, Devere, Deinze (*Devonisa), Diest (*Divusate) and Dieppe (*Divisapa) – a Deba in Spain and the Dees of Wales, Scotland and Ireland. Towns too end up named after springs and rivers of this type: Aberdeen, Deva (Chester) and Devona (Cahors).[86]

Sacred rivers were frequent in the Iberian peninsula, where there was a substantial Celtic population, and inscriptions are found to such rivers as the Durus (Douro) and the Iberus (Ebro):[87] DVRI|C. IVLIV|PVLACES – 'Gaius Julius Pulaces to the Douro'. This is a very provincial inscription: Pulaces is a reasonably familiar name in the Iberian peninsula, though he has gained Roman *praenomen* and *cognomen*, presumably as a freedman in imperial service; the ending -*i* of *Duri* is terrible Latin but good Celtic.

The River Limia (today's Minho, northernmost Portugal, and Galicia, Spain), north of Braga, had somehow become associated with one of the Greco-Roman underworld rivers, the *Lethe* ('Forgetfulness', or in Latin

Oblivio) – perhaps folk believed that drinking from it caused forgetfulness – and it generated much confusion in ancient authors. It certainly terrified a Roman army in 137 BC:[88]

> Decimus Junius stormed cities and subjugated Lusitania right up to the Ocean, and when they refused to cross the River Oblivion, he snatched the standard from the standard-bearer, crossed it himself, and in this way persuaded them to cross.
>
> Livy, *Summaries* Bk 55

River worship like anything else dilutes into folk-custom and folk-belief. An interesting specimen comes from seventeenth-century Estonia, where Grimm reports the existence of a sacred stream, the 'Wöhhanda', running through a sacred grove.[89] Here no-one might cut down any tree or branch, else they would die within the year. The river's source and the stream itself had also to be cleaned to avoid bad weather. But in 1641 a German, one Hans Ohm, arrived and built a mill there, inducing several years of bad weather thereby, which the local Estonians could only end by burning down the mill.

Water worship

How do you worship a spring, a lake or a river? We have seen objects left on trees at wells, but if you have any quantity of water, the obvious, and very widespread,[90] way is simply to deposit objects in it – Excalibur into the lake where the goddess will receive it. Pliny the younger describes how coins can be seen through the clear water of the Clitumnus (*Letters* 8.8; Chapter 6). And an inscription from Narni records coin offerings so copious that a statue, double doors and trimmings could be made from them.[91] So in Gaul rivers have frequently been found to contain offerings, usually of military equipment, and found in bulk particularly near fords, on which more below.[92] Similarly, 'thousands of coins of the Roman period and metal figures of animals, birds and gods have been found in the Thames at London' (Hutton 1991: 230). And when the Olympic Games were held visitors threw gifts into the River Alpheios.[93] *Crossing* rivers was a matter of particular importance for Europeans as for other peoples.[94] At Rome, the reconstruction of the Pons Sublicius called for sacrifices on both banks conducted by the Roman priests, the *pontifices*, whose name, despite all clever theories to the contrary, obviously means 'bridge-makers'. In archaic Greece around 700 BC, Hesiod enjoins us, in a book of moralising instructions,

> never to cross the fair-flowing water of ever-streaming rivers
> by foot before you pray looking into the fine streams
> washing your hands with lovely bright water.

But whoever crosses a river in baseness and with unwashed hands,
at him the gods take offence and give grief afterwards.

Hesiod, *Works and days* 737–41

So it may be regarded as part of common piety to make individual offerings to a river, particularly when crossing them, like Gauls at fords.

It is important above all for an army that crosses a river to make transit offerings (*diabateria*). This is what the Spartan king Kleomenes did unsuccessfully to cross the River Erasinos and march against Argos;[95] he then took his troops by sea instead and slaughtered a bull to the sea, a rare displaced *diabaterion*. More gruesome *diabateria* were offered by the Franks crossing the Po at Ticino in AD 539:

> The Franks, once they had seized the bridge, took the women and children of the Goths that they found and sacrificed them, throwing their bodies into the river as the first-fruits of the war. These barbarians, though they had become Christians, retained much of their previous ways of thought, employing human sacrifice and performing other unholy sacrifices – and divining by these means. The Goths, seeing what was being done, were reduced to panic and fled inside the walls.
>
> Procopius, *Gothic war* 2.25.10 f.

Even the philosophical but religiously conservative Emperor Marcus Aurelius, at the height of the war against the Germanic Marcomanni and Quadi (in the early 170s), could be induced to cast two lions alive into the Danube presumably as an offering for safe crossing.[96] The lions, however, just swam across to the other side and the unimpressed Germans finished them off with clubs.

Likewise, this can be a symbol for the act of 'crossing', as seems to be the case when Achilles is reserving his hair to be offered to the River Spercheios (*Iliad* 23.146) as he crosses into full adulthood. In real life, too, 'Where the Neda comes closest to the city of Phigalia [in Arcadia], at that point the boys of the Phigaleans shear off their hair to the river' (Pausanias 8.41.3). The same symbolism may underlie Aristotle's report that 'amongst many barbarians there is a custom . . . of dipping new-born babies into a cold river', in his view to get them used to endurance from the start.[97] Another transition is into kingship and the first duty of a king in Paionia (Yugoslav Makedonija) was to bathe in the River Astibos.[98]

Rivers in Greece could be worshipped on a more formal basis with the normal accoutrements for a god. In Homer the River Skamandros has its own priest (*Iliad* 5.77) and the Spercheios, though Achilles may intend to slaughter fifty rams 'into' the source, has its 'precinct and sacrificial altars' (*ibid.* 23.148). Sacrifice to a river may therefore be direct (drown-

Figure 3.1 The lions of Marcus Aurelius – unsuccessful *diabateria*

ing), partial (blood only) or indirect (altar). So, at Mykonos on 7
Hekatombaion (in July), ten lambs were sacrificed to the Acheloös, three
at the altar, the rest 'into the river'.[99] A mixture is visible in lines in
which Achilles talks of the practices of the Trojans in honour of the
Skamandros: '. . . to whom you sacrifice many bulls/and send down
whole-hooved horses alive in its streams' (Homer, *ibid.* 21.131 f.). This
may seem like the practice only of a fictional population of supposed non-
Greeks, the Trojans, but in fact it does represent, if rather scaled-up for
the epic, a Greek religious custom of drowning horses – an unusual
sacrificial animal in Greek culture, even if this particular practice is known,
according to Waser (1909: 2777) 'across the whole earth'. Pausanias
(8.7.2) knew that in earlier times 'the Argives used to send down horses
for Poseidon adorned with bridles into Dine', a spring arising off the
coast in the sea which was found in 1847,[100] supposedly the emergence of
an Arcadian river – and a clear anomaly in the landscape, dangerously
subverting boundaries. The religious danger and mystique of rivers is
enhanced by uncertainty about their sources, as in the case of the Nile.
The River Alpheios was supposed to come underground from Sicily; the
Erasinos was supposed to come from Lake Stymphalis in Arcadia via a
mysterious chasm (Herodotos 6.76.1).

It is always good manners to fall in with local custom. Perhaps that was
why, when King Xerxes of Persia was invading Greece, his Magi sacrificed
white horses into the River Strymon, an act surely more in tune with local
Thracian custom than with Persian (*ibid.* 7.113).

4

FOCUS II: STONE AND TREE

Our religious focus now sharpens into those most focal of natural objects, the stone and the tree. These are the natural materials from which more advanced focal objects, the altar and the statue, are in due course made, and they encapsulate all the force of those later objects.

STONE

What a stone is

We are talking here of large, notable stones which are intimately connected with religion. The stone is remarkable because of its size and local rarity (isolation). As trees are grand, powerful and inspiring, stones are mighty, natural and heavier than man can shift – heroes may display their strength by shifting stones that today's men cannot. Indeed, a stone may be preternaturally immobile: it was set up by an Irish saint and simply *cannot* be moved, or, once moved, returns to its place, a common myth exploring the special inanimacy and distinctive mode of being which great stones possess.[1] At a physical extreme, a menhir in Brittany tipped the scales at 350,000 kilograms (de Vries 1961: 185).

Unwrought stones (*arga litha*) may be where they always have been, the products of glaciation or erosion. Some may be struck by lightning and be 'thunderstones'. Others may be alleged to be (but few are) meteorites, alleged fallen from heaven above in order to express the power felt in them:

> Before the consuls could draw lots for their provinces, prodigies were reported: a stone had fallen from the sky into the grove of Mars in the district of Crustumerium, a boy with no limbs was born in the district of Rome and a snake was seen with four feet.
>
> Livy 41.9.4f.

I doubt if this stone actually fell in 177 BC: this has the look of a myth to explain the sacred stone in the grove of Mars.

The unwrought stone may be anointed with oil, an object of reverence. Alternatively it may be used as, and grow into, a sacrificial altar. Following a different track, it may be worshipped as the god, a predecessor of the stone statue – an 'aniconic' (non-representational) object of worship. Wrought (dressed or sculpted) stones may be used in a structure such as Stonehenge or may be the cult statue of the god. Between a fully iconic representation and leaving the stone unwrought lie various geometrical possibilities – pillars and pyramidoid, for instance. Pillars stand on the fertile conceptual margin between stone and tree. And a special category is formed by stalagmites in their mysterious environment.

Feelings about stones

At the Société d'Anthropologie de Paris a session was presented in 1877 on 'The sacred stones of the valleys of the Pyrenees' – in a particular remote valley whose nearest town is Bagnères de Luchon (Haute Garonne), west of Andorra, and in Roman time the spa Aquae Onesiae:[2]

> These sacred stones are most often found in the vicinity of fountains, simple blocks of porphyroid or amphiboliferous granite, left on the mountain by the quaternary glacier and having in previous times served purposes that can no longer be ascertained. Some of these blocks are stones with basins. In any event, they are practically always unworked, rarely presenting any characteristic to distinguish them from other big stones scattered on Mount Espiaut. There are plenty of them that would be passed unremarked by the observer if local traditions and the worship of the inhabitants did not bring them to his attention.
>
> . . . Vainly the priests combat them face to face – they have not succeeded in removing them from all hearts. Vainly they have the stones secretly destroyed, vestiges of such a persistent paganism (particularly those next to which youths and young girls hold their assignations). The inhabitants, when they surprise the

workmen, all come out and prevent the work of demolition. When it has been possible to do it without arousing their attention, they gather together the bits, put them back in place and continue to heap veneration upon them. The fragments have to be dispersed far away from the sacred stone to put an end to the cult it received; the place where it was remains sacred and sometimes the priests set up a cross there to allow religion to benefit from the traditional respect devoted to the place.

It would have been nice to interview a 'pagan' about his trust in these stones and that is precisely what the presenters of the session did:

> One day we asked an old man for some explanations about the sacred stones. He replied to us . . . 'Once upon a time, when people were decent, everyone had *un grana fé* ['a great faith' the peasant spoke in Occitan/Catalan] in these stones: everyone prayed to them and worshipped them. *Jou qu'è tourtem crédut en acquères peyres: qu'en mourire en creyei* ('I myself have always believed in these stones and I shall die believing in them').' Following a remark by the Curé the old man cried out in a voice vibrating with emotion, 'You may not believe in these stones, Monsieur le Curé, but *I* do. I believe in them as all my ancestors did and two of today's men are not the equal of the men of those days.'[3]

Personalising stones

Greek religion in the classical era was generally unable to accommodate nature worship without translating what was worshipped into the more personal language of anthropomorphic divinities. Often, too, the natural object was transferred into a personal world through the medium of a myth told about it.[4] Similarly, a menhir found at Kervadel and later kept at Kernuz (Finistère)[5] had figures of Mars, Mercury, Minerva and Hercules sculpted on it precisely in order to bring it within anthropomorphic religion. This is, as Toutain said, 'a similar procedure to that adopted by the Christians when they engraved, or fixed, crosses on many a megalith'.[6]

In the basilica of St Martin in Tours, quite in the manner of the accommodations of Greek mythology, there was

> a stone on which the blessed man is said to have sat down. A long time afterwards, a priest called Leo moved the holy stone from its place so that he might lay down a tomb for himself. In no time, as he returned home trembling, he was seized by fever, and on the

third day breathed his last. And it was recognised that the Saint had taken offence. We recollect that this, then, happened in our time.

Gregory of Tours, *On the glory of the confessors* 6

This stone is not quite an object of worship and need not necessarily have had a long history (though it may have done). But, psychologically, it continues to be the case, as it had been in pagan times, that the stone is the focus of attention and the bearer of power. In Ireland, too,

> various stones are regarded as sacred because of their association with certain saints, though in many cases the cult is probably much older. Sometimes the stone marks the site of a martyrdom; often it has served as a vessel to transport the saint across the ocean when other means of navigation failed; even more frequently it shows the print of his feet or knees, or traces of the punishment of the enemies who have opposed him.
>
> Plummer 1910: i.clv–clvi

In France, too, a stone may be termed, for example, the *pierre de Ste Radegonde* or *de S. Urbain* or *de S. Vaast* (Reinach 1908: 384), the saint's name registering the primal sacrality of the stone.

Stones and permanence

Stones, being relatively immobile, embody place. An instance is Holystone (Northumberland) in English;[7] in German Holstein presumably means 'hollow-stone' (on whose uses see below). Many personal names end in -stone (Old English *-stan*) which, though not direct evidence of stone worship,[8] is illuminating for the admirable steadfastness associated with stones, which of course also makes them suitable objects to stand on when swearing an oath or standing trial or passing judgement. So Reinach is able to identify a special category of oath-stones ('pierres de serment', 1908: 409). Frazer gets to the root of this when he analyses a passage of Saxo:[9] 'the ancients, when they were about to choose a king, used, fixing stones in the ground, to stand on them and cast their votes, foreshadowing through the firmness of the stones the steadfastness of their deed' (Saxo 1.2.1, pp. 10 f. Holder). On this he rightly comments: 'The common custom of swearing upon a stone may be based partly on a belief that the strength and stability of the stone lend confirmation to the oath' (Frazer 1911: *Magic art* i.160 (= 1905: 73)).

A different fixity is that of death: stones mark graves, in which case they become, as they enter the wrought and iconic age, Greek stelai or the nuanced gravestones of other individual cultures. Their permanence outweighs the bodily disappearance of the dead and offers a vehicle for contact with the dead just as a statue does for the intangible gods. They may also keep the dead in place.

Stones, however, are not totally immovable and they may therefore embody conventional place rather than natural place. They may mark boundaries and in Roman religion a boundary stone (*terminus*) is erected at a chosen spot after, and above, due sacrifice (Chapter 9). This stone is not a mere secular convenience: there is a god Terminus and he has an ancient festival, the Terminalia, held on 23 February as the year is ending and the extra day, if any, is added to February (it was not added at the end). This is a time when society must mark out its social divisions and, apparently, its land divisions anew.

Conversely, in Greek culture stones may mark centrality and be called a 'navel' (*omphalos*), finding a context in the cult of Apollo, god of the Apella, the gathering or assembly in some Greek cultures – presumably somewhere central.[10] Delphi had the most famous *omphalos* stone. But sometimes we overlook them: how many books tell of the stone at the heart of the mystic sanctuary of Demeter and Kore at Eleusis?[11]

Stone as the object of cult

Stones are very frequent objects in cult the world over. One may instantly think of the *Ka'ba* at Mecca, the centre of a whole religion. Interesting, too, is the use which Phoenicians made of conical stones as a focus of cult. These 'betyls' (beth-el, 'house of god', whence the Greek *baitylos*) might be found on altars, or at the centre of the precinct in lieu of a shrine or inside one.[12] Phoenician betyls show how grey the area is between marker, cult object and statue. The important point is that the stone identifies the centre, focuses the religious site – and of course as a result is imbued with its perceived power. Once we concentrate on the stone, even the distinction between an altar and a statue seems secondary.

In Greece the usual sign that a stone is itself an object of cult is when it is 'translated' into person-language: it is given the name of a god. At Megara in the second century AD, 'in the Old Gymnasium next to the Nymph Gates there is a stone shaped like a small pyramid. They call it Apollo Karinos and there is a sanctuary of the Eileithyiai [goddesses of childbirth, usually singular] here' (Pausanias 1.44.2). The shape is reminiscent of the conical Phoenician betyls, but Eileithyiai recall the Cave of Eileithyia at Amnisos (Crete), known to Odysseus (*Odyssey* 19.188), where a stalagmite was marked off for worship.[13] In that case we are clearly dealing with the remains of worship going back before Greeks arrived. And this picture is confirmed by the prominence given, in religious contexts, to stones and pillars on Minoan seal-rings and more generally in Minoan and Mycenaean religion. So here we see a strange form of cult object, somewhat alien to classical Greek practice, perhaps reaching back to Phoenician influence in the Dark Age, perhaps to the pre-Greek populations of Greece and Crete, but in either case representing the continuation by persistent religious tradition of something from a very different past. Sacred stones and barely representational non-statues are in fact felt and respected by the Greeks for the special things that they are. In the sacral landscape of Sikyon,

> after the *heroōn* ('hero-shrine') of Aratos there is an altar [a stone?] to Poseidon Isthmios, and a [statue of] Zeus Meilichios and Artemis Patroa, neither made with any skill – the Meilichios is like a pyramid, the Artemis like a pillar.
>
> Pausanias, 2.9.6

The lack of skill highlights, and reinforces, the fact that these statues are talking a different language. It is important that they should not display that sort of skill which privileges form over material.

There are also a few examples in Roman Gaul of focal stones. At Alesia, according to Toutain, a sanctuary was built around a dolmen-like megalith,[14] as was another (de Vries 1961: 186) at Triguères (Loiret) – not to speak of those that have survived in modern Christian churches, for instance at one corner of the west front of the cathedral at Le Mans, or in various Austrian churches listed by de Vries (1961: 185 f.). We have already seen the Kernuz menhir in Brittany marked as an object of worship. Similarly, in Ireland we have seen stones associated with saints, some of which must have been objects of cult.

In the sanctuary of Endovellicus (Terrena, Portugal; see Chapter 7) was found a curious Latin inscription on a rectangular block of stone, 0.43m tall × 0.17m square: 'To Endovolicus Julia Anus gladly dedicated *it left behind* by the ancestors.' Leite de Vasconcellos (1905: ii.134) interpreted the 'it left behind' (*relictum*) as a vow unfulfilled by the family of Julia, but Toutain (1917: 174f.) argued that it was more likely that the 'it left behind' was the stone itself. He compared it with two other mini-monoliths. One stone, 1.66 × 0.44 × 0.55m, comes from the Roman baths at Caldas de Vizella in Portugal and is dedicated to the spring-god Bormanicus (see Chapter 3); its inscription tells you to tell your slave 'not to smear this stone'. The other, 1.85 × 0.30 × 0.23m, from the district of Paredes de Coura midway between Braga and Vigo, is dedicated to 'Macarius'.[15] 'Without any doubt,' Toutain continues, 'the sacred character of these stones derived from their actual shape and antiquity. Is it rash to suppose that these were ancient standing stones or menhirs?' It probably is rash, but it shows at least the power of the dedicated stone – inscriptions have a greater presence than noticeboards, and themselves, if sacred, can embody or project the power of the god.

Even as late as 1583 we find a stone attested as an object of pagan worship:

> In Samogitia [northern Lithuania] . . . the inhabitants keep up ancient superstitions: the Jupiter of lightning, known in the *patois* as 'Perkunas', old oak trees; 'Szermuksznis' or sorb-tree; elsewhere 'Akmo', a sizeable stone.
>
> *Annual report of the Society of Jesus* 1583, *LPG* 435 (also, Clemen
> 1936: 109)

Indeed, Lithuanians kept stones in their homes as domestic altars:

> Elsewhere they keep stones, not small ones, in their granaries, dug into the ground with the smooth surface uppermost, covered not with earth but with straw and they call them 'Deyves' [*gods*]. They religiously worship them as guardians of their corn and herds.
>
> *Annual report of the Society of Jesus* 1601, *LPG* 433 (also, Clemen
> 1936: 110)

> They worship certain stones as sacred which they keep in their kitchen or stores or granaries, which in their language they call 'Atmeschenes Wête', i.e. 'projecting places' (?). It is a terrible sin amongst them to profane such places or for them to be touched by anyone else except the person who has the right from the (power) above. They pour over such stones the blood of whatever animals they slaughter and they put there a small portion from any meal.
>
> *Annals of the Wendish Residence of the Society of Jesus* 1618,
> *LPG* 455 f. (also, Jouet 1989: 142)

Worshipped stones are quite widely distributed. Choudhury, for instance, mentions in the case of Hinduism stones worshipped as manifestations of Śakti (the creative energy/major female divinity of the universe) which are, according to myth, the dismembered limbs of Satī (1994: 73) and also at wayside shrines (*ibid.*: 84). These latter call to mind the heaps of stones or cairns that are worshipped as *hermaia* – objects associated with Hermes – at Greek waysides (Burkert 1985: 156).

What happens at stones

Stones, like trees and groves, called for recognition and respect. This shines through Apuleius' withering description of the impiety of his opponent Aemilianus in a lawsuit of AD 158:

Up to this age he has made his prayers to no god, frequented no temple. If he is passing by some shrine (*fanum*) he thinks it wicked to raise his hand to his lips in adoration. This is a man who makes no offerings of first-fruits from his crops, his grapes or his flocks to the gods of the countryside who feed and clothe him. There is no shrine (*delubrum*) in the grounds of his villa, no place or grove consecrated. Why mention grove and shrine? People who have been there state they have seen on his property not a single stone which has been anointed or branch which has been wreathed.

Apuleius, *Apologia* 56

It is common piety, then, to set up groves and shrines and to anoint stones with oil and decorate trees as can be seen in the wall-painting of the age.[16] This established place of respect for stones in the apparatus of piety is also attested in the unusual, Epicurean denunciation by the poet Lucretius (*c*. 55 BC):

Nor is it any piety often to be seen turning, head veiled,
To a stone, and to approach every altar,
Nor to fall prostrate on the ground, and to spread one's hands
Before the shrines of the gods, nor to sprinkle altars with much
    blood
Of cattle, nor to tie vow upon vow.

Lucretius, *On the nature of the universe* 5.1197–1201

Stones may also be manipulated and turned, as we will see on the Sacred Promontory in Portugal. But direction matters too. Ireland was sensitive to this: turn a stone clockwise (*diesel*), or circumambulate it, and you will have beneficial effects. To curse someone, go anticlockwise (*tuaithbel*)![17] This is the country where kings did their annual circuit following the path of the sun. Not to follow it is to practise black magic.[18]

Stones with hollows or holes in them invite special use, notably for healing. Grimm (1876: ii.976) cites an instance in Poitou where weak children are placed in the hollow of the stone of Saint Fessé ('tired'?) to regain their strength.[19] In another case, at Minchinhampton (Gloucs) there is a stone, the 'Long Stone', with a hole at the bottom, 'through which children used to be passed for the cure or prevention of measles, whooping-cough and other ailments'.[20] Another use for hollow stones, found in Lithuania, Ireland and Wales, is to collect and hallow rainwater, which might then have healing properties.[21] Such stones might have symbolic force too: sterile women in the département of Ille-et-Vilaine (it includes Rennes) apparently used to rub themselves against hollow stones (Reinach 1908: 407).

TREE

> I used to venerate – my blindness! – statues fresh out of the
> furnace, gods made on anvils with hammers, elephant bones
> [*ivory*], paintings, ribbons on antiquated trees. If ever I saw a
> stone smeared and befouled with olive oil I used to fawn
> before it and address it as though there were some immediate
> force in it; and I sought favours from a trunk that perceived
> nothing. Indeed I was seriously insulting those very gods that
> I was convinced existed, inasmuch as I believed them to be
> wood, stones or bones, or to live in this type of substance.
>
> Arnobius, *Against the pagans* 1.39

What trees are like

We often find an *appreciation* of trees in ancient writers, just as we might
admire one today.[22] In an extraordinary story, Pliny tells of an admirer
who went too far and drifted into fetishism:

> On a hill called Corne in the suburban part of the land of
> Tusculum, there is a grove in ancient reverence (*antiqua religione*)
> dedicated by Latium to Diana. The foliage of the beech forest
> (*nemus*) is sheared as though by topiary. In it an exceptional tree
> was loved in our times by Passienus Crispus, twice consul, the
> orator, later more famous thanks to his marriage with Agrippina
> through which he became stepfather of Nero. He was in the habit
> of kissing and embracing it – not only of lying under it and
> pouring wine over it.
>
> Pliny the elder, *Natural history* 16.242

But, we see, it would be normal to respond to a tree by pouring wine over
it. Some sort of psychological and emotional dimension appears to underlie the languages in which we respond – religious for pagans, aesthetic and
ecological for people today. There is even a legal language: trees have
rights, are often legally protected and the owner of the land may not fell
them. Turning back to the Indo-European language such as we can
reconstruct it, it appears to have been sensitive to two distinct forms of
life, **Hwes*, the 'being' of men and animals, and **bheuH*, the being, or
rather 'growing', of plants.[23] Of the latter, trees are the most striking
specimens – they are the bulls of the plant world. You respond to
*Hwes-life by sacrificing it; **bheuH*-life is more alien and awesome,
requiring the establishment of a symbiosis with our different being.

Writers since Mannhardt in the nineteenth century have seen trees as
participating in a cyclical process of renewal. Van der Leeuw, writing in

the 1930s on the power innate in various forms and circumstances of religion, stressed how the deciduous tree undergoes *repeated* renewal:

> à éprouver la puissance de l'arbre en la voyant surmonter la mort au course d'une suite ininterrompue de renouveaux, l'homme . . . en vint a considérer l'existence de l'arbre, si solidement assurée, comme étant la plus puissante.
>
> Van der Leeuw 1948: §5.3

But, according to Durand (1960: 391), 'the cyclic optimism seems to be reinforced in the archetype of the tree, because the verticality of the tree gives its future irreversible direction and to some degree humanises it bringing it into relation with the significant vertical stature of the human being'. Thus the tree also belongs, where Durand's predecessor Bachelard (1943: 232) had classified it, as an 'image verticalisante' or, as Durand puts it, an 'image ascensionelle'.

Trees live long in comparison with the span of human life, but it is important to remember just how ancient they can be: 'An age of at least 400 years is quite often reached by oaks' (Rackham 1970: 27). Instances can be found of oaks that are much older, as much as 700 years, but other trees rarely live beyond 500, with the possible exception of the yew, though the evidence for this latter is somewhat anecdotal. Most trees have therefore 'always' been there and they have a tallness which dwarfs man, but a verticality that associates them with man. The widespread custom of planting a 'birth tree' rests on the superstitious hope that the vigour and longevity of these human plants will somehow ensure that the child, too, grows mightily and lives long.[24]

However, nothing better measures the value of a tree than cash. Association with religion, in medieval Welsh law of around AD 1300, might increase the official value of a tree, something society needed to know when imposing the penalty for chopping it down: 'The price of a *yew*, i.e. *ywen*, 15d.; if the yew is holy (*sancta*), 20s. is its price' (*Lawcode of Howel Dda, Recension D* in Emanuel 1967: 367). For those who do not remember, 20s. is 240d., sixteen times 15d., and gives some weight to the inviolability of the sacred tree. It is of some interest that the possibility of sacrality is only raised in the case of the yew, though it is not stated what makes it sacred – Jones (1954: 19) talks of association with a saint.

Personalising trees

Trees may be venerable on their own account, particularly if old: 'Even more ancient than the city [*of Rome*] is a holm-oak on the Vatican, bearing a bronze inscription in Etruscan characters indicating that even then the tree deserved veneration (*religio*)' (Pliny the elder, *Natural history*

16.237). But if trees are old and if for modern anthropomorphism they need to be drawn into the stories of people, then a fine solution is to assign the tree a place in history, if Roman, or myth, if Greek. Pliny gives many examples of this (16.237–40). Three holm-oaks marked the site of the inauguration of the settlement of Tibur (Tivoli); a plane tree in Phrygia is where Marsyas was hanged; another plane tree at Delphi and one at Kaphyai were planted by Agamemnon; the olive tree at Argos is the one Io was tethered to; the wild olive at Olympia (veneration – *religio* – is preserved for it even today) is the one supplying Herakles with his first oak-leaf crown; at Troy, trees on the tomb of Protesilaos and an oak on the mound of Ilus go back to those heroic times when Ilium (the city of Troy) was first called Ilium; and the palm tree at Delos goes back to the time of the birth of the god Apollo. Similarly, individual trees 'often prompt Pausanias to recount pertinent events from the legendary past, sometimes including the death of the hero whose tomb they mark' (Birge 1994: 236). Indeed, legend attracted the mind of a Pausanias, but ultimately the function of these myths and legendary associations is to translate the brute religious importance of the tree into the language of anthropomorphic and heroic religion.[25] If Menelaos (this time) planted the tree at Kaphyai, it is so that *you* may sense the importance and resonance of the tree, just as the Michelin *Guide vert* will ensure you sense the aura of this château from the historic events that are alleged to have taken place here under Louis the nth. It is the tree that is important – 'Menelaos' is a translation.

More drastically and especially in highbrow literature with its precious primitivism (see Chapter 2), the tree becomes the residence of a god or the god itself and we erudite may revel in the paradox of incarnation of deity in tree. Silius Italicus knows that the oak at Dodona 'has a *numen* ('divinity/divine power') and is tended [*colitur*, in this case 'worshipped'] with warm altars' (*Punica* 4.691). Ovid gleefully relates how a tree impiously felled in a grove of Demeter bleeds and a wood-nymph is thereby killed (*Metamorphoses* 8.761–73). The allocation of nymphs, rather than full-blown goddesses, to trees is an interesting refinement in the language: the tree belongs to the goddess Demeter, shares somewhat in her power and deserves some of the respect due to her, but it is not actually her and this is what is summed up in the pretty rustic-poetic fiction that a nymph lives within the tree. These nymphs have a propensity for living in *oaks*, so that they may be *dryads* (*drys*, 'oak'): 'The locals say that [the town of] Tithorea got its name from a nymph Tithorea – the sort of nymph that in poetical accounts of days of yore used to grow out of trees, particularly oak trees' (Pausanias 10.32.9).

Nonetheless, Greeks often associated gods and more especially goddesses with trees, something that goes back at least to the Minoan (Bronze Age Cretan) seal stones that depict worshippers approaching a goddess beneath a tree. Artemis, who perhaps more often than other goddesses retained an antique wooden 'statue', a *xoanon*, is frequently so associated.[26] A myrtle tree at Boiai (Lakonia) was worshipped as Artemis Saviour (*Soteira*); in Orchomenos (Arcadia) was the *xoanon* of Artemis of the Cedar (*Kedreatis*); at Karyai (on the borders of Lakonia and Arcadia) was the cult of Artemis of the Nut Tree (*Karyatis*). Near Karyai at Kaphyai there was a cult of 'strangled' Artemis which is associated with a myth of children hanging the statue (*agalma*) of Artemis – presumably from one of the trees in the grove. And the cult of Helen of the Tree (*Dendritis*) in Rhodes was explained by her supposedly having been hanged from a tree there. Aphrodite's statue at Temnos (Aeolid, Asia Minor) was made from 'a flourishing myrtle'. It should perhaps be remembered that a substantial wooden statue inevitably must be made from a tree trunk, the body of the tree. An image of Dionysos was found at Magnesia on the Maeander (Asia Minor), 'inside' the trunk of a plane tree that a storm had brought down. And the tree from which Pentheus of Thebes was wrenched down so that he might be torn apart alive (as in Euripides' *Bacchae*) allegedly required honour 'equal with the god', as a result of which the Corinthians made from it two gilded *xoana* (antique wooden statues) with red faces. To these can be added further instances of Zeus 'In-the-tree' (*Endendros*), in Boiotia Dionysos *Endendros*, on Naxos Dionysos Meilichios associated with a fig tree, and in Sparta Dionysos *Sykites* (of the fig tree).

The Romans used to enclosed trees struck by lightning (we shall see these little enclosures, *putealia*, in Chapter 14). One such in the *Comitium* commemorated the legendary deed of the greatest augur of regal times, Attus Navius, who in response to a challenge had cut a whetstone in half with a razor.[27] The razor and whetstone were naturally buried there, like Lithuanian sacred stones (above). But close by was also the celebrated fig tree of Roman myth, the *Ficus Ruminalis* ('of suckling', or did it originally belong to the faded goddess of suckling, *Rumina*?):

> A fig tree growing in the actual *Forum* and *Comitium* of Rome is revered (*colitur*), sacred because of the lightning-bolts buried there and still more to commemorate the fig tree under which the nurse of Romulus and Remus first sheltered those founders of empire at the Lupercal. It is called *Ruminalis* because it was beneath it that they found the she-wolf offering her *rumis* (that is what they used to call a breast) to the babies, a miracle commemorated nearby in bronze – as though the wolf had of her own accord crossed the comitium while Attus Navius was acting in his role as augur. Nor is it without significance when it dries up and must, through the efforts of the priests, be replaced.
>
> Pliny the elder, *Natural history* 15.77[28]

Fig trees, which live to a great age and are notable for their milky *latex*, are also much venerated in Buddhism.[29] In this case we should not be distracted by the myths. This is a stone and tree combo, where the special shape of the stone and the milkiness of the tree have attracted attention; both have generated, or at least attracted, myths. The tree is tended, and when necessary renewed, by the priests. If it is surrounded by a *puteal*, then originally this may have been understood as a place where lightning had struck and the 'whetstone' might have been considered a thunderstone.

A different way of personalising trees is to draw them into name-giving. Celtic cultures supply many examples: the Irish MacCuill ('Son of Hazel'), Mac Ibair ('Son of Yew') and Dergen ('Son of Oak'). Old Irish *ibor* ('yew') and Gaulish *ivos*, which survives in the French *if*, may possibly account for the tribal name Eburones/Eburovices, and the town of York, *Eboracum*.[30]

In the Pyrenees, that area of Europe that made least apology for rock and tree worship, we find very basic and oddly non-personal inscriptions – to *Fagus* ('Beech') and to the mysterious 'Six Trees'. The only similar inscription is one further afield at Angoulême (Charente) to *Robur* ('Oak').[31] These trees have minimum personality: they are addressable.

Trees do not always have to be personalised and the *bile* of Irish tradition was a mighty tree without such artificial manipulation. Its force lay in its being a *bile feada* ('ancient tree'), or an 'ancient and venerated tree' and out of one such tree the Cross itself was made (afterwards, then!).[32] It might mark a well or fort, five of which are described in fabulous terms in the *Dindshenchas*, an extensive Old Irish collection of texts praising places.[33] To destroy a *bile*, particularly at the heart of a nation where kings were inaugurated, was a supreme act of destruction against those whom it guarded,[34] recalling how the *Ficus Ruminalis* embodied the prosperity of Rome. And when (according to legend around 660) the *Bile Tortan* near Navan (An Uaimh in Irish, Meath) fell in a storm, the great lament over it seems to associate it with the death of a king and tells how it crushed 150 people, gathered at an *oenach* (an annual assembly-cum-fair; cf. Chapter 14) – it was the focus for their meeting.[35] Similarly, the *vårdträd* (ward-tree) in Sweden or *tuntre* (farm-tree) in Norway protected farmsteads.[36] More colourfully, if less plausibly, a single tree is claimed to have opened up to protect two nuns from the attentions of thieves in the life of the Irish saint Samthanna.[37]

Notable trees

Sacred trees can be identified as such because they are different from other trees – taller or of miraculous habits. Willibald tells us of the great Oak of Jupiter (Donar) and its felling.[38] St Boniface is converting the pagans of Hesse around 723; some of them have already accepted the Catholic faith:

> Some were sacrificing secretly to wood and springs, others again openly. Some were practising haruspicy and divination, portents and incantations in secret, others indeed blatantly. Some turned to augury and auspices and practised various sacrificial rites; others again did none of this. Planning to deal with all this, St Boniface attempted the chopping down of a particular oak tree of amazing size which was called the 'Oak of Jupiter' in the former language of the pagans, at a place called Geismar [not far from Göttingen] with the servants of God standing beside him. When, finding strength through the constancy of his mind, he had cut down the tree, a large number of pagans appeared and amongst themselves they vigorously cursed the enemy of their gods.
>
> Willibald the Priest, *Life of St Boniface the Archbishop* 22

Boniface proceeds to calm the crowd by demonstrating that the tree has miraculously fallen into four pieces of equal length. The pagans are naturally at once converted and from the wood an oratory of St Peter is dedicated. This sort of tree has a long history: nearly half a millennium

Figure 4.1 Boniface felling the Oak of Donar

earlier one is mistakenly ascribed to Celts by Maximus of Tyre (it should surely have been Germans):[39] 'The Celts worship Zeus (Jupiter) and the Celtic statue of Zeus is a high oak' (Maximus of Tyre 2.8). It is certainly also suggestive if, as Pennick (1996: 37) says, in southern Germany outdoor Christian services are held 'at notable oaks' at Whitsun and 'gospel oaks' are known too (an unremarkable suburb of Birmingham is so called). Another tree, at Uppsala, was so remarkable that Adam of Bremen thought it worth writing an addendum to his history specially in order to mention it:

> Near that temple is a huge tree stretching its branches wide, always green in winter and summer; what sort it is, no-one knows. There, also, is a spring where pagan sacrifices are practised and a live man submerged. If they cannot find him, the vow of the people will be approved.
>
> T Scholion 138, on Adam 4.26 (Trillmich and Buchner 1961: 470)

Behind the huge column Irminsul (Chapter 7) and these trees at Geismar and Uppsala surely looms a mythic prototype, an Yggdrasil, the world-ash of the Norsemen.

Particular trees were the focus of attention throughout Greece. Pausanias mentions the spring and 'great, fine plane tree' Menelais at Kaphyai, the *agnus castus* (withy) in the shrine of Hera on Samos, the oak at Dodona, and the olive trees on the Acropolis of Athens and also on Delos.[40] One might add the palm tree of Leto on Delos, and the wild olive of Herakles at Olympia. Such trees may be historic, magnificent, or unusual. The olive tree of Herakles at Athens had leaves with the grey side on top; and there was an *evergreen* plane tree at Gortyn (Crete).[41] The degree of interest in such anomalous behaviour may be gauged by Theophrastus' account:

> In Crete there is said to be a plane tree in the territory of Gortyn next to a spring, which does not lose its leaves. The story goes that Zeus had sex with Europa under this tree. And all the nearby trees shed their leaves.
>
> Theophrastus, *On plants* 1.9.5

In Rome, among several sacred trees we may mention the ancient lotos tree in the sanctuary of Juno Lucina, around 500 years old in Pliny's time: this 'is called the tree of the hair because the hair of the Vestal Virgins is brought to it' (*Natural history* 16.235). Indeed, a further ancient lotos tree was to be found in the sanctuary of Vulcan, the Volcanal (*ibid.* 236).

What happens at trees

We have seen Passienus Crispus would have been a normal person if he had poured wine over a tree. That would be libation. Sacrifice at trees turns up in Iceland, where þórirsnepill offered sacrifice, unusually, to a group of trees at Lund ('Grove'). And sacrifice *over* a tree appears in Sweden, where according to legend Blót-Svein ('Sacrifice-Sven') reddened the worship-tree (*blóttré*) with the blood of a horse he had sacrificed.[42] No Greek or Roman would have done that – the blood would have gone over the altar with which the sacred tree was inevitably equipped.[43] However, the most explicit description of tree worship that I have encountered concerns Lithuania. I cite it with the warning that this is only one culture's approach to trees and has its oddities:

> Some have two particular trees: one is an oak, the other a lime. They call the oak masculine and at fixed times put two eggs beneath it. They call the lime feminine and offer it butter, milk, cheese and fat, for the well-being and protection of them and their children. If any are taken ill, straightaway they send the Popus [priest] to the trees to demand of the trees why they are allowing them to be unwell in view of their having made the due gift to them. If they do not get well immediately, they bring the trees twice the said goods and are so freed.
>   . . . They offer in the woods several barrels of beer, more beer or less beer in proportion to the help they have had from the god Cerekling (?). They offer these gifts in this way to the trees. The old Popus, together with the other old men, mumbles a fixed formula and presents and offers gifts. Then, some people run up and lift the barrel of beer on high. The Popus, before they begin to drink, takes a sprinkler [i.e. a branch] from a lime tree and sprinkles the bystanders. Afterwards, fires are prepared in many places and they throw part of the offerings, sc. the fat, onto the fire. They think the gods will never hear them without beer. And in this way, well drunk, they begin to hold dances around the trees and to sing.
>
> *Annual report of the Society of Jesus* 1606, *LPG* 442 f.

Greeks and Romans were happy to light candles and lamps at trees. This is one of those common rituals you only learn about from out-of-the-way sources – some Christian denunciations of Germans and a revealing comment of Servius:[44] 'It is called a grove (*lucus*) because there is no light there (*non luceat*) and not because, as some people would have it, *there are lights there for religious purposes*' (Servius, on Vergil, *Aeneid* 1.441). A number of illustrations from the ancient world show torches or lamps on the structures built to accompany trees.[45] It would be pointless lighting torches during the Mediterranean day and I think we must therefore imagine evening or night ceremonies with that sense of *son et lumière* and a special magic as the leaves glisten in the torchlight.

Trees hold offerings. They may be the recipients of the rags at rag wells or of those of Irish pilgrims (Plummer 1910: i.cliii), a poorer and more self-sacrificing version of what Romans call *vittae* and textbooks call 'fillets', as prohibited by the Emperors in 392.[46] The *vitta* is a woollen band with uses rather like tinsel: it may decorate altars, doorways or trees; it marks sanctity and may be carried in processions or worn by priests. It may even decorate a headband, the *infula*. Ancient landscape painting sometimes depicts trees with votive offerings clinging to their branches; trees and groves were recommended for landscape-painters by authorities like Vitruvius.[47] Whether the offerings were actually for the tree, however, is a different question: in Lithuania they might well have been, as is apparent from a passage above, but elsewhere the trees serve to hold the offerings appropriate to the holy place.[48] Trees can, however, receive attention and it is not out of place for, say, Pliny the elder to say '*colitur*' of the *Ficus Ruminalis*. We should hesitate to translate this 'is worshipped': it only means that it is respectfully and religiously tended. Friends, too, *coluntur*: they are 'cultivated', not hero-worshipped.

Less prettily, trees make display units for sacrificial offerings. Around AD 400, a pear tree in the middle of Auxerre, so the story goes, was the focus of a religious dispute. One Germanus, a young local aristocrat fond of hunting, used to hang the head and antlers of deer he caught in the tree, in accordance with local practice, however much they might deny it, evidently as an offering to Wodan. As his reproofs had no effect, Bishop Amator took direct action and chopped down the tree. Ironically, when Amator was dying, perhaps in 418, he appointed Germanus (St Germain) as his successor. This tale was thought worth three extensive chapters in Henry the Monk's versified *Life of St Germanus* (around AD 880).[49] This is the context also for the Icelandic *blóttré*.[50] It is a practice which must have been known to Greeks and Romans: if a hero in Vergil's epic *Aeneid* (9.407 f.) can appeal for the support of the goddess Diana on the grounds that he has hung the results of his hunt 'from her *tholos* (round temple) or fixed them to the sacred pediments', presumably referring to the heads of hunted animals (like trophies in pubs), then there must be a corresponding practice in country districts, which is after all where a lot of hunting goes on, of suspending animal heads from trees like St Germain.[51] It is important to display one's slaughters, as Poseidonios' Gauls would have told us (Chapter 1), and one's spoils. But in Greek culture by historical times it was armour that was dedicated, nailed up, in temples rather than people that were hanged in groves.[52] Not so at Uppsala:

The sacrifice is like this: from every animal that is masculine, nine head are offered and it is the custom for the gods to be placated with their blood. The bodies are hung up in the grove next to the temple. Indeed, this grove is so sacred to the pagans that individual trees in it are believed divine as a result of the death or gore of the sacrificed. There, dogs and horses hang together with men and one of the Christians told me he had seen 72 of these bodies hung up jumbled together. As for the dirges that are done in this type of sacrificial ceremony, they are various and distasteful (*inhonestae*) and for that reason it is all the better to pass them over in silence.

Adam 4.27

We will see other examples when we come to discuss human sacrifice and crucifixion.

In Rome a distinction was made between a tree that was *felix*, one which bears fruit, and one that was *infelix*, which does not, and laws forbade the felling of an *arbor felix*.[53] But an *arbor infelix* is *damnata religione* ('condemned by religion', Pliny the elder, *Natural history* 16.108) and is therefore the appropriate tree for Horatius to be hanged on after trial by the *duumviri perduellionis* (Board of Two for Treason). This scene from Roman myth-history seems to play before the antique assembly of warriors, the *comitia curiata*, and apparently in a grove, perhaps the *lucus Petelinus*.[54]

The tree, then, sends out signals. Coated with liquid and semi-liquid offerings (wine, milk, blood, fat or gore), it glistens in the dark, thanks to its candles and torches. It proclaims through the gifts dangling in its branches the respect it is owed. And its grimmer colleagues, like crucifixes, advertise judicial death.

Finally, as a prompt to envisaging happy Lithuanian dances around trees in staid old Roman culture, let us read, and think of the implications of, the legendary impiety, and subsequent punishment, of the sinner Erysichthon,

> . . . who treated the power (*numina*) of the gods
> with disdain and did not honour the altars with any burnt
>   offerings.
> He even used his axe to violate the Forest (*Nemus*) of Demeter,
> so it is said, and with iron desecrated ancient groves (*luci*).
> There stood amongst these an ancient oak with the timber of
>   years,[55]
> a forest on its own: *vittae* (woollen ribbons) and commemorative
>   tablets
> and garlands encircled it, proof of the power of vows.

> Often beneath this tree the dryads [oak-, and generally tree-,
> nymphs] danced at festivals;
> often, linking hands one to another, they measured out the
> trunk's
> circumference; the size of the tree filled out
> fifteen armspans [i.e. fifteen nymphs were needed]; and the rest of
> the wood
> was as far beneath this tree as the grass was beneath the whole
> wood.
>
> Ovid, *Metamorphoses* 8.739–50

Nymphs are girls transposed into myth and caught here, Polaroid, in an act of worship.

Pagan tree and Christian objectors

Christians, participants in what was very much an urban religion, did not worship amid nature and found the association of pagans with nature a useful tool for demarcating and branding pagan practice. Trees therefore should be felled and the first feller of pagan trees was St Martin of Tours:

> When in a particular village he had demolished a very ancient temple and was moving on to fell the pine tree next to the shrine, this was the point at which the priest (*antistes*) of that place and the general mass of the pagans began to put up resistance. Though at the command of the Lord these same people had been quiet when the temple was being destroyed, they would not allow the tree to be chopped down. Martin painstakingly reminded them that there was nothing religious about a stump and that they should rather be following the God he himself served. This tree had to be chopped down because it was dedicated to a demon.
>
> Sulpicius Severus, *Life of St Martin* 13.1 f.

Trees, like idols, should be destroyed: according to the *Chronicles* of Cosmas of Prague (1045–1125), one Christian response to Slav paganism was to 'burn down with fire the groves or trees which the people worshipped in many places' (3.1). The people sometimes needed to be persuaded: the demolition of sacred oaks in Lithuania was helped in one case by the sudden departure of a screech-owl 'whom they believed not unreasonably (!) to have been an evil spirit'.[56]

In 597 Pope Gregory was writing to Brunnhilda, Queen of the Franks. Having enjoined her to heal schisms in the Church, he then moved on to paganism:

We equally encourage you to do this also, namely to restrain your other subjects under the control of discipline so that they do not sacrifice to idols, so that worshippers of trees should not exist, so that in the matter of the heads of animals they should not exhibit sacrilegious sacrifices, because it has reached our ears that many of the Christians also meet at churches and – an evil thing to report – do not refrain from instances of worship of demons.

Gregory the Great, Letters 8.4

Presumably he means that the heads of sacrificed animals are nailed up for display and that sacrifices are performed at churches, a practice for which he allows in his advice to Augustine (Chapter 7). As late as April 598, and closer to home, Pope Gregory reproached Agnello, Bishop of Terracina (Lazio):

It has reached our ears that certain people there – an evil thing to report – are worshipping trees and perpetrating many other illicit practices contrary to the Christian faith. And we wonder why your brotherliness is too busy to set this right and punish it.

Gregory the Great, Letters 8.19

The placing of offerings in trees did not die out with the passing of paganism. Maury (1896: 13 f.) refers, if somewhat vaguely, to the practice of hanging images of the Virgin Mary in sacred trees in more modern times. Indeed, at the church at Evron (Mayenne) there had been behind the high altar a tree which had been remodelled with a niche towards the bottom for a silver statuette of the Virgin Mary. This was explained by the following myth:

In 648 a pilgrim brought a relic of the Virgin from the Holy Land and was passing through Evron. Tired by his journey, he rested beside a cool, clear spring and hung up his case containing the relic. But the hawthorn grew while he slept and when he awoke the case had been raised so high that the pilgrim could not get it back. The Virgin, the legend added, indicated thereby that she wished to be honoured at this place.

Maury 1896: 299 n.3, from Gérault, Notice historique sur Evron, son abbaye et ses monuments, 2nd edn (1840): 5

5

AREA I: LAND

From the *focus* of cult, we now move on to the *area* in which rites take place. It is a fact of geography that edges are easier to observe than centres and the result is that a number of the natural, god-given, locations for cult are *marginal*. These include the hills and mountains that in fact divide one landscape from another, as well as the points where land runs out altogether, such as shores and, posing the problem more acutely, offshore islands. Finally, in mountains and at shores, we find caves.

HILL AND MOUNTAIN

What mountains are like

> The dawn, the sun, the moon, the stars, seem to rise from the mountains, the sky seems to rest on them, and when our eyes have climbed up to their highest visible peaks, we feel on the very threshold of a world beyond ... the view of such a temple might make even a stout heart shiver, before the real presence of the infinite.
>
> Max Müller 1878: 176

'Sacred mountains are found everywhere in this world,' observes Van der Leeuw (1948: §5.2). God appeared to Moses on Sinai, he reminds us, and Japanese pilgrims ascend Fuji. Local peoples hold beliefs about the Himalayas, and Tibetans have their beliefs about Kangchendzonga (Jantzen 1988: 191). Incas, too, as grim archaeological discoveries show, conceived mountaintops like Cuzco as the ideal place to lead a child to be slaughtered.

Mountains have two principal characteristics: they are high and they are remote. Their slopes are often wooded and even Thietmar melts a little when he describes the veneration of the huge granite mass of Mount Sobótka (Mount Zobten) as resulting from *qualitatem suam et quantitatem* – its character and scale.[1] But mountaintops are barren, a world untouched by culture, and at the furthest possible distance from human habitation, not least because they typically mark the boundaries of a land, though they may well be visible from afar, these 'présences lumineuses à l'horizon'.[2] So they are 'other', even if this is nowadays becoming obscured by leisure and modern means of communication.[3] Metaphors of height and the theme of ascent to the heavens are such fundamental symbols that they require no explanation.[4] This is the context for mountains, a link between earth and heaven, something of which Mahler was acutely aware when he used cow-bells in his sixth symphony to evoke the last sounds one hears on earth. The peaks of mountains are further differentiated from normal ground by snowlines and by the clouds and mists that enshroud them. Divine powers are instinctively made to live in this divine otherness,[5] in the skies or on the mountaintops, whichever Olympus is. Perhaps, too, in comparison with the human self, itself distinctively erect, mountains are monoliths[6] of incalculable and overpowering height, size and durability. And this regardless of whether they are a 300-metre Mont St Michel or a 4807-metre Mont Blanc.[7]

Worship on mountains: lightning and fire

Toutain observed that some gods in particular tend to be found on mountaintops, citing the Gaulish 'Mercury', Zeus (evidently the lightning-god corresponding to Wodan or Thor) in Greece, and Baal in Phoenicia, and wishing, not inappropriately, to add the Iberian Endovellicus to them.[8] In Galicia various local gods associated with mountains were interpreted as forms of the Roman Jupiter.[9]

One reason to worship a god on a mountaintop is because he is held responsible for lightning and rain. Here a Greek might worship above all the sky-god Zeus, whether 'cloud-gatherer' (*nephelegereta*) or 'of rain' (*hyetios*) or 'sender' (of rain, *aphesios*). In the Germanic landscapes Thor/Donar the god of 'Thunder' often has hills or mountains named after him. In the same way idols of the Russian Perun were revered on hilltops and so was his Lithuanian equivalent Perkunas:

> Among the Samogitae [in northern Lithuania] there is a mountain situated by the River Newassa (Nemunas) on whose peak a perpetual flame used once to be maintained by a priest in honour of Pargnus (Perkunas) himself, who is still believed by the superstitious people to have power over thunder and storms.
>
> J. Ma(e)letius, *LPG* 296 (also, Jouet 1989: 107)

Thunder and lightning are assertive and demonstrative powers that belong with the principal god. So Zeus and Perkunas–Perun are both thunder-gods and sovereign gods. Worship on major mountaintops may, however, without reference to thunder, still denote sovereignty, as, for instance, in the case of the Germanic Wodan. There were many mountains named *Wodansberg* (in the south) or Odinsberg (in Scandinavia). Grimm collected a large number, some of which have undergone Christianising modification, e.g. to Godesberg.[10] In North Yorkshire there was a hill 'Outhenesberg', now 'Roseberry Topping', and in Wiltshire near Alton Priors a Wodnesbeorg, apparently denoting a prehistoric tumulus, the so-called 'Adam's Grave'. Wednesbury (West Midlands), despite its modern spelling, is also this name and has a church apparently built on the site of a pagan temple.[11] These names give a glimpse of the sort of cult that must have existed, though we do not now have the physical remains or direct evidence, except for a brief mention in England which is largely derivative from Martin of Braga but might just be evidence for Odin worship on hills in the Danelaw:[12]

> Then the heathens made him [Mercury] into a celebrated god
> and made offerings to him at crossroads
> and brought oblations to high hills for him.
> This god was honoured among all heathens
> and he is called by another name, Oðon, in Danish.
>
> Aelfric, *On false gods* 136–40

Wodan (cf. Wednesday) is translated into Latin, however inappropriately, as Mercury (cf. mercredi) and it is therefore all the more striking that the most familiar god on mountaintops in Gaul is 'Mercury'. This worship of a Wodan on mountaintops may be the real reason for his identification with the Gallo-Roman Mercury, the usual tenant of mountaintops and their many temples in Gaul, such as the key sanctuary on the Puy de Dôme.[13] Occasionally, though, we see other gods, or at least other god-names. For example, St Martin, on his way from Arthona (Artonne, Puy-de-Dôme) south to Clermont-Ferrand, 'had come to the top of Mount Belenatensis (St-Bonnet) from which the layout of the town of Ricomagus (Riom) could be seen'.[14] Belenus is a widespread Celtic god, the chief god of Aquileia (near Trieste) and Noricum (in effect, Austria); in these regions he is firmly identified with Apollo.

Other gods than Zeus had a place in Greek mountains – for instance, Artemis, goddess of the wild and of maidens making the difficult passage to maidenhood, for which mountains are a suitably marginal location. Greece and Crete are exceptionally mountainous countries and 'mountain' is therefore an immediately available part of their religious language. In Arcadia, the mountainous inland area of the Peloponnese, there were many sanctuaries on or, for practical reasons, near mountaintops.[15] In Crete, back in the Bronze Age, we know of twenty-five peak sanctuaries (Peatfield, in Alcock and Osborne 1994: 21). In the early and middle Bronze Age these were vehicles for popular cult, 'community shrines, not places of remote and arduous pilgrimage' (*ibid.* 25). Later, however, only a limited number of them were retained for use and then in a more elitist and urban context (*ibid.* 23).

A special use of mountains is for fire rituals where the intervisibility of mountaintops may create the sense of a larger community, transcending normal political boundaries (*ibid.* 25). Fire, however, is specially demonstrative and has a certain living force, as Grimm (1875: i.500) stresses. In fact fire and water are rather peculiar words in Indo-European, possessing both neuter forms (represented by the Greek *pyr* and *hydōr* or our *fire* and *water*) and active forms (the Latin *aqua* and *ignis*), rendering them capable of being subjects of sentences in the remote past of Indo-European when it was an 'ergative' language, sharply distinguishing between things capable of being agents and things which could only be acted upon. It is, of course, through the active medium of fire, or of living water, that objects may be offered, made sacred. Thus, in sacrifice burning and drowning are particularly appropriate. At moments of renewal, then, the creation of fire, preferably new fire, on mountaintops has a particular force. This traditionally used to happen at Easter in Holland and northern Germany and Grimm speaks of all the mountains in the vicinity being lit up in this way to create an impressive spectacle.[16] It may seem unduly speculative to say so, but paganism as a whole tends to be concerned with the renewal of the forces on which we depend and of the society in which we live. In Chapter 14 we will see some very particular, and unpleasant, ways in which society can be periodically renewed. But another format may perhaps once have included the extinguishing of fire, centrifugal motion to the boundaries that mountains represent both by their position and their height; and the renewal of fire on them, as though from heaven, so that society may recommence. It is perhaps a sign of some such ritual that the Greek myth of the Danaids, which through the murder of their husbands depicts the extinguishing of marriage and the dissolution of society, is also connected with fire rituals on mountaintops.[17]

It is not always possible for us to recover reasons for the siting of worship on mountains beyond their immediate awesomeness: native cults in Iberia, for instance, were particularly prone to being sited on a summit/hilltop (Toutain 1917: 130) and we can only guess why, as Toutain does with Endovellicus (above). In any case, a distinction should be made between cult-sites on mountains and the predilection for siting temples in places 'with large horizons'.[18] Greek temples were often so sited: for instance, the Parthenon at Athens, or the temple of Hera Akraia ('Of the Heights') at Corinth. Outside Dublin, the Hill of Thor appears to have been one such case and those Gaulish temples on their minor, but horizon-enlarging, eminences (Chapter 14) are others.

SHORE AND ISLAND

Sea: shore and promontory

The sea is not a factor in the lives of many of the pagan nations we encounter. However, it has a great potential for those who do live within reach of it. Greeks are naturally concerned, as a seafaring nation, with its dangers and benefits. From the point of view of this chapter, however, we are not concerned to recite the variety of practices designed to achieve benefits and ward off calamity at sea (any more than in any other department of life) but rather with the sea as a sacred place at which ritual may be performed. Doubtless it is theoretically possible to hold rituals on the sea, on ships, but the real place where the might of the sea is confronted in ritual is where land meets it. It is, for instance, on the seashore that we find Nestor and his sons placating Poseidon with a mighty hecatomb of oxen in Homer's *Odyssey* (3.4–68). This fiction is based on the reality of the sanctuary of Poseidon on the Triphylian coast at Samikon (Strabo 8.3.20).

At times land does not merely meet sea but confronts it. So, near Athens, the 86-metre hill of Mounichia, crowned by its temple of Artemis, dominated the harbour below. Further south, where Attica ends, the temple of Poseidon marked the promontory of Sounion. The Greeks were not alone in this:[19] promontories were also held sacred, for instance, by the pre-Roman inhabitants of the Iberian peninsula.[20] The most striking site is the 'Sacred Promontory' at Cape St Vincent, the south-western tip of Portugal and, according to Strabo, 'the westernmost point not only of Europe but also of the whole world'.[21] Ephoros (fourth century BC) wrote about it and there was a cult there which writers appear to register as a cult of (the Phoenician) Baal/Melqart (= 'Herakles', or 'Kronos').[22] An interesting, if controversial, account is given by Artemidoros (first century BC) who had at least been there himself:

> There is no shrine or altar of Herakles shown there – Ephoros is wrong on this point – nor of any of the other gods. There are just groups of three or four stones in various places which traditionally visitors are supposed to turn around and move, making libations. You aren't allowed to sacrifice nor to set foot in the place at night, because they say gods occupy it at that time. Tourists spend the night in the nearby village, and then go in during the day, taking water with them because there isn't any there.
>
> Artemidoros, in Strabo 3.1.4

The stones have interested scholars and several have seen them as characteristic of Phoenician cult with its baetyls.[23] Leite de Vasconcellos (1905: ii.205) actually visited the area in March 1894 and found local people maintaining superstitions about a number of cairns there and what happened if you removed a stone from them.

A final promontory is that of Arkona on the island of Rügen, where the holiest shrine of the Pomeranian Slavs was sited. To the east, south and north of it, the precipices were its defences, says Saxo (14.39.2, p.564). To the west was an earth and wattle rampart thirty metres high. A site so rich indeed needed defences – for instance, against King Waldemar of the Danes who finally sacked it shortly after Whitsun in 1168. But it also was a striking, and correct, place to site a major shrine.

It is important not to be too pedestrian about our attitudes to such worship. There may indeed be dangers in fabricating a romantic view of nature amongst ancient pagans:[24] according to Van der Leeuw (1948: §5.1) religion cannot have originated in nature worship because nature is a modern idea, not contrasted with human civilisation before Rousseau and the romantics. Nonetheless, the appreciation of something like the sea has some basis in sensibility. 'Just as the grandeur of a mountain humbles the human mind, so does the vastness of the sea,' writes Choudhury (1994: 64), describing the place of the sea in Hinduism and adverting to its shore-temples. Yes, Greeks did not journey to shore-temples to acquire religious merit, but they did think them worth building and worshipped regularly there in honour of the force that lay beyond.

The sea is also a margin to which processions may lead. Here the statue of the goddess may be washed and renewed, typically annually in a form of ritual renewal. At Nauplion, Hera, through the washing of her statue, regained her virginity. And in the Plynteria ('Washing-festival') at Athens the old wooden statue, the revered *xoanon*, of Athene was taken from the Acropolis to the shore at Phaleron where significantly two maidens, the 'washers', had the task of bathing it. The *ephebes* (youths) 'together led out the Pallas [statue of Pallas Athene] to Phaleron and brought it back in [to the city] from there with light [i.e. torchlit procession] and wholly decorously' (Inscription, *IG* 2² 1006.11).[25] This took place towards the end of the month of Thargelion, therefore as a rule in early June.

Worshippers too may be annually renewed. This is attested in Naples as late as 1580 at the summer solstice, to judge by an example which Grimm (1875: i.490) finds described by Benedict of Falco:

> In a populous part of the city lies the church consecrated to St John the Baptist, called 'S. Giovan a mare' (by the sea). It was an ancient custom, today not wholly abandoned, that on St John's Eve towards evening after the day's heat[26] all the men and women went down to the sea and bathed nude.

This is an authentic continuation of paganism as can be seen from startling passages which Grimm proceeds to cite:[27] 'On the feast-day of St John, in a superstitious pagan ceremony, Christians used to go to the sea and baptize themselves . . .' (Pseudo-Augustine, *Sermon* 196 (*PL* 38.1021)); 'Let no-one on the feast of St John presume to bathe in springs or meres or rivers, in the hours of night or the hours of day (*matutinis*) because this unhappy custom still remains from the practice of the pagans' (Caesarius, *Sermon* 33.4).

The feast of St John is at Midsummer on 24 June, but the ceremony sounds as though it incorporates something of the Neptunalia of 23 July (Chapters 3, 10).

Islands

Islands have a special place in Celtic culture. Behind the mythic isle of Avalon, *Encarta* discerns 'a literary tradition of *immran,* journeys to islands, including *The Voyage of Bran* (*c.* 700) and the *Navigatio Sancti Brendani* (*c.* 900–20)',[28] which in turn continue pagan reverence for such locations. One instance is Bardsey Island with its abbey, three kilometres from the Lleyn peninsula (north west Wales), where Merlin sleeps and those who are buried escape hell, a nice blend, as Pennick (1996: 112) says, of Christianity and a pagan Isles of the Blest. Another instance is the special role of Mona, the isle not of Man but of Anglesey, a sacred centre in British religion. Here, at any rate, in AD 61 Britons made a stand against Suetonius Paulinus with their druids imprecating overtime. Following their defeat, their groves on the island, dutifully indicated by Tacitus to be the scene of human sacrifices, were cut down (Tacitus, *Annals* 14.30). More curious still are the goings on related by Poseidonios:

> In the Ocean there is a small island [Belle-Isle?], lying not far out to sea from the mouth of the R. Leiger (Loire). It is inhabited by women of the Namnites [from whom Nantes takes its name] who are possessed by Dionysos and worship this god with secret rites and other sacred rituals. A man may not set foot on the island, but the women themselves sail to have intercourse with the men and return afterwards. It is their custom once a year to unroof the temple and roof it over again on the same day before sunset, each woman carrying a load. If anyone's load falls off, she is torn apart by the others and they carry the limbs around the shrine with wild cries and do not stop until the rage leaves them. It always happens that someone stumbles[29] who must suffer this.
>
> Poseidonios, *FGH* 87F56 (Strabo 4.4.6)

Figure 5.1 An impression of Hiera, the 'sacred island', off the Greek coast at Troizen, with its temple of Athene Apatouria

There is undoubtedly a veneer of Greek religion, with images of Dionysos and his Bacchants crying out ecstatically and performing the *sparagmos* (the tearing apart alive) in ritual of an animal, in myth of a person. This account of a distant people appropriately adopts the mythic version (with overtones of Amazons who visit men only to be serviced by them), something which is easier given that Poseidonios and his doubtless male informants cannot have visited the island themselves. Nonetheless, a sacred isle seems attested by this passage in a concrete and possible enough location. More clearly historical is this:

> And while the pious preacher of the word of God [St Willibrord] was travelling, he reached an island at the border between the Frisians and the Danes, which people who lived near by called 'Fositesland' after a god of theirs, Fosite – because there were *fana* of the same god built on the island. This place was held in such veneration by the pagans that none of them dared to touch any of the animals pasturing there or anything whatsoever. They did not even presume to draw water from the spring which bubbled there, except in silence. The man of God was cast ashore there by a storm and remained for some days for the storms to die down and good weather for sailing to arrive. Paying no attention to the stupid religion of the place, or to the ferocious inclinations of its king, who used to condemn those who violated its sacred rules to a horrible death, he baptised three men in that spring calling upon the holy Trinity and even instructed them to slaughter the animals grazing there for their meals.
>
> Alcuin, *Life of St Willibrord Bishop of Utrecht* 1.10[30]

This, as Adam of Bremen (4.3) tells us, is Heligoland ('Holy Land'), which perhaps reminds one not inappropriately of Holy Island, *alias* Lindisfarne, or more loosely of Caldy Island. The original name of this island recurs in the Oslo fjord where a placename 'Forsetlund' (*lund*, 'grove', not *land*) is found on the former island of Onsøy (de Vries 1956: ii.§518).

Not so far away, the holiest site of the Pomeranian Slavs was the island of Rügen (Chapter 7). On the southern part of this island were the temples of Korenica (now Garz), but the major site was at its northern extremity on the promontory of Arkona (above). And the cult of Earth, practised by remote Suebians (Chapter 9), was sited in a grove on an island in the Ocean, whether Rügen or one off the coast of Schleswig (Chapter 12).

CAVE

Caves have obvious mysterious, deathly and womblike associations. To this may be added their characteristic marginality, which puts them outside the mundane profane world. But caves, like astronomical monuments, are perhaps more prominent in prehistoric religion than in the paganism that we are looking at. Nevertheless, they appear frequently in Irish myth and legend; so, for instance, a whole category of Irish stories is known as 'Caves'.[31] To what extent are they pagan cult places?

A pattern is found in Greece, where caves may feature in local landscapes and be home to country divinities, no less powerful for that, Pan and the Nymphs. Thus, commendable rustics, like the young heroes of Longus' pastoral novel *Daphnis and Chloe*, will be careful to pay their regards to these divinities. But a cave may also need a journey and call something of a pilgrimage into existence. So, for instance, in Bronze Age Crete there are signs that caves quite remotely sited, such as the cave of Zeus on Mount Dikte, were possibly the scenes of warrior initiation; and, descending perhaps from this sort of use, in historical Thessaly the sons of nobles used to visit the cave of Cheiron, evidently at an initiatory moment in their lives.[32] This harmonises with the sense of caves as retreat, which may become psychological and inward in Christian usage. So St Arredius withdrew to a cave in the Auvergne after the death of his father to battle with his inner self and determine the direction of his life.[33]

In Ireland many caves are associated with Christian saints. Here it is a matter for fine judgement whether we should put this down to continuation of a pagan place of veneration or to a new Christian habit of monastic retreat. A very special example of the Irish cave is the one called 'St Patrick's Purgatory' on Station Island in remote Lough Derg (Donegal).[34] According to the myth, Patrick was divinely shown this pit or cave in order to give hitherto 'bestial' pagan Irishmen a hands-on view of purgatory and impress upon them the urgency and depth of conversion that they required:

> The Lord took St Patrick out to a *deserted place*, and showed him there a round pit, dark inside, saying that whoever should enter this pit truly penitent and armed with the true faith and spend the space of one day and one night in it, would be purged of all the sins of his entire life and as he went through it would not only see the torments of the wicked but also, if he stood steadfastly in the faith, the joys of the blest.
>
> Henry of Sawtry, *Tractatus de purgatorio S. Patricii* 129–34
> (Easting 1991: 124), *c.* AD 1180[35] (my emphasis)

Today it is a simpler place of pilgrimage, but the original oracular nature of the site and its faithful transcription of a number of pagan characteristics – lake, island, cave and, until recently, plunges in the lake – and even the way it is embedded in a myth of conversion and is said to be infested with 'demons'[36] suggest it should have had pagan precedent. Otherwise, there has been a spontaneous generation of pagan characteristics within a framework of Catholic control. The oracular character has a sort of parallel at Lebadeia in central Greece, not far from Delphi, where there was a grove and a chasm and cave of Trophonios (Pausanias 9.39). This oracular site had an extensive reputation such that people would travel considerable distances in order to benefit from the dreams in which advice might be offered. No lesser people than the fabulously wealthy King Croesus of Lydia in the sixth century BC and Alexander the Great's father, Philip II of Macedonia, sought the oracle's advice in this mysterious place.[37]

6

AREA II: GROWTH

From the land and all its shapes we turn now to the areas marked by special and vigorous growth, lush meadows and mysterious groves. Groves, as human 'civilisation' advances on its eco-hostile path and destroys other forms of life in its environment, may retreat, like rain-forests, to the margins: 'In Italy, however, the density of ownership has had many immoral outcomes and in particular has resulted in the seizing of sacred groves' (Julius Frontinus, Bk 2 (*RF* i.56)). But they may also, unlike most of the areas we have so far looked at, be central, particularly if we look early at a culture.

MEADOW

A sacred meadow is a specially fertile area of cultivatable land. It is not a well-defined category and it is scarcely possible to identify one archaeologically.

To judge by the placename evidence, German religion seems to have been specially sensitive to meadows – but the placenames are all we have to go on and there is danger that when they are uncorroborated the imagination supplies what the evidence does not. One Germanic word for a meadow is *auwa* or *ouwe* – as in Swans-*ea* (south Wales). A Pholesauwa in the vicinity of Passau (Bavaria) gave rise to a village of

Pfalsau; this is the meadow of a god Phol, who is paired with Wodan in one of the Merseburg curses (*c.* 900).[1] In the north Odin has his meadows – Odense on the island of Fyn (Denmark) and Onsøy, site of Forsetlund (Chapter 5), by the Oslo fjord near Frederikstad.[2]

A different word is more widespread in the Indo-European languages. This is the Indo-European **loukos*, usually denoting open meadowland: Sanskrit *lokás*, Proto-Germanic *laukh* (English 'lea', Water*loo*), Lithuanian *laükas*, Russian *lug*. Latin has specialised this word to denote an area no less sacred – an open space within a forest, a clearing or 'grove' (on which more below).[3] This word gives northern Holland its Vroonloo (meadow of Frô) and Heiloo (earlier Heilgaloo, 'Holy Meadow').[4] In England there is a propensity for leas to belong to *Thunor*, 'thunder', the Anglo-Saxon form of the Norse Thor. To him we owe several instances of Thundersley (Saffron Walden, Rayleigh, others in Hampshire, and a lost *Thunorslēge* in Sussex), as well as a Thunder Hill near Thursley and a Thundersfield, both in Surrey. Thor is not to be outdone, as can be seen from Thorley (Herts), Thurleigh (Beds), Thursley (Surrey), Furzeleigh (Devon) and Thursfield (Staffs).[5] But how much was meant by these names? Was there regular worship of Thor here? Had trees in these fields been struck by lightning? Or were the fields no more than placenames, at most put under the protection of a favoured god?

A particular use of sacred fields was made by the Athenians. Outside Athens, near Eleusis, lay the Rarian Plain (incidentally, one of the few Greek *r-* words that does not begin *rh-*): 'They say the Rarian Plain was the first to be sown and was the first in which crops grew; for this reason it is their custom to use barley from it to make cakes for the sacrifices' (Pausanias 1.38.6). This was the site of one of the three sacred ploughings of the Athenians: 'The Athenians conduct three sacred ploughings, first at Skiron commemorating the most ancient sowing, second in the Rarian land, third beneath the Acropolis at the place called Buzygion ('Ox-yoking')' (Plutarch, *Advice on marriage (Coniugalia praecepta)* 144a).[6] Before the ploughing of the Rarian Plain there was a special ceremony, the *Proërosia* ('Pre-ploughing') on 5 Pyanopsion, late in October, celebrated by the major priests of the Eleusinian Mysteries, the Hierophant and Herald.[7] The sacred fields are evidently representative of what is desired for all fields. Other sacred land existed in Greece, though one cannot guarantee that it was used in the same way. One example is the plain of Krisa between Delphi and the Corinthian Gulf, whose illegal cultivation by the Phocians was denounced by the Delphians and led to the Third Sacred War in the 350s BC.

In later times, the Prussians 'had also sacred groves, plains and waters, such that they did not used to dare to cut (the groves), or cultivate the fields, or fish' (Peter of Duisburg, *LPG* 88 (Clemen 1936: 97)). Baltic and Slav religion tended, at least in the period we know it, to be particularly concerned with prosperous agriculture, 'fertility' as authors tend to call it. Even where a field was not in itself sacred, it might be that it grew well enough to be thought to have a protecting spirit. Typically this spirit would have a name like 'Life Mother', though the Galici (eastern Slavs living on the Dnestr) had a 'life-father' (*zhitnyi ded*) with three bearded heads.[8] Among the Balts we come across the corn-spirit Jumis, an old man in yellow boots who after the harvest must be caught at midday at the end of the field.[9] Such field-spirits are quite commonplace in 'European peasant-lore',[10] but this leads us astray into a very large area of popular belief, including the Romans, who happily present spirits such as *Robigo*, the 'rust' that afflicts corn.

What we have found in this section is that fields and meadows may be made special through religion. How this sacrality is implemented, however, varies. The field may not be available for cultivation at all and is in that case presumably left wild, though it is hard to imagine that it will not need to be tended in some way, if only to eradicate unacceptable plants, such as trees. It may alternatively be cultivated only on certain terms or in a representative way for sacred purposes only. We will never know exactly in what way Thundersfield was sacred.

GROVE

What a grove is like

Grove and temple-culture

A grove is a wooded cult-site. It is a place amid trees, but not of course obstructed by them. If in a wood or forest, it is therefore a clearing.[11] So Actaeon, about to stumble on the awesome sight of the goddess Diana in her grove:

> Wandering through unknown forest (*nemus*) with unsure steps
> Reached the *lucus*.
>
> Ovid, *Metamorphoses* 3.175 f.

Groves are among the most universal features of Indo-European and indeed any pagan religions and they are among the features of paganism most detested by urban Christians.

Germans typically worshipped in groves and, impossible though it might seem, archaeologists have found what appear to be specimens of such cult-sites in bogs in Thuringia and in northern Germany – fenced-off areas with primitive, humanoid posts evidently constituting idols (so-called *Pfahlgötter*), where once woods must have grown.[12] Likewise in a fen at Rosbjerggard in Denmark (north of Hobro), about two metres

Figure 6.1 The forest of Mount Sobótka, possibly the grove of the Alci (cf. also Chapter 12). Photo: Dr Terry Slater, School of Geography, University of Birmingham

down, were found the stumps of pine trees complete with an Etruscan bronze vessel, blackened by the fire, remains of pottery, two large cairns and various smaller ones, a drinking-horn, ox-horns and what may have been two pillar-like representations of gods, for all the world recalling the worship of the Alci in the ancient grove of the German Nahanarvali whom we shall meet in Chapter 12.[13] Celts, too, worshipped in groves until they turned urban and built Gallo-Roman temples instead. Among the Slavs, according to Helmold (1.47, *c.* AD 1167) there existed 'the manifold error of groves, springs and other religious practices.' And groves were the major centres of religion for their neighbours the Balts, too. We have a number of accounts of what happened in Baltic groves, the last attested instance of national paganism in Europe, and can see them proscribed by the Bishop of Samland (the region around Kaliningrad) around 1430 as follows:

> Item, that in future they shall hold no congregations nor cele-
> brations in woods or forests against the statutes of the Holy
> Mother Church and they shall no longer celebrate their *Kresze*
> [fire-festival][14] on pain of strict punishment and exclusion from
> church burial.
>
> Michael Junge, *LPG* 158 (also, Clemen 1936: 102)

Among the Finno-Ugric peoples, groves even lasted until the nineteenth century.[15]

Groves undergo a semantic shift with the arrival of urban life. In origin a people living in rudimentary housing have not yet adopted the metaphor of the god's 'house', the temple. Their gods are located instead amid the towering grandeur of the grove. However much we may try to resist imposing romantic ideas from modern overdeveloped cultures on much simpler lives, it remains evidently true that the grove was a place of perceived power, appropriate for the gathering of the community and the worship of gods. Groves are also ancient places, given the lifespan of trees which we looked at earlier. Such people, then, worship in their clearings. But those who have adopted a temple culture now regard groves as places of worship with non-standard significance, as a sign of some other type of religion. They may be rustic, left behind by the progress of cities; they may be archaic, associated with the history of the nation, as in the case of the Romans; they may be taken as a sign of barbarism and barbaric religion; they may even be taken nobly to reject the anthropo-morphic conventions of the temple culture, as we shall see. But most alarming of all is the Greek castration of the grove: however little we may at first believe Stengel (1920: 18) when he describes a grove as 'a precinct planted [!] with trees', he has in fact accurately captured the true tone of Greek culture. This grove, which I shall refer to as the 'Stengelian grove', remains sacred but is less mysterious, more of an amenity, and well on its way to becoming a public (or private) park or garden. Wild and awesome, carefully planted and tended – these are the two extremes of groves.

The feel of natural groves

Primitive groves are a special instance of woods and forests, which themselves are from one point of view untamed and dangerous places:

> Thus the earth swarms to capacity with wild animals
> Even now, and is full of panic and terror:
> Throughout forests (*nemora*) and great mountains and deep
> woods (*silvas*)
> – places we generally exercise our discretion to avoid.
> Lucretius, On the nature of the universe 5.40–3

They are thus somewhere where human control runs out and are something of another world. This world, however, may also be viewed as old and uncorrupted by the passage of time:

> The bounty of the earth lay long hidden and trees and woods were understood as the supreme gift to mankind. This was where food first came from; the cave was more comfortable with their leaves, and clothing with their bark; even today there are peoples who live in this way . . .
>
> Trees were the temples of the divinities and, following ancient rites, the simple countryside even today dedicates an exceptional tree to a god; nor do we worship more devoutly statues gleaming with gold and ebony than groves and the very silence in them. The different kinds of trees are dedicated to their various divinities and continually tended – the oak (*aesculus*) to Jupiter, the laurel to Apollo, the olive to Minerva [Roman for Athene], the myrtle to Venus [Aphrodite], the poplar to Hercules. Yes, the Silvanuses and Fauns and varieties of goddess, we believe, are assigned to the woods and assigned as their special divinities as though from heaven.
> Pliny the elder, Natural history 12.1, 12.3

From these considerations results the special feel which groves have, presented here by Seneca from the perspective of a Mediterranean climate:

> If you come upon a grove which is crowded with ancient trees exceeding their normal height and which stops you seeing the sky

Figure 6.2 German primeval forest with auroch

because of the shade caused by one branch covering another, the loftiness of the wood, seclusion of the place and your marvelling at such dense and unbroken shade in an open space provide you with the conviction (*fides*) that there is a divine power (*numen*).

Seneca the younger, Letter 41

Other religious sites, too, make sense from the perspective of the grove: trees surround and identify sacrality. A henge, whether stone or wood, is in effect an artificial grove. Greek temples (and those that are modelled on them, such as the Roman, though this feature weakens in Roman designs) are notable for their exterior ring of columns. This ring is indeed distinctive and attractive, but it is not really structurally necessary for the roofing of the *cella* – the columns are no buttresses.[16] I am tempted to the thought that the stone columns, and the tree trunks that we know preceded them, represent the grove that surrounds, and demarcates, the sacred site. In an extraordinary way, we can perhaps see a sublime transposition of the Gothic cathedral with its towering columns and branch-like vaulting, into which light gains oblique entrance.[17] The design of Gothic cathedrals certainly was not based on groves, but it does appeal to something constant and deep-rooted in our psychology. Does the grove recreate the womb?

Grove and garden

The cicadas are stirred by the sun to their midday musicianship and resound through the groves.

Gregory of Nazianzus, Sermon 28.24 (PG 36.60)

For the Greeks, a grove was always an idyllic spot, a place where things grew well and the aridity of the climate was somehow overcome. In the novel of Achilles Tatius (1.15.1, second century AD), an overpoweringly lush garden 'was a (very) grove, a sensation for the eyes' pleasure'. A grove must be luxuriant: how odd, Strabo (7.3.19) remarks, that this bare place on the Black Sea is called the 'grove' of Achilles! And how ridiculous (9.2.33) that any holy site, no matter how bare, immediately becomes a grove in the mouths of poets! As early as Homer nymphs inhabited 'fine groves, the springs of rivers and the grassy meadows' (*Iliad* 20.8 f.). And within shouting distance of the magical palace of Alkinoos (*Odyssey* 6.291-4) lay the poplar grove of Athene, with its spring, meadow, and precinct to Alkinoos himself[18] in the form of a cultivated garden or orchard. Athene's grove is not just pretty – it is mysterious – and Odysseus encounters the goddess herself when he comes there as the sun is setting and prays to her (6.321-7.36).

The Greek grove varies in religious intensity. At one extreme it is quite

Figure 6.3 The temple of Poseidon in its grove. This is on the island of Kalaureia
off the Greek coast at Troizen and is where the orator and statesman
Demosthenes took poison (Plutarch, *Life of Demosthenes*, 29)

simply the grove of a god or goddess. At the opposite extreme, the grove is
scarcely more than a park, even if the power of the park, too, rests in its
mythic, almost Golden Age, dimension.[19] In compromise cases, and they
are frequent, the shrine of the god, goddess or hero is described as located
within the grove. So, at Tainaron, a headland looking out from the
Peloponnese towards Crete, the temple of Poseidon might be found in a
grove (Strabo 8.5.1). Decreasing in piety, the grove may house civic
amenities necessary for the performance of a (religious) festival – the
stadium, as at Olympia, or a gymnasium, or both, like the 'City of
Victory' Nikopolis which Augustus set up beneath the temple of Apollo
of Actium so that every four years they might celebrate the victory by
which he gained undisputed control of the Mediterranean world. Groves
and games go well together: the *alsos* ('grove')[20] in which the Nemean
Games are held (Strabo 8.6.19), the pine *alsos* with its shrine of Poseidon
of the Isthmus 'where the Corinthians used to celebrate the Isthmian

Games' (Strabo 8.6.22), or indeed the *Altis* at Olympia. Thus of the four major panhellenic games, only the Pythian Games at Delphi appear not to be held in a grove.[21]

Greek groves were an expected, almost routine, amenity. Find a Greek city and there, next to the shore, or the harbour, or by the lake, or beneath the hill or mountain just above the cultivated plain, lay the luxuriant, shady grove. The management of the land and its water might produce a landscape, as in Greco-Roman Spain, that was 'well groved and well vined' (Strabo 3.3.1) and the maintenance of a grove, as of any temple within it, would be a clearly assigned responsibility: the temple of Poseidon of Samikon with its grove of wild olives was looked after by the people of Makistia (Triphylia, western Peloponnese, Strabo 8.3.13). It was Kimon, in the early fifth century BC, who 'turned the Academy [the place of worship of the hero Akademos/Hekademos] from a waterless and arid place into an irrigated grove' (Plutarch, *Kimon* 13.7), and Sulla, the Roman dictator of the 80s BC, who chopped it down in rage at the Athenians (Plutarch, *Sulla* 12.3). This was the place that Plato found congenial to discuss philosophy (*Souda* s.v. 'Akademia'), just as Indian Brahmans, very nearly a product of the Greek imagination, would 'sojourn in the grove in front of the city' (Strabo 15.1.59). Plato's philosophy stood in an ambivalent relationship to institutional religion and one would not care to estimate the precise degree of religious ambience implicit in Plato's choice of the grove of the hero Akademos. Later in the fourth century BC, Epicurus, whose own philosophy discounted traditional cult, met in a *Kepos*, or 'Garden', a secularised Academy – though Hephaistos too had a *Kepos* in the centre of Athens.

After the conquests of Alexander the Great, kingship and a culture of royal display borrowed significantly from the long-established Persian kingship which it succeeded. Part of this was the adoption of the demarcated area known in the language of the Medes (the sister nation of the Persians) as a *paridaeza, and borrowed into Greek as a *paradeisos* (our 'paradise').[22] In Persia this had originally been a fruit-bearing area of sacred ground, with a propensity for containing, among other things, fruit trees – a cross, if you like, between a Stengelian grove and a sacred field or meadow, perhaps the Persian vision of a grove (Persians, as good Indo-Europeans, should have had groves too). They next evolve into larger royal lands with facilities for hunting and provision of wild animals, fish and so on. Finally, hunting and animals recede and what we are left with, borrowed into Hellenistic culture, is the grand park, the outburst of artificial natural fertility and beauty, the 'European' garden. So, at Daphne outside Antioch a mega-grove, 80 stades (15 km) in circumference and rich in springs, housed the precinct and temple of Apollo and Artemis and was the site of great festivals (Strabo 16.2.6). And as you sailed into Alexandria with the lighthouse of Pharos on your right, you might see the royal palace, 'its inner buildings provided with all sorts of luxurious living-spaces and groves' (Strabo 17.1.9). Here we meet a Greek terminological problem. A garden is a *kepos*, but that is usually too humble. These new gardens are therefore more usually called *alse*, groves (they are too mainstream to demand the oriental and exotic word *paradeisoi*). But the word *alsos* is not wholly misapplied: parks remained awesome and in a sense sacred; and groves were increasingly beautiful and in a sense places of leisure.

Though the Roman aristocracy and Emperors took up the concept of gardens, the religious sense had largely been lost. Such religion as might be found in painted landscapes or actual gardens scarcely rises above the kitsch. Cicero's closest friend, a man of such culture that he was called 'Atticus' ('he of Athens'), built an *Amaltheion* at Buthrotum, at the southern end of the Albanian coastline:

> The word *Amaltheion* denotes in Greek a sanctuary consecrated to the nurse of Zeus, the nymph (or goat) Amaltheia, who took care of his brief infancy on Mount Ida in Crete. Atticus' *Amaltheion* was shaded by plane trees, the usual tree of gardens and public promenades in Greece, of its gymnasia and its porticoes. This planted area, along or through which flowed a freshwater stream, led to the actual sanctuary. Of it we know only that it 'formed a landscape'.
>
> Grimal 1943: 321 (my translation)

It is difficult to believe that this Epicurean constructed these gardens out of piety to a legendary goat, though its broken-off horn had probably by then become the horn of plenty.[23] Whatever excuses one makes – and writers on Roman religion make plenty – the Roman aristocracy had by the first century BC lost most of their authentic feel for peasant paganism and replaced it with a feeling for aesthetic symbolism.

Unlike the Greeks, the Romans could distinguish between sacred groves (*luci*) and secular gardens (*horti*).[24] So we see *horti* through Strabo's description of Rome as possessing 'groves and three theatres and an amphitheatre' (5.3.8). Yet there may indeed have been something religious, or at least commemorative, about the 'grand grove offering wonderful walks' next to the tombs of Augustus Caesar and his family (also 5.3.8). Augustus himself, after all, with his characteristic sensitivity to archaic religious forms, meant something special by creating, in 2 BC, a *nemus Caesarum* on the banks of the Tiber in honour of his lamented grandchildren and intended heirs Gaius and Lucius.[25]

Yet it is important not to be too sweeping about 'the Romans'. Our evidence privileges the aristocracy and privileges the city of Rome. If we look further afield in place or social level, we find truly sacred groves

Figure 6.4 The grove of Clitumnus. Photo: Ken Dowden

100

continuing in existence and we find the Stengelian (managed, artificial, religious) grove, in this inscription set up by the Montani, the residents of the Seven Mountains that formed the original Rome and whose festival was the Septimontium on 11 December:[26] 'The mayor (*magister*) and priests (*flamines*) of the Montani of the Oppian Mount, from the funds of the Montani of the Oppian Mount, caused the shrine to be enclosed and levelled and trees to be planted' (Inscription, *CIL* 6.32455 (also, *ILS* 5428), first century BC). We can even find the grove beautiful. A prime example must be the grove and river of Clitumnus in the territory of Mevania (now Bevagna, Umbria) visited by the Emperor Gaius 'Caligula' in around AD 39 (Suetonius, *Gaius* 43), and adored by Pliny the younger, whose account is worth recalling:

> A modest hill rises, wooded and dark with ancient cypress. Beneath this a spring emerges . . . so pure and glassy that you can count the coins thrown in there and the pebbles that gleam back. From there, it is driven along not because of any slope in the ground but through its own fullness and, as it were, weight, so far a spring but now a really broad river that will even take boats . . . The banks are clothed with many ash trees and also many poplars . . . Nearby is an ancient and venerable (*religiosum*) temple. Clitumnus himself stands cloaked and adorned in a *praetexta* [toga with border worn by magistrates]; written oracles there indicate he is an active (*praesens*) divinity who even prophesies. Scattered around are several small shrines (*sacella*) and as many gods, each one with his own worship and his own name, some even with springs . . . [The waters of the various streams merge into the river at a bridge . . .] this is the boundary of the sacred and the profane. In the upper part you may only sail, but below you are allowed to swim as well.
>
> Pliny the younger, *Letters* 8.8

Groves and barbarians

Greek groves, though civilised out of all awesomeness, remain an accepted and valued part of the religious landscape. In Rome and Italy the grove is generally a venerable and archaic survival alongside a system of temple-worship (its archaism may be judged from the fact that there are six references to groves in the first, legendary, book of Livy's history of Rome, but none in books 2–5). Otherwise, groves are characteristic of the simpler Roman countryside where there may be no nearby temples – hence Fronto's explanation of his worshipping at hearths, altars, groves and trees (Chapter 2). The groves of other nations are rarely so accepted by Greeks and Romans. Though it is not actually by this stage true of Celts and needs some small print for Germans, Greeks and Romans usually assume they use groves *because they have no temples*: '(because they were) without temples, they used to worship the gods in woods', as an ancient commentator tells us.[27] To emphasise that a nation worships in groves is thus, not quite hypocritically, a denunciation of their cultural *niveau* and a sign of barbarism.

Wholly in tune with this is Lucan's rhapsodic description of a grove at Marseilles in his highly charged epic on the *Civil war* (60s AD):

There was a grove, since the depths of time never violated,
interlinking branches to girdle its dark atmosphere
and chill shades – the daylight world removed far above.
No rustic Pans or (powerful in forests)
Silvanuses and Nymphs owned this grove: it was a place for barbarous
rites to gods. Altars were built from bestial offerings
and every tree was purified with human gore.
If antiquity (in awe at the divine) deserves credit,
birds fear to sit on *those* branches
and beasts to lie down in those haunts; no wind blows on
those woods, nor thunderbolts launched from
black clouds; no breezes stir the leaves
– their own shuddering is innate in the trees. Then copious water pours down
from black springs, and gloomy statues of the gods
lack craftsmanship and stand, hewn trunks, shapeless.
The very decay and pallor resulting from wood now rotten
stuns: divinities consecrated in familiar shapes
do not inspire such fear: so much does it add to their terror
not to know the gods they fear. Before now rumour has it that
often hollow caverns bellowed as the earth moved,
and yews that fell rose again
and fires blazed in woods that were not alight,
and serpents curled round the timbers (*robora*) and embraced them.
The local peoples do not visit that grove for close-up cult
– they yield it to the gods. When Phoebus is at his zenith
or the blackness of night possesses the sky, the priest himself is scared to
enter and fears he may stumble upon the master of the grove.

Lucan, Pharsalia 3.399–425

Marseilles was one of the longest-established Greek colonies and that whole southern region of Gaul was described by the elder Pliny as practically another Italy. This is therefore a particularly ideological piece of writing, bearing little relation to reality. Nonetheless, it delivers some points of substance on groves. The grove is a natural place: it is ancient and virgin. It has not been violated and there is a religious restriction on entry, even if it undergoes rhetorical exaggeration. It has a priest, who has special rights of entry, and there are statues, as there were in Germanic groves. The statues are made out to be crude and not so different from mere trunks, a stage that we know, for instance, Greek statuary passed through (Chapter 7). There is a spring in the grove, a common feature, and of course it is very dark, except presumably in the clearing needed for rites which would impair Lucan's colouring. This is a barbarian grove and the rites therefore embrace human sacrifice: what else would barbarians do in a gloomy grove? The final line reveals that the grove belongs to some specific divinity, though we do not learn who. In the lines which follow this passage Caesar chops down the grove while the 'local Gallic peoples groaned at the sight' (445 f.), an act of which Christians might later approve but which required a brave pagan. Germans have rather infiltrated Lucan's palette: they were indeed responsible for ritual slaughter in groves, as for instance of Varus' army in the Teutoburgerwald (Chapters 9, 14). Another contributor, contemporary with Lucan's writing, is Suetonius Paulinus' destruction of the groves of Anglesey in AD 61:

> Afterwards he imposed a garrison on the defeated and chopped down their groves, devoted to savage superstitions: they considered it right (*fas*) to make burnt offerings at altars with captive gore and to consult the gods using men's innards.
>
> Tacitus, Annals 14.30

It is striking that the chopping down of this grove leads, as though it were the result, into the revolt of Boudicca ('Boadicea'). Well might the 'brave hands' of Lucan's characters proceed to tremble before the 'majesty of the grove if they were to strike the sacred *robora* (wood/oak)'. In another passage Lucan (1.453–4) gives us a fine display of 'attitude' when describing druids, taking rather a jaundiced view of their supposedly philosophical nature and more impressed by their participation in barbaric rites (human sacrifice) and by the fact that they 'inhabit tall forests, in remote groves'.

This type of picture is influential. Claudian, as late as AD 400, is still writing this sort of poetry:[28]

> So that far away through the vast silences of the Hercynian Forest
> one may hunt safely and groves which ancient
> rites made savage and oak-wood in the shape of barbarian
> divinity might be hewn with impunity by our axes.
>
> Claudian, In praise of Stilicho 1.228–31

Pliny the elder also knew 'the expanses of the Hercynian Forest oak trees, untouched by time, as old as the world' (*Natural history* 16.6). It is the ideal site for stylised description, an indiscriminate name for a large unknown forested area in Europe whose leading characteristics are (a) to be as old as time, (b) to know no geographical limits, and (c) generally to represent the unknown. As knowledge became better this forest moved off in the direction of southern Germany and Bohemia, and the Teuto-burgerwald could be peeled off from it. A peculiar passage found in Caesar's *On the Gallic war* tells us it was nine days' journey wide and even sixty days' journey did not exhaust its length – no-one had ever found where it began.[29] But there were fabulous creatures there, including oversize goats with no knee-joints called *alces*, presumably 'elks'. You catch these creatures by weakening the trees they habitually lean against in order to sleep – because, once fallen over, they cannot get up again.[30]

But the Greco-Roman imagination also had a soft spot for primal Golden Age simplicity and merit found at the ends of the earth. In the far north fabulous nations mix imperceptibly with remote Celts. Here Pliny the elder and the geographer Mela know from their common Greek source[31] that there are nations permanently high on religion and festivals. The fabulous Arimphaioi and Hyperboreans are sacred peoples, who have the forests, *nemora*, for their homes, and 'live in the groves and woods', *qui habitant lucos silvasque*. These peoples are at one with nature and religion and seem never to have fallen from the Golden Age. To win asylum, you have only to escape to them. A different fantasy is the elegant, but silly, belief of Tacitus that Germans deliberately avoid temples and statues and choose instead to worship in simple groves (Chapter 7).

Groves and placenames

Latin sometimes associates the *lucus* ('grove') with the *nemus*, a rather wilder wooded area, a forest.[32] This word is occasionally used contingently of groves. It only denotes a grove in the case of the *nemus* of Diana near Aricia, not however the 'grove of Diana', but the 'forest of Diana' (which, so it happens, is her grove). Because of misunderstanding of this Latin word, the Gaulish word *nemeton* has almost universally, and wrongly, been supposed primarily to mean 'grove'. In fact it denotes a 'sanctuary' (we do not know any Gaulish word for a 'grove' as such) and so I will discuss it in Chapter 7 and deal there with those Celtic towns that display *nemeton* names as a result of their urban development beginning with a shrine. In Celtic lands, however, the Latin *lucus* may apply to a few, more grove-like sites. Lugo (Galicia, in Celtic Spain) owes its name to the *Lucus Augusti*, where Augustus appears to have taken over the veneration previously given to native gods. This became a centre where the *conventus Lucensis* met under 'the priest of Rome and Augustus at Augustus-Grove', the *sacerdos Romae et Augusti ad Lucum Augusti*.[33] Similarly, Luc-en-Diois (Vendôme) was the *Lucus Augusti* on the road from Milan to Vienne and once the second city of the Vocontii after Vasio (Vaison la Romaine).[34] A rarer, native *Lucus* placename was the *Lucus Bormani* near Diano Marina (in Liguria, northern Italy), commemorating the Celtic god Bormanus, the god of warm springs (Chapter 3).[35]

For a clear example of 'grove' placenames in Celtic, we must turn to Ireland, where a *doire* is an oak wood and the 1851 Census showed nearly 1000 'townlands' called *Derry*.[36] This is the same sensitivity that we find around Rome, where local placenames attested to groves of particular types of tree that had once grown there, *Corneta, Lauretum, Aesculetum* (cornel, laurel and oak respectively), though of course we cannot necessarily suppose that all had been cult places.[37]

A *lucus*-grove might become a place, testifying to its power as a focus, like Lugo or the *Lucus Feroniae* near Capena. The latter was already very notable in 211 BC when Hannibal made a detour in order to plunder it:

> [It had] a temple at that time celebrated for its wealth. The people of Capena and others who lived near it brought first-fruits there and other gifts according to availability and kept it adorned with much gold and silver.
>
> Livy, 26.11.8 f.

At this stage it was evidently managed by Capena (and Cato in his *Histories* referred to 'the grove of Capena') but later it was a site chosen by Julius Caesar in 46 BC for a wholly new town, the *Colonia Julia Felix Lucoferonia*, which Augustus then developed.[38]

Something of the sense of landmark which made this possible is shown in the case of another grove of Feronia outside Terracina (or 'Anxur') in a *Satire* of Horace describing his journey to Brindisi: this was the place they reached at lunchtime where they could wash their hands and faces, in holy water.[39] And Vergil describes 'Feronia rejoicing in the greenery of her grove'.[40] On the western shore of Lake Fucinus in the territory of the Marsi there was a *Lucus Angitiae*, celebrated in Vergil's *Aeneid* (7.759), which also went on to become a town, the modern *Luco dei Marsi* (Abruzzo). 'The site', comments Smith,[41] 'is now marked, as is so often the case in Italy, by an ancient church.'

Greek groves, too, are landmarks. The grove of Athene is the place at which Odysseus is directed to wait. 'Holy (or mighty) Onchestos' on the shore of Lake Kopaïs in Boiotia is notable for its 'splendid grove of Poseidon' (*Iliad* 2.506). By the days of Pausanias, the town may be ruined, but the grove with its temple and image of Poseidon of Onchestos survived (9.26.7) and remains of that temple can be visited today. A grove *mérite un détour*: Pausanias, our second-century Michelin *Guide vert*, is careful to mention groves as noteworthy sights on eighty-four occasions and Strabo the Geographer refers fifty-three times to particular groves, or to groves in general, in the Greco-Roman world.

Even when still on the continent the English (*Angli*) were worshipping in groves. We know this from Tacitus' account of the Nerthus religion (Chapter 9). The Old Norse for a grove was *lundr*, an element preserved in many British placenames deriving from Norse languages (especially in Lincolnshire). Philippson (1929: 189) cites twenty-four instances. Plumbland, ten kilometres north of Cockermouth (Cumberland), is the most interesting because of this comment:

> There is a *church* in the place which is called Plumbelund . . . so called after the forest (*nemus*) that surrounds it, hedged around as it is by the most close-packed abundance of woods on every side . . . because in the English idiom a forest given over to peace is called a 'lund'.
>
> Reginald of Durham, *The admirable virtues of St Cuthbert* 129
> (my emphasis)

In this church the local Cumbrians kept all their valuables.

The power of groves

Ancient groves

Trees in ancient and modern times often, individually and in groups, mark boundaries, but they are also often *left* at boundaries. A wood is therefore something ancient which one may expect to find undisturbed at margins. It may be little more than a fact of life, as in Greek boundary-forests mentioned by Pausanias: 'The few stands of trees that are unequipped with either legends or monuments grow in border territories' (Birge 1994: 233).[42] But the boundary-grove may also mark the religious power of the margin. This becomes clear in the work of the Roman land-surveyors, where groves are perceived as typically situated at the junction of two or more properties; at, for instance, *trifinia* and *quadrifinia*. Each property in turn has three Silvanuses – a Silvanus is a loosely personified god embodying the power of the untamed countryside (*silva*, 'wood'). One of the three, the Eastern Silvanus (*Silvanus orientalis*), regularly has a grove at the boundary of the property. In other cases a temple is found between properties and must have, as presumably groves in some sense had, one entrance from each property.[43]

In Italy before the Empire, groves had had a considerable cultural and religious significance, so that Cicero might appeal grandly to 'Alban mounds and groves' (*For Milo* §85), something of whose political role we will see in Chapter 14. Groves know how to belong in history. So, annually on 19 and 21 July the Romans celebrated the *Lucaria* 'in a very large grove which lay between the via Salaria and the Tiber, because when they had been defeated by the Gauls [in 390 BC] and were trying to get away from the battle, they hid themselves there' (Festus, *Excerpts from Paulus* 106 L).[44] The story is aetiological and, regardless of whether it is historically true, indicates the psychological dynamics of the grove and its festival. The ancient grove protected its people.

One of the most important of these groves was the one at Aricia (Lazio, south of Rome). Sanctified by its *antiqua religio* (Ovid, *Fasti* 3.264), it lay at the margins of the territory of Aricia, on the north-eastern side of modern Lake Nemi. Nemi, now notable for delicious strawberries, recalls through its name the '*nemus*', beneath today's Mount Artemisio, itself obviously named after the precinct of Diana, in Strabo's Greek the 'Artemision'.[45] Here is a wonderful pagan sense for sacred place, the *nemus* and the lake, the so-called 'mirror of Diana', the *speculum Dianae* in which, Latte romantically speculates, you might see the stars and moon.[46] It was fed by revered springs, including a nymph no lesser than Egeria herself.[47] This, then, is the grove implausibly associated in ancient writers with the mythic Greek cult of Artemis Tauropolos with its cruel human sacrifices and melodramatic story of the near-sacrifice of Orestes by his sister Electra. But the local practice, too, was cruel if we believe the tale that Strabo tells with relish:

> In fact, a barbaric, Skythian, custom prevails at the shrine. The priest is appointed by murdering the person previously appointed priest and he is a runaway [slave]. So, sword-in-hand, he is always looking around in case he is attacked, prepared to defend himself.
>
> Strabo 5.3.12

This is the fabled *Rex Nemorensis*, 'King of the *Nemus*', which Frazer used in his *Golden Bough* as a starting point for the detection of supposed king-sacrifices and allied customs all over the world and especially all over Germany (where Mannhardt had collected the folk-evidence). The ceremony which underlies these grotesque garblings probably occurred once a year: 'Now the day was at hand when smoke rises from the Aricine *nemus* of Trivia [Diana depicted as Hekate, goddess of crossroads, witches and hellhounds], a place suited to its fugitive kings' (Statius, *Silvae* 3.1.55 f.). There were other striking rituals in the *nemus* too – the mystery-cult of a figure Virbius (supposed to be the same as the Greek Hippolytus) and torchlit processions of womenfolk every 13 August to the *nemus*, an awesome sight.[48]

Inviolability

Powerful groves should not be maltreated; in particular they should not be cut or improperly entered. This is immediately apparent in an ancient inscription in archaic, olde worlde, Latin, found near Spoleto and dating from around 250–200 BC:

> Let no-one violate this grove nor convey nor carry out anything that is in the grove nor set foot in it [or possibly 'cut it'] except annually on the day of the rite; on the day when it is done because of the rite it shall be permitted to enter (cut) it with impunity. Whosoever violates the grove shall give a purificatory offering of an ox to Jupiter; whosoever violates it knowingly and maliciously shall give a purificatory offering of an ox to Jupiter and shall be fined 300 *asses* [a unit of currency]. The chief magistrate[49] shall be responsible for the exaction of the offering and fine.
>
> Inscription, *CIL* 1^2.366

Fines, in civilised lawgiving (cf. Chapter 1), replace more drastic measures exemplified for us by Festus' (*Excerpts from Paulus* 57) definition of a 'capital grove' as 'a place where any violation is paid for with the life of the violator'! God's law too was brutal: the Spartan king Kleomenes burnt down a sacred grove at Argos in which fugitives had sought refuge ('having no respect for the actual grove, he burnt it down') and this doubtless caused his grisly death.[50] More routinely, the very Arval Brethren, whose job it was to tend the grove of the Dea Dia, had to perform piacular rites when they pruned and thinned the grove. There may even be a worry about entry to the grove; after all, nothing taken into the grove of Marica at Minturnae might be brought out again. This sort of prohibition can be seen in the inscription above and extended even to groves as pleasant as those of the Greeks. So Strabo's expensive grove at Tralleis (see below, p.114) might only be entered by priests and the ill. It was *adytos* (no entry on religious grounds) and *olethrios* (deadly) for others. Even in Irish saints' lives 'to cut any of these sacred trees or groves is sacrilege'.[51]

Entrance to groves, as we can see, is particularly subject to taboos. An extreme case is provided by a German tribe:

> The Semnones tell that they are the most ancient and noble of the Suebi,[52] and confidence in their antiquity is reinforced by their religious practice. At a fixed time the peoples of the same name[53] and same blood come together in deputations into a wood[54] sanctified by the auguries of their fathers and through ancient awe: slaying a man in public, they celebrate the gruesome opening

of their barbarian rite.[55] There is also another rite displaying their respect for the grove: no-one may enter unless he is tied and bound, as a subject and displaying the power of the godhead. Should he by any chance fall, he may not rise back to his feet: they roll out over the ground. The whole superstition is based on the idea that their race originates here and the god who rules all is here, while everything else is dependent and obedient.

Tacitus, Germania 39

The same atmosphere infuses the groves of thirteenth-century Lithuanians[56] and Prussians:

On the Dusii[57] demons and how, once one body has been taken away, they substitute another

Now follows the section on the Dusii or Dusiones, which is the third type of demon.

> We have seen many aspects of the Dusii demons. These are the ones for whom the pagans used to preserve groves which had been planted long ago. Even today pagans in Prussia consider woods sacred to them and, not daring to set foot in them, never enter them except when they want to sacrifice to their gods in them.
>
> Thomas of Cantimpré, *The universal good of bees* (1263) 2.57.17,
> *LPG* 48 (also, Jouet 1989: 149)

Oliver the Scholastic (d. 1227) comments on Baltic 'groves that no axe has presumed to violate'.[58] And when a hare crossed the path of the Lithuanian king Mindaugas (ruled *c*. 1238–63), he would not ride into the grove before him or break a twig.[59] (Horses were not allowed in Diana's *nemus* either.)[60] Indeed, this whole feeling that groves were a dangerous place to enter is reinforced by Adam's observation about Slavs in the eleventh century: 'Even today among them, even though everything else is shared with us, access to groves and springs alone is prohibited – they say they are polluted by Christians entering' (Adam 4.18). Precisely because groves may not normally be 'violated', it is specially powerful to remove a branch for religious purposes and to use the leaves of trees to form garlands, one of the most important ancient indicators of engagement in a sacred activity. So, for instance, druids 'do not perform any rites without oak leaves' (Pliny, *Natural history* 16.249). Tacitus tells us of divination among the Germans performed with 'a branch cut from a fruit-bearing tree' (*Germania* 10.1). Servius tells us that in the grove of Nemi there was a certain tree from which no branch might be broken off, except by a newcomer to challenge the existing holder of the kingship of the grove, and also, presumably a fact about Greek mystery-religion, that 'without a branch one may not approach the rites of Persephone'.[61] Branches are a significant part of the apparatus of Greek religion. They are used, for instance, in supplication, as at the beginning of Sophocles' great play, the *Oedipus Tyrannus*. Combining the grove of Nemi with Greek mystery-religion, Vergil's Aeneas, to enter the Underworld, must follow the Sibyl's instructions and tear the Golden Bough from a tree in the grove of Juno Inferna[62] (*Aeneid* 6.133–211). We have perhaps looked too long at the 'golden' and too little at the 'bough' and 'grove'. It is a psychologically revealing feature of Greek mythology, however, that it so reduplicates the quest as one for gold in a grove: we may think also of the golden apples of the Hesperides (which in a later poet's telling are painted in Vergil's colours)[63] and the Golden Fleece at Colchis in the grove of Ares – a practically unworshipped god, incidentally, and a most unlikely, if colourful, grove-holder.

The inviolability of the grove may also on occasion benefit those who enter it, as for instance when it offers asylum. Partly this is a question of simply hiding (as the Romans supposedly did in the Lucaria), or as the Argives tried to when King Kleomenes burnt down their grove. But Marius found asylum in the grove of Marica at Minturnae, and Gaius Gracchus fled, if in vain, to the grove of Furrina.[64] Romulus himself had created as an asylum 'the place which is now fenced off as you go down [the Capitol hill], Between-Two-Groves' (Livy 1.8.1).[65] It is a natural step from asylum to the granting of freedom:

> (Feronia) is also a goddess of freedmen, in whose temple they used to receive the *pilleus* [*freedman's cap*]. In her temple at Terracina there was a stone seat inscribed: 'Let deserving slaves sit down and rise free.'
>
> Servius Auctus, on Vergil, *Aeneid* 8.564 (possibly from Varro)

Feronia was very much a goddess of groves, as we have seen, and she is also associated from our earliest evidence (third century BC) with slaves and freedmen.[66] They may find safety and transition to a better status in her grove.

The grove may also exercise a more magical liberating power, as in groves of Juno and Diana or, as Strabo puts it, Hera of Argos and Aetolian Artemis, among the Veneti on the River Po where his informants adopted the mythic register and told him that 'the wildlife is tame and deer mix with wolves and will let men come up and stroke them' (Strabo 5.1.9). The wild becomes tame and the Golden Age is restored in the anomalous surroundings of a sacred area. It was much the same for temple fish (Chapter 3).

Divine ownership

If you subscribe to a religion which is in any way anthropomorphic, then it is likely that the grove will belong to a particular god. Thus Greek groves are owned by gods and, given the stress on growth and fertility, very frequently by goddesses: in Pausanias six groves are Demeter's and four or five Artemis'. Similarly, the Italian equivalent of Artemis, Diana, and goddesses capable of identification with her characteristically possess groves: 'every oak is sacred to Jupiter and every grove to Diana,' says Servius.[67] The new temple of Diana on the Aventine in Rome was positioned on the only hill that remained wooded: 'There was a grove beneath the Aventine, black from the shade of the holm-oak (*ilex*) – looking at it you would say "there is a divinity in there"' (Ovid, *Fasti* 3.295 f.). Rome had once been more wooded, as we can tell from its placenames such as 'Between-Two-Groves'.[68] The Aventine hill actually lay *beyond*, outside the *pomoerium* or religiously determined boundary of the city, and was rather cut off by marshy ground.[69] There were other groves just outside the city: the *Lucus Petelinus* at Rome, perhaps the same as the *Aesculetum* and, by the Porta Capena, the grove of the Camenae, goddesses identified by intellectual Romans with the Greek Muses, though maybe in real life they were spring goddesses. Here, legend told, King Numa had his assignations with his mistress, the spring-nymph Egeria. This was the grove from which the Vestal Virgins drew water for their temple. Similar are the groves of Feronia in central Italy. The actual *Lucus Feroniae*, as can be deduced from the lack of evidence for settlement there, was on the western side of the colony Lucoferonia.[70] And the grove at Terracina was at the third milestone from the town, just as the grove of the Dea Dia was at the fifth milestone from Rome along the Via Appia. In Greece Pausanias tells us of fifteen instances of groves within a couple of kilometres of Greek cities (Birge 1994: 241) – for instance, the grove at Kolonos where Sophocles' Oedipus finally disappeared from mortal sight.

At Minturnae (above the Gulf of Gaeta, north of Naples) beneath the city lay a 'holy grove exceedingly revered' (Strabo 5.3.6), the grove presumably of the local goddess Marica in which Marius took refuge 'which they revere and they take care that nothing which is taken into it shall be taken out again' (Plutarch, *Marius* 39). One of our most colourful inscriptions is a record of proceedings in the grove of the Dea Dia. Finally, the birth-goddess *Lucina*, identified with Juno in historical times, is thought at least by Pliny to be the goddess 'of the Grove' and certainly had a grove in Rome – perhaps she had been Juno Lucina from the start.[71] One should probably resist, however, any comparison with Celtic instances of a goddess *Nemetona*; she is not 'grove/shrine-goddess', but the goddess of the Nemetes, the tribe in whose territory her inscriptions are mostly found and who give rise to Slavonic names for the Germans.[72] Juno's husband

Jupiter owned groves too – the erstwhile *Fagutal* where there had been a 'beech-grove' of Jupiter Fagutalis and surely the *Aesculetum* ('Oak-Grove'), given that the *aesculus* was 'sacred to Jupiter'.[73] In the same way Zeus, the Greek Jupiter, and his local consort Dione, whose name corresponds to the Latin Diana, owned the oracular grove at Dodona.

Germans too appear to have assigned groves to specific gods: for instance, the grove of Baduhenna where 900 Romans were allegedly slaughtered by the Frisians in a battle of AD 28 that went on continuously from one day to the next (Tacitus, *Annals* 4.73.4). Somewhere near the Weser there was a 'wood sacred to Hercules' (*Annals* 2.12), perhaps meaning Donar?[74] Certainly, in Dublin in later times (Dublin was captured in the ninth century by Danes) there was an oak wood sacred to Thor (*Coill Tomair*), whose destruction is referred to in an eleventh-century Irish text: 'Brian remained in that place [Dublin] from Christmas till the festival of Brigit [1 February] . . . the wood of Thor[75] was burned by him and hewn down, and passages and fortresses cleared by him' (*Cogadh gaedhel re Gallaibh* ch.70, transl. Todd 1867: 117 (except 'wood of Thor')); '"The battle, king, is like the forest of Thor, surrounded by flames after the seven battalions, over 30 days, had cleared the thick undergrowth and felled the young trees and only the tall trees and the majestic oaks were still standing"' (*Cogadh gaedhel re Gallaibh* ch.113 (Todd 1867: 199), following the French transl. of Marstrander 1915: 247). Just as in the case of Romans fleeing Gauls, this forest north-east of Dublin appears to have been where the Norwegians sent their wives, children and flocks when this final attack of the Irish under Brian of Munster was upon them. The burning of the forest took place around Christmas of the year 1000. As Marstrander (1915: 247) comments, 'Among all ancient peoples, the forest, wherever it was situated, was the principal place of refuge against the attack of an enemy.'

The fearsome grove of the Semnones was not only their own place of origin but the haunt of 'the god who rules all (gods)'. And a miscellaneous set of tribes of no special distinction, according to Tacitus – English readers will note they contain the Anglii – shared worship at an inviolate grove on an island in the northern sea, sacred to Nerthus, *id est Terram Matrem*, Mother *Earth*.[76]

Groves may on occasion be associated with the world of the dead. The grove at Tralleis (Strabo 14.1.44) is a grove of Pluto and Persephone, a grove to which people came for healing. At Aquileia there appears to have been a grove of Dis (= Hades) and Era ('Mistress', i.e. Persephone).[77] Lucan paints in these colours when he depicts the Marseilles grove as a sort of shade-inhabited underworld. The grove at Lerna belonged to Demeter and Dionysos: these gods offered a mystery-rite there, rites fundamentally about death and afterlife, and the site was even supposed to be an entrance to the Underworld. A special aura is given to mystery-rites when they were, as often, held in a grove.[78] The grove at Kolonos outside Athens housed the shrine of the *Semnai* ('Awesome' goddesses, identified with the Furies), where nonetheless Oedipus is presented by Sophocles, a native of Kolonos, as seeking asylum.

Groves, however formidable, are at least demarcated. Forests are altogether more impressive and may call into existence a divinity to empower them – the *dea Arduinna* of the wooded 'high' (*ard*) Ardennes or the *dea Abnoba*, the mountain-goddess of the Black Forest:[79] 'To Arduinna, [Mars] Camulus, Jupiter, Mercury, Hercules, Marcus Quartinius Sabinus son of Marcus, citizen from Reims, soldier of the 7th Praetorian Cohort of Antoninus Pius Vindex paid his vow gladly' (Inscription, *CIL* 6.46).

If the divine inhabits the grove it may also speak.[80] The grove of Apollo at Pagasai in Thessaly was also the site of an oracle.[81] That too may be why the only priest that Odysseus encounters was 'living in a wooded grove of Phoibos Apollo' at Ismaros in Thrace (*Odyssey* 9.200). The oracle of Apollo at Klaros, too, was in a sacred grove.[82] Perhaps the most famous oracular tree is the oak of Zeus at Dodona in Epirus, where his priestesses, the 'Doves', are supposed to have divined from the rustling of the leaves, though, of course, one tree does not make a grove even if Vergil got a good line out of it: *habitae Grais oracula quercus*, 'oaks considered oracles by Greeks' (Vergil, *Georgics* 2.16).[83] At Olympia, where the swelling River Alpheios and its tributary the Kladeos flowed along two sides of the sanctuary, rose the marshy and therefore lush *Altis*, the grove of Zeus, also an oracular site according to Strabo.[84] The original wooden pillars of the temples presumably came from the grove itself, in a sense perpetuating the trees, and certainly one pillar in the temple of Hera was still in Pausanias' time made of oak (5.16.2). Here, however, in historical times the only actual grove was one of wild-olive trees beyond the perimeter, amidst which the Stadium had been built (Strabo 8.3.30).

Roman history told more grandly how voices might issue from groves:

> Shortly before the capture of the city [of Rome by the Gauls in 390 BC] a voice was heard from the grove of Vesta, which sloped down from the foot of the Palatine to the New Road, saying that the walls and gates should be renovated.
>
> Cicero, *On divination* 1.101

This was a time for voices: Livy reports a 'voice from heaven' announcing the imminent arrival of the Gauls (5.51.7). To have a grove, though, is to have heaven near by. And further back, before the death of King Tullus, 'they thought they heard a huge voice from the grove at the peak of the [*Alban*] Mount, saying that the Albans should perform their rites according to ancestral ritual' (Livy 1.31.3).

Inside the grove

What would you find if you dared disregard all prohibitions and step into a grove? In fact, much of the apparatus that we would associate with a temple and any other sanctuary, and that begins with the water supply, which temple-sanctuaries need for purificatory purposes, but trees need in order to live.

Greek and Italian groves are characteristically next to a river or a lake, or endowed with springs. The spring-nymph Egeria watered the grove of the Camenae outside Rome and the grove of Diana at Aricia, and Horace washed in the water of the grove of Feronia at Terracina. The trees of a grove are thickly packed, creating a roof of leaves shading you from the sun. They may be wild: so, around the cave of Demeter the Black at Phigaleia in Arcadia, 'there is a grove of oaks and cold water comes up out of the ground' (Pausanias 8.42.12).

Having entered the grove, we should be sensitive to the particular varieties of tree we find there. Beyond the 'Hall' of the Mistress (*Despoina*, a Persephone-type queen of the Underworld), where mystery-rites are held in a rather isolated area of Arcadia, is 'a sacred grove of the Mistress whose perimeter is formed by a wall of stones, and within it grow trees including an olive and holm-oak (*prinos*) growing from one rootstock – this is not a product of agricultural skill' (Pausanias 8.37.10). Wild too, perhaps, are Athene's poplars in the *Odyssey* (above) and the 'tall poplars and willows that lose their fruit' in the grove of Persephone on the other side of the River Ocean, appropriately for the land of the dead (*Odyssey* 10.509 f.). But 'willows that lose their fruit' point to the tamer sort of grove, where in Stengelian splendour the grove is actually a plantation of cultivated trees. Such, for instance, was the situation 'at Gryneion [in Phrygia] where there is a very beautiful grove of Apollo, of cultivated trees and of all the non-fruit-bearing ones that offer some pleasure of smell or sight' (Pausanias 1.21.7). This delightful place was the site of an oracle of Apollo, though it did little good to the local inhabitants, who were sold into slavery by Alexander's general Parmenion (Diodoros 17.7.9). The grove at Didyma near Miletos (Strabo 14.1.5) and that of Plouton and Kore near Tralleis (on the River Maeander in Asia Minor, Strabo 14.1.44) are even described as 'expensive'. It was part of the special Greek delight in groves that they would actually plant them and ensure a lovely collection of trees, foreshadowing the secular gardens of the Romans, and indeed of Europe. The Stengelian grove may seem uniquely Greek, but presumably the same attitude is evinced by Thomas of Cambrai's comment (see above, p. 109) that pagan Prussians used to revere groves 'planted long ago' – unless the word 'planted' is a malicious attempt to undermine the power and authenticity of the groves by denying that they are genuinely ancient.

More primeval groves will have more natural trees. The fictional grove of Lucan contains yew (*taxus*), a notable evergreen,[85] various types of oak, rowan, alder and cypress. It is a well-populated mixed forest. Vergil speaks of the 'huge oak (*aesculus*) whose leaves adorn the groves of Jupiter' (*Georgics* 2.15 f.). Druids, too, by their very name, whatever its derivation, are associated with the oak (Chapter 12): hence Pliny's comment that they seek out groves of oak (*robora*) for their own sake and do not perform any rites without oak leaves (see above, p. 109). We should be alert to the sensitivity of pagan peoples to the variety of trees and to their perceived properties, which are attested, for instance, in old Irish texts and more recent folk-custom.[86]

> Yet, different soils bear different produce.
> By rivers willow-trees, in dense marshland alders
> are born, sterile rowans on rocky mountains.
> Shores are most fruitful for myrtle groves. Finally, open
> hills are enjoyed by Bacchus [i.e. vines], North Wind and cold by
> yews.
>
> Vergil, *Georgics* 2.109–13

But beyond trees we would find typical cult apparatus. The Germans of Tacitus seem to keep portable statues in their groves (Chapter 7), indirectly supported by Lucan's fictive but Germanising Marseilles grove with its crude aniconic 'gloomy statues of the gods' and grim altars reeking with human blood. Similarly, in the Teutoburgerwald Germanicus found the altars of the Cherusci, on which the officers of Varus' army had been sacrificed (Tacitus, *Annals* 1.61). Valuable offerings too lay inviolate in groves, as we can see from injunctions not to remove things from groves and from Hannibal's plundering of the *Lucus Feroniae*. Valuables include sacred animals, even white horses grazing, ready to divine (Tacitus, *Germania* 10.2).

Trees are also good for hanging things on, as we saw in Chapter 4. In the Greek temple culture the standard word for 'dedicate' is *anatithemi*, which means 'I put up' and clearly many dedications were attached to temple walls. The origin of this, however, is surely a practice of leaving offerings in the trees of groves in the days before such temple buildings had appeared. Thus, for instance, in the *Odyssey* the prospective murderer of Agamemnon, Aigisthos

> burnt many thighs on the gods' sacred altars
> and hung up many dedications, woven cloth and gold.
>
> Homer, *Odyssey* 3.273 f.

Homer on the whole tends to suppress temple culture (it is too modern for epic) and what may well be meant here is that Aigisthos hung his offerings in trees. Clearly, if you do not have a temple building (much less, a treasury to house gifts) it is hard to identify where gifts should be left: to leave them on the ground is feeble, to hang them in trees is a matter of display and simultaneously advertises the power embodied in those trees. Typically such gifts would be hung somewhere near the altar, the focus of the sanctuary.[87] In later times it was common enough for those rescued from shipwreck to dedicate their clothing in trees and it may be that the tree continued long to be associated in particular with vows and fulfilment as we saw in the case of Erysichthon's tree (Chapter 4).

But other, more grisly offerings might hang in trees too. We will have to wait until Chapter 14 to see them.

7

TECHNOLOGY: STATUES, SHRINES AND TEMPLES

With this chapter we now enter advanced paganism, where the statue becomes the focus and the temple distracts attention from the sacred enclosure. These artefacts are also items which modern urban dwellers readily associate with paganism and which ancient and medieval urban critics of paganism knew should be destroyed. In some sense a paganism with statues and temples was less frustrating and easier to eradicate than a paganism with groves and springs; it at least conformed to a Christian pattern and offered targets. It also brought real paganism nearer to the biblical idea of paganism.

STATUES

The place of statues

A remarkable, and unread, speech of the Greek philosophical orator Maximus of Tyre (late second century AD) discusses the question of *Whether we should set up statues to the gods*. With great bravura he observes the huge variety of ways in which nations represent god and concludes that our conventional notion of the statue is only one semiotic method among others for finding signifiers by means of which mentally to approach divinity. But the fact is, 'there is no nation, not barbarian, not Greek, not by the sea, not inland, not nomadic, not urban, that can bring itself not to establish some symbols of the status of the gods' (Maximus of Tyre 2.9). Statues are for thinking about the gods and not even the most unidolatrous of Christians can ineffably think the ineffable. Statues, too, are a language and perhaps the Romans were on to something when they used *signum*, a sign, to mean 'statue'.

Statues may not be an inevitable part of pagan religion – trees and stones, and cairns (*hermaia* in Greece, Chapter 4) demonstrate an alternative semiotic – but they are usual when gods are sufficiently personally conceived. This is a two-way process, because the existence of anthropomorphic statues, however crude, encourages anthropomorphic perception of the gods. So the motor for the development of Greek free-standing sculpture was very largely the determination to produce ever more anthropomorphic cult statues; and in return Greek pagan religion becomes arguably the most completely anthropomorphic of any paganism. We in our turn remain, even at a popular level, closer to Greek paganism (and its Roman imitation) than to any other and therefore perhaps have unrealistically anthropomorphic expectations of all paganisms. The dominant model in our imaginary apparatus is of the very human god of Greek mythology frozen in a cult statue and worshipped in a marble temple surrounded by pillars. The cult statue in this picture is at least life-size and maybe larger.

In fact statues develop from, and indeed are made from, trees and stones, themselves foci of worship (Chapter 4). Stone sculpture is very hi-tech and the commonest development therefore is from the tree to the statue. Trees, as such, tend not to be personalised; rather it is 'the stock or carved trunk, that is, the tree artificially wrought upon in some rude way'.[1] These sawn trunks may serve as a dummy for clothing and as the raw material for conversion into human form. But there remains a distinction between those statues that are sculpted to look like a person ('iconic') and those which are less worked and in which there is no attempt to personalise the raw material ('aniconic'); there are also stages in between, where, for instance, the head is sculpted but the rest is a mere column.

A whole trunk, if I may draw the unromantic parallel of a telegraph pole, is also in its way an impressive thing and turns up in Rudolph of Fulda's account (AD 865) of the Saxons defeated by Charlemagne in the 780s:

> They exhibited the worship of leafy trees and springs. They also worshipped in the open air a trunk of wood of no small size, raised erect, calling it in their native language 'Irminsul', which in

Latin means 'universal pillar' (*universalis columna*) on the grounds that it holds everything up.

Rudolph of Fulda, *The translation of St Alexander* 3 (*MG ScrGerm* 2.676)[2]

Irmin-sûl is the pillar (German *Säule*) of a god Irmin, after whom are named the Hermunduri, who massacred the Chatti (Chapter 9).[3] In its massiveness this pillar recalls the oak of Jupiter at Geismar (Chapter 4). Turning to folk customs, it is hard in this context to ignore the maypole, which seems particularly prevalent in Germanic countries, though whether this actually descends from ancient paganism, we do not know.[4] What is certain is that 'Jupiter columns' have been found in north-eastern and central Gaul, but particularly on the middle Rhine. These columns are ornate Gallo-Roman stone constructions: the base is decorated with Roman gods, sometimes part or the whole of the column, too; at the top typically there is a horseman, whose rearing horse is supported by a giant emerging from the front of the capital.[5] This product is best related not to trees but to pillars, the replication of tree-trunks in stone.

Greek culture, which had seen, and preserved instances of, most stages in the development of the statue, distinguished between different types of statue.[6] Some were little more than a pillar (*kion*), as in the pointed pillars of Apollo Agyieus ('of the streets'):[7] 'Agyieus: the altar which is stood in front of the doors in the shape of a pillar' (Hesychios, *Lexicon*). Beyond this lay one of those very old and rudimentary, but portable, wooden statues called a *xoanon* – something which has been 'shaven' (*xeo*); in origin this seems to indicate barely more than that its bark had been planed off (aniconic, then) but in fact some attempt, seeming rudimentary in sophisticated retrospect, had been made to create at least a face. These antiques were greatly revered and were often thought to possess strange powers.[8] Some statues are called a *bretas*, an atmospheric, poetic word for an old wooden statue, though the difference between that and a *xoanon* eludes us.[9] Finally, there is the statue proper, generally referred to as an *agalma*, 'adornment', which is an ornate, artistic statue.

It is important not to be too hastily evolutionist about this process. Statues, or at least statuettes, go back to the Neolithic era, as archaeology has shown. In the Bronze Age statuettes have been excavated even in Jutland (de Vries 1956: i.§83). It is therefore no surprise if, as Tacitus appears to say, the Germans kept idols in their groves:[10] 'They take certain images (*effigies*) and ensigns/statues (*signa*) from their groves and carry them into battle' (Tacitus, *Germania* 7.2). This passage has given rise to a certain amount of discussion and it is not clear what the ambiguous term *signa* denotes; it may be representations of gods in bestial form, which are used as standards in battle.[11] But it does look like evidence for portable and therefore not very large statues. The concept was clearly known to Germans, as we can tell from the fact that Athanaric, king of the (Visigothic) Tervingi, around 370 paraded a wooden idol for Christians to worship; perhaps it was an idol of Terwing, their ancestor.[12]

Old English terms for statue can be surprisingly fluid: *wēoh* (Northumbrian *wīg*), very common in this sense, and *hearg*, much rarer, also denote the arrangement in which such an idol might figure – a shrine in which to house an idol, or cairn on which to mount it.[13] This fluidity is rather offputting to Latinate minds and it is bewildering to follow the term *vi/wēoh* in Germanic languages as it vacillates between grove, temple, *fanum*, idol and god (Grimm 1875: i.54) – the problem really is that it comes from a root meaning only 'dedicate/consecrate' and therefore has a range of applications into which it has settled.[14] Placename evidence is perhaps best regarded as denoting the actual holy site and is therefore dealt with under temples below. However, the primary use at least of *wēoh* in Anglo-Saxon is to denote statues which evidently existed and had a smith to make them (the *wīgsmið*), an altar to stand on (the *wīgbed*, unless that is just a 'consecrated table'), were viewed as offerings (a *wīggield*, '*wīg*-offering') and were the foundation of idol worship (*wīgweorðing*).[15] These are authentic terms for authentic objects, but in denunciatory retrospect a statue became a 'devil-offering', *deofolgield*, a very frequent term indeed, drawing perhaps not only on real Anglo-Saxon statues but replicating in Old English the required clichéd denunciation of Latin *idola* and *simulacra* – that is what pagans worship (Chapter 8). Thus both ideology and historical fact underlie the references of Gregory and Bede (below) and the proscriptions of church councils: pagans worship idols which should be removed from their *fana*.[16] As a result, however much one may suspect the lack of empirical evidence in the Christian portrait, it would be hypercritical to dismiss it altogether. As we shall see, Coifi is supposed to have initiated the destruction of Edwin's idols and at Edwin's palace at Yeavering there is significant archaeological evidence for a set of three statues.

Impressive statues and Christian destruction

Statues come in all shapes and sizes, from miniature ('statuettes') to colossal. The best-known larger examples come, of course, from Greece, where, for instance, the great sculptor Pheidias built two huge 'chryselephantine', gold and ivory-adorned, statues for major shrines. The Athene Parthenos at Athens was around 11.5 metres high and it was said that if the 12-metre enthroned Zeus at Olympia had stood up he would have taken the roof off![17] The extreme is represented by the statue that gives us our word 'colossal', the Colossus at Rhodes, the statue of the local god

Figure 7.1 Pheidias' statue of Zeus at Olympia, seen as you step through the colonnade into the temple

Helios ('Sun' – the Greeks did not generally worship Helios as a god). At 30 metres tall with around nine tons of iron and fifteen of bronze, it took twelve years to build and was over twice the height of the Zeus of Olympia; erected in 292, it collapsed, taking several houses with it, in an earthquake of 226 BC.[18] It lay, a fallen masterpiece, for almost a millennium, until finally it was sold for scrap in AD 654 and taken away, Brodersen (1996: 89) tells us, on 980 camels.

Romans, too, were impressed by colossal statues and Pliny the elder pauses to give us some information on them. In the AD 60s Zenodoros built a statue of Nero 106.5 Roman feet high (31.5 metres) which, after the damnation of Nero's memory, was dedicated instead to the Sun, like the Colossus. But before that – and this seems to be how Zenodoros got the Nero commission – he had built another statue: 'But every size of statue of that type was surpassed in our own times by Zenodoros when he built the Mercury at Clermont-Ferrand in Gaul. It took ten years and had a budget of HS 40 million' (Pliny the elder, *Natural history* 34.45). This is the celebrated Mercury shrine on the Puy de Dôme which was plundered by Chrocus in the third century (below).

121

Figure 7.2 An impression of the awesome scale of Pheidias' statue of Zeus at Olympia

Impressive north European statues arrived much later, around the tenth century. So, 11th-century Irish Christian texts denounce the 'dumb gods of wood and stone' worshipped by Norsemen in Ireland, which were regularly dressed in luxurious clothes, perhaps raided from Mediterranean Christians. One text alludes to their richness as follows: 'his flank and his sweet, transparent hands sparkled like white silver encrusted in the drapery which clothed the idol around' (Marstrander 1915: 243). More colossal were the statue of Redigast (below) and those in the temple of Uppsala:

> This race [the Swedes] has a particularly striking temple, called Uppsala, not far from the city of Sigtuna or Birka (Björkö). In this temple, which is all made of gold, the people worship the statues of three gods. The most powerful of them, Thor, has his throne in the middle of the room; the places at either side are taken by Wodan and Fricco [usually identified with Freyr]. The significance of these is as follows: Thor, they say, presides in the air and governs thunder and lightning, winds and rain, good weather and crops. The second, Wodan, i.e. frenzy, conducts wars and provides man with strength against his enemies. The third is Fricco, who dispenses peace and pleasure to mortals. And his statue is made with a huge *priapus* (penis). Wodan they sculpt armed, as our people do with Mars; Thor with a sceptre appears to replicate Jove. They also worship men who have become gods, whom they reward for their great deeds with immortality.
>
> Adam 4.26

This statue of Thor was prominent at the meeting of the Thing and around 1030 was the subject of an attack by an overenthusiastic Christian from England called Wolfred:

> He began to anathematise (curse) the idol of the people, by name Thor, that was standing in the council of the pagans [i.e. the Thing]; at the same time he picked up an axe and chopped the image into pieces. And he indeed 'for deeds of such daring' instantly was stabbed with a thousand wounds, and he sent his soul onward to heaven, worthy of the laurel of martyrdom.
>
> Adam 2.62

Christians regard it as a prime characteristic of pagans that they have statues and as an equal and opposite duty of the missionary to smash them. Almost universally the word they choose is *idolum*, our word 'idol', a Greek word for an 'image' used particularly by the Septuagint to refer to pagan idols and maybe to highlight the offensiveness of their attempt to reproduce the divine form. The statues they actually confronted could on occasion be very substantial and the wrecking of them by Christians, like the wrecking of statues of Lenin in modern times, might be no easy job. St Walfroy (Vulfilaicus the Deacon) is reported as giving this account to Gregory of Tours:

> 'Then, I called together several of them [the peasants] so that, as I didn't have the strength to smash it myself, I might with their

assistance pull down this huge statue. I had already broken up the remainder of the statuettes, which had been easier. Lots of people congregated at this statue of Diana, ropes were attached and they began to heave. But their labour made no impression. Then I hurried to the basilica and casting myself down on the ground I pleaded tearfully for the Divine pity that, as human effort was not strong enough to overturn it, the Divine strength should destroy it. Leaving after my prayer, I went to the workmen and taking hold of the rope, as we began our very first heave, immediately the statue crashed to the ground. I broke it up with iron hammers and reduced it to dust.'

Gregory of Tours, *Histories* 8.15

It is a good story and by imitation flatters Sulpicius Severus' St Martin: 'Constantly fasting and beseeching, [Martin] prayed to the Lord that, as human hand could not overturn that temple, Divine strength should destroy it' (Sulpicius Severus, *Life of St Martin* 14.4). Cliché this may be, but the physical destruction of pagan technology was a powerful enough image and a memorable enough deed to allow its standardisation. It transposed into modern life the meritorious act of Moses in reducing the Golden Calf to dust (cf. Chapter 8).[19]

On Rügen, the statue of Rujevit at Garz (in German, Karentia/Korenica in Slavonic) was around three metres tall and that of Svantovit at Arkona was at least eight metres, a remarkable statue, itself an important factor in the religious power of the temple:[20]

A huge idol stood in the temple, surpassing in its size any human stature, amazing with its four heads and necks; of them two seemed to look from his chest and two from his back. But whether positioned at front or back, one [of each pair] seemed to direct its gaze left and the other right. His beard was depicted shaven and his hair shorn – so that you might think that the energy of the craftsman had emulated the hairstyle of the people of Rügen. In his right hand he carried a horn adorned with various metals. The priest, expert in the rites, used to fill this with wine once a year, to judge from the actual state of the liquid the bountifulness of the coming year. His left hand was depicting holding a bow, with his arm drawn in to his side. A tunic was carved reaching down to his shins. These were made out of a different kind of wood and were joined to the knees with so secret a joint that the position of the joint could not be made out except by looking very carefully. The feet could be seen touching the earth but their base lay hidden inside the ground.

Saxo 14.39.3, p.565 Holder

Figure 7.3 What Svantovit might have looked like

Polycephaly, the possession of many heads, is common enough in mythology (as of Cerberus) and indicates in various ways the diversely powerful otherness of divine creatures. It is particularly associated with Slav religion ('they sculpt many gods with two or three or even more heads', Helmold 1.84) and Triglov ('Three-head') is certainly a popular god in Pomerania.[21] Down the road from Arkona, at Garz, Porenutius had four faces and another on his chest, Porevit five heads, and the oaken statue of Rujevit seven faces![22] Greeks and Romans did not on the whole go for this model: perhaps Janus, god of the door, of peace and war, and of the new year that begins in January, with his two faces is the only godly exception.[23]

The destruction of this statue of Svantovit was no easy matter for Waldemar, King of the Danes:

> He ordered the ancient statue of Zvantevith, worshipped by the whole nation of the Slavs, to be brought out and instructed that a rope should be tied to its neck and that it should be dragged through the midst of the army before the eyes of the Slavs and be chopped in pieces and put on the fire [because it was wooden, a tree-trunk]. He destroyed the *fanum* with all its religious awe and plundered its wealthy treasury.
>
> Helmold 1.108 (2.12)

> On the next day, Esbernus and Suno, on the orders of the King, set about destroying the statue but it could not be dislodged without crowbars. So they instructed the workmen to tear down the curtains covering the shrine and to get on with the job of felling it. They warned them to work carefully in view of its enormous mass when it came down in case they should be crushed by its weight and be thought to have paid the penalty to the angry god. In the meantime a huge crowd of townspeople had gathered around the *fanum* hoping that Svantovit would attack those responsible for such a crime with the full hostile force of his divine power. Now they cut through the bottom of the statue's shins and it fell face-forward against the nearby wall. In order to pull it out, Suno encouraged his workmen to demolish the wall but instructed them to take care that in their eagerness to fell it they did not overlook the danger to themselves and accidentally expose themselves to being crushed as the statue fell. So the statue collapsed on the ground with a great noise. In addition a great quantity of purple cloth hung round the temple, with rich splendour, but so decayed that it could not withstand being touched. There was no lack, either, of unusual horns of woodland wild animals, not less amazing for their own nature than for their adornment. And a demon, in the shape of a dusky animal, was seen to leave and suddenly to remove itself from the sight of the bystanders.
>
> Saxo 14.39.31 f., pp.574 f. Holder

Not just the statue but the religious outlook of the people of Rügen is being physically and dangerously dismantled in this passage. As the statue is demolished it must not be perceived to exercise any power as it falls –

St Martin had once stood under a sacred tree as it fell to demonstrate much the same point. Conveniently the demon, masquerading as the god Svantovit, is seen to leave, but you were too late to see it yourself.

These statues are not just impressive, they are also magnetic and increase the 'pull' of the site. They are therefore an important factor in the pretensions of given sites to more than local significance, whether on Rügen or at Olympia.[24]

TEMPLE, *FANUM, ECCLESIA*

What a temple is

Unnecessary. The fundamental cult activities of sacrifice and prayer need no building. What it is useful for is the dedication of more advanced offerings than can be hung in trees, and for the more civilised housing of a probably more carefully sculpted cult statue in a society that is becoming more comfortable with urbanisation. The temple is where the god *lives* and that is what the Greek word for temple, *nāos* or *neōs* means (*naiein*, 'dwell').[25]

So temples are a product of wealth, because of the volume of offerings, of settled life and ultimately urbanisation, because they are cost and effort expended in a given place to produce a form of 'housing', and of progress to an increasingly anthropomorphic understanding of gods. By the end, temples become the most characteristic visible sign of developed paganism and a *Description of the city of Rome*, dating perhaps from around 400, counts 455 of them, against only 44 public toilets.[26]

There is also a terminology of temples. A *templum* itself is a mighty structure, typically of stone, found in a civilised city, an *urbs*; the temple is the *aedes* when it is viewed as a house or dwelling-place, which the word also means, and in this it is rather like the Greek *nāos*. You might find a *fanum* (**fas-nom*, see Chapter 2) anywhere, particularly in the countryside. Somewhere in between, with a measure of hoary respect, is the *delubrum*, which was associated in antiquity with the word *deluere*, to 'wash off, purify' by means of the sacred running water. Christians on the whole, unless they strike exceptionally lucky, destroy only *fana*.

The shape of temples

Temples can be designed to reflect more natural sacred sites. Hindu temples imitate the shape of mountains and mountain ranges, while internally they may reproduce the feel of a cave, particularly in the unlit, specially holy back room (Choudhury 1994: 63, 78–81), a room whose significance is further enhanced by its name, the *garbhagrha* ('womb chamber'). We have looked at how the usual ring of columns around the Greek temple echoes the grove (Chapter 6) and will comment further on them below when considering the design of Gallo-Roman temples.

Hindu temples are miniature universes, usually square and mapped out according to a *yantra*, a sacred diagram, to act as an image of the world.[27] In the Greek and Roman cultures, to my knowledge, such microcosmic temples occur only in the cult of Mithras, where the temple is called the Cave and represents the world; it contains astrological symbols and a representation of a primal act, Mithras' slaying of the Bull, which brought our Age into existence; sometimes its floor is decorated with the symbols of a set of seven grades which lead the soul through its heavenly ascent.

However, the shape of the temple is more normally determined by the fact that it is the metaphorical house of the god, where he lives through the medium of his cult statue and where he keeps his possessions in the form of cult offerings. So a first model for the temple is house architecture of whatever style and level prevail among the wealthier classes. Among those who have little, or value settled life little, the god's house may be only the *casula*, hut, that the *Indiculus superstitionum* declares serves as a *fanum* among the Germans (Chapter 8). In north European paganism the rectangular hall that kings found satisfactory enough may serve as a model. So in Scandinavia we find wooden rectangular temples, some of them as large as 30 × 15m with a central hearth. In buildings this large in a non-Mediterranean climate, worshippers gathered inside around the hearth and the walls might be spattered with the sacrificial blood.[28]

Further back, the standard Greco-Roman temple too has its origins in a chieftain's house, having the luxury of a porch or anteroom, the *pronāos*, before you reach the main room, the so-called *cella*, and frequently an inner room, *adyton* ('not-to-be-entered'), beyond it. This structure is characteristic of the central buildings of the Bronze Age palaces of Crete and mainland Greece and there are cases of apparent continuity from buildings of this structure with a palace function to buildings on the same site of a similar structure which serve as temples – for instance, at Thermon (Aetolia) – unless, as Tomlinson has argued, the similarities between the Bronze Age *megaron*, as this type of hall is called, and the later temples is due to their both reflecting on grandiose scale a basic hut structure.[29] Long after houses have adopted a different pattern, of rooms around an open courtyard, this hut structure lives on, amplified and archaic, as the imposing form of dwelling appropriate to a god. Its rectangular shape is due to the difficulty which Greeks long experienced in roofing large structures. They could have overcome it, if they had wished, though probably at the cost of a forest of columns, as in the *Telesterion* ('Hall of the Rites') at Eleusis. With the invention of the arch in late Hellenistic times, domes also became possible, but the traditional rectangular model for the temple was by then long established and the dome of the Pantheon in Rome is in effect a showpiece exception. Its shape is specially appropriate to convey the cosmic overtones of a temple devoted to All the Gods (Pantheon).

In the Roman Empire it is of interest when the established Greco-Roman design does *not* provide the model. Apart from Roman-style imports, often in the bigger centres, Gaulish religion appears in particular to have its own agenda for temple structure which it sets down in defiance of Greco-Roman expectation. In both Gaul and Britain there are a considerable number of *square* temples. Lewis in 1966 counted 35 in Britain and 138 in Gaul and they have been continually discovered since then (Fauduet 1993: 64, if without regard to squareness, roundness or polygonality, claims 650 temples with galleries). They often seem to consist of a tall central *cella* with clerestory windows and, outside, a gallery all around it – rather as if a Christian nave had been constructed with the wall on the inside of the aisles, not the outside, or as if a Greek temple had been built square and only the *cella* covered by a pyramidal main roof, with no pediment, or like an inside-out cloister.[30]

Our best surviving example is the so-called 'temple of Janus' at Autun, in fact an astonishingly complete *cella*.[31] To give rough figures, the central *cella* of typical British examples is around 7 metres square, with a gallery around 2 metres wide, but that of continental examples is on average 1–1.5m larger per side of the square.[32] Why these galleries? Writers have conjured up the image of a rite of *circumambulation*, for which there is no direct evidence.[33] It *is* found in Hindu religion:

> While visiting a temple it is customary for a worshipper to go round the central structure of the temple on foot in a clock-wise direction to complete the circle before gradually penetrating inwards. This circular journey is known as *pradkṣina* (circumambulation). Because of the importance of this journey, many temples are furnished with ambulatory passageways.
>
> Choudhury 1994: 79 f.

A similar practice is seen in the ritual around the *Ka'ba* in Mecca. In a more specialised way, in some cases in Germany, there used to be a custom of taking the funeral procession once or thrice around the church in whose graveyard the corpse was to be buried.[34] In all these cases it seems to serve to associate the circumambulated with the location, as an act of aggregation.[35]

This may, however, be a dangerous hypothesis. We have discussed the feel of the ring of columns surrounding Greek peripteral temples without needing to invent, in this case non-existent, rites of circumambulation. The only explanation I know of from antiquity takes the pleasant amenity view: Vitruvius talks of its allowing the visitor to 'take a walk (*ambulatio*) around (*circa*) the *cella* of the temple' (3.2.5), not a ritual. Similarly, the 'ambulatories' of great Christian cathedrals provide a space for the visitor to take in the religious ambience and a certain thrill as one passes the tomb of St Cuthbert, but do not provide tailor-made space for a ritual of circumambulation.

Sacrality, practicality and aggrandising are all influences. *Practicality*: the colonnade gives the visitor somewhere to sit, out of sun or rain, when the *cella* was closed, which indeed it might be for most of the time. It is somewhere for Vitruvius to walk. *Sacrality*: perhaps, as Lewis (1966: 24) has suggested, we should observe a progressive sacrality of space and the possibility that worshippers would be admitted to the gallery but not to the *cella*, something which in effect happened at Arkona (below). I think that something not wholly dissimilar, if perhaps less a question of grada-tion, is happening in the case of the Greek peripteral temples: the columns serve to demarcate, *visually* circumambulate and appropriate the sacred house; they offer a concentricity that deepens the sacrality of the final central *cella*. *Aggrandising*? There is some tendency to claim the holy site as a centre (Chapter 14). The shape of sites and of temples reinforces that claim. This is particularly strong in the Gaulish case: the temple, or main temple, is normally found at the centre of Gaulish sanctuaries[36] and the shape of the Gaulish temples themselves seems determined, whether round, square or polygonal (approximations to round?), by the intention to represent centrality.[37] Round temples are a fascinating concept for Greeks and Romans: Hekataios of Abdera's Hyperboreans beyond Gaul have a spherical temple (presumably 'round' is meant!) and Macrobius' Thracians have a round one, which may actually have existed.[38] But the Romans have the problem that a round temple cannot be inaugurated because the whole process of augury depends on the observation of quarters and it is a mystery how the round temple of Vesta can have come into existence.[39]

Square temples are found in other traditions, too, whether by coinci-dence of religious 'vocabulary' or by indirect influence of the late Roman Celtic temples (Lewis 1966: 55). Some Icelandic sacred places, *hörgr* (i.e. *heargs*), are formed by two concentric squares – one at Sæból has a 6-metre-square building in a 13.5-metre-square precinct, and the 40–70 centimetre post-holes of the Swedish temple at Uppsala seem to tell a similar story.[40] On the island of Rügen, the temple at Arkona (below) was 20 metres square and those at Garz were also square; and when Grand Duke Gediminas, in the later thirteenth century, remodelled a Christian cathe-dral at Vilnius for pagan use in the cult of Perkunas, it, too, was square.[41]

Cultures tend to have rules of thumb for the orientation of temples based on east and west. Most Gaulish and British temples try to face east, and if not directly east, then south-east rather than north-east, presum-ably because they were targeted on sunrise – from which one can work out

Figure 7.4 The interior of the Parthenon, misconceived. The ceremony should be taking place outside the temple, seen through open doors by the statue. This Parthenon is halfway between a European cathedral and an opera house

the point in the year at which the decision was taken: the temple at Aubigné-Racan was planned on 23 April or 19 August![42] The Roman architect Vitruvius, on the other hand, declared on the whole for west-facing temples – like the Parthenon, though plenty faced east:

The direction which the sacred temples of the immortal gods should face is to be established as follows. If there is no reason to the contrary and a free choice, the temple and the statue which is to be located in the *cella* should face the western region of the sky, so that those approaching the altar to sacrifice or make offerings should face the direction of the eastern (*orientem*, 'rising') sky and the very statues should seem to rise up and look upon those making prayers and sacrifices, because it seems necessary for all altars of the gods to face east.

Vitruvius, On architecture 4.5.1

Christian churches, too, typically face west and the great door of cathedrals is the West Door.

Contents and decoration

Technically a *fanum* or temple does not need to be more than a storeroom and indeed in the Bronze Age palaces of Crete it can be hard to tell the difference between a cupboard and a shrine. On the other hand, worship at an outdoor altar is rather a Greek and Roman thing, as far as we can tell, and the *fana* of northern European paganism, whether because of the weather or because of the Christian model, look as though worship took place inside. That was where the *wīgbed*, altar (apparently, 'statue-stand'), was (de Vries 1956: i.§266). The natural outcome of this would be greater attention to the interior decoration of the shrine, quite apart from any Norse tendency to throw blood at the walls. Saxo (14.39.4, p.565) tells us that only the priest might enter the shrine at Arkona and that even he had to hold his breath there while he swept, rushing in-between to the door. But unless he had the lungs of Caruso, only the curtained-off inner sanctum can surely have been subject to this restriction and even there the great statue was well enough known.

It is worth mentioning in passing that unless Germanic temples were much larger or much more numerous than is generally thought, there cannot have been a great percentage of the population who were active *hearg*-goers: it may be that it is a sign of nobility and wealth that you and your closest followers can worship together in a purpose-built shrine.[43] Only the *hof* of late Icelandic paganism seems to be on a suitable scale, capable of seating 100 men; and *hof* is found in a score of Icelandic placenames, though not in Sweden or Denmark.[44] Apparently major shrines like Uppsala and Arkona are suitable only for occasional major gatherings of tribal leaders (much like an EU summit), for intermittent 'pilgrimage' when confronted by personal problems, generally of health, or for the storage of treasure and the funds of the Thing – Svantovit at Arkona received a coin annually from every man and woman and a third of any spoils in war.[45] So specific buildings may not always have been needed. In Norway farm buildings were frequently pressed into use: they too were *hofs*.[46]

Idols so frequently inhabit pagan temples that Christians must take a view as to whether it is sufficient to smash the idols or whether the temple should be smashed too (below). In Greece and Rome it is unthinkable to establish a temple without having some cult statue to complete the metaphor of ownership and focus the visitor's religious attention. These statues might all, naturally, consume great effort and expense, as we have seen above in the case of huge statues. Norse statues were frequently decorated with gold and silver and carried a golden ring on one arm, as the priest did during the rite (so he *was* a god, too).[47]

As we have seen, to dedicate something in Greek is to 'put it up' (*anatithenai*) on display, which in the temple culture means to affix it to the inner wall. Object-tourism is well established in Greece from early in historical times: Pythagoras (fl. *c*. 520 BC), after all, recognised the armour he had fought in when he had, in an earlier existence, been the Homeric warrior Euphorbos in the Trojan War.[48] It was not long before temples at the major national sites could not cope with all the offerings and 'treasuries' were therefore built at places such as Delphi and Olympia. At least as early as the fifth century BC the terrible crime of *hierosylan*, sacrilegiously stealing from a temple, had come into existence. This was not just *kleptein*, robbing, but plundering and stripping, *sylan*, as one might, more justifiably, strip the armour from a corpse, it was 'sacred stripping'. Such dedication of objects is, of course, not exclusively Greek or Roman, as we can see from the lake at Toulouse (Chapter 1), but a building for their storage is something more than that. Among the Pomeranian Slavs, the 'wealthy treasury' of the temple at Arkona was worth plundering (Helmold 1.108 (2.12)), because of course it held the contributions made by all Slavs in the region for its operations and upkeep. Inside, this temple exuded opulence: four posts in a square had hanging between them huge six-metre sections of luxuriously expensive purple cloth, screening the great statue of Svantovit himself.[49] The purple, as we have seen, had become old and fragile but was still magnificent, and the same method of screening was used also in nearby Garz.[50] The Frisian shrines, too, were rich:

> After this Albric sent Ludger and with him other servants of God to destroy the *fana* of the gods and the various instances of idolatry among the nation of the Frisians. They, fulfilling their orders, brought great treasure which they found in the temples. The Emperor Carolus (Charlemagne) took two-thirds and instructed Albric to take one-third for his purposes.
>
> Altfrid, *Life of Ludger* 1.15 (*PL* 99.776)

The *outer* decoration of temples varies enormously. One extreme is the staggering expensive Greek temple with its sculptured pediments and friezes for visitors to marvel at – as a Chorus does when it arrives at Delphi in Euripides' play *Ion*. The exterior of these Greek temples, too, would be highly coloured, even gaudy to our eye, though the paints have almost entirely faded away by now and we have a quaint picture of restrained, philosophical Greeks setting up temples of bare white marble! In fact the exterior marble surface, a stucco veneer of marble if it was too expensive, was painted bright red and blue.[51] In barbarian paganism there were also some exceptional temples which were highly decorated. The wooden temple at Arkona, with its red roof, was a remarkable sight:[52] 'The exterior of the temple gleamed with detailed decorations, embracing various representations in a primitive and unrefined artistic style' (Saxo 14.39.2, p. 564 Holder). The temple at Uppsala was no less striking as you looked down on it from the surrounding hills. Strange and marvellous, it had a golden chain hung from its gables and all around it (Adam 4.26). Similarly, Thietmar (6.25) tells us of the vivid decoration of the temple of 'Zuarasici' among the Redarii.

Shrines, vocabulary and placenames

The Gaulish *nemeton* (Old Irish *neimed*), usually thought of as a 'grove', through confusion with the Latin *nemus* (forest, grove), in fact denotes any holy enclosure, with or without palisade and with or without a temple; it may also denote the temple itself.[53] Its Latin translation is *fanum* and its relationship to the concept of 'grove' may be judged by the fact that the Irish for a grove is a 'wood that is *nemed*', *fidnemed*. Comparison of related words in Greek, Lithuanian and German suggests rather that the Indo-European verbal root **nem-* referred to assigning areas for use – for instance, as pasturage. *Nemeton* is visibly not a basic noun like *dunon* or *briga*, but an adjective derived from the verb and should mean 'assigned (area)', very close to the phrase *locus consecratus* ('consecrated area') that Caesar uses twice in Gaul.[54] This is a common origin of terms denoting a precinct, as we can see from the Greek *temenos* (if it is an area 'cut off', set aside, for a king or a god) or the Latin *templum*, in origin meaning the same as the Greek *temenos* but later denoting the holy building itself.[55] *Nemeton*, therefore, in the neuter means an 'assigned/sacred' thing, and like the Greek word *hieron*, 'sacred (thing)', may denote either a sacred area or the sacred building.[56] The Gaulish placename *Vernemeta*, Vernantes (Maine-et-Loire), is explained by Venantius Fortunatus in the sixth century as *fanum ingens*, 'great shrine'.[57] The Celtic word is also found in Old Irish *neimed*, which is used to translate the Latin *sacellum*, a 'simple shrine', and which is explained as follows in the most authoritative dictionary: 'In Irish lit. *a* *sanctuary,* in early Christian lit. prob. a small chapel or oratory (or else the spot on which such stood) . . . Prob. in this sense in place-names: Nemed' (*DIL* s.v. 'neimed'). In modern Irish this has become *neimheadh,* 'a sacred/privileged place/thing'. It may also be present in Welsh in the archaic but rather obscure *nyfed,* claimed by some to mean 'shrine'.[58] I think it is quite clear that the Gaulish meaning was substantially the same as the Old Irish and that it no more denoted a grove than the Old Irish did.

The sacred area, contingently, because of Celtic religious practices, can on occasion be a grove, and that is why the word is so used. The Galatian *Drunemeton* is 'Oak-shrine' and *Nemetobriga* in Hispania Tarraconensis is 'Mountain with a temple'.[59] Why then does the *Indiculus superstitionum* (6, see Chapter 8) refer to 'groves which they [Saxons] call *nimidas*'? This is the sole instance of this word in Germanic and must show a word *borrowed* by neighbouring Saxons from Celts. It is not so much evidence for a community of vocabulary and culture between the ancient Celts and Germans as a border phenomenon: these were neighbouring tribes with some bilingualism (as we shall see in the case of Ariovistus, Chapter 12) and the Saxons in all probability moved into a previously Celtic land- scape. As d'Arbois de Jubainville said long ago, 'The Saxons respected these sacred places and kept their name.'[60]

The Celts often enough oriented themselves by reference to the shrine, as we can see from placenames across Europe.[61] An example in Latin is provided by *fanum Martis,* the modern Famars (Nord, west of Bavay), a type of name found elsewhere in France, Italy and Britain (*Fanum Cocidi,* Bewcastle on Hadrian's Wall). On other occasions shrines in Celtic lands were felt distinctive enough to require the word *nemeton.* In Britain we know of *Medionemeton* ('Centre *fanum*') near the Antonine Wall in Scotland; *Vernemetum* ('Great *fanum*') in Nottinghamshire; *Aquae Arne- metiae* ('By-the-*fanum* Spa') at Buxton (Derbyshire). This last site is close to the 'Bull Ring' henge, which looks as though it must be the *nemeton* in question: henges either were perceived once to have been shrines or, more likely, actually continued in use. A striking example has been a site in Devon, west of Crediton, where close to North Tawton, the probable location of *Nemetostatio* ('*nemeton*-post'), a henge was found by aerial photography and is evidently the monument to which the placename refers.[62] A little to the north, near South Molton, lie King's Nympton, George Nympton, Bishop's Nympton, all named, it appears, after local rivers, the Yeo and Mole, once known as 'Nymet' or 'Nemet' and themselves therefore named after a *nemeton.* In Gloucestershire, three kilometres from Uley we find a place Nymp(h)sfield. It is important to have early forms of placenames to avoid just guessing: in this case evi- dence going back to Domesday and to a charter of 872 produces the form *Nimdesfelde,* the field of the *nemeton.*[63]

In Gaul there are many cases: Nemetocenna or, perhaps the short form, *Nemetacum*,[64] the ancient name of Arras, *Nemetodurum* ('*Nemeton* market'), which gives us Nanterre, and *Nemetoialos* which seems to lie behind Nampteuil-sous-Muret (Aisne).[65] Particularly striking in our Roman context is the Gaulish '*Nemeton* of Augustus', *Augustonemeton* (Clermont-Ferrand), in effect a *fanum Augusti* to correspond to the *Lucus Augusti* we find elsewhere. There was a people, the Arnemetici, hailing presumably from a Gaulish Buxton, at Jonquières (near Beaucaire, Gard).[66] And there are other examples where the word *nemeton* has survived as a placename – for instance, *Nimy* next to Mons (Hainaut, Belgium).[67] In other Celtic lands we hear of *Nemetobriga* ('*Nemeton*-burgh') near Puebla de Trives in Galicia (province of Orense), and *Drunemeton* ('Oak *nemeton*') in Galatia (Asia Minor).[68] Even as late as 1031, in the *Cartulary* of the Abbey of Quimperlé (Finistère), reference is made to a wood 'which is called Nemet'.[69]

Temples in less developed cultures

Temples indicate a settled way of life and a fairly advanced economy. In Gaul Roman rule confirmed and entrenched these conditions, with the result that the development of a temple culture was greatly accelerated. Already shortly before Constantine,[70] Chrocus, King of the Alamans, invaded Gaul

> and all the temples (*aedes*) which had been constructed in ancient times he demolished to the foundations. Indeed, coming to Clermont-Ferrand [or 'into the Auvergne'],[71] he burnt, demolished and razed that shrine which in the Gaulish language is called 'Vasso Galate'. It was a wonderful and solid piece of work. It had a double wall: inside it was made of small stones, outside of sculpted blocks. That wall was thirty feet thick. Inside it was decorated with marble and mosaic; the floor of the temple was also laid in marble and above it was roofed with lead.
>
> Gregory of Tours, *Histories* 1.32 (30)

This is the site at Dumium, le Puy de Dôme, with the colossal statue of Mercury (above). The fame of this site reached as far away as Bitburg (near Trier) where we have an inscription 'to the god Mercury *Vasso Caleti*'.[72] *Vasso Caleti* seems to mean 'tough (?) servant', with *vasso* as in our word 'vassal', Welsh *gwas*.[73] Temple-building was part of a cultural wave. Gaul had been ahead of the game even before the Romans arrived and under Rome served as a vanguard and as a model for the temple culture. In Gaul there was substantial building of native-style temples from around 50 BC to around AD 200, with only a few later; in Roman

Britain it was spread more thinly across the first to third centuries AD, with a tail in the fourth.[74]

Moving more clearly away from the Roman Empire to the east, we immediately encounter the Germans, who had been much less settled and 'developed'. In Tacitus this leads to an extraordinary 'Noble Savage' misapprehension, sharply redolent of Poseidonios on druid-philosophers. These quaint primitives failed to have Greco-Roman temples out of theological principle:

> They do not think it in accordance with the grandeur of the heavenly beings to confine gods within walls or to represent them in accordance with human features. Groves and woods they consecrate and they call by the name of the gods that remote being that they see through reverence alone.
>
> Tacitus, *Germania* 9

This is a rhetorical, pseudo-philosophical point of view, whose immediate ancestor lies in a passage of Cicero where he accounts for the Persian king Xerxes setting fire to the Greek temples in 480 BC:[75]

> Then again in Greece, as among us, magnificent shrines are consecrated with anthropomorphic statues, which the Persians thought impious (*nefaria*). For this one reason Xerxes is said to have ordered the shrines of the Athenians to be set ablaze, because he considered it impious to confine within walls the gods, whose home is this whole universe.
>
> Cicero, *On the state (De re publica)* 3.14

Perhaps Cicero had read the same lost passage of Poseidonios. Gibbon, however, had not and presented a more realistic, if trenchant, interpretation of German architecture:

> Some applause has been hastily bestowed on the sublime notion, entertained by that people, of the Deity, whom they neither confined within the walls of a temple, nor represented by any human figure; but when we recollect that the Germans were unskilled in architecture, and totally unacquainted with the art of sculpture, we shall readily assign the true reason of a scruple which arose not so much from a superiority of reason as from a want of ingenuity.
>
> E. Gibbon, *Decline and fall of the Roman Empire*, ch.9
> (London 1776; London 1910: i.223 f.)

Peoples who are not settled, urban or specially wealthy will not have temples, however hard we, or the Greeks and Romans, find it. Temple-lessness is not unique to Germans. Among the Russians, too, there is no evidence for pagan temples (Unbegaun 1948: 405). In Iberia there is a remarkable absence of temples to native gods (Toutain 1917: 169) and even at the Sacred Promontory in Portugal there was neither temple nor altar.[76] So far we may incline, then, to the view of Rowell (1994: 134) that 'we should not build temples where the pagans did not'.

Yet by the end of antiquity at least, Germans did have sufficiently 'hard' concepts of gods to allow equations such as 'Mercury = Wodan' and to know that thunder was the business of Donar; and they did have idols which might in principle have been stored in temples, with such treasures as they made themselves or raided from others.[77] The archae-ological record is as silent as Tacitus, who mentions a German temple only twice.[78] One is that of Tamfana (*Annals* 1.51), barely across the Rhine, in the Celtic-influenced zone (did they call it a *nimid*?). The other is on any grounds exceptional: it is the temple of Nerthus in her grove on an island in the Ocean (Rügen? cf. Chapter 12); the temple is sufficient to put a statue in, and has not been seen by any reliable witnesses who have not been sacrificed (Chapter 9)! Early temples were doubtless built of wood, like churches of those times as in the case of Bishop Bruno of Verden (Bishop 962–76): 'who built an outstanding church, exceeding others in its size and quality, at Verden [near Bremen] out of wood because he had no stone – and

Figure 7.5 The Germans were not an urban people: Roman soldiers destroying their huts. From the column of Marcus Aurelius in Rome

Figure 7.6 Athens in the time of Hadrian. Contrast this reconstruction with the German huts in the previous illustration

sensibly enough was put in charge of it' (Thietmar 2.32 (21)). Such temples will have left little trace, but the archaeological silence is still deafening and Tacitus must be right about pagan Germans of his time. However, in later, more developed days of paganism we might expect a significant spread of the Gaulish notion of the *fanum* among the various peoples of Europe. Gallo-Roman Euroculture must account for the *fanum* that St Gall found at Köln (*Colonia Agrippina*) around 525:

> There was in that place a *fanum*, packed with all manner of adornments, in which the local barbarians displayed offerings and filled themselves to vomiting-point with food and drink. There, too, worshipping images as though they were God, they sculpted limbs in wood corresponding to where they were in pain. When St Gall heard of this, he straightaway hurried there with only one clergyman, lit a fire when none of the foolish pagans were present, applied it to the shrine and set fire to it. Seeing the smoke from the shrine (*delubrum*) rising to heaven, the pagans looked for the person responsible for the fire and, finding him, drew their swords and gave chase.
>
> Gregory of Tours, *Lives of the Fathers*, 6 'St Gall', 2

This cultural seepage continued: Franks could be found worshipping in *fana* in the sixth century (see below on St Radegund) and Germanic peoples around Antwerp in the seventh (see below on St Éloi).

In this context, perhaps Bede's portrait of *fana* in England is not implausible, though not a single specimen has been discovered by excavation, except Yeavering: it is not hard to believe that there had been structures satisfying the basic requirements for *fana* if nothing beyond.[79] In the 780s, *fana* were adequately impressive in Saxony: 'That the churches of Christ which are currently being constructed in Saxony and are dedicated to God should have no less honour but greater and more excellent than the *fana* of idols had' (*Capitulary of Paderborn* §1 (*MG LegesII* 1.68). Similarly, Thietmar (6.25), who ought to have known, tells us that, in addition to the great shrine at Riedegost, every locality cf the Pomeranian Slavs had its temples and statues and we have specific mention in texts of a dozen between Szczecin and Kiel.[80] And Saxo tells us that the Svantovit of Arkona had many other shrines tended by priests, if obviously of less authority than the priest of Arkona.[81]

Words and placenames imply something, too. The Germanic term *harug*, Anglo-Saxon *hearg*, oscillates between *fanum* and wood/grove (Grimm 1875: i.54 f.). It is connected with the Latin *carcer*, a prison (as in 'incarcerate') or starting stall for horse races, and must therefore originally have referred to some sort of enclosure.[82] The whole picture becomes redolent of the Celtic *nemeton* that authors have too readily associated with the concept of 'grove' in order to match classical ideology. What can we therefore deduce when the term is used? Any precinct would satisfy the *Lex Ripuaria* (the lawcode of the Ripuarian Franks, probably around AD 633) where formal oaths are regularly to be taken *in haraho*.[83] But something more substantial and noteworthy is suggested by a number of English placenames of the form *Harrow*. Typically these 'harrows' seem to be situated on relatively high ground (Wilson 1992: 8), making a name like Harrow much the equivalent of 'Godshill' (Kent and Isle of Wight).[84] So what was on these raised pieces of land? Were there *fana* as we might perhaps have found at the various *Mediolana* of the Gauls, themselves on eminences? It is surely likely.

The grander pagan temple culture, particularly the habit of major centres, apparently spread from Scandinavia[85] – too late for Christian England. Adam describes for us the great shrine at Uppsala, focus of the Swedes (cf. Chapter 14). The Norwegian colony at Dublin was responsible for a significant temple of Thor, built of wood like most church buildings of the time (Marstrander 1915: 244). Moving out from Scandinavia, we come to the Danish temple at Lederun, and then to the temple of the Scandinavian Forseti on Heligoland ('Fosetesland'), destroyed around 785. The Slavs in Pomerania and Mecklenburg had a great centre at 'Rethre', apparently on an island in the Tollensesee (at Neubrandenburg):

> Among these [Slavonic tribes] the central and most powerful of all are the Retharii and their well-known city is Rethre, a seat of idolatry. There is a large temple there built in honour of the demons, of whom the chief is Redigast. His statue is made of gold and his bed of purple. The city itself has nine gates, surrounded on all sides by a deep lake. A wooden bridge provides access and it is only those wishing to sacrifice or to seek responses[86] who are allowed to cross . . . To this temple it is four days' journey from Hamburg.
>
> Adam 2.21

There is another account in the crabbed Latin of Thietmar, a couple of generations earlier, which gives more detail, though with some differences:

> There is a certain city in the land of the Riedirierun called Riedegost, triangular [lit. 'three-horned'] and with three gates, which on all sides is surrounded by a great wood, untouched and venerated by the inhabitants. Two of its gates are open to all entering. The third, which faces east and is the smallest, shows a crossing (bridge?) placed next to the lake and very grim [*horribile<m>*, is there a hint of human victims being led down this path?][87] to look at.

> In it [*eadem*, namely the *insula* 'island' which Thietmar has forgotten to mention, obviously not the *urbe* 'city'] there is nothing except a *fanum* carefully constructed of wood, which is held up by the horns of various beasts instead of foundations.
>
> Thietmar 6.23 (17)

Thietmar goes on to tell us of marvellous statues of gods and goddesses sculpted into the walls, with their names on them, dressed in helmets and breastplates. Their flags are kept here except when carried by infantry in war. He calls the main god Zuarasici and the town Riedegost; Adam calls the god Redigast and the town Rethre. 'Zuarasici' is an authentic god-name, son of Zvarog: Russians were alleged in sermons to 'address prayers to the fire, calling it Svarožič'.[88] So Adam is wrong (and he is followed by Helmold, often *verbatim*), or the names had moved in the seventy years between Thietmar and Adam, or they were fluid epithets not firm names. The temple is in any case equipped with a priesthood who in some obscure way draws auguries from the behaviour of a fine sacred horse led over two crossed spears, much the same mode of divination as is ascribed by Saxo to the shrine of Svantovit at Arkona (14.39.10, p.567).

These were some of the peoples whom Adam claims Otto the Great reduced to 'tribute and Christianity', establishing Magdeburg as their metropolis in 968.[89] A century later, however, on 10 November 1066 Archbishop John of Hamburg, captured by pagan Slavs at Mecklenburg, mocked and mutilated, suffered the last indignity of having his head dedicated on a pole to Redigost at Rethre (Adam 3.51). Such an atrocity, incidentally, is perhaps more a statement of rebellion against Saxon power than of theology and of the rejection not so much of the missionary Gottschalk as of the Saxonised princely Gottschalk.[90] This temple was finally burnt down in 1068 and the city destroyed in the 1120s.[91]

Where exactly was this shrine and town? It is an enigma that the archaeologists have been unable to find it given the fairly specific type of site the authors imply. The conventional view before Schuchhardt was that the temple was on an island, 'Fisher-Island', and that the wooden bridge leading from city to island, 420 metres of it, had been found. I am not convinced that this view is false. Schuchhardt, however, the excavator also of Arkona, claimed in 1923 to have found Rethra on a mountain further away, the Schlossberg at Feldberg, and asserted (a) that the island showed no traces of a shrine but was in fact a military site, the *castrum Wustrow* mentioned in archives, (b) that Thietmar's word *tricornis* meant not triangular but 'three-towered' and (c) that the Schlossberg site satisfied this description. There can be no doubt that Schuchhardt found a significant sanctuary, complete with square temple, and maybe it is not likely that another would exist so close. On the other hand, it seems that

Thietmar's description, as well as Adam's, actually refers to an island and good authorities have rejected Schuchhardt's view.[92]

Finally the temples of Garz and especially Arkona arguably provided the last major examples of pagan temple culture in Europe. Arkona must have been the effective successor to the destroyed Rethra.[93]

CONTINUITY

Instances

In Britain Lewis concludes that 'many rural Romano-Celtic temples probably had their roots in the pre-Roman Iron Age' (1966: 49). Few country shrines in Britain seem to service villas and therefore the likeliest reason for their existence is that the sites were already holy before the villa culture (*ibid.* 50). Only temples in the towns would be likely to be founded on new sites. This view gets some support from the limited evidence for the reuse of henges which we have seen above.

But it is examples of continuity from paganism to Christianity that are at first sight numerous. To cite a few at random: at Avebury (Wiltshire) a mere glance at the map shows the Christian church sited at the heart of the third-millennium BC megalithic henge and the medieval church at Knowlton (beautifully illustrated in Woodward 1992: pl. 1) is similarly situated. Countless Greek and Roman temples, particularly in the west, were turned to Christian purposes – the Parthenon, the temple of Castor and Pollux in the Roman forum, the Pantheon (into a church of All Saints with barrowloads of relics), and the temple of Athene at Syracuse, now the Duomo.[94]

Hill- and mountaintops do not lend themselves to alternative sites: it is clear where the notable point is and that is where the Christian church as well as the pagan site will be. The chapels of St Elias took over from the worship of Zeus on Greek mountaintops (Nilsson 1955: 74). In Portugal the shrine of Endovellicus near Terena (Alentejo, around 150 kilometres east of Lisbon) was situated on a hill now named after San Miguel da Mota and whose (now destroyed) chapel appears to have succeeded the pagan shrine.[95] St Michael the Archangel is indeed the normal Christian possessor of hill- and mountaintops and is the standard selection to replace any local divinity. Three times between 706 and 708 St Aubert, Bishop of Avranches, was told in a dream by St Michael to found the shrine on Mont St Michel.[96] That is the story, but why exactly should St Michael be so concerned to be worshipped there? A preference for worship on mountaintops and eminences was already displayed by the 'Mercury' (to give him his Latin name – we have no other that is consistent) of central, northern and eastern Gaul. Sometimes we only know this because the village is called, for example, Mercurey.[97] True synthesis is reached with the village of St Michel Mont Mercure (near Pouzauges, Vendée) – a nameless Celtic god is translated 'Mercurius' into Latin and, apparently, 'St Michel' into Christian.[98]

A final example concerns the temple at Uppsala. Adam tells how 'recently' one of the priests at Uppsala became blind and (a testimony to the power of Christianity to worry late pagans) put it down to offending the god of the Christians. Immediately, he had a dream in which the Virgin appeared to him and traded him sight for Christianity. OK, he said. 'To which the Virgin replied, "Know that assuredly this place where now so much blood of the innocent is poured forth very soon is to be dedicated in honour of me"' (Adam 4.28). Thus the shrine at Uppsala was effaced and Uppsala became, what it is now, the seat of the Archbishop of Sweden.

What are Christians to do with temples or *fana*?

To build is an activity of assertion and display: it is the job of temples to proclaim civic paganism, something which is naturally anathema to Christians, who saw their own religion as very different. They embodied that difference in their terminology for sacred buildings. So Gregory of Tours (*Histories* 4.48) recalls how an earlier generation of Franks (before 573) 'were converted from shrines (*fana*) to churches (*ecclesiae*)', that is, became Christians. Temples (if grand) and *fana* (if smaller) must in some sense give way to *ecclesiae* ('churches').

Destroy the **fana***!*

An obvious reaction is physical destruction, an act of cultural deletion, perhaps of vandalism. Thus we have seen that the Sarapeum at Alexandria was actually destroyed (Chapter 1), though in a locally motivated riot. Some Emperors insisted on demolition of '*fana*, temples and shrines', whereas others such as Arcadius and Honorius viewed, particularly, stone temples as valuable public buildings that should be preserved so long as the idols were destroyed.[99] Martin of Tours, with his ugly looks, filthy clothes and untidy hair,[100] a direct and no-nonsense man, had a speciality in demolition, reducing any number of Gaulish shrines to rubble. This speciality is raised to the status of myth by Sulpicius Severus' biography and in his wake Gregory of Tours stresses how 'at this time the *beatissimus* Martin set about preaching in Gaul . . . This man destroyed *fana*, repressed heresy, built churches' (*Histories* 1.39); 'he caused many pagans to be converted and demolished their temples and statues' (10.31.3, AD 371/2). This even reaches an Old English sermon, which tells us that *He manig tempel and deofolgyld* ('statue') *gebraec*.[101] Martin prefigures and establishes the powerful imperative that Caesarius of Arles (470–543) enunciates when stamping out the last vestiges of paganism 150 years later: 'Therefore, do not allow a *fanum* to be repaired; rather, wherever it is, strive to destroy it and scatter it. Chop down sacrilegious trees to the roots; pulverise the altars of the devil' (Caesarius, *Sermon* 54.2). A couple of generations later, St Radegund (518–87), 'hearing that a *fanum* was used for worship there by Franks, gave orders to her servants that the shrine should be burnt down, judging it wrong that the God of heaven should be disdained and diabolical contraptions venerated' (Fortunatus (revised Baudonivia), *Life of St Radegund* 2.2). Let us also not forget St Éloi, who did good work around Antwerp *c.* 650 and 'destroyed several *fana* with apostolic authority protected by the shield of Christ'[102] – that is, with a letter from the Pope and 'moral' support from the Merovingian king, Dagobert I. Later, in 755, Wynfrith or, as he liked to be known, St 'Boniface', 'having smashed the sacred power (*numen*) of the *delubra*, constructed *ecclesiae* with immense energy' (Willibald the Priest, *Life of St Boniface the Archbishop* 35).

They are all Martin.

Build churches!

So you have destroyed the temple, but what then? You must continue the example of Martin (or Radegund) and build a church:

> Such was the strength of his virtues and of his example that now there is nowhere in that region which is not filled with thronging churches or monasteries. For wherever he had destroyed *fana*, there he would immediately build either churches or monasteries.
>
> Sulpicius Severus, *Life of St Martin* 13.9

Indeed, on Mount Beuvray (the Gaulish Bibracte) a classic square Gallo-Roman temple was ultimately replaced with a chapel of St Martin, which the antiquarian Bulliot attempted to trace to Martin himself, imagining a scene from Sulpicius Severus to play on that great mountain.[103] The chapel was certainly constructed out of the stones from the temple (Fauduet 1993: 96) and it is a remarkable religious site; processions used to wind their way up the mountain to the annual fair until the nineteenth century.

The constructive response is found repeatedly in the history of the conversion to Christianity. Ludger and his companions, reaching the island Fosetesland perhaps around 785 (cf. Alcuin on Willibrord, Chapter 5): 'destroyed all the *fana* of the same Fosete which were built there and in their place built *ecclesiae* of Christ' (Altfrid, *Life of Ludger* 1.19 (*PL*

99.779)). A special point is made by using the material of the old religion to construct the buildings of the new:

> Unwan [Archbishop of Hamburg 1013–29] gave instructions that all pagan rites, whose superstition was still flourishing in this area, should be eradicated; in this spirit, he had the church buildings in his diocese renovated from [the wood of] the groves which our marsh-dwellers used to frequent with stupid reverence. Out of these he ordered the basilica of St Vitus to be built outside the city and the chapel of St Willehad which had been burnt down to be repaired.
>
> Adam 2.48

It is, however, uneconomical to destroy one building only to replace it with another. More often Christians reverted to the pragmatism of Emperors Arcadius and Honorius, which resulted in the continuity of the holy place. Initially Pope Gregory's view was indistinguishable from Martin's, that the Anglo-Saxon shrines should be destroyed. So he advises King Ethelbert in a letter (11.37) of 22 June 601: 'Hasten to extend the Christian faith among the people subject to you, multiply the zeal of your righteousness by their conversion, attack the cult of idols, demolish the buildings of *fana*.' But within a few weeks, on 18 July 601, he was writing to Abbot Mellitus:

> Since Almighty God has brought you safely to the most reverent man, our brother, Bishop Augustine, tell him what I have decided after long reflection on the case of the English, namely, that the *fana* of idols among the same people should not at all be destroyed, but the actual idols which are in them should be destroyed. Let water be consecrated and sprinkled in the same shrines, let altars be built, and relics deposited there, because, if the same *fana* are well built, it is necessary that they should be transferred from worship of demons to the service of the true God so that while the nation itself does not see its shrines destroyed, it should lay aside the error from its heart and, recognising the true God and adoring him, meet at those places that are usual and familiar. And since they usually sacrifice many oxen at a sacrifice to the demons, in this matter also they should have a certain change in ceremonial so that on the day of dedication or the feast day of the holy martyrs whose remains are placed there, they should make temporary buildings around those same churches that have been converted from *fana* out of tree branches and celebrate a ceremony with religious feasting. But they should not any longer sacrifice animals to the devil. And let them slaugh-

ter animals in praise of God for their eating and give thanks to
the giver of everything from his sufficiency so that, while exter-
nally some joys are maintained for them, they may seem to be
more readily consistent with their interior joys. From tough
minds without doubt it is impossible to chop off everything at
once, since he who tries to climb to the top must rise by steps and
paces not by leaps.

Gregory the Great, Letters 11.56

This is a fairly clear indication, incidentally, that at least in the mind of
Pope Gregory the relics of saints were meant to occupy the psychological
space of the pagan statue.

It is not clear what Gregory thought a *fanum* was and it cannot be said
that we know securely what an Anglo-Saxon *fanum* looked like, though
Bede seems clear enough that shrine buildings actually existed.[104] Anglo-
Saxon *fana* are, however, extremely elusive for modern archaeologists.
Philippson (1929: 185) observed that there were no known instances of
Anglo-Saxon, or even Germanic, *fana* being taken over as churches, only
instances of their destruction, as, for example, at the critical point where
Northumbria is gained for Christendom and the classic motif, 'pagan
destroys his own shrine', is memorably deployed by Bede:[105]

> and when (Paulinus) asked the said priest (Coifi) . . . who should
> first profane the altars and *fana* of the idols together with the
> fences with which they were surrounded, he replied, 'Me.' . . .
> Nor did he delay immediately to approach the *fanum* and profane
> it by throwing the lance he was holding into it. And, much rejoicing
> at the recognition of the cult of the true God, he bade his
> companions destroy and set fire to the *fanum* with all its fences.
> The place once belonging to the idols is shown not far to the east
> of York, across the River Derwent, and is today called God-
> munddingaham (Goodmanham), where the priest himself,
> through the inspiration of the true God, polluted and destroyed
> those altars which he himself had consecrated.
>
> Bede, *Ecclesiastical history* 2.13 (of 627, under King Edwin)

Since Philippson's study the situation has not improved greatly. Possibly
an instance of continuity has been found at Maere in Norway, but
frustratingly there is no sign of the great temple at Uppsala in Sweden
except for a few post-holes. In England it remains almost impossible to
find a *fanum* at all, let alone one that has been reused as a church. A
number of structures have been identified in Anglo-Saxon cemeteries, but
they are all tiny and do not count in our eyes as *fana* (the *Indiculus* does,

however, describe *fana* as mere *casulae*, 'huts'). What would a *fanum* then be for? A cupboard in which to keep statues, maybe?

In most cases the likeliest explanation for the absence of evidence is that Gregory's advice was heeded and that the construction presently of stone churches, alien to the local tradition, has effaced the traces of most of the wooden structures that preceded them.[106] Gregory's advice to those who would convert pagans will have endured. Just as Boniface in 736 specifically asked Nothelm in Rome for a copy of Gregory's correspondence with Augustine of Canterbury on a marriage question, doubtless others looked up the records for his *fanum* policy.[107]

The sole case of Anglo-Saxon continuity in fact appears to be a building known as 'D2', excavated at Yeavering (Northumberland), Edwin's capital. D2 is 10.5 × 5.1m, has side entrances in the middle, a pit 1.8 × 0.3m with animal bones, mainly cattle, and three intriguing post-holes in a line across the building towards the other end. They appear to correspond to the position of statues and if the statues were primitive enough, they may be 'statue-holes' not post-holes. The trio would then correspond to the trio in the temple at Uppsala. In any case it does appear that the building continued in use after Edwin's conversion *but without the statues*.[108]

8

CHRISTIAN PAGANISM

With this chapter we move from where it happens to what happens, from sacred place to ritual. We may approach this topic in a number of ways. One way is the study of archaeological remains, but generally in this book I have chosen to look at a different source of evidence, namely what people tell us about pagans. Some pagans, Greeks and Romans, tell us about themselves. Sometimes they tell us about other pagans. But one overwhelming and characterful source for the activities of pagans is those who sought to destroy, stamp out and repress every last vestige of paganism. For Christians, paganism was a professional interest. But that does not, as we shall see in this chapter, make them scientists of paganism. In a remarkable way Christians were unable to comprehend the variety and chaos that always make paganism what it is.

CHRISTIAN KNOWLEDGE

Textuality: coming down from Sinai

Why are song and dance so obviously pagan for Christian writers? Somewhere in the intertext lurks the image of Moses descending from Sinai, hearing the 'voice of people singing' (*cantantium*), seeing the idol, the golden calf, and the 'dances' (*choroi*), a passage overtly recalled by Gregory of Tours:[1]

Figure 8.1 The Golden Calf of the Israelites, as depicted by Poussin. Courtesy: The National Gallery

But this generation [of Franks] has always seemed to serve fana-
tical cults and utterly to have failed to recognise God. They have
fabricated for themselves the forms of woods and waters, birds
and beasts, and other elements too, being in the habit of worshipping these as God and offering sacrifice to them. Oh if only that
terrible voice might reach the fibres of their hearts, which spoke
through Moses saying, 'Let there be no other gods but me. You
will not make anything sculpted nor shall you adore a likeness of
all the things which are in heaven and on earth and which live in
the waters; you shall not make and you shall not worship them'
[Exodus 20.4–5 from Gregory's memory] . . . What if they had
been able to understand what punishment overtook and overwhelmed the Israelite people for the worship of a 'molten calf',
when *after their feasting and songs (cantica), after their indulgence
(luxurias) and dancings (saltationes)* with filthy mouth they
uttered, concerning the same piece of sculpture, 'These are your
gods, Israel, which led you from the land of Egypt' [Exodus 32.4].

Gregory of Tours, *Histories* 2.10

Every Greek philosopher is returning from Plato's cave to exhort prisoners trapped in a material world and, just so, every church father and every
bishop is Moses, once more bringing his Israelite captives out of Egypt,
those would-be inhabitants of a promised land.[2] Or he is descending from
Sinai with the Word of God, only to find a backsliding people scarcely
worthy of God's Law. To this vision the evidence must conform. By nature
Christianity, certainly of this period, is a cult of the *word*. Daily historical
lives are woven into the greater tapestry of the Bible and writing constantly cites, assimilates, reincarnates the biblical text. Mere songs, *cantica*, are specifically held side by side with the biblical text by Caesarius
(*Sermon* 6): best practice is to read the Bible for three hours a night, live it
and be drawn into its *imaginaire*; but even rustics can do some good, if
instead of learning 'diabolical amatory *cantica*', and 'sending shameful
cantica into the darkness of the devil', they learn such things as the Lord's
Prayer and *Psalms* 50 and 90. For Caesarius *cantica* and *ballationes*
('dancings') are repeatedly denounced[3] and his denunciations become a
new scripture, extending the original scripture, like subclassing in C++.
Caesarius above all others created the litany of pagan practices whose
quasi-biblical authority was a much greater attraction than scientifically
observing for oneself the paganism of one's parish. It barely mattered
whether pagans did do this now, had done it once, or some other pagans
had done it once. The fact was that any diffusion of energy from the
Church was a recreation of the mood of the erstwhile enemies of right
religion and was therefore correctly damned through the authorised versions of Moses and Caesarius. Caesarius, after all, was Archbishop of

Arles, not the lovely Provençal town of today, not just a significant Roman city, but a seat of Empire replacing Trier in 395 and the see of at times the most important bishop in Gaul. Caesarius was, therefore, as Boudriot emphasises, for forty years the bishop of the 'Gallic Rome'.[4]

Education mattered too for those great men of the Church whose job it was to lead congregations of somewhat fragile Christianity and to convert pagans. There were no courses in contemporary paganism, but plenty in the Bible, and the church fathers were thoroughly drilled, with an emphasis on learning by heart that would appal even the most conservative educationalists today. So these were the views of paganism that they could recite and could recognise, that dictated their mental structures.[5] Ancient and medieval authors, however great, often disappoint by our critical standards. Augustine, in arguing against paganism himself in the wake of the sack of Rome in 410, directs much of his discussion against Varro, who had himself in the late 50s and early 40s BC been doing essentially antiquarian work. Thus Augustine's opponents were in fact out of date half a millennium earlier. In fairness to him, however, it must be said that there are modern authors who imagine that something called 'Roman religion' was being practised throughout the Empire and that its character is that of the religion described by Varro. We shall see this in the case of the 'Vulcanalia' denounced by Martin of Braga.

Paganism is thus something very unspecific for most Christian authors. It occurs in an eternal synchrony as blanket paganism; there is no diachronic sense, no sense of change in time. It is an enemy with a single identity, that of failure to be Christian: 'there are three religions in the world: Jewish, Pagan and Christian' (Vigilius of Thapsa).[6] Paganism in principle knows no geographical variations. It is simply daemonic or diabolical, more successfully repressed or less relentlessly resisted. There is therefore a quasi-Platonic Form of Paganism, a universal paganism which corresponds indeed to important features of much pagan practice, but it is not designed to be empirical. The hand of God is recognised because we already knew it; likewise, the ways of paganism are not discovered but recognised.

Specificity

The question then arises as to whether *any* local observations are made by Christian writers for themselves. On the whole Boudriot (1928: 5–8), followed by de Vries, thought not: they simply repeated the hallowed version of Caesarius. I think that if an extreme position is to be adopted, this is the correct one. But we can soften its hard lines a little.[7] The sites alleged for pagan worship, particularly when they have been returned to the Stone Age by Christian occupation of towns (that is why 'rustics' and 'pagans' are co-terminous), can only be those sites routinely but correctly named by Christian authors. So the Franks of Gregory of Tours, the Saxons of Rudolf of Fulda and the Slavs of Helmold, Priest of Bozova, all display, in Helmold's words, 'the manifold error of groves, springs and other religious practices among them' and the Christians, whether they knew it or not, were right to be indiscriminate on these topics.[8] Furthermore, even Caesarius' comments are not based on nothing and have some limited specificity, some perhaps more than others – dressing as a stag on New Year's Day (but where – in Arles, in Italy, all over Europe?), more than generically worshipping at trees and springs.

Gradually, as missionary activity becomes more genuine and less a question of answering an application to join the European Union, churchmen pay more attention to what they are up against. The result is still not fieldwork or scientific scholarship; rather, it is a modified synthetic vision of paganism, part cliché, part actuality, nowhere better illustrated than in the mid-eighth-century *Indiculus superstitionum et paganiarum* or *Index of superstitions and pagan practices*. This is a *breviarium*, a list of topics to act as an aide-mémoire, which forms for us a fascinating set of chapter headings, but alas no chapters, listing for reference the supposed practices of pagans. As it, at least the first half, is evidently designed for the German market and as it is found together with a formula for Germans to renounce paganism (below), it is presumably part of a missionary kit. It is not always clear what is meant and I have inserted one or two explanations in brackets as well as references to other points in this book where individual practices are discussed.[9]

1 Sacrilege at the tombs of the dead [feasting, Chapter 13].
2 Sacrilege over the deceased, i.e. *dadsisas* ['sung lament for a corpse', Chapter 13].
3 *Spurcalia* in February. [This word merges a Germanic word for 'piglet', *Sporkel* (evidently from Latin *porcellus*), with the Latin *spurcalis* 'foul, impure'. February was still called *Sporkelmonat* in lower Germany in the nineteenth century. It would be a reasonable guess that the sacrifice of pigs was somehow involved in the cleansing away of the old year, maybe even of the dead, as in the Parentalia of pagan Rome.][10]
4 Huts, i.e. *fana* [Chapter 7].
5 Sacrilege at churches [dancing or sacrifice, see below].
6 Rites in woods, which they call *nimidas* [Chapter 7].
7 What they do at rocks [Chapter 4].
8 Rites of Mercury or Jove [Wodan and Donar, cf. the *Renunciation* below, possibly also with worries about the names of weekdays, Wednesday and especially Thursday].
9 Sacrifice to any of the saints.
10 Amulets and ligatures.

11 Springs of sacrifices [Chapter 3; this may mean no more than 'offerings thrown into springs', according to Dölger 1932: iii.16 n.43].
12 Enchantments.
13 Auguries – birds', horses' or oxen's dung or snortings. [Tacitus (*Germania* 10) already notes the propensity of Germans for using 'auguries and lots' and draws attention also to their use of bird flight and song and the noises horses make. Whether these actually continued into the eighth century is another question. Chapter 12.]
14 *Divini* (people with alleged special powers) or lot-casters [Chapter 12].
15 Fire from rubbed wood, i.e. *nodfyr* [Germanic for 'need-fire', Chapter 1].
16 The brain of animals [for divination?].
17 Observations of the pagans at the hearth or at the beginning of any matter.
18 Indefinite (*incerta*) places which they worship as sacred.
19 The bed-straw which good people call holy Mary's [referring to herbs popularly known as *Muttergottesbettstroh*].[11]
20 Ceremonies performed to Jove or Mercury [the same as 8].
21 Eclipse of the moon, what they call *vince luna* ['win, Moon!', a cry of encouragement to the poor thing, cf. Maximus, below].[12]
22 Storms, horns and shells.
23 Furrows around villas [to keep witches away, according to Boretius 1883: 223 n.16].
24 The pagan (running) race that they call *yriae* (?), tearing their clothes and shoes [one suggestion is *Friae* instead of *yriae*, to refer the races to Freia, goddess of fertility].
25 The fact that they make certain dead people into saints [in order to have graveside binges, cf. Zeno below?].
26 Idol made of dough [Chapter 12].
27 Idols made of rags [Chapter 12].
28 Idol that they carry around the fields [Chapter 9].
29 Wooden feet or hands, in the pagan manner. [As left at sacred places for the healing of that part of your body; objects depicting parts of the body have been found in a score of Gaulish sanctuaries, even plaques depicting eyes.][13]
30 The fact that they think that women command the moon, (so?) that they are able to remove the hearts of men, according to the pagans.[14]

Indiculus superstitionum et paganiarum (*MG Leges* 1.19 f.)

In between, the case of St Martin of Braga is particularly striking and difficult. His denunciations contain much that is routine (Janus was only a man . . .). But it is possible that he exceeds his inheritance from Caesarius.[15] This is how he talks of those who revert to paganism:

Lighting candles at rocks and at trees and at springs and at crossroads – what else is this other than cult of the devil? Celebrating the Vulcanalia, observing the Kalends [the first of the month], decorating tables, laying out laurel [above the entrance to the home], watching the foot [lifting clods people have trodden on in order to practise magic on them],[16] tipping corn and wine over a log in the hearth, and dropping bread in a spring – what else is this other than cult of the devil?

Martin of Braga, *Reforming the pagans* 16

Does he mean observing *every* Kalend – if so, this is new – or is he only sloppily carrying forward Caesarius' obsession with the 1 January? Martin certainly has it in for 1 January: it is not the proper beginning of the year, only the vernal equinox is.[17] When he talks of lighting candles, is there genuine observation here? A fifth-century church council had already pronounced: 'If in any bishop's territory, the faithless light torches (*faculas*) or venerate trees, springs or rocks, if he fail to eradicate this, let him regard himself as guilty of sacrilege' ('*Second Council of Arles*' 23, *CC SL* 148.119 (after 442)).[18] Are crossroads a new detail or just more sloppiness? Regardless of the commonplace nature of the observation, however, this custom does seem to have continued in Martin's Galicia until relatively recent times.[19] Throwing bread in springs may be distinctive, even if it does not seem specially so to Burchard who adds it to his German collection.[20] Some customs are obscure[21] and I suspect that the automatic relating of the 'Vulcanalia' to the Roman festival of that name practised on 23 August, unless mindlessly inherited from an Italian sermon, is beside the point: surely it refers to some bonfire ritual, like the well-known custom of bonfires on St John's Eve (i.e. midsummer):[22]

On 21 June during the day, the mayor issues a notice that a vehicle will pass through all the streets on the morning of the 23rd to collect the wood that each occupant is willing to contribute for the bonfire of St Jean. No-one evades this obligation, everyone contributes with conviction.

Teacher in the département de l'Aisne, in Bertrand 1897: 406

Elsewhere (Chapter 3) we have seen how an apparent mistake of Martin's, about *Lamiae*, may instead mean that he had more knowledge of local pagan worship than we do.

But meticulous research always has its limits. Adam, looking back late in the eleventh century to the pagan Saxons who were 'converted' by Charlemagne, quotes Einhard. His 'Einhard' turns out actually to be Rudolph of Fulda, 200 years before Adam, who had, when not plagiarising Einhard, added some details to Tacitus' description of 'the Germans' of three-quarters of a millennium earlier. This 'superstition of the Saxons' is then in turn what 'the Slavs and Swedes seem still to keep up following the pagan rite' (Adam 1.7). Paganism is a single describable thing, to which only details – such as Adam's wonderful evocation of the sanctuary at Uppsala (4.26) – can be added. Thus there is accretion but not discrimination in the evolving picture of paganism from Maximus of Turin around 400 to Burchard of Worms's anthology of 'decrees', the *Decreta*, in the eleventh century.

WHAT PAGANS DO

Let us now look at the beginnings of standardised paganism. First, here is Zeno of Verona, denouncing the sort of paganism that his Christians may carelessly indulge in around, let us say, 370:

> The following also displease God:
>
> - those who run around tombs, who offer sacrificial meals to the stinking cadavers of the dead ['banquets in honour of sacrilegious rites in such funereal places' were banned by the Emperors in 407 and the bishops instructed to prevent it];[23]
> - those who out of love for overindulgence (*luxuriandi*) and drinking in disreputable places [tombs?] have suddenly produced [i.e. invented new] martyrs for themselves [to celebrate boozily] through their wine-bottles and cups;
> - those who observe days [see Audoenus below and compare reports of Lithuanians being fussy about which days they do various things];[24]
> - those who make 'Egyptian' [ill-omened] days out of favourable ones;
> - those who try to find auguries and seek their well-being/ salvation in the violently torn-open stomachs of cattle . . . [Broader questions of morality follow.]
>
> Zeno of Verona, *Sermon* 1.25 (15).11

Somewhat more broad-brush is Maximus around, say, 410:

> And so, anyone who wants to share in the divine should not be a comrade of idols. It is joining the idol to inebriate the mind with wine, to distend the stomach with food, to rack the limbs with dancing and to be so engaged in wicked actions that you are forced into ignorance of the nature of God. . . . If we are the

Figure 8.2 Greek maidens 'rack the limbs with dancing', as described by Maximus

temple of God, why is the festivity of idols worshipped in the temple of God? Why where Christ lives, who is abstinence, temperance and chastity, do we introduce feasting, drunkenness and debauchery?

Maximus of Turin, *Sermon* 63.1

Pagans, then, are people who eat, drink, make merry and dance. They worship idols in temples. They fuss about auguries and divination from cattle. They perform rites at tombs (*parentalia*) and perhaps they hold feasts at those same tombs. And they have holy days at variance with the Christian.

An interesting halfway house is presented by St Eligius (Éloi, *c.* 588–660). He views paganism at Rome as a matter of antiquarian interest, speaking of the long-gone days 'when the Romans held dominion over the whole world':

Each five-year period used to be called a *lustrum*, because when it came to an end and the census had been completed, the Roman people used to gather and celebrate a sacrifice and the city of Rome was *purified* (*lustraretur*) with candles and lamps in honour of the infernal god and particularly of Februus, i.e. Pluto who was said to be lord of the underworld [this is a doubtful equivalence], from whom the month of February got its name, in whose last part [the period of the Parentalia] i.e. the Kalends [!, Eligius awkwardly identifies these rites with New Year rites] this used to be done. Now, it was for this reason that they used then to sacrifice to the infernal gods, because they believed that it was under their protection that they had subjugated the peoples of the world. But now the Christian devotion has beautifully converted the error of empty superstition to the true religion of faith.

Eligius, *Sermon* 2 (*PL* 87.602)

So distant is Roman paganism for Eligius that one cliché, the Parentalia that had endured in family observance and taken some stamping out, is identified with another, rites to celebrate the New Year at the January Kalends and the synthesis is held falsely to be the heart of Roman paganism. But at the same time, in the sermon that is attributed to him by St Audoenus (Ouen, *c.* 600–84), he can still rattle through the following list, as though it mattered to his audience, which itself is ideologically conceived, perhaps even fictionalised, as one in constant danger of relapse into stylised paganism. It may be school of Caesarius, but there are some updates:[25]

- Don't consult soothsayers, people with special powers, lot-casters, enchanters, however ill you are.
- Pay no attention to auguries or snortings [of animals], or birdsong when you are on a journey.
- Pay no attention to the day you leave home or return.
- Don't wait for a particular day or phase of the moon to begin something.
- Don't perform stupid rites on the Kalends of January, [dressing up as] calves, stags, or games.[26]
- Don't lay on feasts at night, or give New Year presents, or drink to excess.
- Don't believe foul [or 'fire-divining'?][27] women or sing in a corner.
- Don't, at the feast of St John or any saint's feast,[28] do dance of any sort (*ballationes* or *saltationes* or *choraulae*) or diabolical songs.
- Don't invoke any name belonging to *daemones*: Neptune, Orcus, Diana, Minerva, or the Genius.
- Don't take a holiday on Thursday (Jove's day) or in May or a day of moths or mice.
- Don't, at *fana*, rocks, springs, trees, *cancelli* [railed off/marked out areas], or crossroads, light lamps or make vows.
- Don't hang things around the necks of people or animals – even Christian objects.[29]
- Don't do lustrations or chant over herbs or make your flocks go through a hollow tree or through holes in the ground.
- Women shouldn't hang amber from their necks or incorporate it in their clothing.
- Don't shout at the eclipse of the moon.
- Don't call sun or moon 'masters' (*domini*) or swear by them.
- Don't go in for fate, fortune and what your birthday means [astrology].
- If you're ill, don't go to enchanters, people with special

powers, lot-casters, soothsayers, to springs or trees or cross-roads, or turn to diabolical amulets.

- Generally be restrained with respect to speech, diabolical amusements, dancing.
- Chop down 'sacred' trees and springs [*chop down?*].
- Ban model feet from crossroads and if you find them, burn them!
- Imitate the good . . . go to church every Sunday, don't chatter in church.

Paraphrase of part of sermon of Eligius,
in Audoenus, *Life of St Eligius Bishop of Noyon* 2.15 (16)

Eating and drinking

Paganism is about eating. Sacrifice is the key ceremony of paganism – that is why Jarl Hákon, who reinstituted paganism in Norway around 970, was known as *blótjarl* – 'sacrifice-earl'.[30] Eating, typically communal, is the normal outcome of sacrifice and therefore, even in the dying days of paganism, this kernel survives to be denounced. The most influential denunciator was undoubtedly Caesarius, who as Archbishop of Arles from 502 to 542 presided over a number of church councils which propagated his images of paganism and manufactured them into cliché.[31] 'I appeal to you . . . not to go to those diabolical feasts which take place at a *fanum* or at springs or at certain trees' (Caesarius, *Sermon* 54.6).

If we now look through the rulings of councils, we see that eating is a significant part of their worries about paganism:[32]

§20 Catholics who do not completely maintain the grace of the baptism which they have accepted and return to the worship of idols, or who, with a taste for illegitimate obstinacy, take food which has been immolated for the cults of idols, should be banned from the assemblies of the Church; likewise those who feed on animals killed by the bites of beasts or choked by any disease or accident.

Council of Orléans, 23 June 533

§15 If anyone, after receiving the sacrament of baptism, goes back to consuming food immolated to demons, as though he were going back to vomit, if he does not comply with a warning from a priest to correct this collusion, he shall be suspended from the Catholic communion as punishment for his sacrilege.

§16 If any Christian, as is the way of pagans, shall by any chance swear by the head of an animal, wild or tame, moreover invoking the divinities of the pagans, if he does not comply with a warning to desist from this superstition, until he corrects his guilt, he shall be expelled from the company of the faithful and from the communion of the Church.

Council of Orléans, 14 May 541

§23 In fact, we have learnt that there are some people to be found who follow the ancient error who celebrate the first of January, though Janus was a pagan man, a king indeed but he could not be God. Therefore, whoever believes in one God reigning together with the Son and the Holy Ghost cannot be said to be a complete Christian if over and above this he maintain some pagan practices. There are also those who at the feast of the Chair of St Peter offer mashed food to the dead and, returning to their own homes from Mass, go back to the errors of the pagans and after the Body of the Lord take food consecrated to a demon. We call upon pastors as well as priests to take care that, whenever they see persons persist in such foolishness or perform deeds incompatible with the Church at any rocks, trees or springs, the designated places of the pagans, they should with their sacred authority expel them from the Church and not allow people who maintain the practices of the pagans to share in the holy altar. For what do demons have in common with Christ, when they appear to add to, rather than purge, their sins which require punishment.

Council of Tours, 18 November 567

§1 It is not permitted on 1 January to do the calf or stag or to observe the practice of New Year's gifts but on the day itself every kindness should be practised as on other days . . .

§3 It is not permitted to make special offerings in one's own home nor to have wakes on the feast-days of saints nor to discharge vows among bushes or at sacred trees or at springs, except if whoever has made a vow keep vigil in a church and make the vow for the register (?) or for the poor and does not obstinately have sculpted things, a wooden foot or man, made.

Synod of Auxerre, unknown date, perhaps c. 585

§16 We have ascertained that auguries are being so observed by Christians that it may be compared with the similar crime of the pagans. There are also some who eat food together with pagans, but it has been decided that these should be kindly admonished so that they may be recalled from their earlier errors. But if they fail to, or become involved with acts of idolatry and immolation, the penalty for them shall be a period of penitence.

Council of Clichy, 27 September 626 or 627

We have already seen how St Gall, the Auvergnat (*c*. 490–554), not the more famous comrade of Columban, burnt the *fanum* at Köln.[33] Similar rituals to those witnessed by St Gall are stressed in the account which St Walfroy gave of the cult of a 'Diana'[34] in the land around Trier, as presented by Gregory: '"I preached to them . . . that also the very songs (*cantica*) which they uttered amid their cups and copious overindulgence (*luxurias*) were without value"' (Gregory of Tours, *Histories* 8.15, cf. pp.123 f. above). Finally, Charlemagne, as we saw on p. 43, in order to lay claim to the manner of a Roman Emperor, contemplated with displeasure 'anyone [who] should make a vow at springs or trees or groves or make any offering in the pagan manner and eat in honour of demons'.[35]

Looking now to the intertext of drunkenness, Caesarius may be our guide. In a virtuoso, concordance-like display of passages relating to drunkenness (though he misses Noah, Philo's core example) he mentions our old favourite and another which serves to feed in the keyword *luxuria*, the opposite of asceticism:

> Moreover, the Jewish people, about whom it is written, 'The people sat to eat and drink, and they rose to play' [Exodus 32.6], after they had taken more wine than they should have, sought to make idols for themselves, and in honour of the same idols began to arrange dances and in frenetic manner to distort their limbs in various styles of dance (*saltationes*) . . . Also, the apostle Paul advises us against the evil of drunkenness, saying, 'Do not get drunk on wine, for in this is self-indulgence (*luxuria*)' [Ephesians 5.18].
>
> Caesarius, *Sermon* 46.5

So here we have in close association eating, drinking, dancing, idolatry and *luxuria*.

Dance

An enduring memory of one holiday is of the Catalan *sardana* outside the church when mass is over. The Catalans are lucky they do not have Caesarius of Arles to contend with:

> These unhappy and wretched people who neither fear nor blush to practise dances (*ballationes et saltationes*) before the very churches of the saints, even if they go as Christians to church, they return pagans from the church, because *ista consuetudo balandi de paganorum observatione remansit* (the custom of dancing is a left-over of the practice of the pagans).
>
> Caesarius, *Sermon* 13.4[36]

161

Figure 8.3 The *sardana* outside the church of Madremanya (Girona) after Sunday mass. Photo: Ken Dowden

It is a grave pronouncement, but the late and unsanctioned verb *balar* (*ballare* is said first to appear in St Augustine, but it may be later) shows the authentic place of dance even then in Occitan culture.[37] Folk ritual not sanctioned by the Church is 'paganism'. Any Christian father with insight will see that it is *really* the Jews worshipping the Golden Calf.

But dance also offends against a code of restraint which had been active (and generally is) in western upper-class society. Even Cicero had told a jury that

> just about no-one dances sober, unless perhaps he is mad, nor in isolation nor at a restrained and decent dinner. Long-drawn dinners, luscious locations, many exquisite pleasures – dancing is the final companion for these.
>
> Cicero, *For Lucius Murena* 13

This is not far from Caesarius' description of bad behaviour in church:

> What sort of Christian is that who scarcely ever comes to church, and when he does, doesn't stand in the church or pray for his sins . . . after he has got drunk, he rises to dance (*ballare*) like a frenetic madman in a diabolical way, to dance (*saltare*), to sing

shameful, amatory, indulgent (*luxuriosa*) words. This sort of man would not hesitate to commit theft or fear to engage in adultery, to give false evidence, to curse, to perjure.

Caesarius, *Sermon* 16.3

Christianity, which had taken root in the cities, imposed an ascetic urban code of restraint as it advanced towards the fields. 'Typical of the Christian ethics of that time', writes Schmitt (1991: 66), 'was the interiorisation of the notions of sin and shame that led to a greater distrust of the body and, along with it, of gestures.' Thus dance is an offence against the Christian gestural code. This theme is a recurrent one in the history of Europe: in the Renaissance, too, the nobler classes sought to distinguish themselves by restraint in gesture and by adopting courtly dance styles that could be distinguished from their rustic cousins (Burke 1991: 76 f.).

Pagans, therefore, dance and sing because (a) that is what pagans do, as we learn from the case of the Golden Calf, and (b) they are bad and lower-class people, probably *rustics*!

Particular customs

New Year's Day[38]

The celebration of the New Year on 1 January was a particular concern of the Church, given that it seemed within a week to undo Christmas. The quotation above (pp.156 f.) from Maximus (*c.* 410), denouncing eating, drinking and dancing, comes in the context of New Year celebration; it should not be celebrated anyway, because Janus was just a man of long ago, who founded the settlement on the Janiculan Hill (Maximus of Turin, *Sermon* 63.2). Janus was a king (Council of Tours, 567), feared and worshipped as a god because people then did not know God (Alcuin, 790s).[39] Martin of Braga (570s) even found it necessary to argue that this was not the beginning of the year at all – the vernal equinox was (*Reforming the pagans* 10). On this day, as we have seen, according to Caesarius of Arles in the early sixth century, men dressed up as women or as stags at some unspecific place. In conformity with the archbishop's views, the Synod of Auxerre (580s, above) prohibits 'doing the calf or stag'. Two hundred years later Alcuin tells his readership that people *used* to dress up as animals or as women.[40] He throws in some augury too 'and what's more they used to have full plates for eating ready all night, thinking that they could make 1 January last all year'. This is why the Universal Church declared a public fast on that day![41]

Thursday

Thursday is the day of Jupiter, *dies Jovis, jeudi*. We are told that pagans, particularly spinning women, who I suppose are more superstitious than men, refused to work on this day. This idea first appears in Caesarius:

> Let no-one on day five [*quinta feria*, as in Portuguese] presume to practise the observance, in honour of Jove, of not doing any work. I call upon you, brothers, to stop any man or woman ever following this practice, lest he be judged by the Lord to be among pagans rather than among Christians, because they sacrilegiously transfer to Thursday (Jovesday) what they should practise on the Lord's day.
>
> Caesarius, *Sermon* 19.4

It recurs in Martin of Braga and will in due course feature in a *Penitential* apparently by Bede and in the omnibus edition of Burchard of Worms.[42]

The moon

This is a very interesting *topos* that has a clear point of origin. It goes back to Maximus, who was disturbed by a great clamour one evening in Turin:

> A few days ago when I had been hitting hard at a number of you about lust and greed, the same evening there was such an outcry from the people that their irreligiosity penetrated heaven. When I asked what all this shouting was about, they told me that the moon was in trouble (*laboranti*)[43] and your shouting was to help it, to assist its giving out (i.e. eclipse) with your cries. I really laughed and was taken aback by your empty-headedness. There you were, supposedly dedicated to the Christian God, bringing assistance, shouting in case through your silence you should lose a heavenly body, as though in His weakness and infirmity, unless He were assisted by your voices, He could not save the luminaries that He had created! How well you do, who exhibit such concern for the Divinity, that with your help He can rule heaven! But if you want to do a proper job, you will need to stay awake all night every night!
>
> Maximus of Turin, *Sermon* 30.2

There can be no doubt that this was on 6 December 401, referring to a total eclipse that reached its maximum shortly after midnight, at 00.38 Rome time, to be precise.[44] It was the latest and greatest of a series of three eclipses in only a year and the previous year there had been a comet too – all of which set pagans jittering, as we know from Claudian, whose eclipse is certainly this one:

> Terrifying, the perpetual trouble of the moon and black Phoebe [moon]
> on frequent nights bewailed through bronze-resounding cities.
> They don't believe the sun has been denied and his sister [moon] cheated
> as the globe of the earth comes up.
>
> Claudian, *Gothic war* 233–6

So they cried out in a howling lament at the moon and clashed cymbals – and that is what Maximus came across. But by Caesarius, *Sermon* 52, this has become a *topos*: 'and what sort of thing is that, when stupid men think they must help the moon as though it was in trouble' and so on. Caesarius, however, has improved the orchestration, with a reference to the use of trumpets and bells at such moments.[45] And it will pass on from there into the *Indiculus*, which frets about lunar eclipses because that is an established cliché thanks to Maximus, but wholly ignores the much more frightening solar eclipse!

Laurel

There is also, however, a sense from Martin's words that it was becoming unclear what counted as paganism. Laurel on your home seems fairly harmless, but 'what else is this than cult of the devil?'

CATECHISM: RENOUNCING WHAT?

Caesarius makes reference to the 'sacrament of baptism' and then offers a gloss as to what is renounced in this catechism:

> Do you renounce the devil, his ceremonies and works? . . . *I renounce them* . . .
>
> What the 'ceremonies of the devil' are, practically everyone knows; however it is necessary to tell you some of it in part:

- All spectacles, frenzied, bloody or shameful, are ceremonies of the devil.
- Slavery to the gullet or to drunkenness, subjugating the unfortunate soul to lust or indulgence (*luxuria*) – these certainly belong with ceremony of the devil because in such actions his will is fulfilled.

- As for adultery and murder, theft and perjury, what need is there to say they go with the ceremony or works of the devil when no man can be ignorant of this.
- Together with this go the observation of auguries, calling in enchanters, and looking out soothsayers, lot-casters, people with special powers (*divini*) – there is no doubt that all this belongs to the ceremony or the works of the devil.

Caesarius, Sermon 12.4

Later, in the mid-eighth century, we find a formula of renunciation for the use of missionaries, the so-called *Abrenuntiatio*. This is the script for registering the conversion of a German-speaking pagan:

- Do you forsake the Devil? [*Forsachistu Diabolae?*, German] and he shall reply [*respondeat*, Latin]: I forsake the Devil [German].
- And all devil-idols?[46] and he shall reply: and I forsake all devil-idols.
- And all the Devil's works? and he shall reply: and I forsake all the Devil's works and words, Thunaer and Woden and Saxnote [the eponym of the Saxons][47] and all the fiends that are his companions.
- Do you believe in God the Father Almighty? I believe in God the Father Almighty.
- Do you believe in Christ the Son of God? I believe in Christ the Son of God.
- Do you believe in the Holy Ghost? I believe in the Holy Ghost.

MG Leges 1, p.19

A slosh of baptismal water, a nice new linen baptismal garment and the job is done. When a barbarian adopts Christianity, he abandons old gods and their associated rituals and habits. But for those who are not yet good Christians, in a civilised place like Arles, it is a matter of extirpating the sources of backsliding – consulting diviners; eating, drinking and enjoying oneself (especially communally); spectator events that are too close for comfort to the old festivals; and immorality generally, because the image of the Golden Calf displays the meeting point between pagan celebration and failure of self-control.

9

PAGAN RITE

We have seen how Christians typecast pagan rituals and, like them, I am going to focus on pagan actions rather than pagan words, even if that leaves aside the interesting and complex question of prayer which Versnel has so resourcefully discussed for the Greco-Roman world.[1] The words of prayer, in any case, can only be rendered effective by the definitive act of libation or the brutal act of sacrifice. These are the twin pillars on which Indo-European paganism rests, corresponding to the human need for food on the one hand and drink on the other. Libation, the pouring of a drink-offering, often from a special, valuable vessel, is a core Indo-European religious practice (Chapter 12).[2] But the evidence we have for European paganism outside Greece and Rome does not cast much light on it and obviously one cannot find the remains of a libation by archaeology, though one does find, for example, jugs in Gaulish temples.[3] The most we can do is observe the close connection of libation, so much more flexible, after all, than the business of sacrifice, with prayer: in the older Indo-European languages you often 'pour out' prayers, by transference from the act of libation that so frequently accompanies them.[4] That said, we will move directly to the single most important feature of paganism, sacrifice.

SACRIFICE

veitstu hvé biðja skal? do you know how you should pray?
veitstu hvé senda skal? do you know how you should 'send'?
veitstu hvé blóta skal? do you know how you should sacrifice?
veitstu hvé sóa skal? do you know how you should slaughter?

Hávamál 144[5]

We do not know the origins of sacrifice any more than we know the origins of religion, but in the form that we have it, it seems to be a feature not of hunting society but of agricultural society. That would place its origins, for Europe, around the seventh millennium BC.[6] Its most typical form is the slaughter of a tame, farm animal, which is subsequently eaten. Indeed, sacrifice may be defined as the way in which the killing and eating of animals is sanctioned, just as in Jewish and Muslim religions meat must be kosher or halal, and to speak of sacrifice is to speak of dietary habits: if ancient Egyptians did not generally sacrifice pigs, an oddity that strikes the Greek historian Herodotos (2.47), then that means that, like their neighbours and kinsmen the Jews and other peoples of that area,[7] they did not generally eat pork. Sacrifice is the religion of the thinking, or at least feeling, carnivore and the way in which it achieves approval for meat-eating is surprisingly simple: the animal is offered to superhuman beings 'first'. Of course, it cannot actually be given to the gods because the whole point is that man shall have it. Thus there is a degree of fiction about sacrifice. Gods preferably only receive a token part of the animal: blood or inedibles. Hesiod related for the Greeks a myth of how once at a banquet Prometheus had tricked the gods into accepting the inedible parts of the animal, thigh-bones wrapped in fat, as an explanation for the gods' standard portion at sacrifices (*Theogony* 535–69). This portion however, was, burnt on the altar and the smell went up to heaven where the gods enjoyed it.

Blood is visible through this book. Some nations are literally blood-thirsty. The Scordisci (below) supposedly drank blood from skulls, and Celts and others certainly used skulls as drinking cups. In a Norse temple you drank some of the blood as you feasted on the meat. The rest of the sacrificial blood (*hlaut*) is kept in a basin (*hlautbolli*) to be spattered over the walls with sacrificial branches (*hlautteinnar*) like a holy water sprink-ler.[8] So meek a word as to 'bless' in fact originates from sprinkling the person with blood, *blædsian*.[9] In Lucan's fictional grove at Marseilles, the trees drip with gore (Chapter 6) and in a rather opaque comment of a scholiast on Lucan the Celts are said to hang victims to Esus in such a way that the blood drips over them and the body rots (Chapter 11). Horace's spring at Bandusia will be treated to blood from a goat (Chapter 3), just as a Welsh spring may appear where a beheaded virgin's blood drips (Chapter 3). Priestesses may divine from how human blood pours into a vessel (Chapter 1); divination from human blood as the victim dies is known elsewhere among Celts and Balts (Chapter 12). The Slav gods enjoy blood, particularly of Christians, and the priest tastes some of it to increase his oracular efficacy, presumably by sharing in the divine nature (Chapter 14); in Greece only the dead taste blood to give them strength, except for a curious parallel which has puzzled classicists when the mythical dead prophet Teiresias, addressing Odysseus, connects blood-drinking with accurate prophecy: "'but stand back from the pit and hold back your sharp sword, so that I may drink and speak accurately to you'" (Homer, *Odyssey* 11.96 f.).[10] Altars, above all, have blood poured over them in most pagan cultures and the Roman Epicurean poet Lucretius denounces the common belief that it is pious 'to sprinkle altars with much blood' (Chapter 4). Similarly, Lithuanians poured blood 'of whatever animals they slaughter' over their granary stones (*ibid.*). Indeed, after Vladimir set up pagan idols on the hills around Kiev, the hills now flowed with blood (Chapter 11). And even if it is only legendary, Vortigern will need a child's blood to sanctify the ground for his fort (Chapter 14).

Why sacrifice?

In modern times *theories* of sacrifice have been vigorously promoted and discussed. There is a certain justification for this in that the last person who can give an account of sacrifice satisfactory to current western thinkers is the person who actually practises it.[11] However, I am not going to spend much time on this topic: I am concerned in this book to keep as close as I can to primary evidence, which takes up plenty of room on its own account and is of absorbing interest. In bare terms most pagans sacrifice because religion is embedded in their community, and sacrifice, they are taught, is the means by which religion is conducted. However much we may seek to understand their thinking, we should not project on to them the anxiety for self-justification and self-assessment so characteristic of late twentieth-century management culture. Pagans were not continually reinventing or re-evaluating their institutions, and their security in some part derived from the stability which unchanging institutions gave them in a physically more hostile world than our own. On the other hand, sacrifice would not have survived unless it was felt satisfactory and the features which made it so satisfying can be reviewed. Death (of the animal) is an instant and shocking (or thrilling) event which is fit to form the climax of a ritual; it is also, usually, a group event in which aggression is channelled and guilt dispersed; it unites the murdering group and offers the shared and special meal. Sacrifice, therefore, reinforces the communal identity as well as offering various psychological experiences which we can perceive readily enough through comparison with modern times – violence of the football hooligan, comradeship of guerrillas, or Christmas dinner as feast of family integration.

Sacrifice has some pagan ideologies, too, which can lead to deviation from the central, food-based, pattern. One instance is the sense, if rarely overtly expressed, in which the life force of the animal is sent (back) to the gods. Animals have even been skeletally reconstructed by those Siberian hunters who eat them, as though there were a concern not to deplete the stock which is needed in order to survive. Animals must be recycled via the gods and the blood poured over their altars, statues, trees or walls.

Another, more visible concept is that the sacrifice is a *gift* which is given to superior authority to encourage it to look favourably on us. Crudely this has been described as *do ut des*, 'I give (to you) in order that you give (to me)', and those of philosophical disposition have worried about the notion of attempted bribery of the divine. Yet, as modern business knows, it is a fine line between the bribe and the legitimate gift, the friendly gesture meant to encourage a responsive attitude on the part of others. Gifts still have their power, but perhaps in materially simple cultures they are of special importance and are a recognised medium of reciprocal social bonding.[12] The gods are thus drawn into human society. If, however, sacrifice is a gift to gods which a society assures itself exist, then it ceases to be exclusively a medium for the preparation of food and the requirement that it should provide a meal may not always be binding. Thus, first, the whole victim may be consumed by fire, as in the Greek *holocaust*, whose original meaning this is – a 'total-burn', as opposed to a part-burn where the token part is burnt and the remainder provides the feast; in the Anglo-Saxon of Caedmon, this is a 'burn-offering', *bryne-gield*.[13] Second, human sacrifice may occur as an extreme gift but without any necessity that the victim should be eaten. Indeed, the ghastly account transmitted by Caesar of alleged druidic practice implies a combination of human sacrifice and holocaust:[14] 'Others have idols of grotesque size, whose wickerwork limbs they fill with living men and then set fire to so that the men die overcome by the flames' (Caesar, *Gallic war* 6.16.4). In other instances the head of the human victim might be removed for display, as at the portals of the *fanum* at Gournay-sur-Aronde (Oise), but we have no notion what happened to the body. Cannibalism is rare and in many cases mythical or defamatory. Human sacrifice, so far from being a primitive mode of sacrifice, which the Greeks thought Orpheus had taught them to abolish, is in fact a developed and special outgrowth from the institution of sacrifice, not at all typical.[15]

Sacrifice is one particular form, the most dramatic, of offering something to divinity. The occasions on which it occurs are therefore those when such 'payment' is felt necessary. These may be regular payments, an annual one maybe to a particular god on his feast day, or a nine-yearly one to secure the goodwill of the Thing-god as the community reasserts and recreates itself. Or they may be prompted by the exigencies or special nature of an occasion, perhaps to seek approval for a course of action enunciated in prayer, to share the proceeds of a hunt or a battle. They may even be promised in advance and paid later as an act of thanks. 'One should sacrifice to the gods for three reasons – for their honour (worship, *timē*), or out of gratitude, or out of need for something beneficial' (Theophrastos, *On piety* fr.12). It is not clear that any paganism can fail to have any one of these three occasions for sacrifice. So, among the Germans, the Hermunduri promised the gods their tribal enemy and paid up (below); of the Saxons, we are told: 'Their custom is on their return [before they raise anchor] to kill every tenth prisoner of war by drowning or crucifixion, the sadder for the fact that it is done out of superstitious ritual' (Sidonius Apollinaris, *Letters* 8.6.15 (*c.* AD 470)). However barbaric, these are thank-offerings. I therefore do not understand de Vries's allegation that the Germans may not actually have practised 'thank-offering' (1956: i.§282), unless he means that the fulfilling of a vow does not count as thanks. We simply have, as he observes, no evidence for minor personal offerings. The Saxon offering is, of course, also a beginning-of-dangerous-journey-offering and has a parallel in a highly coloured allegation of Dudo of St Quentin, a writer wont to lapse into verses (quite good ones). He tells us that in olden days the Norsemen used to select a man by lot for sacrifice to Thor whom they then drowned in the sea: they smashed in his skull and divined by his heart and innards, smeared their heads with his blood and sailed off (*PL* 141.620 f.).

Foundations and the division of territories are particularly tender moments which require the utmost support from the gods to sanction the new departure that is now being made. We shall see Vortigern ready to sanction the moment by child-sacrifice in Chapter 14. But for now let us rest content with the agreement of boundaries between Roman land-owners. The Roman surveyor Siculus Flaccus tells us how ancient Romans dug pits (*fossae*) and sacrificed at them.[16] The burnt remains and ashes were put in the pit together with blood, incense, grain, honeycombs and wine. 'Once the fire had consumed all the food, they located the (boundary) stones above the still warm remains.' This ceremony was performed, he stresses, by *all* the landowners whose properties' limits were marked by the stone, thus binding them by religious means to recognition of boundaries.

A final aspect of sacrifice, if not quite a reason for it, is the widespread assumption that as the victim is killed simultaneously a supernatural message can be discovered from its physiology. This is divination, by inspection of livers of sacrificial animals or of death throes of human victims.

171

What to sacrifice

The animals which are sacrificed in European and Indo-European pagan-ism satisfy a number of conditions. They should be domesticated, not wild. Greeks hesitate to sacrifice animals so domesticated that they are seen as working partners; so dogs are rarely sacrificed in Greece or Rome,[17] nor are horses or plough-oxen. But the prime sacrificial animal remains one that lives with man and, together with men, is perceived by Indo-European language as contrasting with the whole category of 'wild' animals.[18] It has, of course, been bred for food. In some cultures there may be a taboo against a particular animal, notably the pig, as we have seen in Judaic and Egyptian culture. However, pigs are less commonly sacrificed than one might expect in Greek religion, too (Bremmer 1996a: 251 f.), though piglets are common. Oddly, it seems preferable that an animal should be capable of having horns (Indo-European *ker-w/n-)[19] – like oxen, sheep and goats which can be left as trophies of sacrifice and signs of sacrality.

Cattle-sacrifice is costly and magnificent, but both Indian and Iranian cultures came eventually to reject it – Zarathustra, for instance, for quite unclear reasons, singled it out for condemnation.[20] Horse-sacrifice is very special among certain Indo-European nations, especially in association with the creation of a king, who has notional sex with a mare which is subsequently sacrificed (and need not lie about it).[21] Not only was there the well-known Indian *Aśvamedha-*, but there appears to be a closely equivalent Gaulish word, *Iipomiidvos* (probably pronounced *Epomeduos*), and other reflections in the descendant cultures such as the Irish.[22] The Roman sacrifice of a horse in October, the *Equus October*, with its ritual battle over the head and race with its dripping tail, may also be an outgrowth of this custom.[23] A horse-sacrifice is the greatest amplification of sacrifice possible without resorting to human sacrifice.[24]

Sheep and goats are the staple sacrifices in Greece, as may be seen, for instance, in the Erchia calendar on pp. 211 f.[25] In Gaul, though other animals might be of higher status, according to Méniel it is the pig whose remains are most represented in archaeology and, according to Brunaux, sheep and pigs, though it varies between sanctuaries, just as Greek gods varied in their tastes.[26] With the coming of Rome, the sacrifice – and eating – of horse and dog fell into disuse, though before then dogs in particular had been eaten in significant numbers.[27]

In different ways some pagan sacrifices seek to be representative or comprehensive. In desperation the Romans might order a *Ver sacrum*, 'sacred spring', in which they sacrificed to Jupiter specifically for the welfare of the Roman state for the five-year period from now, 217 BC.[28] These offerings, at least according to Livy (22.10.3), were of all stock – pigs, sheep, goats, cows – born that spring starting from the day specified

Figure 9.1 Suovetaurilia: from the forum at Rome. Photo: Ken Dowden

by the Senate and People. A not wholly different sort of sacred spring is found at Uppsala where the Swedes sacrificed a variety of animals, including at least dogs, horses and hens, and a man on each of nine days (Chapter 14). Less overwhelming, but also of great antiquity, is the sacrifice known by the strange Roman jumbo-term, actually a regular pattern in Sanskrit, the *suovetaurilia*, 'pigsheepbull (offerings)'; other nations, too – for instance, the Greeks and the Indians – practised the sacrifice of particular combinations of animals, in which scholars of the Dumézil persuasion have attempted to discern Indo-European tripartite ideology (Chapter 12).[29]

The action of sacrifice

For such a frequent activity, we have very little direct evidence for how sacrifice was done except in Greece and Rome. Although it is not my purpose in this book to add to the literature on Greek and Roman religions where they cannot be usefully linked to other European paganisms, we cannot do without a brief visualisation at this point.

Even in Greece, the model for sacrifice is shaped from a few scenes in the great epics of Homer that stand at the beginning of Greek culture

Figure 9.2 Suovetaurilia. Note how engravings were done.
Compare with Figure 9.1

rather than from any direct historical account.[30] From it and a few other sources we can piece together the procession, with doomed animals, to the holy place. The focus is the altar. The participants stand in a ring around victim, officiants and altar. Their hands are washed and they are silent, holding some barley groats. A prayer is said, to activate the god and establish the purpose of the ceremony. The barley groats are flung forward, as though stoning the victim, and a lock of hair is snipped from it. It is now sacred and can be slaughtered. At the moment of slaughter, apparently, the womenfolk regularly and ritually scream – theirs to channel the emotion. The blood goes over the altar, the innards are inspected for signs, for example, by looking at the zones of the liver, 'hepatoscopy', and various inedible parts are burnt on the altar fire for the god; other vital parts are roasted in order to be ritually 'tasted' by the privileged participants. The rest of the meat is for feasting on and, though epic heroes had it roast on spits, everyday classical folk generally had it boiled. J.-L. Durand even finds meaning in the carcase-geography of butchery.[31] In any event, no part is wasted and the hides and sometimes the meat are a perk of the priests and the sanctuary. Conversely, it is not at all clear that an animal can be eaten *unless* it has been sacrificed first.

Fire is a vital means of crossing the metaphysical divide and communicating with the gods and its place is on the altar. Though the actual word does not extend to Greek, there is a community of Indo-European words connecting altar, fire and ashes: Latin *āra* is an altar (often coupled emotively with *foci*, hearths) and their neighbours the Oscans had 'fire-altars', *aasai purasiai* on the Iguvine tablets; Hittite *ḫašša* is a sacrificial fire-place, as is an Old Norse *arinn* (Finnish *arinna*, 'hearthstone'); more broadly English *ashes* and Sanskrit *ása* (also 'ashes') come from the same root.[32]

What do you do at this altar? In Greek you *thyein* a victim, a word belonging to the family that includes Latin smoke, *fumus*, and the sulphur that Greeks used for fumigation, *theion*.[33] More generically, you *hiera rhezein* 'work holies/victims', you perform an action which somehow transmutes human into divine surroundings, charges the field around you, makes it *hieros*, the key vibrant term for 'sacred'.[34] Similarly, in Latin you *sacra facere*, *sacrificare* for short: you 'do' the sacred, or possibly 'make' the offering sacred, causing it to cross over to the divine world by means of sacrificial warp drive.[35] In German languages you are most commonly engaged in *blōtan*, doing a *blōt*, and you may gather for the *miðsumarsblót* or for the *dísablót*, the offering to the *dísir* which formed part of, or even constituted, the nine-yearly gathering at Uppsala (Chapter 14).[36] You do not *blōtan* a victim; it is *with or by means of* the victim that you *blōtan* and its peculiar force may be felt distantly in a word possibly derived from it, to *bless*.[37] Indeed, in Old Norse you may *blōtan* a temple (*hof*) – or Thor.[38] The word is mysterious and in shape is somewhat contaminated with the word 'blood' (*blōþ*), though in origin it has nothing to do with it. A word which performs similarly is the Old Latin word *mactare* ('slaughter, sacrifice'), which appears to mean to 'magnify' so that (originally) you *mactare*'d a god with the offering; and there is another instance in Sanskrit, where you *yaj-* a god with an offering.[39]

It used to be thought that there was no Indo-European term for 'sacrifice', but it is becoming clear that in fact there was – it was a 'to-bring', **adbher-* or **obbher-*. Irish sacrificial offerings are *adopair* and Welsh are *aberth*, resting on proto-Celtic **opber*, a thing brought. In Italic languages, so often close to Celtic, Latin has *offero/oblatum* and the Iguvine tablets, in Umbrian, a different Italic language, name an official as an *ařfertur*. The same structure is visible in the Old English *tifer* or *tiber*, 'to-bear', amounting to 'sacrificial animal' and there are even some comparable words in Sanskrit.[40] We will again see the extent to which common Indo-European vocabulary can be reconstructed in the course of our discussion of priests (Chapter 12). Slavonic languages use a word *zhertva* (Russian), which, understandably when one thinks about it, is related to the Latin word *gratus*, 'grateful, pleased'.

BEYOND SACRIFICE

Non-sacrificial offerings

Anything of value may be given to a god, even if these elemental drink- and life-offerings have always been primary. Food-offerings may include first-fruits or cooked foods, such as breads and cakes. We know of these for Greek and Roman culture. If perishable offerings are rarely detected by archaeology, nonetheless they must have been made by many of our nations. And sometimes circumstances conspire in our favour, as when cereal grains are found fossilised in the rust of a weapon left at the sanctuary of Mirebeau (Côte-d'Or).[41]

Gifts associated with one's sense of one's own identity are central, such as model limbs denounced in the *Indiculus superstitionum* (Chapter 8).[42] Personal objects such as hair, clothes and jewellery may be left, and found, in shrines. Armour and weapons, too, may be dedicated, though preferably an enemy's rather than yours. One frequent gift is coinage. Though it does raise other issues, image for the issuer, maybe even adornment or display for the user, all the same it overtly declares value. Once invented, therefore, it is a visible 'sacrifice' in our sense. The use of coinage was particularly prominent in Gaulish religion. So, in Belgic Gaul, Fichtl (1994: 40) identifies a dozen sanctuaries in each of which over eighty coins were found and in Britain a further dozen country shrines have come up with between 123 and 2370 coins from the end of antiquity (Lewis 1966: 47). Similar deposits have been found in shrines in other areas of Gaul, though interestingly some coins seem locally minted, specially and rather badly, for the purpose, like the 4000 found at Morvillers-St Saturnin (Somme, forty kilometres west of Amiens).[43]

If we find objects today, how do we tell that they were offerings? An interesting set of criteria has been developed by V. Rey Vodos, which I loosely paraphrase:[44]

1   because of an overt dedication;
2   on the basis of the types of objects found together with each other;
3   because of where precisely they are found in a given sanctuary;
4   because of the remarkable number of the objects in question.

Location, then, and heaping up both matter. This is to put objects of value or significance out of human circulation. They will be restricted to holy ground – dedicated on a temple wall, deposited in a lake or river.

Attitudes to sacred property varied from nation to nation. Of course, once sacred it was not meant to be removed: in Latin that was *sacrilegium*, originally 'gathering up sacred items', and in Greek *hierosylia*, the despoiling of sacred items (Chapter 7). On the other hand, provided it was done rightly, states might 'borrow' sacred wealth, as when the Athenians borrowed the gold plates from Athene's statue to finance the later stages of the Peloponnesian War. Gauls, conversely, seemed to Greeks and Romans to take their religion more seriously, and Caesar and Strabo both report, evidently from Poseidonios, what they think is a noteworthy fact, that Gauls would not touch sacred property.[45] Caesar adds that anyone who did was tortured to death, which brings us back to castration on the Frisian seashore (Chapter 1).

How to offer things that aren't alive

Food offerings at least burn or decompose. So Greeks would burn cakes and breads at an altar, in a pit or on a grave; or they might throw them into the sea or a river.[46] In household cult Lithuanians placed 'a small portion from any meal' on their granary stones (Chapter 4) and Romans put a preliminary portion of their meals in the hearth fire for their household gods.

But, most interesting, it is possible to 'kill' inanimate things by spoiling and destruction, like the huge numbers of 'ritually damaged weapons' found before Romanisation at Gournay-sur-Aronde (Oise) – 200–300 each of swords, scabbards, shields and chains.[47] From a sceptical point of view this removes the temptation to rob the shrine of them, and of course it makes the act of giving final and irreversible,[48] but also it dedicates them to the god by an act of para-sacrifice. So, in west-central France, there are a number of shrines where dedicated coins have first been defaced. And this too is an important element in the frenzy of destruction that followed the massacre by the Cimbri of the armies of Caepio and Mallius in 105 BC:

> The enemy, having become masters of two camps and a huge amount of booty, in some new and unheard-of grim offering, took everything they had captured and destroyed it. Clothing was torn apart and cast aside, gold and silver thrown into the river [Rhone], the breastplates of the men broken up, the *phalerae* (ornaments) of the horses destroyed, the horses themselves drowned in the eddies, the men with nooses around their necks were hanged from trees, so that no booty might be recognised by the victor nor pity by the loser.
>
> Orosius, *History* 5.16.5 f.

Finds made in 1943 at Llyn Cerrig Bach in Anglesey cover a similarly staggering range. Above the lake which had once existed there projected, three metres up, a rock shelf:

> From this vantage point had been thrown numerous weapons, chariot fittings, slave chains, tools, and at least fragments [broken, then?] of cauldrons, trumpets, and pieces of fine bronze work decorated in the insular La Tène style. A large quantity of bones, representing ox, horse, sheep, pig and dog, were also found, and these appear to have been sacrificed animals rather than domestic refuse.
>
> Powell 1980: 178

Green (1986: 142) sensitively draws attention to the special character of the surrounding landscape with its 'rocky outcrops and small lakes'. It evidently awoke some religious sense which we now only perceive through anomalous remains.

Finally, let us remember that even living things can be offered to the gods without killing them. Instances are sacred animals, temple attendants and monks, all of which are sacred because confined and maybe through dress and decoration.

Dance and song

Among the many things we should envisage with ancient sacrifices is the role of music. Unaccompanied music is perhaps a rarity except for those amusing themselves, such as shepherds. More often music is accompanied by words, dance or both. Music is by its nature a thing which is performed before audiences, even if it is not always. And audiences in the sort of societies we are looking at are the community at leisure, in celebration mode. That almost certainly means religion.

Dance[49] is not something that was invented, but is found everywhere and is part of human nature. As the first Roman professor of rhetoric wrote, 'Singing and dancing exists among all nations in some form' (Quintilian, *Education of the Orator* 2.17.10). Dancing in groups is affirmative, assertive and socially bonding. Within the context of paganism, it is therefore most commonly going to be found in what are classified as religious activities, just as today it plays a large role in folk and popular culture. Christians were not off-target in attacking *saltationes* and *ballationes* (Chapter 8).

In Indo-European culture, there evidently had been dance-groups of a nominal size of fifty, consisting, for instance, of youths or of maidens. In Greece in the historical period we find this size of group in the chorus (dance-group) that performed dithyrambs, dance-hymns for Dionysos with a substantial mythological element in the words. These dances were generally round dances and customarily dances were single-sex: hence the mild shock in Strabo's (3.3.7) observation that 'in Bastetania [Andalucía, Spain] *women* dance intermingled with the men and take hold of their hands'.

Almost everywhere we turn in ancient Greek religion we find dance groups, *choroi*. The chorus in Greek tragedy, itself part of a festival to Dionysos at Athens, is one instance of the penetration of religious dance into the cultural life of Greece. Within festivals dances at particular locations might be required. So, for instance, in the procession from Athens to Eleusis for the Mysteries, there were a number of points at which a dance had to be performed.

Particular groups of people might have a duty to dance. So there were various women's guilds in Greece which had a duty to perform at the biennial festival ecstatic dances for Dionysos. We know these broadly as *Bacchae* or *Maenads* but they had other names, too, such as the *Thyiads* who went specially all the way from Athens to Delphi to join in the celebrations there. Dances with weapons are well known the world over from ethnological study and the Greeks, too, had such a dance, the *pyrrichē*, perhaps named after the red colour of the military costume in which they originally danced, though depictions show them nude with shields.[50] At Athens's major civic festival, the Panathenaia, among the contests was the pyrrhic dance, in which there were three competitions, one for boys, one for beardless youths and one for men – and the prize for each competition was an ox and 100 drachmas.[51] Such a soldier's dance seems almost sanitised beside the sword and spear dance of Tacitus' Germans: 'They have one sort of entertainment, the same at every gathering: nude youths, who regard this as fun, dance leaping amid swords and threatening *framea*'s [a type of German spear]' (Tacitus, *Germania* 24). Sword-dances have continued into modern times in Germanic countries.[52] Otherwise in German culture the evidence for dance is fairly feeble, though there can be no serious doubt that it took place (de Vries 1956: i.§302). And this is typical of the fragmentary basis on which perfectly ordinary and common activities are transmitted to us. We have seen Lithuanians dancing around trees at their beer-festival (Chapter 4) and Strabo reports, probably out of Poseidonios but ultimately on rather shaky authority, that the Keltiberians and their northern neighbours performed dances in front of their houses under the full moon.[53] These are mere glimpses of a widespread practice.

At Rome, dance looks more restricted from the aristocratic vantage-point that our evidence imposes upon us. It tends to get wrapped up with popular secular entertainment and associated with women and perverts (*cinaedi*). Even so, various priestly colleges had a duty of dance. The Arval Brethren performed a *tripudium* (apparently an agitated three-step dance – it is also used to describe what sacred chickens do) and the *Salii* were warrior-priests of Mars and Quirinus who had to perform with archaic figure-of-eight shields and spears. *Salii* means 'leaping' and the principal verb for dance in Latin, *saltare*, is derived from this root.

HUMAN SACRIFICE

Human sacrifice is not a mark of civilisation. Indeed, as Burkert says, 'with human sacrifice, religion and morality part company' (1985: 248). It is to the limited credit of the Romans that they banned it in 97 BC,[54] though why, after all, was it necessary to ban it? Modern European law does not.

Human sacrifice is 'only' execution?

Was there human sacrifice, or is it just a thing that civilised people say barbarians do, fixing on killing which has other motivations? The distinctions between capital punishment, contravention of the Geneva Convention in war fury, and human sacrifice can be slight at times.

The selection of victims often suggests that it is mere capital punishment in disguise. Traitors and defectors were hanged on trees (Tacitus, *Germania* 12). 'Hanging was a frequent method of executing capital punishment, especially, it seems, in the case of persons guilty of adultery or seduction' (Chadwick 1899: 17). Unworthy, unmanly offenders were drowned by the Germans, the very manner of death somehow fitting their crime: 'Cowards and unwarlike and those who have used their bodies disreputably, they drown in mud and marsh, putting a wicker hurdle on top' (Tacitus, *Germania* 12). One may speculate that the celebrated British corpse from the peat bog at Lindow (Cheshire), known therefore as 'Lindow Man' or more popularly as 'Pete Marsh', was a not wholly dissimilar execution dating perhaps from around 550 BC.[55] He is generally said to have suffered from ritual overkill – axed, garrotted, his throat cut – though the accidents of excavation and a tight torque may dilute this Gothic story somewhat.[56] The cause, however, may well have been some criminal offence rather than a hunger for human sacrifice. Diodoros (Poseidonios) reports of the Gauls that 'they also use prisoners as sacrifices for the worship of the gods' (5.32.6 = *FGH* 87F116), and Caesar (*Gallic war* 6.16.5) says that druids chose criminals: 'Punishment of those convicted of theft, robbery or some crime they think particularly pleasing to the gods [ironic!], but when this sort of supply runs out, they even turn to the punishment of the innocent.' If the innocent were actually sacrificed, this would be conclusive refutation of the capital punishment view of human sacrifice, but were they? When the pagans of Iceland in 1000 needed two men for each quarter (farthing) to sacrifice, they selected 'certain worst men' and threw them off cliffs.[57] These are certainly odd preferences for pleasing victims: a believer in real human sacrifice would have to believe that 'slaves and criminals were not the persons originally chosen to serve as victims', unless we can believe that they are selected for their marginality.[58]

It is possible to devise a rationale for human sacrifice, as Caesar, or Poseidonios, does in the case of the Gauls: they allegedly employ druids to conduct human sacrifice when gravely ill or in battle or other extreme danger: 'because, unless a man's life is given for a man's life, they think that it is impossible to placate the will of the immortal gods' (Caesar, *Gallic war* 6.16.3). The test is: what came first, the need to sacrifice, or the disposability of the men? There are less decisive passages than one might expect, but a number talk of acquiring victims by purchase, which argues clearly for the need to sacrifice. Is this passage of Adam (4.17) what we are looking for?

> The people themselves are wholly ignorant of the God of the Christians. They worship dragons [household snakes?] together with birds, to whom they even sacrifice live men. They buy them from merchants, very carefully checking they have no blemishes on their body, which they say leads the dragons to reject them.

There are, however, some problems with the historicity of this account which Adam gives of the 'island' of Aestland, that is, Estonia, which is just before you reach the Amazons! But there is, sadly, something historical in it, when we compare Pope Gregory III writing to Boniface in 732 about baptised Germans who realise their assets unethically by selling slaves to pagans for human sacrifice, something which casts ghastly light on the prohibition on the sale of slaves to pagans in the Laws of the Frisians, and possibly also in the Laws of the Alemans and those of Canute.[59] The instances of lottery which we will presently see discourage the view that this is just another tabloid scare story. On the other hand, there is not much credibility in the allegation of *Gutasaga* that in olden days the inhabitants of Gotland used to sacrifice their sons and daughters.[60] A later writer might well think those pagans used to.

Battle and hanging

Instances of atrocity in, or following, battle are part of this 'religious' picture. Germanic peoples did on occasion dedicate the whole army of their enemy before battle, typically by throwing a spear over it or otherwise dedicating them to Odin,[61] something which perhaps casts different light on the antique Roman rite of declaring war by having one of the priests called *fetiales* throw a spear into their neighbours' land. There are a number of instances, all appalling:

> But the war turned out well for the Hermunduri and catastrophically for the Chatti, because the victors had consecrated the opposing line to Mars [probably *Tiwaz] and Mercury [Wodan], and according to this vow the horses, the men, everything were for slaughter.
>
> Tacitus, *Annals* 13.57 (event of AD 58)[62]

A similar vow seems to underlie the vow 350 years later of the Ostrogoth king Radagaisus, a real monster according to Orosius: 'He was a pagan and a Scyth[63] who, as is the way of barbarian peoples like this, had vowed to drink to his gods the whole blood of the Roman race' (Orosius, *History* 7.37 (event of AD 405)).

Back in AD 9 had occurred the event which subsequently gave the Emperor Augustus nightmares, the massacre of his legions under Quinctilius Varus in the Teutoburgerwald. Six years later the charismatic Roman imperial general Germanicus 'was seized by the urge to pay his last respects to the soldiers and their leader' and this is what he saw:

> Alongside lay broken weapons and horses' limbs, and at the same time their [the horses']⁶⁴ heads nailed up on the tree-trunks. In the nearby groves were the barbarian altars, at which tribunes and centurions of the first rank had been slaughtered. Survivors of this disaster, escaping the battle or shackles, told how legates had fallen here, standards been seized there, where Varus got his first wound, where with unlucky right hand and a stroke of his own he had found death, on which platform Arminius had harangued, how many gallows there had been for the prisoners, what (burial) pits, how he had arrogantly mocked their standards and eagles.
>
> Tacitus, *Annals* 1.61 (event of AD 15)

And we have already seen how the armies of Caepio and Mallius had been hanged by the Cimbri in 105 BC.⁶⁵ These events form a pattern: they are not just coincidental atrocities but a view of warfare as sacrifice and the appropriate form of dedication of the sacrifice is to hang it in a tree or on an artificial one, the gallows. This ultimately is the reason why the last form of capital punishment in Britain, effectively abolished in 1965 under Harold Wilson, was hanging. The gods of such hanging varied: we have seen a place for *Tiwaz, the Germanic Zeus, and at Uppsala for Thor, but elsewhere there is an overwhelming case for Mercury–Odin–Wodan, the god of *frenzy* (German *Wut*), often enough described as *Hangaguð*.⁶⁶

If somewhat garbled, it is this sort of ritual that Procopius describes in his history of Justinian's Gothic Wars. He speaks of a part of the Eruli, a Germanic tribe, some of whom, defeated by the Lombards, emigrated through the Slavs and Danes northwards across the sea to a land of the midnight sun which he calls Thule. It is clearly Scandinavia (Chadwick 1899: 17). There they settle next to the Gauti (cf. Goths, Gotland). In 'Thule' this is the religion:

> They worship many gods and daimones, those of heaven and the air, those of the earth and the sea, and other daimonia said to be in the waters of springs and rivers. They perpetually sacrifice [to gods] and offer [to infernal powers] all sorts of victims, but for them the finest victim is a man whom they take prisoner in war. This man they sacrifice to Ares [the Greek name for the god of

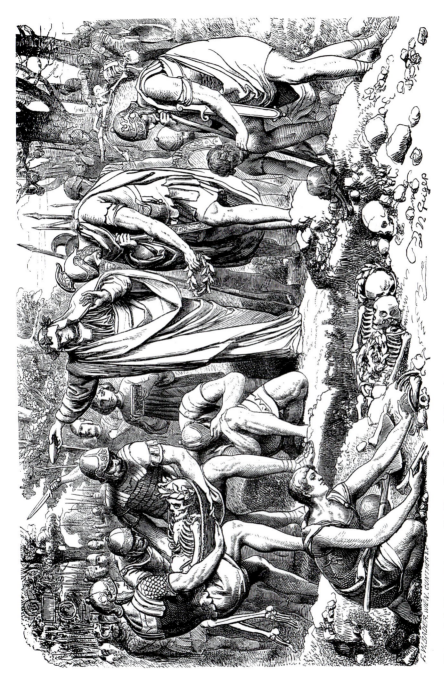

Figure 9.3 Germanicus collecting the bones of Varus' army

war] since they think he is the greatest god. They offer the captive not only by sacrificing him but by hanging him from wood [possibly a tree is meant, more likely a gallows] or throwing into thorn-bushes or killing him in some other piteous form of death.

Procopius, Gothic war 2.15.23–5

The importance of hanging on a tree is such that it figures in an extraordinary moment of Norse mythology, where, in Hávamál, a poem not earlier than the tenth century, the human sacrifice and Odin – Wodan, the god to whom sacrifice is made, are blended:

> I wot that I hung on the wind-tossed tree
>> all of nights nine,
> wounded by spear, bespoken to Óthin,
>> bespoken myself to myself.

Hávamál 138, transl. Lee M. Hollander

Similarly, in Snorri's Ynglingasaga (Heimskringla 1.10) Odin, rationalised as an early king, has himself wounded with a spear and lays claim to all who die in battle, claiming he will await them in Asgard. Marking the victim with a javelin, then, 'was probably regarded as a substitution for death in battle', because 'the slaying of an enemy in battle under ordinary circumstances seems to have been regarded as a sacrifice to Othin' (Chadwick 1899: 28, 8).

It is hard for civilised moderns to enter into the furious mentality of German tribes that lived by war and would have died of shame, but if you believe that immortality is achievable through war when you are killed in battle (Chadwick 1899: 11), then those who escape are worthless deserters from immortality who have in effect tried to cheat the gods of the offer of their lives. Human sacrifice is a monstrous act of assertion that also restores to the gods what is theirs. Similar battle customs were also found among the Scordisci in Thrace in the fourth century AD who sacrificed prisoners of war to 'Bellona and Mars and greedily drank human blood from the hollow bones of the head' (Ammianus Marcellinus 27.4.4). In Thrace they might be, but of course they were Celts, the proud owners of a place Capedunon, maybe 'Shanty Town', and their 'Thrace', at least in Strabo's time, was nearer Croatia.[67] It is not just an act of excess, however, to sacrifice a captive, but it is also thought right or even a duty. So Tacitus (Annals 14.30) tells us that British Gauls on Anglesey thought it right, fas, to sacrifice captives; Caesar tries to find a rationale for Gaulish human sacrifice (above); and Pliny the elder thinks that those who practise it consider it an extreme of religious duty (religiosissimum).

Hanging might seem particularly Germanic, but there are other instances. Is it 'cultural' seepage in the case of Celts or did they have this practice from the beginning when we are told that in honour of the Gaulish Esus, equated with Mars, 'a man is hanged in a tree until his limbs have decomposed in gore'?[68] Whatever it is, decomposition is a Gaulish, bone-collecting, speciality.

Related to the question of human sacrifice is the case of the 'scapegoat'. This is the use of a person to take all the religious bad luck or impurity that threatens a community of worshippers on a sort of exchange basis, not entirely different from the philosophy outlined by Caesar in the case of illnesses above. It looks as though the hero of Petronius' comic novel *Satyrica* had undergone such a ritual:

> This expression comes from a custom of the Gauls. In Marseilles, whenever they were suffering from a plague, one of the poor would offer himself to be fed for an entire year at public expense and on pure foods. After this he would be decorated with vervain and sacred clothes and be led around the whole city with curses, so that the evils of the whole city would fall upon him. Like that, he was thrown out. This can be read in Petronius.
>
> Servius, on Vergil, *Aeneid* 3.57 (Petronius, *Satyrica* fr.1)

Expulsion is the outcome of Greek scapegoat rituals. It may be hostile and it may involve stoning but instances of killing seem ill-founded or fictional (Bremmer 1983: 315–18). All the same, human sacrifice may be only a different way of achieving the same object, unloading impurity.

For human sacrifice, the god may choose his own victim, by lottery. The Saxons sacrificing, before sailing, selected their victims by lot.[69] So it is told of Willibrord and his party on Fositesland that the lot steadfastly refused to fall on any of them, save only one, unfortunately for him but evidently not for this improving story.[70] Lottery and human sacrifice are again associated in a passage of Helmold about the religion of the not so distant Pomeranian Slavs, as we shall see in Chapter 14.

Divination and other reasons

There are some clear contexts for human sacrifice. One example is when the slaves entering the grove of Nerthus in the course of the ceremony must be drowned (Chapter 12). Though it is in the nature of things unwitnessed, it is hard to pronounce it incredible. Another, more disturbing if anything for its futility, is human sacrifice used for divination, as we saw in Chapter 1 in the case of the Cimbri, the *cupa* and the priestesses[71] and as we see again in Tacitus' reference to the practice of Britons on Anglesey (*Annals* 14.30). But perhaps the most explicit example is found in Diodoros' account of the Gauls, based on Poseidonios, where he discusses their use of prophets and means of divination, then continues:

> But particularly when they are looking into some important matter, they have an extraordinary and incredible custom: consecrating a man, they stab him with a dagger in the area above the diaphragm. As the stabbed man falls they interpret the future from his fall and from the contortion of his limbs and in addition from the flow of blood, trusting in ancient and age-old observation of these things.
>
> Diodoros of Sicily 5.31.3 (Poseidonios, *FGH* 87F116)

A very similar story is told of the Lusitanians:

> The Lusitanians are given to sacrifice, but though they look at the entrails, they do not cut them out. They also look at the veins on the flank and judge by feeling them. They also do entrails in the case of prisoners of war, covering them with cloaks; then, when he has been struck in the entrails by the diviner, they divine first of all from his fall. And they chop off the right hands of captives and dedicate them.
>
> Strabo 3.3.6 (Poseidonios)[72]

Divination by human sacrifice appears, then, among Celts, among Cimbri who by their name ought to be Celts[73] and among the Lusitanians, a race whose language displays some Celtic characteristics.[74] We have also seen it attributed to Franks crossing the River Po in 539 (Chapter 3) and in 1286 it could still happen among the Prussians, we are told in a gruesome account (those who have the stomach may read the footnote).[75]

From these examples, but particularly from the recurrent pattern of human sacrifice at the Germanic Thing, it becomes clear that occasional bans on human sacrifice, such as that at the Synod of Liftinae (Hennegau) in AD 743 on sacrifice to Donar (de Vries 1956: i.§283), were not unrealistic or purely ideological. But if sacrifice is generally about eating, then human sacrifice is clearly not normal sacrifice or the climactic peak of sacrifice. It is something different and deviant, indeed something demonstrative. Sometimes it may be found within what is already a killing environment – war or execution. But where it is not, it exceeds the conventional language of sacrifice and that is why it is found at the periodic, nine-yearly, festivals of the Thing at which the global reintegration of society is achieved (Chapter 14).

There is one final occasion for human sacrifice and that is at the tomb of a great man when servants might join, or rather be made to join, their master. The voluntary death in this case is that of the wife, which we

Figure 9.4 A romantic vision of 'Germanic Sacrifice to the Dead'

know, as a result of practice in the Indian subcontinent, as 'suttee', though in fact this is a regular part of Indo-European funeral rites for great men (Gimbutas 1974). This was practised among the western Slavs and Procopius' Eruli, too:

> When an Erulian man died, it was necessary for his wife, if she laid some claim to virtue and wished to leave behind her a reputation, to fasten a noose and, not long after the burial of her husband, to die. If she failed to do this, in future her lot was to be inglorious and be an offence to the relatives of her husband.
>
> Procopius, *Gothic war* 2.14.6 f.

In addition, from opera we may recall Brunnhilde's immolation as the Rhine waters get ready to rise and that story, too, has its basis in saga.[76]

MANIPULATION OF PLACE

Study of religions worldwide would generate a psychologically fascinating book on uses of place. Pilgrimage is already beginning to attract attention among anthropologists, but it would be good also to look at parade and procession and at the outward projection, whether on to town or country, of movement-grids that are ideological in nature. Here, however, I only have time to point up one or two aspects of place that are of religious interest – a selection and a sketch.

Procession

The divinity is represented by the idol (or the icon) and its association with the worshippers and its pervasion of the community is demonstrated by parading it through and around the communal space.

One form involves parading an idol in a cart. This is what we see in a rare description of barbarian ritual in classical times (for the location, see Chapter 12):

> They [part of the Suebi, including Lombards and Angli] worship in common Nerthus, that is Mother Earth, who they think inter- venes in human affairs and rides among the people. There is on an island in the Ocean a holy wood and in it there is a cart dedicated, covered with cloth, which only the priest may touch. He realises when the goddess is present in the shrine and follows the goddess with great adoration as she is drawn by female oxen. At this time the days are joyous, and the region that she judges worthy to offer her hospitality on her arrival celebrates the

festival. They do not start wars, nor take up arms; every weapon is shut away. Only at this time do they know or like peace and tranquillity – until the same priest returns the goddess to her temple, having taken her fill of mixing with mortals. Presently, the cart and cloth and, if you are prepared to believe it, the divinity herself are washed in a secret lake. Slaves do the work – and are immediately drowned in the same lake. This leads to a mysterious fear, a sacred ignorance, of what it is that they see only as they are about to die.

Tacitus, Germania 40

The function of this circumambulation of the goddess Earth is to embrace and unify all her very fragmented peoples in this part of the world, as well as spreading the divine influence and protection. This is an important function of grove rituals, to which we will return in Chapter 14. Later, in the north, we hear similarly of the priestess at Uppsala going around in a cart with the statue of her supposed consort Freyr.[77]

In Gaul St Martin knew about a ritual presumably current around Tours:

> He thought [wrongly, as it turns out] that profane sacrificial rites were being conducted, because rustics among the Gauls in their wretched idiocy had a custom of carrying statues of demons covered in white veiling around their fields.
>
> Sulpicius Severus, Life of St Martin 12.2

This is a similar custom to the one that Simplicius, Bishop of Autun, encountered in the late fourth century:

> They say that in this city [Autun] there was a statue of the Berecyntian [Mother, i.e. Cybele, the Great Mother] . . . On one occasion, when they were carrying it in a waggon for the well-being of their fields and vineyards in the wretched way of paganism, the aforesaid Bishop Simplicius was there, looking on from near by as they *sang and danced* in front of the statue.
>
> Gregory of Tours, On the glory of the confessors 77 (my emphasis)

Simplicius brought all this pagan jollity to a dead halt: the statue falls and the draught animals are rooted to the ground.[78] The practice is still known to the *Indiculus*, as we have seen, when it refers to an 'idol that they carry around the fields'. Nor did the practice die out: de Vries refers to the folk-practice of taking saints' statues around newly sown fields (1956: ii.§323).

Pilgrimage

Dillon (1997: xviii) defines pilgrimage as 'paying a visit to a sacred site outside the boundaries of one's own physical environment' and, so understood, it is clear that there were many instances of such behaviour in ancient Greece.[79] One thinks of visits to oracles such as Delphi and Dodona, to healing shrines such as that of the doctor-god Asklepios at Epidauros, and of distant Greeks and even foreigners such as Romans attending the Eleusinian Mysteries at Eleusis, on the fringes of Athenian territory.[80] In the case of oracles and healing shrines, the desired object of the journey tends to be a little more concrete than mere spiritual merit. However, no-one will deny a spiritual quality to pilgrimage to Lourdes and we should not deny it either to the visits of the hypochondriac Aelius Aristides (later second century AD) to Asklepios at Epidauros; these on his own account possess a spiritual quality, as though he needed to be ill in order to maintain his spiritual communion. Clearly, too, the Mysteries at Eleusis were patronised in order to achieve better hope after death, not as a healing centre, and once was sufficient, as for the *hājj*. Thus we should not be blind to the special spiritual quality of sites visited by ancient pagans. However, out and away the commonest reason for long journeys to shrines, if that is what a pilgrimage is, was health, though sometimes, particularly in the case of oracles, you might seek to resolve problems beyond human means, notably childlessness, the very reason Oedipus' parents consulted the oracle at Delphi. Similarly, Hindus practising *tīrthayātrā* (journey to pilgrimage sites) need to be exhorted to keep their minds on spiritual merit, because 'the majority seek more earthly rewards such as health, happiness, children, success, cure from diseases' (Choudhury 1994: 75).

Christian pilgrimage only reaches its fully developed form in the eleventh century: it is then that we find full-scale and habitual pilgrimage, to a nominated destination, typically Rome, Tours or the rising Santiago de Compostela.[81] The word 'pilgrimage' itself derives from the Latin word *peregrinatio*, at first (1) any trip or stay abroad, then (2) an enforced period abroad (exile), then (3) a Christian penance most appropriately carried out in a holy place abroad, and finally (4) a voluntary act of piety (nevertheless, one that is punishing in nature)[82] consisting in the visiting of a holy place abroad. In classical Latin it scarcely gets beyond meaning (1). Christian pilgrimage has its clear precursors in the fourth-century Roman Empire and maybe earlier,[83] but penitential pilgrimage seems to originate in Irish and British areas in the sixth century AD[84] – to such an extent that continental Europeans used *Peregrinus* as a term for 'Irish missionary'![85] It is interesting that the beginnings of medieval pilgrimage are so closely associated with this part of the world. One form of such pilgrimage is the quest for an offshore island characteristic of several saints (Plummer 1910: i.cxxii). There is the deepest suspicion that this goes back to pagan custom (Chapter 5).[86]

It is not only Christians who consider some sites of more than local significance and journey there from religious motives. Indeed, in the modern world the most striking instance of pilgrimage is the duty of *hājj* which is laid upon every Muslim. Yet this pilgrimage has its origin, apparently, in pre-Islamic custom (Bennett 1994: 94) and is a visit to a sacred stone, the Black Stone in the *Ka'bah* at Mecca, complete with circumambulation (*tawaf*).[87] This looks like an instance of a long journey which culminates in appropriating its objective by circumambulation.

Pilgrimage is a very interesting manipulation of geographical sense. Not only does it instantiate some primal sense of 'the difficult journey'; it implies a doctrine of 'arch-focus', overriding more local and regional geographies of the sacred. Simultaneously it constitutes a fundamental challenge to the geography of states and social groupings – and not just because pilgrims so often cross borders. Pilgrimage to Rome might seem an exception to this challenge, but in fact it reinforces it, because it was only after Rome had lost all genuine imperial power that it became a place for pilgrimage. Pilgrimage, indeed, has the habit of avoiding major political centres – we need not expect pilgrimages to Washington or Brussels.

10

PAGAN TIME

Religion observes time, and regulates time. In our lives religion marks birth, marriage and death. But religion also defines absolute time through the 'religious year' and its calendar. Without a calendar, festivals cannot be held and cannot punctuate, and give sense to, time.

> We cannot conceive of time except on condition of distinguishing its different moments . . . The divisions into days, weeks, months, years, etc., correspond to the periodical recurrence of rites, feasts and public ceremonies. A calendar expresses the rhythm of the collective activities, while at the same time its function is to ensure their regularity.
>
> Durkheim 1915: 10 f.

There are greater things than mere years – grander periods of time and indeed the renewing of time itself, ritually replayed creation.[1]

TIME-RECKONING

Lunar months

Years, months and days are the fundamental units of time-reckoning. A word for 'month', related to our word 'moon', is fundamental in the Indo-European languages:

Tocharian A *mañ*, B *meñe* 'month', Latin *mēnsis* 'month', Umbrian *menzne* '*mense*', Old Irish *mí* (from **mēnsos*) together with Gothic *mēna* 'moon', Lithuanian *ménuo* 'moon, month', Ionic Greek *meís*, Doric Greek *mēs* 'month' (from **mēns*), *mēnē̄*, Armenian *amis* 'month' (from **mēnsos*), Albanian *múaj* 'month' (from **mōn-*).

Gamkrelidze and Ivanov 1995: i.371 (with abbreviations expanded)

Though the moon itself may have gained a new name (Latin *luna*, from *luc-na*, that which gives light; Greek *selēnē*, from *selas-na*, that which gives light), the word for 'month' endures better. The actual reconstructed Indo-European root for 'moon', **meHn* or **meHs*, is evidently derived from the root **meH*, 'measure', where it is the measuring of time that is the issue.[2] It is unlikely that a society that had months would refrain from naming them and in practice they are frequently named after the festivals which take place during them, because that is the principal reason for observing months in the first place. Among the Greek city states, month-names are a bewildering mixture of conservatism, several being named after festivals that are no longer held, and innovation; there are common themes and styles of calendar but certainly no overall Greek calendar. Nevertheless, Greek and other months are part not just of local tradition but of a tradition that goes back to Indo-European times. Indeed, I think we are able to identify one Indo-European month, a spring month for festivals renewing time.

In some Greek calendars a month *Agriānios* (or *Agriōnios*) is found, named after the festival Agriānia (Agriōnia) in which society is dismantled, the household dissolved and the sexes separate, in order evidently to establish a new beginning for society.[3] Meanwhile, in Sanskrit texts, we learn of a festival *Āgrahāyana* which is perceived as introducing a new year or a new *yugá*. Finally, in Gaul, a month in the Coligny calendar (see below), is known as *Ogron(ios)*.[4] To Greek scholars *Agriānios* seems like 'wild'-month, to ancient Indian scholars *Āgrahāyana* seemed like 'begin-year', and to modern Celtic scholars *Ogronios* is the 'cold' month. Too many explanations, too localised: this is an example, maybe the only one, of an inherited Indo-European month-name (Dowden 1989: 196) and maybe of an associated Indo-European festival.

A month, the time taken by the moon to return to its original phase, lasts 29.53059 days. So to maintain a true lunar month, months should oscillate between 29 and 30 days, which is why months may be paired into a 'full' month and a 'hollow' month, male and female.[5] Even then, every three lunar years, another day would have to be inserted. And every thirty lunar years that day should *not* be inserted. Who is to decide when the next month begins? Once, the Romans had allowed a pontifex to observe when the moon first became visible and the first of the month, so observed, was ever after the 'Kalends', because on that day the priest

193

stood before the (obviously monthly) assembly and *proclaimed* which of two dates the Nones of the month would fall on: 'On the fifth/seventh day I proclaim (*calo*) you, Juno Covella ['hollow Juno', apparently referring to the shape of the first quarter of the moon]' (Varro, *The Latin language* 6.27). But in historical times the strict connection with phases of the moon was given up. The Muslim calendar, by contrast, ignores the solar year, a source of considerable difficulty in 'dating' Muslim festivals, generally achieved by using tables.[6]

Intercalation and periods of several years

The solar year, the time taken by the earth to orbit the sun, lasts on average 365.24225 days. Twelve lunar months ('lunations'), the lunar year, is 10.87517 days short of this. How is this problem to be resolved? A process known as 'intercalation' comes to the rescue: this is the periodic insertion of an additional ('intercalary') month into the year.

After what periods is intercalation best done? To answer this question, I wrote a simple program, assuming that the lunar months are kept in step with the phases of the moon. It looked at half-year periods up to 5 years and at whole numbers of years up to 110, and gave the results in the table below. I have included the 106-year cycle for its particular accuracy but otherwise omitted numbers of years greater than 30; nor have I included multiples (e.g. of 19, 11 or 8) where their factors lead to better results, except in the case of 30 (6 × 5).

From the table it can be seen that 2.5 years is an attractive interval: it is the most accurate way of intercalating only one month. If 2.5 years is a difficulty, then its multiple, 5 years, is within an acceptable range. Nine years is not a particularly good interval (+9.29 days adrift) but its multiple, 27 years, allows very accurate correction with one extra intercalary month. Similarly, 4 years, the period of our leap years and of many major

After how many years do you intercalate?	How many months do you intercalate?	That leaves the year how many days adrift?
19	7	−0.09
106	39	+1.07
30	11	+1.42
11	4	+1.51
8	3	−1.59
27	10	−1.68
2.5	1	−2.34
3	1	+3.09
14	5	+4.60
5	2	−4.69

Greek festivals, is very inaccurate in itself, leaving the year almost half a month adrift (13.97 days, much worse than anything in the table), but its multiple 8 makes excellent correction, the basis of the Greek *enneateris* (nine-year cycle, counting inclusively).[7] Seven years is poor in itself (−12.47 days), but is a factor of 14.

Nineteen years is clearly the ideal, if unattractive in some respects: it is a prime number and the year would have got too far out of step if one waited till year 19 to intercalate the seven months. But you can, of course, pay by instalments and that is why the Metonic cycle (named after its Greek discoverer, Meton, the late fifth-century BC Athenian astronomer) is operated by the Jews as a system of twelve normal and seven leap years. As the most accurate solution, a nineteen-year cycle also commended itself to the Council of Nicaea to solve the thorny problem of managing Easter.[8]

I think it must be this process of adjustment of the lunar year that leads to the recognition of larger time periods. These are clearly found among the European, and Indo-European, peoples. In India there was the *yugá*, a cycle typically of five years, though it could also refer to a generation, a lifetime or a cosmic age.[9] In Rome there was the *lustrum*, a period of five years marked by the actions of the censors who were in effect responsible for renewing society at this interval: they conducted a classification of the population (*census*) and a ceremony of purification (also, *lustrum*) to renew the compact with the gods (*pax deorum*).[10] In addition Romans used a word *saeculum* (French *siècle*) to denote longer periods such as a generation, a lifetime or a century (or even a cosmic age when Greek thought made that necessary) and they held a religious festival *à la grecque*, the *ludi saeculares* or 'saeculum-games', to celebrate the beginning of a new age, though generally it was politically massaged.[11] In Greece the intervals between certain festivals were every two years ('trieteric'[12] festivals of Dionysos) or every four years (penteteric festivals, which became the common pattern for inter-state festivals such as the Olympics). Occasionally, they might be every eight years: the enneateric festival at Delphi recreated, for instance, Apollo's primeval defeat of the monster Python and King Minos in Crete communed with Zeus every ninth year (Chapter 14).[13] Among the Gauls, the Coligny calendar was designed to cover five years and Diodoros (5.32.6) tells us that they held particular festivals involving human sacrifice every five years. In fact, as we can see from the Coligny calendar, the Gauls, like the Hindus, inter-calated a month every two and a half years, therefore twice in the five-year cycle.[14] Pliny further tells us that the druids observed a *saeculum* of thirty years, which is the best point to refine a five-year system with an extra intercalary month, as the table shows – it would take another 600 years before correction of the thirty-year periodicity was required.[15]

In our final chapter we will see powerful ceremonies enacted by the

Irish every seven years and by the Danes and Germans every nine. These ceremonies will indeed be festivals of renewal.

Weeks

Weeks, from the Latin *vicem* 'change, succession', help man to impose order on time, to break up the raw continuity of nature into the segmentation of culture.[16] Weeks were not part of traditional Greek or Roman time-reckoning, though they had long been a practical necessity for Jews if they were to observe the Sabbath. Judaism, however, scarcely accounts for the fact that weekdays are named after the planetary gods![17]

Latin planetary god	Latin day	Castilian day	French day	Old High German god-equivalent[18]	English day
Sol	dies Solis	[domingo]	[dimanche = *domenica* 'Lord's' day]	Sunna/ Sunnūn	Sunday
Luna	dies Lunae	lunes	lundi	Mānin	Monday
Mars	dies Martis	martes	mardi	Ziu[19]	Tuesday
Mercurius	dies Mercurii	miércoles	mercredi	Wodan	Wednesday
Jupiter	dies Jovis	jueves	jeudi	Donar	Thursday
Venus	dies Veneris	viernes	vendredi	Frī/Fri(j)a	Friday
Saturnus	dies Saturni	[sábado]	[samedi = *Sabbati dies* 'day of the Sabbath']	[Sambaztag = 'Sabbath day'][20]	Saturday

This is clearly a pagan planetary system, which is why Martin of Braga tried to stamp it out in Portugal and indeed succeeded. There the days are now numbered in the Latin ecclesiastical[21] manner, without reference to planetary gods, for example *terça-feira* (Tuesday). The planetary nomenclature belongs with astrology as an orientalising development in Greek science, to be attributed to Assyrians or Egyptians at will, though, so far as we know, it was only implemented in the Greco-Roman world. There are traces of it as early as the first century AD and Trajan included the planetary gods in the decoration of his Baths in Rome (*c.* 115).[22] Like the closely related astronomical religion of Mithras, with its use of the planetary gods as powers to protect each grade of initiate which also emerged in the late first century AD, the week and its gods did not catch on in mainland Greece, but did capture the imagination in the Roman west and may have been fortified by their reception in Rome and specifically adopted and developed there. The impression of the historian Cassius Dio, writing early in the third century, was that the week had first been common in (Greek) Egypt and had only recently spread from there to the rest of the Empire (37.18). However that may be, the Romance languages speak for the thoroughgoing adoption of the pagan week in western Europe: it spread to Gaul, perhaps around 300; from there it seems to travel to south-west Germany where there was the most intensive intercommunication with the Roman world; and still at an early date the Germanic peoples as a whole adopted this pagan system of time-reckoning.[23]

So the week was already firmly established when Constantine paid it particular attention, presumably to facilitate Christian observance of the Lord's day. He could not displace the venerable 'Sun' of Sunday because it was too entrenched and because the solar cult had been favoured by Emperors in the late third century, in particular Aurelian; in any case, through religious metaphor it was not incompatible with Christianity, as Constantine's coins showed.[24] Constantine was concerned to make Sunday a day of rest except for such things as the freeing of slaves.[25] It was obviously before him that Romans had taken up the regular custom, denounced by Caesarius of Arles and Martin of Braga, of reserving Thursday, *dies Iovis*, as a day off work in honour of Jupiter.[26] Caesarius and Martin still consider it necessary to urge *instead* that Sunday should be used as a day of rest, just as the 'unhappy Jews celebrate the Sabbath with such devotion'.[27] Thus it appears that the reason we have a sense that work should cease on Sunday is ultimately a pagan one, to replace Thursday.

CALENDAR AND FESTIVAL

Festivals can in theory be held as the result of events – for instance, to celebrate a victory. But most festivals, and those most central to religion, are held at particular dates and therefore require a calendar. Calendars come into existence because of the need to maintain festivals and that is why time-reckoning is in origin a matter for priests.

A Gaulish calendar

The longest Gaulish inscription is a five-year calendar beautifully inscribed in Roman capitals of perhaps the second century AD in sixteen columns on a sheet of bronze 1.48 × 0.9m. Found in 1897 at Coligny (Ain), it is known therefore as the Coligny Calendar and is now kept in the fine Musée Gallo-Romain at Lyon.[28] It was a sensational find and retains a place in the hearts of, sometimes indiscriminate, Celtic enthusiasts.[29] It is not, however, unique: a few pieces of a very similar calendar have been found (and some lost again!) near Villards d'Héria (Jura) on the

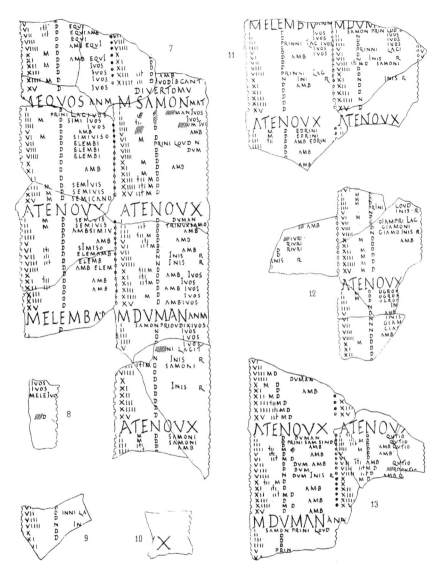

Figure 10.1 The Coligny Calendar, the text (*Revue des Etudes Celtiques* 19 (1898), Plate II)

other side of the Ain. The Coligny Calendar, we have seen, deals with two two and a half-year periods. Each period is headed by an intercalary month, to restore the coincidence of the solar and the lunar years. So that the reader may gain some feel for this calendar, I print the sequence of months for each

Figure 10.2 The Coligny Calendar. Photo: Ch. Thioc, Musée de la Civilisation Gallo-Romaine, Lyon

Summer? half of year		Winter? half of year	
Samon-	30	Giamoni-	29
Dumann-	29	Simivisonn-	30
Riuros	30	Equos	30
Anagantios	29	Elembiu	29
Ogron-	30	Edrini-	30
Cutios	30	Cantlos	29

half of the year[30] and its entry for a sample month, the second instance of the month ('M') abbreviated 'Samon-'[31] – Samonos, maybe, or possibly (sounding now like some Greek months) Samonios. The month Samon- is *mat*, as are all 30-day months; 29-day months are, the opposite, *anm(at)*: though *mat* has therefore been argued to mean 'complete' (a bit like the Latin *maturus*, 'mature'), the word is basic Celtic for 'good' (Welsh *mad*, Irish *maith*) and it surely means 'religiously OK', the equivalent of the Latin concept *fas*.[32] The month rises fifteen days to ATENOUX, which in a perfect lunar calendar would suggest the night of the full moon (or alternatively the new moon), though Gauls were supposed to have started the month on the 6th! The meaning of the word is disputed, but, again, it is best not to dismiss clear relatives in Celtic languages, in this case the Middle Irish *athnughudh* 'renewal', which argues for the *new moon* in mid-month.[33]

The calendar forms the whole basis for the denounced practice of 'observing days' (Zeno of Verona, see Chapter 8). Against each day is a small hole so that a nail or peg may mark which day it is today. We learn the religious quality of each day (presumably, D) or, where it is important, night (N, a reasonable guess). And then there is the case of the three wickets, one with a bar through it: they are always three and they have a tendency also to come in three sets; one wicket is marked with a crossbar and in sets of three it tends to be 1, 2, 3 in order that gets the crossbar (but does the sculptor always get it right?). The most plausible explanation for this mystifying symbol is that it marks one of three *parts* of the day as either *mat* or *anmat* – unless it is the other two parts that are *mat/anmat*![34] These days, nights or part-days are then marked *M*, surely *mat*, or *AMB* – *anmat*, but what is the *B*? Whatever it is, the days that are *AMB* are typically the 5th and 11th before Atenoux, and *all* the odd days after, except the first, showing typical superstitious prejudice against odd numbers.

From Greek and Roman calendars we might expect festivals to be named, but there are few examples and where they are mentioned they are presumably of very special significance – like the *Trinux Samo* – as much as the sculptor could get in of what we find elsewhere, *Trinux Samoni sindiu*, 'Threenight of Samon- today'. We also find what we do

M SAMON MAT

• I	N		DVMAN IVOS
• II III M	D		IVOS
• III I II	D		DVM IVO[S]
• IIII M	D		
• V	D		AMB
• VI M	D		
• VII	PRIN LOVDIN		
• VIII	D		DVMA
• VIIII III M	D		
• X M	D		
• XI	D		AMB
• XII M	D		
• XIII III M	D		
• XIIII III M	D		
• XV III M	D		

ATENOUX

• I	D	DVMAN
• II III	D	TRINVXSAMO
• III	D	AMB
• IIII III M	D	
• V III	D	
• VI III M	D	
• VII	D	AMB
• VIII	N	INIS R
• VIIII	N	INIS R
• X III M	D	
• XI III	D	AMB IVOS
• XII III M	D	IVOS
• XIII	D	AMB IVOS
• XIIII M	D	IVOS
• XV	D	AMB IVOS

not expect, a constant cross-referencing of months, particularly to the paired month,[35] in the case of Samon-, the following month Duman(ios). It would be most honest finally to say that *INIS R* and *IVOS* are anyone's guess.

This is fascinating, but exiguous: the rest of the calendar has a reference to Lugus (the Mercury of Lugdunum, Lyon) and maybe one to Taranis (the Celtic Thor); but at least we see a religious care to maintain time and to map out the specific religious quality of every day in a perpetual system of five-year cycles. These, then, are the lore-systems that ancient priestly figures might be thought to learn and pass on. De Vries (1961: 206) observes, after all, how the Irish druid Cathba taught his pupils to distinguish favourable (*maith*) days from unfavourable and it might be to such purposes that the druids' supposed astral knowledge was directed: 'There is much besides – on stars and their motions, on the scale of the world and the heavens, on natural science, on the force and power of the immortal gods – that they debate and hand on to the next generation' (Caesar, *Gallic war* 6.14.6).

Finally, a deduction about priestly activity. This calendar has been alleged not to work.[36] There is danger of taking too much on trust here, so let us look at the facts. The Coligny year without intercalation adds up to 355 days, the correct number given that a lunar year is 354.36708 days and that correction can only be made by dropping days; it is, in fact, proof that lunar synchronisation was sought. Intercalation is itself going to have to be flexible to maintain the lunar cycle (sometimes 29, sometimes 30 days) and cannot be specified definitively in a five-year calendar. Indeed, after thirty years an intercalary month would have to be dropped. The calendar, so far as these marginal problems go, simply offers a *maximum* set of months. In practice, priests obviously elided surplus days, particularly from the ends of intercalary months but also on occasion from normal 30-day months as they judged necessary (the category exists: the 29-day months simply have the thirtieth slot marked '*divortomu*', presumably 'dropped'): they performed the activity presupposed in the Roman word *kalendae* (see above). There is no need for exotic theories about strange goings-on in bits of the calendar that don't survive – that wouldn't work anyway.[37]

Duration of festivals

For us a day begins chronometrically at midnight, though we also believe that day comes first and night afterwards: it is sleep that divides one day from another. Caesar, too, seems to be looking through our eyes:

> The Gauls profess that they all descend from Father Dis [the lord of the dead][38] and they say that this is handed down by the druids. For this reason they mark the extent of every instance of duration not by a count of days but by a count of nights; they observe birthdays and the beginnings of months and of years on the basis that day follows on from night.
>
> Caesar, *Gallic war* 6.18.1 f.

Yet it is difficult to know what to make of this comment, as the Greeks, including presumably Caesar's source, themselves reckoned the start of a day from sunset. Perhaps rather the point is that the Gauls have carried through the logic of starting with nights into period-reckoning and into when celebrations are conducted. This manner of reckoning continues into modern Celtic languages: the Breton next day is the *antronoz*, and the Welsh week a *wythnos* ('eight-night') and fortnight a *pymthegnos* ('fifteen-night') – yes, *fortnight*, in which 'the ancient Germanic reckoning by nights is preserved' (Onions), 'for [the Germans] do not calculate the number of days like us, but the number of nights' (Tacitus).[39] ('The Indian solar day', however, 'begins and ends at sunrise.'[40]) And so it is that the Coligny Calendar describes the three-day festival held in the month of Samon- as a *Trinux*, 'three-night'.[41] It is night when the moon may be observed, the foundation of their time-reckoning.[42] I would hazard the guess, based on the agreement between Gaulish, ancient German and Greek cultures and the centrality of the moon to Indo-European time-reckoning, that the Indo-Europeans, too, counted by nights, began the day at nightfall and had night-festivals.

Three-day festivals are well known. The Irish equivalent at Samhain of the *Trinux* in Samon- is of three days' duration and so was the lake-festival in the Gévaudan (Chapter 3) and a grand Lithuanian festival described by Jan Długosz (Chapter 14). Enneateric festivals at Delphi, which might be expected from their periodicity to be festivals of renewal, consist of three days in a row;[43] and various Athenian festivals concerned with transitions for society and for its members were of the three-day type – the Anthesteria, the Thesmophoria and probably the Apatouria. Three-day duration allows a sense of 'there and back again' and allows transitions to be accomplished. More exotically, the Lemuria in Rome, a festival concerned with the returning dead, was held on three non-consecutive days, odd ones which we Gauls sense to be *anmat*: 9, 11 and 13 May. The Romans, those inventors of the secular, on the whole distinguished games (*ludi*) from festivals, just as they could distinguish gardens from groves (Chapter 6): games might run on for a week, but the festival, or the religion, had its appointed day.

Night-festivals, however, in the sense that they are held *at night*, are well enough known in Greece (*pannychides*, 'all-nighters') and indeed the Agriōnia is one of them, to such an extent that it is in some places called the Nyktelia ('Night-festival').

An English calendar

We English may have no Coligny Calendar to call our own, but we do have Bede, who in his *Reckoning of times* (15) with commendable spirit adds the Old English calendar to his account of those of more esteemed, classical, nations.

> The ancient peoples of the English – it does not seem fitting to me
> to speak of the yearly observance of other nations and yet to stay

silent about my own – reckoned their months according to the course of the moon. This is why, like the Hebrews and Greeks, they derive the name from the word for moon: the moon is called *mona* and a month *monath*.

Bede, *On the reckoning of times* 15

Bede then lists the months and their correspondences as shown below.

Giuli (II)	Jan	Lida (II)	Jul
Sol-monath	Feb	Weod-monath	Aug
Rhed-monath	Mar	Haleg-monath	Sep
Eostur-monath	Apr	Winter-monath	Oct
Thrimylchi	May	Blod-monath	Nov
Lida (I)	Jun	Giuli (I)	Dec

Giuli (Yule *Gi* is pronounced 'Y') is both December and January, just as the Gothic November was also *Fruma Jiuleis* ('first month of Yule').[44] We are, then, in the presence of a double-month system. Bede regards Giuli (II) as the first month (because the Romans so regard January?) and states explicitly, carrying this view through:

> They began the year from the eighth day before the Kalends of January [on the Latin method of counting, this is 25 December], when now we celebrate the birthday of the Lord. And they called the night which is now sacred to us [Christmas Eve] in pagan language *Modranicht*, that is 'night of mothers', because, I imagine (*ut suspicamur*), of ceremonies which they [mothers?] stayed awake to keep on it.
>
> In normal years, each season of the year had three months, but in leap years, that is, when the year consisted of thirteen lunar months, they added the extra month to summer so that three months at a time were called *Lida* and for that reason this year was called *Thrilidi* . . . Also, overall (*principaliter*), the entire year was divided into two seasons, viz. winter and summer. They assigned the six months in which days were longer than nights to summer, and the other six to winter. As a result they called the month with which they began wintertime *Winterfylleth*, a name made up of the elements 'winter' and 'full-moon', because obviously they gauged the beginning of winter from the full moon of that month.
>
> It would not be irrelevant to take the trouble to explain what the other month-names mean. The months *Giuli* get their name

from the turning of the sun towards increasing day-length ['turn', then, as in the German Sonnen*wende*, 'solstice'] because one of them precedes [the solstice] and the other follows.[45] *Solmonath* may be translated the month of cakes because in it they used to offer them to their gods. *Rhedmonath* is named after a goddess of theirs, Rheda, to whom they used to sacrifice in that month. *Eosturmonath*, which is now called the paschal (Easter) month, once got its name from a goddess of theirs, Eostre, for whom they used to celebrate festivals in it . . . *Trimilchi* was so called because in it they used to milk their flocks three times a day. Such once was the richness of Britain – or of Germany from which the nation of the Angli came into Britain. *Lida* means 'gentle' (*blandus*) or navigable, because in both of these months the calmness of the winds is gentle and the seas may be sailed. *Weodmonath* is the month of weeds because at that time of year they are prolific. *Halegmonath* ['holy month'] is the month of rites. *Winterfylleth* may be translated by making up a new word 'winter-fullmoon'. *Blotmonath* is the month of sacrifices [*blōt* means 'sacrifice', not 'blood'] because in it they used to vow to their gods the cattle they were about to kill.

Thanks be to you, good Jesus, who have turned us aside from these futilities and granted us the privilege of offering you sacrifices of praise!

Bede, On the reckoning of times 15

We have no idea on what authority Bede makes these statements about a religion which had passed by his day, but they are what we have. Could there have been a goddess Eostre, otherwise totally unknown? Could the year really have begun in the middle of a double month, or might it have begun at the beginning of Yule, shortly before 1 November, the date of Samhain? But could they really have intercalated (in Lida) at a point other than between years? Does the winter and summer division of months correspond to the *Samon-*, *Giamoni-* division of the Coligny Calendar? The interrelation, however, of calendar and religion shines through clearly, even to the great *blōt* in which stock-rearers slaughtered the animals they were not going to keep for the winter. This is, in the words of a law of King David I of Scotland (ruled 1124–53), 'the Tyme of slauchter'.[46]

Equinoxes and other times

To what extent are pagan festivals arranged around solstices and equinoxes? Their observation seems to have continued, after all, into our tradition of quarter-days, which combine ritual with the timing of legal sessions in a way strongly reminiscent of the Germanic Thing (Chapter 14); the quarter-days are, for the record, Lady Day, Midsummer's Day, Michaelmas and Christmas, 25 March, 24 June, 29 September and 25 December, respectively. Ordinary or regular meetings of the Thing, the basis for the major festivals of the Germanic peoples, tended to take place three times a year, in winter, spring and summer, at least among the Franks, the Anglo-Saxons and the Norwegians.[47] These times mark approximately the extent of the English ritual year observed in folk and supposedly religious customs before the Reformation, which Hutton has studied for the period 1490–1540, continuing the argument of Phythian-Adams that a ritual year, 'or rather half-year' in early Tudor England 'commenced with Christmas and ended around Midsummer' (Hutton 1994: 5). It is even arguable that there are really only three seasons inherited from Indo-European times – winter, spring and summer.[48]

If we believe Bede, we start the Germanic year with the *winter solstice* and Yule, even if we have little but folk-practice on which to reconstruct its events.[49] We see its character as a festival of the dead in Chapter 13. A *spring equinox* festival might intelligibly be held at the first full moon following the equinox; the first Sunday after that is what we call Easter. Why is this great Christian feast held after the equinox, and why must it wait for a full moon? In every ninth year this same equinox was the time for the festival of the Swedes at Uppsala. This periodicity, together with the offering of every type of animal life and the union of all the Swedish peoples to celebrate this rare, key event, suggests a festival of renewal of society itself (cf. Chapter 14). *Midsummer* festivals are known from Scandinavia, where Olaf Tryggvesson forbade attendance at the *miðsumarsblót*. They are also amply known from popular tradition: there often appears to be a substantial pagan dimension to the observance of the feast day of St John the Baptist (24 June) and in German culture it has been explicitly connected with the *Sonnenwende*, 'solstice', for example, in the phrase *sant Johans sunwenden Tac* ('St John's solstice day').[50] These are naturally not the only occasions of Germanic periodic observance. May festivals, if they go back to paganism, are not equinox or solstice observances but rather fall between quarter-days, like the Irish Beltane.[51] And the last quarter might not have a meeting of the Thing, but in England, as we have seen, September was *halegmōnath* and a number of Germanic agricultural festivals seem understandably to have been held then.[52] The harvest is, after all, a naturally occurring moment in the solar year for a festival and it is this, presumably, which fixes the annual Lithuanian gathering to October, given the overwhelmingly agricultural nature of that country's paganism. Not so far away, the annual festival of the Pomeranian Slavs at Arkona was held 'after the harvest' (Saxo 14.39.4, p.565).

The Athenian year began in June with the new moon after the summer solstice.[53] Thus, the nearest the Athenians had to a midsummer festival was their great festival of integration, the Panathenaia, which began on the third day of the waning moon, 28 Hekatombaion, usually some time into August on our calendar and in any case the birthday of the goddess Athene.[54] The festival took place annually, but with greater ceremony and on a grander scale every *four* years. With this latter periodicity the festival was known as the *Great* Panathenaia and aspired to be counted among the great inter-state Greek festivals, the Olympic, Nemean, Isthmian and Pythian, all known for their substantial sporting and cultural competitions. It then must have run on to the end of the month and the new moon. It began, as the day started, at nightfall and the first part was a *pannychis* ('all-night') to be arranged by state religious officials and doubtless including the torch-race to light the altar-fire of Athene. Certainly, there would have been lots of artificial and celebratory light. Youths and maidens, separately as was the Greek custom, danced and sang through the night on the Acropolis. At dawn a *paian*, a majestic hymn to Apollo, was sung, and then the procession (*pompe* – 'escorting' the goddess) got under way. The huge procession incorporated every category in the community. At its head were the cattle, a hekatomb (a set of 100 oxen). The procession wound its way up the Acropolis and culminated in the huge sacrifice and the presentation of a new robe to Athene – just as in Elis the 'Sixteen' (women) wove a new robe for Hera every four years.[55] This robe was carried up the Acropolis, extraordinarily, on the mast of a ship-float, which was finally parked next to the Areopagus. The robe was not for the huge new statue of Pheidias, but for the antique and revered olive-wood statue, the *xoanon* (Chapter 7), of Athene Polias, which on another occasion, the Plynteria, would even be taken down to the shore and ceremonially renewed by washing. Following this, sport, if to our puritan eye rather secular and too redolent of the Public Holiday, nonetheless formed an essential part of the religious grammar of renewal, invigoration and celebration.

Three months on from the Panathenaia, were the festivals which regulated and celebrated citizenship for males, the Apatouria, and females, the Thesmophoria. This is the month of Pyanopsion, around October/November. The winter in Athens was very quiet in terms of festivals, but it was brought to a close with the Anthesteria, a colourful if difficult festival of Dionysos, celebrating the new wine, and apparently chasing out the dead, in Anthesterion (February/March). And the spring was well and truly launched with the City Dionysia in Elaphebolion (March/April), most notable to us for its drama competition at which most of the Greek tragedies were first performed. Athens had many other festivals, indeed more than any other Greek state, some said. But these are some of the major ones and can be seen to be broadly staggered across the year, standing in some tenuous relationship to a quarter-day pattern.

Athens is only one Greek state and though there were broad similarities among, say, Ionian Greeks and Dorian Greeks, each in principle had its own cycle of festivals and its own calendar to go with it. The Dionysos festivals in particular can be more basic in some other states. In central Greece, in Boiotia, the trieteric (two-yearly) and at times enneateric (eight-yearly) festivals held in the spring month of Agrionios define the community and reinstate the marriages that are formative for it. In their periodicity they recreate the society in a way which corresponds to some extent to the Swedish festival at Uppsala. Further south, at Sparta, as in other Dorian states, there was a festival of great importance for the state, the Karneia, held for Apollo Karneios, at least in a special form, every four years.[56] Representatives of twenty-seven men's groupings, *phratries*, gathered for a sacrificial banquet beneath parasols and there is a tradition that the rituals of the Karneia were designed not only to draw together the community at harvest-time, but to celebrate 'military life'.[57] (So much so that the Spartans could not leave it to attend the Battle of Marathon in 490 BC!) The festival was held in the first half of the month of Karneios, August/September, half a month after the Panathenaia, and lasted for nine days – from the 7th until the full moon.

The ancient calendar of Rome began its year in March, which is why, for example, the seventh month is *Septem*ber and why the month whose days are altered for leap years is February, on this count the last month. Originally they may not have counted months after December at all; indeed, it has been thought, wrongly to my mind, that before 449 BC there simply were only ten months of thirty or thirty-one days in a year and that after six such ten-month years the lunar year was back in synchronisation with the solar year, the period of *five* solar years, a *lustrum*, having then been completed.[58] Several March festivals are conducted to arouse the god of war, Mars, and begin the campaigning season.[59] Similarly, in October the weapons are purified, a horse sacrificed and the campaigning season closed. The rest of the calendar lacks this clarity of purpose and has become a very antiquarian matter by the time of our sources, though naturally there are quite a number of agricultural festivals of various types.[60] The nearest we have to other popular festivals at quarter-days are: a month late on 23 July, the Neptunalia, with its erection of huts called *umbrae* ('shades') made out of leafy branches and its focus on springs and streams in danger of drying up, a powerful festival still being denounced in late antiquity (Chapter 3); and the Saturnalia on 17 December, when masters and slaves exchanged roles and when presents were given. Any connection the Roman calendar may have had with the articulation of primitive society or even with agriculture has become obscured or effaced, unless, as Wissowa said (1912: 204), the

Saturnalia originally closed the sowing season.[61] However, the one festival clearly relevant to the year's progress is that of the personified year or perhaps new year, Anna Perenna, on 15 March. This was held just outside the city, at the first milestone on the Via Flaminia, in her apple-grove alongside the River Tiber. The poet Martial (4.64.16) mystifyingly says she enjoys virgin blood, but he may simply be building upon the red of the apples. Certainly, in classical times it was a festival of singing, dancing and drinking which would have been bad for the blood pressure of Caesarius.[62]

The Irish calendar, as it emerges from traditional literature, notoriously operated a displaced system of quarter-days, out of step with solstices and equinoxes but including May Day. The days in question are Samhain (1 November), Imbolc (1 February, perhaps a less major festival, certainly more obscure), Beltane (1 May) and Lugnasad (1 August). These names have been the subject of unreliable speculation since their earliest attestation. *Imbolc* was tortured to mean 'Ewe-milk' (in the form *Oimelg*); and *Samhain* is supposed falsely to mean 'Summer-end' (*sam-fuin*),[63] though that is where November may have been perceived to be – and, for the Welsh, 1 November is *Calan Gaeaf*, 'the Kalends of Winter'. On the other hand *Beltane* may indeed refer to fires for a god such as the Gallo-British Belenos; and *Lugnasad* may plausibly be connected with the god Lug. If, however, I am happy to link this much Irish evidence to Gallo-British, I do not intend to construct an indiscriminate romantic 'Celtic' calendar and festival system, an idea which Ronald Hutton has blown out of the water.[64] Calendars in fact vary quite easily in what one might think unitary cultures, as we can see in particular from the month names of Bronze Age Greece, which bear little relation to later Greek calendars.

At the same time, however, it is very tempting to connect the Irish Samhain with the month *Samon-* of the Coligny Calendar, whatever it means (see also Chapter 14). I can get no further than that one of the following statements must surely be true and that the rest are false:

1 Irish *Samhain* is the Gaulish *Samon-* and the latter, like the former, is around November. The Gaulish month *Giamoni-*, which is at the opposite side of the year six months away and therefore on this view in May, either, surely impossibly, celebrates winter's end (*réca-pitulation d'hiver?*)[65] or despite appearances does not have anything to do with the Indo-European **gheim/ghyōm* 'winter'.[66] A November *Samon-*, however, successfully places the month *Ogron-* at a similar point to the Greek *Agrionios* (cf. above) and fits the preference of Duval (*RIG*3: 403) for a 'cold' February/March rather than a 'cold' October, if that is what the word was taken to mean. It also makes sense of the Irish Lugnasad in August if, in Gaulish times, the feast in

honour of the divinised Emperor Augustus at Lugdunum (Lyon), a loyalty religion for Gaulish notables, was deliberately placed on the day of Lug's festival – the Emperor may then plausibly be seen as hijacking local religion for his own purposes.

2   *Samon-*, not in this case November, is indeed named after summer and *Giamoni-* after winter. The connection with the Irish Samhain is illusory. The real connection is with the words denoting 'June' in modern Irish, Welsh and Breton that derive from *medio-samonios* (midsummer).[67] The summer start to the year would then be like the Athenian calendar (and not too distant from the point at which Anglo-Saxons intercalated). As a variant, we could even suggest outrageously that Irish Samhain in fact derives from *Giamoni-* and that the *Samon-* of Coligny was May!

3   *Samon-* is indeed named after summer and *Giamoni-* after winter and that is why some Gaulish personal names are derived from these months rather than others.[68] The Irish Samhain is in fact the Gaulish *Samon-* but the Irish calendar had drifted relative to the solar year (Greek calendars, too, were always out of step with each other). This view is also supported by the non-equinoctial/solstitial timing of Irish quarter-days. In that case the Irish were not as meticulous as the Gauls who maintained the two and a half-year system of the Coligny Calendar for accurate intercalation, if indeed even they succeeded. If we assume the summer and winter months to be around five months late, then we are looking at the equivalent of a period of around fifteen years of relentless lunar years (with months called 'summer' and 'winter'!) without maintenance, perhaps not impossible, particularly in the early years of Irish Christianity.

There are only a few possibilities and we simply have to choose between them. I feel that Lug and *Bel-* and Samhain and *Samon-* add up to some continuing Celtic tradition, though I do not believe that the Gauls had the Irish quarter-days.

Obviously, then, equinoxes and solstices can play a part in positioning the more prominent festivals in a year. However, from this brief review it seems that in developed societies festivals have a momentum of their own and it is sufficient if they punctuate time at spaced-out intervals. These intervals may well be quarterly on occasion and may well recognise the seasons, being driven therefore by agriculture as much as by astronomy. We may perhaps detect a falling-off of interest in astronomical observation in late, developed paganism, visible both in the orientation of monuments and in the timing of festivals.

THE CALENDAR OF ERCHIA ('THE GREATER DEMARCHY')

A table of the sacrifices, month by month, of one Athenian village

Column A	Column B	Column C	Column D	Column E
METAGEITNION 12th: to Apollo Lykeios, in the city a sheep, no rem(oval) 12 (drachmas). On the 20th, to Hera Thelkinia, on the Pagos at Erchia a lamb, all black, no removal, 7. BOEDROMION 27th: to the Nymphs, on the Pagos at Erchia a sheep, 10. PYANOPSION 14th: to the Heroines, at the Gate at Erchia a sheep, no removal, priestess to receive sk(in), 10. GAMELION 7th: to Kourotrophos, in the Delphinion at Erchia a pig, 3; to Apollo Delphinios, at Erchia a sheep, 12. On the 8th: to Apollo Apotropaios, at Erchia near Paiania a goat, 12.	METAGEITNION 12th: in Eleusis in the city, to Demeter a sheep, 10. On the 16th: to Kourotrophos, in Hekate's (shrine) at Erchia a pig, 3; to Artemis Hekate, at Erchia a goat, 10. BOEDROMION 4th: to Basileus [King], at Erchia a ewe-lamb, white, holocaust, no wine, 7. On the 27th: on the Pagos at Erchia, to Acheloös a sheep, 12. GAMELION 9th: at the Erosouria on the Acropolis at Erchia, to Athene a ewe-lamb, 7. On the 27th: to Kourotrophos, in Hera's (shrine) at Erchia a pig, 3; to Hera, at Erchia a sheep, priestess to receive skin, 10.	HEKATOMBAION 21st: to Kourotrophos, at the property of the Sotidai at Erchia a pig, no removal, 3; to Artemis, at the property of the Sotidai at Erchia a goat, no removal, skin to be burnt, 10. METAGEITNION 12th: to Zeus Poleis, on the Acropolis in the city a sheep, no removal, 12. On the 25th: to Zeus Epopetes, on the Pagos at Erchia a pig, holocaust, no wine, 3. BOEDROMION 27th: to Alochos, on the Pagos at Erchia a sheep, 10. GAMELION 8th: to Apollo Apotropaios, at Erchia a goat, to be handed to the Pythaistai, 12. On the 27th: to Zeus Teleios, in Hera's shrine at Erchia a sheep, 12.	HEKATOMBAION 21st: to Kourotrophos, on the Peak at Erchia a pig, no removal, 3; to Artemis, on the Peak at Erchia a goat, no removal, skin to be burnt, 10. METAGEITNION 12th: to Athene Polias, on the Acropolis in the city a sheep, 10. BOEDROMION 5th: to Epopos, at Erchia, a pig, holocaust, no wine, 3. On the 27th: to Hermes, on the Pagos at Erchia a sheep, 12. GAMELION 27th: to Poseidon, in Hera's (shrine) at Erchia a sheep, 12. ELAPHEBOLION 16th: to Dionysos, a goat, to be handed to the women, no removal, priestess to receive the skin, 12.	METAGEITNION 19th: to the Heroines, by the Rush at Erchia a sheep, no removal, priestess to receive the skin, 10. BOEDROMION 5th: at Erchia, to Epops a pig, holocaust, no wine, 3. On the 27th: to Ge, on the Pagos at Erchia a pregnant sheep, no removal, 10. POSEIDEON 16th: to Zeus, on the Rock at Erchia a sheep, no removal, 12; to Zeus Horios, at Erchia a pig, no removal, 3. GAMELION 7th: to Apollo Lykeios, at Erchia a sheep, to be received by the Pythaistai, 12.

THE CALENDAR OF ERCHIA ('THE GREATER DEMARCHY') (CONTINUED)

Column A	Column B	Column C	Column D	Column E
ANTHESTERION, at the Diasia: in the city at Agrai, to Zeus Meilichios a sheep, no wine until the innards, 12. ELAPHEBOLION 16th: to Semele, at the same altar a goat, to be handed to the women, the priestess to receive skin, no removal, 10. THARGELION 4th: to Leto, at the Python at Erchia a goat, 10. SKIROPHORION 3rd: to Kourotrophos, on the Acropolis at Erchia a sheep corresponding to an ox (?), 10. TOTAL [. . . .]	MOUNICHION 4th: to the Herakleidai, a sheep at Erchia, 12. THARGELION 4th: to Apollo Pythios, at Erchia a goat to be handed to the Pythaistai, 12; to Apollo Paion, on the Pagos at Erchia a sheep, 12. SKIROPHORION 3rd: to Aglauros, on the Acropolis at Erchia a sheep, 10. TOTAL 108	ANTHESTERION 2nd: to Dionysos, at Erchia a budding (?) kid, 5. MOUNICHION 20th: to Leukaspis, at Erchia a sheep, without wine, no removal, 12. THARGELION 4th: to Zeus, on the Pagos at Erchia a sheep, 12. SKIROPHORION 3rd: to Zeus Polieus, on the Acropolis at Erchia a sheep, no removal, 12. On the 16th: [. . . .]	MOUNICHION 21st: to the Tritopatores, at Erchia a sheep, no wine, no removal, 12. THARGELION 4th: to the Anakes [Dioskouroi], at Erchia a sheep, 12. On the 19th: to Menedeios, at Erchia a sheep, no removal, 12. SKIROPHORION 3rd: to Poseidon, on the Acropolis at Erchia a sheep, 12. TOTAL 110	On the 8th: to Apollo Nymphegetes, at Erchia a goat, 12; to the Nymphs, on the same altar, a goat, 10. THARGELION 4th: to Hermes, in the Agora at Erchia a ram, the herald to make the sacrifice to him and to receive the privileges in the same way as the Demarchos, 10. On the 16th: to Zeus Epakrios, on Hymettos a lamb, no wine, no removal, <7>. SKIROPHORION <3rd: to Pandrosos, on the Acropolis at Erchia a sheep, 10 . . . . > TOTAL . . . . . >

Bulletin de Correspondance Hellénique 87 (1963): 603 ff.: transl. N.R.E. Fisher, slightly modified by K. Dowden

11

A FEW ASPECTS OF GODS

In this chapter I raise some questions about gods that we encounter as we look at pagan cult. This is not, however, a book about specific gods or a book about mythology and there are significant difficulties in writing about pagan gods. It is no use just listing names and supposed functions ('the Romans believed in Neptune; he was the god of the sea . . . '). It is tedious and uninformative for paganism because paganism is not primarily credal and there is accordingly even less justification for starting from official beliefs about the divinity than there is for Christianity, Islam and Judaism; to tell the god is not to tell the religion. Pagan polytheism is in fact a very complicated ideology and we need a lot of evidence to understand why their systems of gods were configured as they were. It is maybe only in the case of Greece and possibly Rome that we have sufficient evidence. At the other extreme, with respect to the Slavs we only know about gods among those along the Baltic coast and among the Russians. We have little information, often eked out by imagination, about Czechs, Poles or south Slavs.[1]

CHRISTIAN CONTRASTS

Pagan plurality

Early Christians needed to distinguish themselves from pagans, which is what they otherwise would have been. So the creeds of the early Church to an extent define paganism: 'I believe in one God, the Father Almighty . . .' (*Nicene creed*). Pagans, by failing to be Christian, fail also to 'believe in one God'. Characteristically, pagan systems embrace a great variety of gods and pagans are 'polytheists'. Because they do not believe in one god, there is no need for that god to be 'omnipotent' ('all-powerful, almighty'): gods may exist in various grades and at various levels of importance and competence. Their functions and geographical areas may be, and usually are, circumscribed.

One thing that seems, however, to be universal about European pre-Christian societies is that they always have gods. We can be reasonably confident, therefore, that when Strabo (3.4.16) reports that 'according to some people the Galicians do not have gods', these sources are either fantasising about a place that is for them the ends of the earth or have learnt something odd about their religion (perhaps they have no statues or priests) and got the wrong end of the stick.

In teaching ancient cultures, one often has the harmless fantasy of interviewing a genuine ancient pagan. We have a document which comes very close to this in the case of Baltic paganism, a Jesuit report from workers in the field in AD 1606, from which we earlier saw a report on how to worship trees with beer (Chapter 4). This extract casts light on polytheism, Christian procrustean beds and a number of other issues:

> One of our priests made an expedition on Quadragesima [six weeks before Easter] up to the very boundaries of Moscow, particularly to Rositen and Lucinus [Rēzekne and Ludza, in eastern Latvia],[2] places where the Lothavi [Latvians/Lithuanians] are still miserably going to their death without recognising God – just like the pagans of ancient times. They are idolaters and they worship trees and have groves, to which on certain occasions, namely around Easter and around the feast of St Michael [29 September, close to quarter-days, then] they offer various kinds of gifts. He negotiated for many days, not without hard work and weariness, with a certain ninety-year-old man of that locality, Popus [*pop*, in many Slavonic languages, means 'priest'],[3] to have him confess – which he finally did. This was the man on whom everyone blamed their idolatry, on the grounds that they had learnt and observed from their family that he should be trusted because he was an old man. He had, with two old men at his side, managed their ceremonies and made offerings to the trees.
>
> After confession he was finally questioned on the ceremonies or gifts which he offered to the grove and on his objectives in doing so. He replied along these lines: 'We poor people, destitute of the entire Divine Word and of priests such as we understood they have in other areas of the faithful, were obliged to find solutions for our needs. Since we had heard that our ancestors worshipped particular trees and by offering them certain gifts were released from their illnesses and enriched with all sorts of goods, we were merely obliged to do the same to avoid being reduced to nothing.'
>
> Asked how many gods he had, he replied that there were

various gods corresponding to the variety of places, persons and needs. 'We have', he said, 'a god with responsibility for the sky; we also have a god who governs the earth. Though this one is supreme on earth, he has under him various subordinate gods. We have a god who gives us fish; we have a god who gives us game; we have a god of corn, fields, gardens, herds – namely horses, cows and various animals.'

> *Annual report of the Society of Jesus* 1606, *LPG* 441 f. (also, Clemen 1936: 111–13)

In his confession the old man is made to claim that his paganism was based in a distorted way on Christianity. Such propaganda, plausibly uttered by the victim, should not be believed, as its purpose is to discredit paganism by denying its authentic roots. We see this happening also in the case of Svantovit, who is alleged to be a perversion of St Vitus, whereas in fact, though *svanto-*, like *sanctus*, means 'holy', his name is one of a sequence of god-names which end *-vit* and is nothing whatever to do with St Vitus, that specialist in epilepsy and rabies about whom nothing historical is known (Attwater and John 1995: 353 f.). But the Christian matrix is more extensive: the *popus* is being required to format his religion as a set of claims about gods, which are mere statements of function, whereas the real action is in the groves.

Do the pagan gods exist?

This may seem an extraordinary question to ask, but if one agrees that they do not, certain conclusions follow. Pagans obviously thought they existed in some real sense, if not perhaps exactly as they were depicted in art, literature or oral tradition. Anthropomorphism, even to the most hardened idolater, is always to an extent metaphorical and no-one would be more surprised than a devout pagan to see a god in the flesh – even the heroes of Greek epic were somewhat taken aback.

I have encountered no examples of Christians denying the existence of pagan gods. Of course, St Martin might deny there was any *religio* ('religious force') in a tree stump (Chapter 4) and others would deny it for idols, generally denounced as mere artefacts made by man (Chapter 7). But there are clear statements about the nature of pagan gods in the Greek Septuagint and particularly in the Latin versions of the Bible with which our European Christians were familiar and in which they had been schooled: a song of Moses in Deuteronomy (32.17) tells us that 'they sacrificed to *daemonia* and not to God' and Psalm 95.5 tells us that 'all gods of the pagans are *daemonia*'. I am, of course, not concerned with what the Hebrew original actually said, because our authors were not reading the Hebrew.[4] The Septuagint was good enough for Paul, it seems:

'What pagans (*ethnē*, 'gentiles') sacrifice, they sacrifice to *daemonia* and not to God and I don't want you to become partners with *daemonia*' (Paul, Letter to the Corinthians 1.10.20 f.). For the Christian fathers and bishops, like, for instance, Cyprian (executed 258) and, following him, Zeno of Verona (d. 380) who quote these two passages, the gods were equally *daemonia* – as they were for Honorius and Theodosius when they forbade sacrifice 'to demons' in 423.[5] *Daemonia*, a Greek word, is the diminutive of *daemon*, denoting minor gods and spirits who are held responsible, for instance, for evil in the world by some Platonic thinkers, as God himself could not by his nature be responsible for evil.

Martin of Braga (*Reforming the pagans* 3, 7) claims that these gods are fallen angels who prevailed upon impressionable newly created men to worship them, vices and all.[6] This view derives ultimately from a passage of Luke's Gospel (10.17–20) where seventy-two Christian workers report back to Jesus that they have been formidably successful and 'even the *daemonia* are obedient to us in your name', to which Jesus replies, somewhat riddlingly, that he has seen 'Satan falling like lightning from the sky'. Thus, the *daemonia* are associated with the fall of Satan, itself recapitulating a passage of Isaiah (14.12–15) describing the fall of Lucifer. This, then, is the intertext driving a baptismal catechism, referred to in one sermon of Caesarius, 'renounce the devil and his ceremonies *and his angels*' (*Sermon* 178.1). Because the devil, who assuredly exists, is an 'angel separated from God through his pride' (178.2). A contemporary of St Martin of Braga, St Aridius, found some of these *daemones* when he came to a village Argentomagus,[7] an unhappy place redolent of B-movies:

> In fact this was a profane place, consecrated to the cult of the demons of ancient superstition. In this place the Christian people who inhabited it could not bear the misery, because they were subject to various illnesses, or even were continuously harassed by these very demons. Though the man of God, Aridius, had wanted to escape the attention of the people and he was praying in secret, there was a disturbance among the mass of ill people, calling upon him by name, because the petulant crowd of demons was unable to conceal itself from the arrival of the holy man.
> Gregory of Tours, *Life of St Aridius the Abbot* 28 (*PL* 71.1133)

He, of course, cures the population of its illnesses/demons, but it is clear that these demons are real enough and that they are the same demons that had been the object of pagan worship.

It has always seemed to me that the European pagans of antiquity are unfairly dealt with by the religious of modern times. The past quarantines them into a fantasy zone where they may be denounced at will. Were they in the present, in some Pyrenean village, the anthropologists would descend and many modern Christians would wonder whether they did not approach God in their own way. If, after all, God is not crudely to be regarded as some anthropomorphically individualised being, then perhaps a plural and polytheist approach might not be inappropriate and in some sense the pagan gods might be thought to 'exist'. Polytheism is then a language for communication with the Other. Monotheism is another language. Perhaps translation is possible.

If, on the other hand, we are convinced, as I am, that the pagans were wholly deluded in supposing various gods to exist and that ontologically, in the cruel light of day, they were worshipping nothing, then what purpose was served by this apparently futile activity and what principles governed their construction of gods? Their religious world becomes a fictional expression of myths buried deep in their subconscious and of the needs of individuals, family and the society in which they live. To turn Freudian, there is something parental about gods, who are typically the progenitors of a society (or at least of those who are important within it). Older, bigger, more powerful, apparently rational but in fact inscrutable, to be appealed to for the help which surely they should give, to turn down apparently reasonable requests for some inscrutable adult reason or because one simply hadn't pleased them enough – these are the gods and these are the adults every child knows. Not without reason does Burkert (1996: 30) talk of the special role of the father for the human animal and of gods as superfathers and supermothers.[8] The creation of gods may be viewed as an outcome of a conditioning to parental author-ity by nature and upbringing, followed by the awful burden of adult responsibility – a moment depicted in ancient epic when Aeneas, founder of the Roman nation, his direction wavering, uncertainty gripping him, loses his father Anchises (Vergil, *Aeneid* 3.710).

DIVINE FUNCTIONS

Sets of gods

The gods of a given society inevitably reflect that society's priorities. Thus, most obviously, a warring society will have a war-god. And an agricultural society will have a corn-goddess and perhaps field-spirits. After an evolu-tion from times long beyond our grasp, the actual systems which societies have accumulated are of very great complexity. Furthermore, given the conservatism of religion and the entertainment of folk ceremonies and festivals, however outmoded on any strict view, we cannot be too deter-minist about the allegedly perfect match of polytheist system to society.

But there is also a problem of discovery: we do not have a complete knowledge of *any* European pagan festival and god system. The closest we come is the knowledge we are able to patch together of the Athenian festival system, some of whose festivals emerge from time to time in this book. Out in the villages there were more intimate systems, of which a remarkable example survives in the 'Erchia Calendar', a list of sacrifices to be made, divided into five columns so that the cost of them might be borne evenly by five wealthy members of the community (see pp.211 f.). One thing that comes clearly out of this calendar is the splintering of gods: there are spirits at all levels, like the 'Heroines at the gate', and there are gods individualised by a special epithet, like Zeus Epopetes. As paganism is not usually doctrinal, it is not standardised either. So across Greece local splintering produces huge numbers of versions of gods, even where the basic identity of those gods is shared by a whole nation. We tend not to notice this ourselves, as we privilege particular classes of writer and have a pre-processed notion of Greek and Roman mythology deriving from a lowest common denominator system used (and presumably invented) by the poets. The Roman poets, in particular, are to blame here, because they grafted on to very diverse Italian and Roman systems of gods an anaemic set of Greek fictions. The sea? Call for Neptune (Greek: Poseidon). Hunting? Diana (Artemis). Corn? Ceres (Demeter). Trade? Mercury (Hermes). Wisdom? Minerva (Athene). Fire? Vulcan (Hephaistos). War? Mars (Ares). Sex? Venus (Aphrodite). More sex? Her son, Cupid (Eros). Naturally, these functions had some basis in cult, though there is no significant cult of Eros, or oddly of Ares. Indeed, so profoundly did the poets invade the general imagination that this interpretation of cult was reinforced. But paganism as a whole did not deal in neat sets of twelve gods, however convenient we may find it.

Multiplicity and miscellany are the enemy of writers and of all people seeking quickly to understand an area as complicated as pagan religion; I have enough problems in this book itself! How useful, then, for Caesar, or Poseidonios, that the Celts worship a short list of gods:

> Of gods they worship Mercury most. His are most statues, he (they say) is the founder of all skills, he is the guide on roads and journeys, he has greatest power over making money and trade. After him, they worship Apollo, Mars, Jupiter and Minerva. They have much the same ideas about them that other nations have: Apollo gets rid of illnesses, Minerva passes on the first stages of arts and handicrafts, Jupiter holds sway over the gods in heaven, Mars governs wars. To the latter, when they have decided to engage in battle, they generally vow whatever they capture in war; they sacrifice the animals they capture alive and they gather the rest of the goods into one place. There are many states in which you can see mounds built up of these goods in holy places [i.e. *nemeta*] and it does not often happen that anyone ignores

218

religious propriety and dares either to conceal on his person what he has taken or to remove what has been deposited – and the most serious punishment, with torture, is reserved for this offence.
Caesar, *Gallic war* 6.17 (cf. Poseidonios *FGH* 87F33, Chapter 1)

How useful, too, for Lucan and for his ancient commentator ('Scholiast'), who fleshes out his bare mentions with one account (A) equipped with precise information predating Roman control, evidently from Poseidonios, and from another (B) that is making it up as it goes along, but at the same time keeping roughly in step with Caesar (all the easier if Caesar himself was following Poseidonios):[9]

[A1] Mercury in the Gaulish language is called 'Teutates' and is worshipped by them with human blood. Teutates Mercury is appeased by the Gauls like this: a man is put head first into a full *semicupium* (half-barrel) so that he may be drowned. [A2] Hesus Mars is placated like this: a man is hanged in a tree until his limbs have decomposed in gore. [A3] Taranis Father Dis[10] is appeased among them in this manner: men are burnt in a wooden container.

Also we find this explained differently in other authors: [B1] Teutates is Mars . . . they think [B2] Hesus Mercury, because he is worshipped by traders, and [B3] Jupiter Taranis, who presides over wars and is the greatest of the gods in heaven, accustomed once to be placated by human lives, but now to rejoice in those of sheep.

Commenta bernensia, on Lucan, 1.445

Three seems to be quite a common number and was even thought by Grimm to be the basic, original model of polytheism, from which sets such as twelve later emerged.[11] Caesar's Germans worship Sun, Vulcan and Moon (*Gallic war* 6.21.1). Tacitus' Germans worship Mercury, Hercules and Mars (*Germania* 9.1) and their descendants 700 years later must renounce 'Thunaer and Woden and Saxnote' (Chapter 8). From modern books we learn that thirteenth/fourteenth-century Lithuanians worshipped Perkunas, Andai and Teliavel (or Kalevelis), provided you set aside the great many other 'spirits'.[12] But is three a common number for religions, or for people who write about religions, like Dumézil with his conception of the three ideological levels, 'functions', of Indo-European society or Plato's analysis of the ideal society in a proto-Dumézilian triadic way (Chapter 12)? We have a large amount of inscriptional evidence for god-names in Gaul and Spain, a very substantial source of shallow knowledge. In Gaul these name 375 gods, 305 of them once (Taranis appears seven times, as well the father of the Gaulish nation, and the Celtic Thor, might).[13] In Spain there are more than 300, but few who appear anywhere else (Epona the equine goddess, Cernunnos with the stag's antlers, Sucellos with the Thor-like hammer, and Lug).[14]

Is it, then, wholly imaginary to impose so few gods on this utterly fragmented evidence? Possibly not. The comments of Caesar seem to reflect a defragmentation taking place as a result of contact with the Greco-Roman world. It is undoubtedly true that Mercury, under that Roman name, was worshipped all over Gaul.[15] And some gods by their Celtic names, though poorly attested in these inscriptions, are in fact widely distributed. The most obvious is Lug, known from personal names and placenames widely across Europe. There are up to sixteen places that may once have borne the name *Lugdunum* ('fort of Lug') – for instance, Lyon, Laon and Leiden – and other similar names such as that of Carlisle (Luguvalium).[16] He was used for (Mercury's) functions of commerce and crafts in Ireland, as Lugh Lámh-fhada ('long-handed'), and gave his name to the Irish pagan quarter-day *Lugnasad*.[17] The apparent proliferation of god-names seems partly to be the result of inscriptions focusing on epithets of gods and partly of their submerging gods, such as Lug, under their Latin names, such as Mercurius, because inscriptions are, after all, written in Latin. What *can* be translated is: *don't say Lug, say Mercury.* Something similar is found in Lithuania where the standard god Perkunas can be known instead by his title *Diviriks* ('chief of the gods').[18]

Triads do, however, appear in cult from time to time. The Greek Apollo, Artemis and Leto are a set; the Roman Jupiter, Minerva and Juno are worshipped as the Capitoline Triad in the temple of Jupiter Optimus Maximus on the Capitoline; Isis, Osiris (alias Serapis) or Anubis and Horus (alias Harpokrates) form the travelling triad of Egyptianising divinities in the Roman Empire. And at Uppsala we saw three statues in the Thing, of Thor, Wodan and Fricco (Chapter 7). So the structures of the human brain simplify the proliferation of pagan gods, both in accounts of them and sometimes in cult itself. Three is sometimes held to be the maximum number of items that we can focus on simultaneously.

Lightning

If we are to enter into the mentality of European pagans, we cannot fail to notice how frequently a god of lightning is prominent in their systems. Though pagans can be unclear about where exactly gods live, it is common enough for them to be thought of as superior and therefore above. The sky is accordingly specially associated with them and the awesome activity of thunder and lightning seems a very immediate confrontation with the divine. It is hard not to conceive of lightning as a physical object and accordingly there is a whole fictitious category of 'lightning-bolts' and 'thunderstones'. Greek Zeus and Roman Jupiter continue an Indo-

European god of the sky and have power over thunder and lightning. The German equivalent is *Tiwaz (who gave his name to *Tues*-day) but he appears to have been more a god of war and assembly; for a real equivalent we must turn to Donar/Thunnor/Thor and, in Gaul, to the metathesised Celtic equivalent Taranis.

But it is with a final god that the mystery of oak groves is finally unravelled.[19] The Russians venerated Perun, god of lightning, the same word in Old Slavonic as *perunŭ*, 'thunderbolt', and derived according to Slavists from the root found in Old Church Slavonic *pero*, 'strike'.[20] The god repeatedly appears to be the most prominent of the Slav gods. Procopius, who for Slav history counts as the remotest antiquity, comments in his history of 545 that the 'Sklavenoi and Antai' (i.e. the Slavs) 'think there is only one god, lord of all, the maker of lightning, and they sacrifice oxen and all victims to him' (Procopius, *Gothic war* 3.14.23). This in turn is the same god as the Lithuanian thunder-god Perkûnas, who lives on mountaintops and strikes, above all, oak, with which he is closely associated. Naturally, he is found in Latvia as well, as Pêrkôns, a real mace-wielder:

> *Perkons struck at the oak*
> *With nine flashes*
> *Three flashes cleaved the trunk*
> *Six cleaved the top.*[21]

The name Perkûnas is itself very suggestive. It is echoed, slightly off-target, in Norse mythology (Fjorgyn, *mother* of Thor) and in the name of the Hercynian forest (were they oaks, then?) or possibly in the Gothic word for a 'mountain-range', *fairguni*, echoed by the Old Church Slavonic wooded hill, the *pregynja*.[22] There is a Vedic (Old Sanskrit) equivalent, Parjānua, master of storms. But, above all, the name Perkûnas itself seems to have built into it an Indo-European word for 'oak' which we see in the Latin *quercus*.[23] Even odder, the Greek Zeus, whose name at first sight has nothing to do with *Perkûnas* has a traditional epithet *terpikeraunos* ('who enjoys lightning') which seems to invite the redistribution of its phonemes into Perkûnas-shape, just as the word *keraunos* ('lightning'), a word otherwise of opaque etymology, has much the right phonemes in much the wrong order.

A final element in this swirling pool of data is supplied by stones. A Lithuanian *akmuõ* is a 'rock, stone', rather like a Sanskrit *aśman*, 'boulder'. In Greek it is more technical, an 'anvil', *akmōn*, but in some passages of older poets it seems to be a 'thunderbolt'.[24] Fire and the thunder of hammer-strokes then conjure up a smith-god in heaven – Taranis, Tanaris, Thor or Thunder – or Indra striking rocks with his *vájra*, releasing water or light.

So there appears to be a number of key elements found in association with each other in Indo-European language and religion: oak trees, lightning, stones, anvils, thunder and the god of lightning or thunder. A god of lightning is connected with oaks and with the forests on the mountainside in which oaks are situated. Somewhere here are large stones which are struck by lightning or by hammers, in which case they are anvils (unless they are clouds smitten above and sparking lightning). Finally, let us think of the mountain tops where lightning strikes and the god's statues are found, and of stones sent from heaven, as thunderbolts (we prefer meteorites), which may even be the god himself – Jupiter Lapis, Zeus Kappotas, or the Lithuanian Akmo that a sixteenth-century traveller came across.[25]

What is going on? Are oaks disproportionately susceptible to lightning strikes, as the forestry evidence of Nagy suggests?[26] They have this reputation: who has not heard of the 'blasted oak' or of 'oak-cleaving thunderbolts' (Shakespeare, *King Lear* II.i)?[27] An investigation in Germany in 1899 covering 50,000 acres of forest showed that though oaks constituted only 11 per cent of the trees, they were casualties of lightning in 58 per cent of cases. Why? Oaks are no more likely to be struck than any other tall tree, but it is what happens next that matters. Trees are fairly poor conductors of electricity and so lightning in a thunderstorm prefers to travel along the trickle of water down the tree's bark, its natural lightning-conductor. Careful examination of an apparently unaffected beech may show a scorch line. But oaks have rough bark which inhibits the flow of water and as a consequence the lightning charge travels only part of the way down the trunk (the water goes no further), then leaps to 'the sap inside the tree with shattering effect due to the sudden internal release of steam by the heat generated. The top part of the tree appears as if it has been blown off by an explosion' (Malan 1963: 151).[28]

Among natural, unplanted, groves we are at the mercy of nature's forests for the variety of trees available. But we can now see why the oak figures so often. I recapitulate where we have already seen oaks: at Drunemeton, the Galatian placename; at Dodona in Greece in connection with the oracle of Zeus; the grove of oaks around the cave of Demeter the Black at Phigaleia (Arcadia); as the material from which an ancient column of the temple of Hera at Olympia was made; in the *Aesculetum* outside Rome in which the *Lex Hortensia* was passed. Oak is clearly foregrounded. Some Greek philosopher, probably Poseidonios, was determined that 'druid' should derive from the Greek word for an oak, *drys* (as in fact it may, Chapter 12), and should shin up oaks to collect the mistletoe. Already in the fourth century BC Theophrastos (*On plants* 3.7.6) finds it necessary to point out that mistletoe can grow on other trees than oaks. He, too, observes (3.8.5) that 'some Aeolians' had decided that only one variety of oak, the broad-leaved oak, was struck by lightning, even though it was not the tallest; presumably this was the variety with the roughest bark.

Thus the oak enters the ideology of god-construction. It is the tree with which the god of lightning so immediately and so devastatingly communicates.

12

PRIESTS

Priests – we all have a gut sense of what they are for; and if we do not find them indispensable in our personal lives, we at least imagine that pagan societies could not do without them. Somewhere in our shared imaginations lurk two powerful images of the pagan priest: first, the mirage of the druid, the archetypal pagan priest, with white robes and matching beard – and a starring role in the Astérix theme park or at the Eisteddfod; second, the priest or priestess of the goddess, standing before his or her classical temple and the statue of his or her god, a priesthood which turns out to be rarer than we might suppose.

This book would not be possible if there were not a certain uniformity in European paganisms, in places of worship, sacrificial ritual and so on, but priests provoke the greatest difficulty for this method. 'Priest' itself is a term which cloaks a variety of different activities in different pagan societies.[1] This is why 'there is no single Sumerian or Akkadian word corresponding to our word "priest"' (Grabbe 1995: 54) and why Beard and North (1990: 44) deny 'that the wide range of those [Roman] officials traditionally entitled "priests" should be seen as a single subject for analysis'). So, before we do anything else, let us look at the actual functions fulfilled by 'priests' and suchlike.

THE NEED FOR PRIESTS

What a priest is

Ultimately, sacrifice is the chief business of the priestly class.
Lincoln 1981: 62

In the modern age priests are often guides and exponents of a credal system. But pagan religion is about ritual more than creed and we must not, therefore, be disappointed if its priests busy themselves with the performance of ritual rather than the exposition of a system of ideas:

> Another type of responsibility is that concerning the gods, as when priests and those responsible for the rites are concerned with preserving existing buildings and restoring those that have collapsed and all the other arrangements for the gods. This responsibility in some places turns out to be a single one, as in small cities, but in other places there are multiple responsibilities which are separate from the priesthood, e.g. *hieropoioi* (rite-doers) and *nāophylakes* (temple-wardens) and treasurers of the sacred moneys. Following on from this responsibility is the one which is demarcated for all the communal sacrifices that the law does not assign to priests but which derive their status from the communal hearth. Some call these *archōns* (magistrates), others kings, others *prytaneis* (members of the presidency).
>
> Aristotle, *Politics* 6.8 (1322b18–29)

This is nuts and bolts religion, a matter of buildings and arrangements.

It remains, however, a fact about religious history that people have generally felt more comfortable with a triadic, mildly distanced, relationship with the divine than with a dyadic one. Persons whose profession it is to mediate between men and the divine, to cope with and transform this relationship, negotiate a difficult boundary and reduce the risk of error and catastrophe that is inherent in private, amateur contact. 'Priest' is only one term: there are others, too, who specialise in one way or another in the sacred, notably prophets and diviners. They may be individuals or groups, private vendors or public authorities, central or marginal. Sacred and magical functions are distributed differently, too, in different societies, and 'priesthood' itself is an umbrella term which *we* use to cover a range of personnel that individual societies may wish to distinguish and approve. The varieties of religious professional are for cultures rather than dictionaries to determine.[2]

All the same, there is a finite range of functions performable by professionals, which cultures in effect select and bundle:

- The *rememberer* preserves traditions, whether narrative (myth), teachings (doctrine) or practice (ritual). 'The [Israelite] priests were the ones with leisure to pursue intellectual activities . . . they had the opportunity to learn, teach, study, and preserve traditions' (Grabbe 1995: 65).

- The *advisor* gives advice on the basis of tradition and who may pronounce whether this or that ritual is now required.

- The *authority* is a variety of the advisor who hears cases and arbitrates (usurping legal functions, we might feel). This may be characteristic of a 'theocratic' state, as in Iran today, and possibly in the case of the Levites in ancient Israel.[3]

- The *performer* performs ritual authentically in the light of tradition and with the particular authority that derives from specialism; the ritual may be regular (festival), or occasional to meet special needs (drought, famine, war); the most important performance is of sacrifice.

- The *validator* must be present for the ritual to be conducted with authority.

- The *functionary*, a lesser, more menial professional, carries out certain necessary functions – for example, butchery, song or dance (like Egyptian women, who could not be priests).[4]

- The *warden* maintains the paraphernalia of religion – temples, offerings, bones and any cult objects.

- The *interpreter* interprets signs on the basis of a body of specialist knowledge; signs may appear in nature, especially in the skies (portents, augury), or in dreams, or in things revealed by sacrifice (e.g. haruspicy, the investigation of inner organs). By interpreting signs he, of course, gives advice.

- The *showman* has, and exploits, special psychological powers. He uses altered consciousness to gain access to prophetic truth (advice, again) or to deal with problems categorised as spiritual – the shaman's recovery of ill souls or disposal of dead souls, or exorcism. Sometimes this state will be depicted as a temporary departure of the spirit from the body, sometimes as possession by a spirit or a god.

Together with what we would normally call priests I have included space for prophets, seers and shamans. I have excluded magic, because by definition it is not capable of being institutionalised within religion, though plainly actions which we or others might dismissively categorise as magical can be performed by priests as ritual – or by individuals who happen to be recognised religious professionals as acts of, for example, medicine.

There are some other vital distinctions to be made before we proceed. People sometimes distinguish between *cultic* and *non-cultic* religious specialists (Grabbe 1995: 2), those involved in cult and those who are not. Though this leaves some grey areas (When is a *seer* 'cultic'? Is he cultic when he inspects a sacrificed victim in front of a community?), 'cultic religious specialist' more or less identifies what is commonly meant by 'priest'. Priests themselves may be attached to a particular god, or not. If attached, I label them *tied* priests; if not, then *free* priests. Tied priests are liable to be associated with a particular sanctuary or temple, like, for instance, Egyptian chief priests (the *ḥmw nṯr* or 'servant of the god').[5] Free priests are liable to find their context in another way, namely, that of belonging to a class or caste, like brahmans. This leads in turn to questions of *hierarchy*. This is what the *Oxford English Dictionary* (2nd edition) refers to as 'an organized body of priests or clergy in successive orders or grades', a sense first attested in English in 1619 (hierarchies of angels go back to Wycliff *c.* 1380) and clearly devised for the Christian Church. In pagan cultures a hierarchy may be present, partly present or absent. Free priests are perhaps more readily hierarchised (tied priests, like teachers of minority subjects, cannot be promoted); the *sites*, however, of tied priests may achieve this purpose by themselves being hierarchised: so, for instance, Rome is a suitable place for the Pope (though even that could be challenged for a while at Avignon).

A final set of distinctions concerns the ways in which priests may be viewed and their place in the stratification of society. Priesthood may be a question of aristocratic privilege, or of individual choice. Diviners may be official, but they may also be unofficial and influential only with 'lower' classes. Deuteronomy 13.1–5 even identifies prophets who should be put to death![6] As paganism declines, is rejected by those in charge, its priesthood loses recognition except among non-powerful classes and declines into something less institutionalised. So an old person may be considered to have some special knowledge or skill. One instance of this is the pathetic old Lithuanian interviewed by Jesuits who is obliged by the forceful propaganda of the authorised and educated to recognise the error of his ways (Chapter 11).

Priestly specialism, development of the state

Knowing how to bridge the gap between man and god is, for many societies, a skill which like any other may be practised by specialists: so priesthood, in its widest sense, may be viewed as one offshoot of increasing specialisation in the distribution of skills in the community. This is an evolutionary theory, held, for instance, by Frazer – at least, he believed that 'magic' became a specialism and as magicians realised magic did not work, they turned to ritual, where failure could be accounted for by unwilling gods.[7] The predictive value of this rather *a priori* view is that priests will turn out to be specially characteristic of developed and wealthy societies and in particular of those where the development of the state has led to the creation of a system of public offices. In societies that are poorer and where the institution of the state is less developed, we shall expect less formal priesthood and homelier, more part-time, religious specialism.

If religious specialism is undeveloped in a given society, religion itself will still be important and its operation will be entrusted to those who already have greater authority than others. So, as we shall see below, in a household the head of household – what the Romans called the *paterfamilias* ('father of the household') – will play the most significant role. In a community the holders of power – the aristocracy (where one has developed) and the king (if the society has developed this far) – will have some important role in the preservation and implementation of cult.[8] The special role of the king in cult, on behalf of the whole state, is reasonably well known in the ancient Near East, Egypt and Israel, even if a *modus vivendi* had to be reached between kings and very developed bodies of priests.[9]

With the advance of specialism, although anyone may know by tradition and upbringing how and when to, say, sacrifice a chicken, and although many religious duties will continue to be performed by persons in authority, greater needs, involving the whole community, will require greater skills. Routine needs, too, particularly at community level, will be more efficiently met by the appointment of specialists. One way in which this can happen is for particular extended families to specialise in certain rites. In Athens and Rome this leads to rites performed by particular *clans*, always resulting in control by those of noble birth (there are no clans of the ignoble). But more generally this leads to the emergence of priests with a recognised authority. Priests cannot be separated from the development of the community of which they form a part. The more a people advances towards statehood, the more it will have officials both secular and sacred. The more that statehood involves the building of fixed cities, and the more they thrive economically, the more there will be sacred buildings and a need for sacred personnel to manage them – buildings and priests will justify each other's existence. On the other hand, public positions need not exclude other activities by the holders of those positions and priesthood need not be a full-time job.[10] But religion is conservative, too, and even within what to our view is a state the priesthoods of earlier units of organisation, principally the clan, continue.

A corollary of these propositions is that the development of priest-hood is a *measure* of the development of statehood. Thus, the Egyptian or Mesopotamian states would lead one to expect, what one finds, a clear sense of priesthood. And if the Celts of Gaul display a more developed priesthood than the Germans, it follows that they have advanced further towards the state, as indeed they had. It is accordingly likely on *a priori* grounds that the druids are a late development and that talk of a priestly class at Indo-European level rests too much on anachronistic assumptions. It is then an interesting social *development* if 'a king or a warrior cannot sacrifice for himself but must employ a priest to do so for him'.[11]

Religion may, then, be conducted at a variety of levels: at that of the individual, the nuclear family, the extended family, the notional family (kin, clan), the village, the city, the state. Within every context other than that of the individual, persons may come to be assigned specialist sacred authority and skills.

Religion in the home, without professionals

In the home no professional is required. Though household worship rarely reaches the historical record, it probably occurs as standard in all paganisms. So in this sense every pagan father is a priest and the home is the first and most important school of paganism for every child.[12] Best known is the Roman cult of little figurines of Lares (minor gods of the property) and Penates ('cupboard'-gods, gods of the house and its sup-plies), especially from the excavation of real houses at Pompeii. Greek houses, too, had their worship of 'Zeus of the courtyard', *Zeus Herkeios*, but for so well evidenced a culture, remarkably little is known of this more intimate form of worship.

Elsewhere we are largely dealing with hints, like the Anglo-Saxon *cofgodas*, 'room-gods', apparently the equivalent of the Roman Penates. The same gods are seen in the German *Kobold*, perhaps in origin a *kofe-walt*, a spirit that has power over the room. This in turn appears to be the word that, via Norman French, has become our *goblin*, showing how pagan gods can degenerate if not properly maintained.[13] A glimpse into the religious past of goblins is given by Johann Maletius (*LPG* 296):

> The same [Baltic] nations worship certain visible spirits that they call *Coltky* in Prussian, *Cobili* in Greek (?), *Coboldi* in German. These spirits, they believe, live in the hidden parts of houses or in woodpiles and they feed them lavishly with every manner of food, because they are supposed secretly to steal corn from other peo-ple's granaries for those who feed them.

Great state or tribal occasions may be happening three times a year or once every eight or nine years or whenever, but day in, day out, each family unit is a religious state in miniature, its head of household the chief priest, worshipping incessantly, at every meal and on every occasion of any importance. This relentless domestic worship, so taken for granted that we rarely see it, is the true basis of pagan religious sentiment. Central to it was worship at the hearth fire, tended perhaps by the daughters of the household. Offerings from each meal were placed here by Romans and doubtless by many other Indo-European peoples. Other, less technically and materially advanced, nations may not have had little idols like the Romans, though they might have made them of dough or rags, such as the *Indiculus* envisages (Chapter 8); or they might have humble wooden figures such as the Norwegians kept into the nineteenth century to bring fertility and luck to their houses. North European pagans called them by a plethora of diddy names, often taking care, for instance, to leave them a saucer of milk.[14] These are the tip of an iceberg of spirits worshipped locally, domestically and in the fields. And if we were to visit a pagan house, maybe we should not be surprised to meet a sacred snake either – they are found from Minoan Crete to Lithuania: '*Of the snakes, or as they themselves call them Puken, kept in their houses, with every manner of good thing brought to them, so that they will make them rich*' (section heading in Paul Einhorn's account of Lithuanian paganism, *LPG* 474 f.).

PRIESTS AND GOVERNMENT

Dumézil and his many followers have supposed a priestly function was present and, indeed, dominated the hierarchy of classes (or ideas) in proto-Indo-European society. This theory has its foundation in the observation of the Indian and Iranian departments of Indo-European and is quickly sketched by Bruce Lincoln:

> the tripartite social system that hardened into the Indian and Iranian systems of social class (Skt. *várṇa-*; Av. *piština-*) was already well-established among the Indo-Iranians. This system separated priests, warriors, and commoners and ranked them hierarchically in that order. The priests were placed at the head of the social system, above kings, warriors, and all others, and their position seems to have been hereditary.
>
> Lincoln 1981: 60

Whatever one thinks of Dumézil's theories and their verifiability, it remains an interesting part of his analysis that the priestly and the kingly are tightly associated. In this section I look at the relationship of priests to secular authority. Are priests kings? Are they hand-in-hand with kings? Are they a separate oligarchy from the ruling oligarchy? Or is it just the same oligarchy wearing different, usually pointed, hats?

King-priests

In a number of historical European cases the king appears to retain what we might regard as an extraordinary amount of sacral power and actually is a priest. What, for instance, was a *lauchma* (Latin *lucumo*) among the Etruscans? The twelve of them in the times of legend had the discipline of haruspicy dictated to them by one Tages; and their number gives the impression that they are the leaders of the twelve constituent towns of the Etruscans. *Lucumo* also is the name of the (Etruscan) King of Rome Tarquinius Priscus *before he became king* at Rome (Livy 1.34). Another source says *lucumo* is the title of the Etruscan kings. It seems that this can only add up to one thing: *lucumo* is the sacred title of the Etruscan king, as inheritor of the Etruscan divinatory doctrine.

Perhaps something of this was left among the Thracians, who lived north of Greece, in a swathe of land including modern Bulgaria. 'Until Classical times the Thracians lived in open villages; only in Roman times was urban civilization developed.'[15] This is the sort of society where we would be surprised to find a developed priesthood and certainly the evidence we have is remarkably silent about any Thracian priests. Kings seem still to have performed priestly functions or at least that seems to be what underlies the comment of Polyainos (7.22) that 'priests of Hera' were chieftains among the Kebrenioi and Skaiboiai. Even as late as Trajan (98–117), a Greek historian, Kriton, interpreted this combination of functions as a cunning ploy:[16] 'The kings of the Getai, instilling superstition and concord in them through trickery and showmanship, aim at great things' (Kriton, *FGH* 200F7). Such a performance had also been put in by Vologaises, the leader of the insurgent Bessoi against Rome in 12 BC and 'priest of Dionysos' (Cassius Dio 54.34).

Goths and Irish had their priests, but traces remain of the sacrality of the king. The Gothic king was credited with a magical charisma (Wolfram 1988: 108). The Irish *ard rí* was sacred enough to be hedged in with specific sets of *geisi* (taboos):[17] for instance, the King of Tara might not let the sun rise on him in Tara, break a journey on a Wednesday at Mag Breg, travel over Mag Cuilinn after sunset, and so on. Even the four lesser kings were subject to their own *geisi*.

Turning to Greece, the two kings of Sparta had particular religious duties. Elsewhere in Greece,[18] as in Rome, kings had gone by historical times, but the abolition of the monarchy had called into existence particular magistrates to replace them whose sole duty it was to officiate at certain rites:

So kings in ancient times held complete power over matters in the city, at home and abroad; but later, whether the kings themselves gave up their powers or the masses took them away, in most other cities [other than Sparta] sacrifices were all that was left to the kings.

Aristotle, *Politics* 3.14 (1285b 13–17)

In Athens we find the *basileus archon* ('king magistrate') and at Ephesos 'even today his [Androklos'] descendants are called kings and have certain privileges: front seating at games, purple robes – a mark of the royal family – a staff instead of a sceptre, and [control of] the rites of Eleusinian Demeter' (Strabo 14.1.3). This type of development is also found at Rome, where the *rex sacrorum* ('king [in the matter] of rites') is all that is left of the former kings, and, further afield, even among the Sumerians, where the *en* (king) gave way to *en*-priests and priestesses chosen from the royal family.[19]

The king must have been as impressive as he was powerful. His special status may have had as a corollary a certain grade-inflation suggesting that there was something divine about him.[20] It has been argued (Walcot 1963) that the Mycenaean (Bronze Age Greek) king had a claim to divinity comparable with – and maybe influenced by – that of the Egyptian pharaoh. It has also, however, been argued that in the case of Greek culture and Greek mythology, the sacred role of kings was taken up in a sort of propaganda as the institution of kingship faded. Seer-kings were then inscribed into myths – for instance, the archetypal seer Melampous, about whom a late heroic poem was written.[21]

Kings and priests

The king is a figure apart and usually, however far back we go, we find a separate priest or priests associated with him, but distinct from him. Among the Getai, Strabo tells us there was an institution of a priest called 'god' who advised the king (7.3.5). In later times Goths are referred to under this name, something which is usually thought to be a confusion and a mistake. I am not so sure: it is among the Germans that the name of 'priests' at times comes close to that of 'gods' – for example, the Gothic *gudja*. These Getai are surely Goths[22] and their god-priests go back very far; indeed, as long ago as 339 BC (the account dates from *c.* AD 100):

As a result the gates were suddenly flung open and the priests of the Goths who used to be called 'gods'[23] came out to meet them with citharas and white garments, singing to their native gods in suppliant tones that they should be kind to them and drive back the Macedonians.

Dio of Prusa (Dio 'Chrysostom'), *FGH* 707F3,
in Jordanes, *Getica* 10.65

What were these priests doing in a town, Odessos (Varna, on the Black Sea coast of Bulgaria), whose 'gates' could be 'flung open'? Does the town supply the environment for priesthood to develop and thrive?

This brings us to the vexed question of the priesthood of the Germans, a people well known not to live in cities (Tacitus, *Germania* 16.1): 'The Germans differ considerably from this pattern [that of the Gauls]: they neither have druids to be in charge of ritual nor are they eager about sacrifices' (Caesar, *Gallic war* 6.21.1). Caesar denies a priestly class to the Germans, but he does not deny that they have individual priests. His view also, probably Poseidonios', is that among the Germans religion as a whole is less developed and foregrounded than it is in Gaul and he marks the differences from the Gaulish model:[24]

> They [the druids] attend rituals and deal with public and private sacrifices, and give guidelines on religious practice . . .
> The whole nation of Gauls is *specially devoted to religious practices* and for this reason those who have serious illnesses or who are involved in battles and dangers either sacrifice men in place of sacrificial victims or vow that they will so sacrifice, *and they use druids as the officials for these sacrifices.*
>
> *Ibid.* 6.13.4, 6.16.1–2

Nonetheless, Tacitus (*Germania* 7) mentions how in Germany punishments, tying up and flogging require the *authority* of the priests, not the kings, and how it is they who must call for silence at the bimonthly (new moon, full moon) meetings of the Thing. Furthermore, they are the only people authorised to bring their statues out of the groves into battle, clearly implying a warden function for the grove. Talking of ritual that would be conducted in the home by the *pater familias*, he says that when it is conducted publicly the *sacerdos civitatis* ('state priest') is required to perform it.

Though most scholars today would doubt the propriety of describing any German social structure as a *civitas* ('state'), nonetheless this does give a sense, which is supported elsewhere, of a singular, elevated 'priest', in this case also a *diviner*:

> They pay particular attention to auspices and lots. Their method for lots is straightforward: they cut off a branch from a fruit-bearing tree and chop it into sticks; they then distinguish the sticks by certain marks [the origin of runes?][25] and scatter them randomly and haphazardly on a white cloth. Next, if it is a public consultation the priest of the *civitas*, or if it is private the actual head of the household (*pater familiae*), prays to the gods and looking up to the sky picks up single sticks three times. Once they

are picked up, he interprets them according to the mark that had
previously been put on them.

Tacitus, *Germania* 10.1

The 'state priest', the single key priest, of the highest standing, reappears
in later periods. So Ammianus Marcellinus (28.5.14) reports: 'The most
important priest among the Burgundians [also Germanic] is called
"Sinistus" [evidently the Burgundian for "Oldest"] and holds the post
for life, threatened, like the kings, by no changes.' *Sinista* is also used by
Ulfila to translate *presbyter* ('elder/priest') into Gothic.[26] King and priest
come close together in Jordanes' account of the Goths when he states that
both kings and priests belong to the *pilleati*: the *pilleus* is a type of felt
cap, a sign of the ruling class, where the mass of the population went
bareheaded.[27] In Rome, too, it was a sign of some religious officials, the
flamines and apparently the *haruspices*[28] (as well as of mere freedmen) and
we might just be in the presence of Indo-European costume. Much later
again we come across the English priest Coifi, instrumental beside King
Edwin of Northumbria in the conversion to Christianity, and the 'state
priest', if ever there was one.

Pagan Slavonic priests are not at all well known to us,[29] but they existed
and, according to Helmold (1.108 (2.12)), they had an importance exceeding even that of the king: 'Their king is of moderate importance in
comparison with the *flamen*. The latter seeks responses and investigates
the outcome of lots. He depends on the decision of the lots, but the king
and people depend on his decision.' This is, however, a somewhat tendentious reading of the dynamics of lottery and really states little more
than the obvious. It is, in the end, a variation on the conceit of Tacitus
(*Germania* 10, below) attributing importance to horses. All the same, the
stress on a singular priest comparable in authority with the king repro-
duces the Edwin and Coifi model, or the 'state priest' model which Tacitus
attributes to the Germans.

Oligarchy in Gaul – 'no sacrifice without a philosopher'

Once societies start turning from kingship to oligarchy, the question arises
of how sacred power is to be wielded. In medieval Iceland the forty or so
priestly *godar* actually became its rulers. But perhaps a more normal
expectation would be that they adopted Aristotle's structure: 'the leadership of the city is divided into priests and magistrates' (*Politics* 7.12,
1331b4 f.). This appears to be the case for the Gaulish druids, but as
our understanding of them is dependent on how we read Poseidonios'
account of the whole system of Gaulish priests, it is there that we had
better start.

Poseidonios had evidently declared, as Strabo, Diodoros and Ammianus (who got it from Timagenes) tell us:

Among all the Gauls, just about, there are three classes [*phyla*,
'tribes'] which are especially revered: *bardoi, wateis* and *druidai*.
The bards specialise in hymns and poems, the *wateis* in sacred
ritual and accounts of natural science [*physiologoi*], the druids in
addition to natural science also practise moral philosophy. They
are considered the most just and for this reason they are entrusted
with private and public judgements . . . They – and the others –
also say that souls and the kosmos are indestructible and that one
day fire and water will supervene.

Strabo 4.4.4

There are among them also poets of songs whom they call *bardoi*.
These, singing with instruments like lyres, hymn some people and
foulmouth others. And there are certain philosophers and theo-
logians [*theologoi*], exceedingly revered, whom they call *druidai*.
And they also use diviners [*manteis*, a Greek word] considering
them worth great attention. These foretell the future by bird-
watching and through the sacrifice of victims and have the whole
population under their control. Particularly when they are dealing
with great matters, they have a surprising and incredible practice.
Sprinkling a man, they strike him with a sword above the dia-
phragm and as the stricken man falls they gain an idea of the
future from the way he falls, how the limbs collapse and also from
the flow of blood, having confidence in an ancient and time-
honoured observation of these details. It is further their custom
that no-one may perform sacrifice without a philosopher.

Diodoros of Sicily 5.31

As these men gradually became civilised, there grew strong
among them the study of praiseworthy doctrines, begun by bards
and *euhageis* [Greek for 'pious', but probably a mistake in transcription for *wateis*] and druids. Bards sang the brave deeds of
illustrious men composed in heroic verses with the sweet melodies
of the lyre. The *euhageis* examining . . . [*the manuscript makes no
sense here*] and tried to set forth the loftiness of nature. The
druids, more elevated in their genius and devoted to association
with their colleagues, as the authority of Pythagoras decreed,
were raised up by research into secret and lofty matters and,
looking down upon things human, pronounced souls immortal.

Ammianus Marcellinus 15.9.8 (Timagenes?, *FGH* 88F2)

These authorities are not multiple independent witnesses, but regurgita-
tors of a single witness and a single philosophical mind, that of
Poseidonios. The latter, a Dumézil *avant la lettre*, identified and privileged
three classes, though his terms for them and his emphasis on training do
receive some support from later Irish tradition with its *bard, faith* and
drui.[30] The life of bards might not be very different from that of seers:[31] as
Bremmer (1996b: 102) says of Greek poets and seers, they 'were dependent on kings, were inspired, led itinerant lives, were often represented as
blind, and pretended to possess supernatural knowledge'. The Gaulish
bards evidently *remember* and elaborate oral tradition and show us what
had happened to the epic lineage that led in Greek culture to Homer and
in Serbian to *guslars* like Radovan Karadjić. The philosophers, without
whom no sacrifice can take place,[32] are a wonderful mirage imposed on
Gaulish culture by a Poseidonios no less fascinated by the appalling
barbarisms of which this society was capable – divination by human
sacrifice, or the nailing up of heads we saw in Chapter 1. They are
'Pythagorean' because Pythagoras' most distinctive doctrine was that
the soul is immortal. So what we can extract from Poseidonios is that
there were, at least, two classes of priest: augurs-diviners (*wateis*) and
druids who superintend sacrifice, undergo training in the tradition which
they preserve, and exercise particular social authority. In Roman terms
the *wateis* are the college of augurs and the druids the college of *pontifices*.

Wateis is evidently the same as the Latin *vates*, a rather olde-worlde
word denoting a prophet or a seer, but in any case implying some inspiration: the Gothic word is *wods*, 'frenzied, possessed', as in the Germanic
Wodan or the daemonic *Wütende Heer* that is let loose at Yule (Chapter
13). *Vates* is also a term appropriated by Augustan poets to dignify their
calling.

The word 'druid', which must have been **druis* (plural **druides*), invites
etymology and learned guesswork. If we assume that the word is built
from roots inherited from Indo-European, then it looks very much as
though this is a compound word of which the second element is **weid*,
'know', a root which is sometimes found among religious specialists,
particularly when they have a divining function, as we shall see later in
this chapter. But *what* do druids know?

Dru-, according to Thurneysen and recently Le Roux and Guyonvarc'h,
was allegedly an intensive prefix, so that a *druid* is very knowing – and
Drunemeton, uncomfortably, is an arch-shrine.[33] A second possibility was
suggested long before the age of critical scholarship, to all appearances by
Poseidonios:

> The druids – that is what they call their *magi* – consider nothing
> more sacred than mistletoe and the tree on which it grows,
> provided it is an oak. Indeed, they seek out oak groves on their

own account and do not perform any rites without oak leaves, so that according to the Greek interpretation it may seem that this is how they got the name 'druids' [i.e. from Greek *drys*, 'oak']. In fact, they think that whatever grows on the oaks has been sent from heaven and is a sign that the tree has been chosen by the god himself.

Pliny the elder, *Natural history* 16.249

It might seem poor method to interpret Gaulish from Greek (Pliny does not particularly back the interpretation) and perhaps it reminds us also of the *Semnones* who are the most revered (Greek *semnoi*)[34] of the Germans. However, this same root is in fact found in Celtic languages (*derwo-*, as in the placename 'Derry') and the interpretation is not impossible; *druneme-ton* is, then, entirely plausibly, a 'cult place with oaks/trees', i.e. one of Pliny's oak groves.[35] The loss of the 'e' probably falls under the standard rules for Indo-European (see n.35 for this technical point) and, short of the druid being an expert in skinning or stripping (**der*),[36] the tree/oak root is one of only two possibilities.

The other possibility goes back, it seems, to Indo-European metaphor: 'The hardness and solidity of oak wood may have given rise to the range of notions "true", "firm", "steadfast"' (Gamkrelidze and Ivanov 1995: i.526). And it does appear that, for instance, our word 'true' goes back to the same root as 'tree' (**derw-*). In Celtic languages both meanings are found and consequently it is impossible for us looking at Gaulish, or indeed for a Gaul speaking it, to distinguish between 'oak-expert' and 'truth-knower'[37] as the meaning of 'druid'. So both *oak* and *true* are valid for speakers of the language and it is not for us to dismiss the inevitable associations of the two by sternly dismissing 'false' etymologies. Finally, more subjectively, the word looks as though it was originally put together in Indo-European rather than Celtic and it may therefore be very archaic, though of course not necessarily in origin denoting the institution of druiddom as the Gauls had it.

Roman *pontifices* could sit as a panel of judges, religious magistrates, to determine points of sacred law. They decided what was *fas* (religiously right), as opposed to *ius* (legally right). The druids hold a very similar position, except that they appear to make less distinction between *fas* and *ius* – *mat* (Chapter 10), it seems, covered everything:

They attend divine rites, manage public and private sacrifices, and are authorities on religious observance. A large number of youths come eagerly to them in order to learn, and they [the druids] are greatly respected by them. They decide in just about all public and private disputes and they also make the decision if a crime has been committed, a murder done, or if there is a dispute over inheritance or territory, and in addition determine the rewards and penalties. And if either a private individual or a people does not comply with their decision, they ban them from sacrifices – which is the most serious penalty they have.

Caesar, *Gallic war* 6.13.4–6

Such knowledge requires long training and in the case of druids it got it – twenty years in some cases according to Caesar.[38] This may have been quite a widespread model, to judge also by Germanic culture. There, too, according to Grimm (1875: i.73) *ê(w)a* represented both *fas* and *ius*. From it is derived an '*ewa*-guardian', Old English *aeweweard*[39] (Old High German *êwart* or *êwarto*), and, more judicial, an '*êwa*-speaker', Old Saxon *êosago* (Old High German *êsago*).

In any case, the druids are *rememberers*, of all sorts of traditions, poetic, doctrinal, medicinal, and *advisors* both on the basis of divination and on legal matters. And they come close to the Roman *pontifices*, no casual comparison. The Roman pontificate was an expression of power and was reserved for the Roman aristocracy (as was the augurate). The druids represented a power structure which the Romans had not encountered before, though it strangely mirrored their own at home. In particular its strength derived from its being a *free* priesthood with some collegiate sense, not safely quarantined to local shrines and deities. We shall doubt-less never quite recover the motivation the Romans had for the abolition of the druids – the version for public consumption focused on human sacrifice – but the effect was the abolition of the *free* priesthood and the inevitable consequence, which writers ancient and modern have failed to notice, the elevation in importance of the *tied* priesthood. This latter must already have been in existence, even though Poseidonios apparently did not register it, because of the foundation since around 300 BC of great sanctuaries (Brunaux 1996: 27). Now, an increase in wealth, due to European integration, promoted the building of shrines and temples which in turn demanded further personnel. Their name will emerge below, under the 'Temple priests' section.

So an influential, culturally dominant sacred oligarchy, comparable in status with the magistrates and rulers of the Celtic states – sometimes even supplying one, as in the case of Divitiacus – was displaced with the advance of Roman power. The parallel oligarchy model was finished and would not be restored until the rise of the bishops of medieval Europe.

Oligarchy at Rome

The government of the Roman Republic ('509 BC' to, say, 31 BC), whatever the outward constitutional forms, was oligarchic, involving the control of effective power by a tiny aristocracy at Rome itself. This aristocracy simultaneously occupied all priesthoods, which were perceived as a matter of extra status and privilege for ambitious individuals and not as vehicles for professional lifetime devotion. The priesthoods themselves were tightly organised. The pontifical college may originally have consisted of the three major *flamines* (of Jupiter, Mars, Quirinus) and the twelve minor *flamines*, tied priests. Established before a temple culture, these *flamines* were assigned to gods, not to particular temples, though their gods are often obscure. If we look for cult-sites, it is only by antiquarian speculation that we can reach some possibilities – perhaps of groves inside and just outside the city. The obscure *flamen Furrinalis* is evidently the priest of Furrina whose grove lay on the Janiculum and whose annual festival, presumably celebrated in the grove, was the Furrinalia on 25 July.[40] He looks like the priest of the grove. It is also possible that the cult-place of Pomona, the Pomonal in the Ager Solonius between Rome and Ostia, was itself a grove (like the Fagutal of Jupiter) of fruit trees and the *flamen Pomonalis* would be in charge of it.[41] These are certainly archaic priest-hoods, as we shall see presently from the taboos on the *flamen Dialis*.

The way in which the Roman oligarchy responded to the proliferation of temples, on the Greek model, was usually not to institute priests, but simply to extend the oligarchic board of religious management, the number of *pontifices* without specific portfolios. The *pontifex* is the aristocratic member of an oligarchic board of *free* priests (literally, a 'bridge-maker', Chapter 3) and is multi-functional: he is a *rememberer*, an *advisor* and indeed *authority* on whether a course of action is *fas*, a *performer* and, through his staff, a *warden*. A more specific term for a warden is *aeditu(m)us* ('temple-person'). Normally this is a minor *tied* official, but interestingly it turns up in late antiquity as a post, the *aedituus Beleni*, of which an antiquarian Gaul may be proud, on which more below.[42] If, however, we want an *interpreter* of anything other than divine law, we must turn to various diviners – *augures* or, less authorised, *haruspices* (see below on 'Divination'). For the detailed execution of religious rituals, another board, originally of two men, finally of fifteen, was established: the *IIviri* or *XVviri sacris faciundis* and these were also the officials who consulted the Sibylline Books for the Senate and recommended innovations in religious practice. Thus, the Senate, the body through which the oligarchy operated, managed the state apparatus of religion and its calendar of ancient festivals. It was at once a secular and a sacred body.

Rome is very distant from the Greek temple-culture model (below). In Latin *sacerdos* is usually thought of as the basic term for 'priest'. It is an ancient term, given that its second element (*-dot-*) can only be explained from the prehistory of the language,[43] and in origin means 'one who disposes *sacra* (things holy)'. Perhaps this *performer* was generally a subordinate figure of whom we hear little before the same term comes to be applied to *foreign* (Greek-style) priests. In this use, as the equivalent of the Greek *hiereus*, the word is not used very often before the Empire[44] and, when used, tends to be applied to the *tied* priest of a god at a particular temple, as we see in this second-century BC Roman play set in the Greek city of Cyrene:

AMPELISCA: Is this, please, the *fanum* of Venus?
PTOLEMOCRATIA: It is. And I am the *sacerdos* of this *fanum*.

Plautus, The Rope 284 f.

TEMPLE PRIESTS, GROVE PRIESTS

Greece

The classic model for the temple priest is the Greek. The Greeks of historical times built temples as copiously as any nation. Indeed, groves as a result are so certain to contain temples that we do not hear of priests of temple-less groves. Each temple was dedicated to a specific divinity, more rarely to two or more, and each and every temple would have at least a priest or priestess. At the same time, anything that is done by a Greek priest can in principle be done by someone else with sufficient authority – for instance, a magistrate or a general. Indeed, so baffling is the needlessness of Greek priests that Burkert has provocatively described Greek religion as 'almost a religion without priests'.[45] At this point a Hindu view helps, one not so different from the Greek view once you subtract the scriptures that the Greeks – and ancient pagans universally – did not have: 'When a priest presides the rite will be more elaborate and in accord with scriptural prescription than when a head of household officiates. Rites without a priest are not invalid, but are less prestigious' (S. Weightman, in Hinnells 1985: 218). The priest was an honoured figure in Greek society, whether he gained the post by election, lottery (let the god decide), purchase (a contract with a view to such perks as hides of sacrificial animals) or, much more rarely, inheritance. He must have looked magnificent in his white (sometimes purple) costume, long hair and staff. The priestess, allowed to wander the streets no more than any other Greek woman, was seen only in the context of rituals where she might represent the goddess she served – with shield and helmet, or carry the sacred goatskin of Athene, the *aegis*.[46]

There is a wealth of information, especially from inscriptions, about what priests did – enough to write a book on (and it is time someone did). The priest is the Aristotelian manager of the temple and its resources: he or she does the cleaning or more likely directs it after the mess of sacrifice and has the authority to determine where all those gifts will be stored and who may sacrifice when, what and how. If it is important the priest may conduct the sacrifice in person and utter the correctly worded prayer. This is less onerous than it sounds: the shrine may, after all, be open only one day a year for the annual festival. At oracular shrines the business will occupy more of the year (though Delphi closed down for three months at winter, while Apollo spent time among the fabulous northern race of Hyperboreans) and it will require a correspondingly greater staff to manage answers and assist arrivals who do not know the local rules. At Delphi the Pythia, Apollo's priestess, will even be required to enter a trance (a delicate thing which on one occasion killed a priestess who was not in the mood) – but that is exceptional. Priestesses, however, were not in themselves uncommon, particularly in a country with so many female divinities. Thus there was a priestess of Athene at Athens, and a priestess of Hera at Argos, whose tenure was the basis for counting years in some older Greek systems. Children, too, might be 'priests', particularly for a year as they approached adulthood. Children and old women (as at Delphi) were free of sexual taint.

Greek 'priests' perform a variety of tasks and have a correspondingly various list of names, of which I give some samples here.[47] The *hiereus* or (feminine) *hiereia* is one who deals with *hiera,* things holy, primarily sacrifices. *Kleidouchoi* ('key-holders') hold the keys of sacred buildings and this large key is in itself a grand display item. *Hiereus, hiereia* and key-holders go back to the Bronze Age Mycenaean texts.[48] Further wardens include such people as *nāophylakes* and *neokoroi* ('temple-guardians/attendants'). Beyond these we hear of persons appointed for particular duties by the state (cf. Aristotle above): such are the *hieropoioi*, whose job it is to organise sacrifices and the disposal of the carcasses, and various managers (*epimeletai*) and sacred finance officers (*hierotamiai*). Other cults might need further specialists: for the Mysteries at Eleusis, there was not only a *hiereia* of the goddesses twain (Demeter and Kore-Persephone) but the 'sacred announcer', *hierokeryx*, the torch-bearers (*dadouchoi*) and, most important of all, the 'revealer of the holies' (*hierophant*), who conducted the great mystic ceremony and, the supreme illumination of the Eleusinian Mysteries, in a flash of blinding light, so it is said, waved an ear of corn. Beyond all these lay the various authoritative 'interpreters' of religious requirements (the *exegetai*), dream-interpreters (*oneirokritai*), and old-fashioned or legendary seers (*manteis*) and their more modern counterparts, oracle-mongers (*chresmologoi*) and liver-examiners (*hepatoscopoi*).

Germans

Among the Germans we have seen slender but persuasive evidence for a state priest. Tied priests are naturally even more difficult to find, as we required settled religious sites dedicated to particular gods. One such is the cult of Nerthus which we have seen (Chapter 9) on an island somewhere in the region of Schleswig-Holstein and Pomerania, possibly even, as Gibbon thought, the island of Rügen, a predecessor to the later cults of the Pomeranian Slavs. There the priest 'realises when the goddess is present in the shrine', implying that he is in charge of the calendar, and processes with her ox-cart. He is the priest of a named goddess in a particular grove, operating within a festival pattern which would be familiar to Greeks, but for the human sacrifice. This model recurs in the 'ancient grove' among the remote eastern German Nahanarvali (or Naharvali).[49] That grove belongs to the Alci,[50] divine twins on the Indo-European pattern (the Greek pair are the Dioskouroi), and its ceremonies are conducted by a transvestite priest (*Germania* 43). Transvestism is a marker of 'difference' among religious specialists, found commonly among shamans and, possibly as a survival of this Germanic sort of culture, in Lapland;[51] perhaps, then, the priest of the Alci is not only a performer, warden, rememberer and authority, but a rare instance of a *showman*. This site, maybe the communal shrine of the Lugii group of tribes, may in fact be at Mount Sobótka (Zobten in German) in Silesia, south-west of Wrocław (Breslau), mentioned by Thietmar as a centre of pagan veneration.[52] If so, we can see, as possibly in the case of Rügen, almost a millennium of pagan continuity from the Germans of Tacitus' day to the Slavs of 1017, and a continuation from there on into more modern Christian worship. The word 'sobótka' in fact refers to St John's fire, the fire lit at summer-solstice ceremonies, something which we frequently see cross the pagan–Christian divide. Given the persistence of pagan holy places, it may be that we should view these two dedicated groves and their priestly attendants not so much as part of 'Germanic' culture, but as part of an areal culture which later Baltic and Slavonic religions bring more consistently to our notice.

Remaining evidence for tied priests in Germanic culture is found in particular elements of vocabulary. An OHG *parawari* must look after a *paro*, a type of sacred grove (OE, *bearo*). An OHG *harugari* looks after a *harug*, a shrine (Chapter 7), as does an OE *herigweard*, of which we hear once.[53] There were other Germanic terms for priests, too, some of them old enough to be shared between OHG and OE and therefore to antedate the arrival of the English in Britain. Most broadly, the priest may be a 'godsman' (OE *godesman*, MHG *gotesman*) or similar simple term, thought possibly to underlie Tacitus' vague *ministri deorum* ('servants of the gods', *Germania* 10.2).[54] Even simpler equivalents are the Gothic *gudja*, used by Ulfila to represent 'priest' in the New Testament, and the later Old Norse *goði* – so that the priest of the *fanum* is the *hofgoði*, responsible for the building (*hof*) and for the organisation of the sacrificial feasts. The priest may also, as *performer*, be named after 'sacrifice': if a sacrifice in OHG is *bluostar*, he is therefore a *bluostari*. This translates the Latin *sacerdos* well, maybe too well: was it simply *invented* by the

Figure 12.1 A Christian church at the top of Mount Sobótka today. Photo: Terry
Slater, School of Geography, The University of Birmingham

glossary in which the word is found for just that purpose? Certainly, it is a
late formation (de Vries 1956: i.§277). This is in fact a danger in working
with mere vocabulary – that it had no application except to translate the
concepts of other cultures. So, if the *Heliand*, an Old Saxon poem written
between 822 and 840, presents a *wihes ward*, guardian of the *wēoh* (in this

case a temple),[55] does it follow that there were any temples, or guardians of them, or that, if there were, they were called *wihes wardas*? If Zachariah is the only attested *aeweweard*, were there any *aeweweards* at all, or is the translator struggling to render Judaic concepts in Anglo-Saxon? Another hopeless case is the alleged Lithuanian *blûtekirl*, 'sacrifice man': he is found once, sacrificing, needless to say, in an OHG rhyming chronicle about Lithuania, but the word is plainly not Lithuanian and seems to be in fact Old Swedish! What on earth is it evidence for?[56]

Gauls

For a culture according to popular literature so devoted to groves, it is remarkable that in Gaul there is no adequate evidence for priests whose function it is to manage specific groves.[57] But if it is the case, as we have argued, that the tied priesthood was a later development in Gaulish religion and that it benefited from Roman repression of the oligarchic free priesthood, then we can make some sense of the rise of the *gutuatros* (Latinised as *gutuater*).[58] This priest is known from four inscriptions from mid-France, dating, of course, from after the abolition of the druids, three from Saône-et-Loire (two at Autun, one at Mâcon), and a third from Le Puy-en-Velay (Haute-Loire, 130 kilometres south-east of Clermont).[59] The Mâcon inscription is obscure but is dedicated to a person who appears to have been the *gutuatros* either of an unknown 'god Moltinus' (whose name seems to mean 'mutton'!) or of the god Mars Ultor, but in either case a *tied* priesthood. The Le Puy inscription gives us a more functional '*gutuatros* of festivals' as though it were his sacred duty to arrange them. The term is also known, before the abolition of the druids, from Aulus Hirtius' completion of Caesar's *Gallic war* (8.38), but Hirtius thinks wrongly that it is someone's name – it cannot have been in the Poseidonian textbook! It is therefore no surprise that it is hard to relate him to Poseidonios' three classes of (*free*) professionals, though the attempt has been made: because Hirtius' *gutuatros* (but none of the others!) is found in the vicinity of the Carnutes and druids met there, he has been alleged to be an alias for a druid, perhaps when engaged in some particular activity; even by the standards of paganism this is a feeble argument. The *gutuatros* is plainly a distinctive post to be proclaimed on an inscription. The natural supposition is that the *gutuatros* belongs to the organised temple culture which continued to rise in importance after the loss of the druid–oligarchic model. He is, I think, what Ausonius calls an *aedituus* (above) and represents an assimilation of Celtic religious practice to that of such safer subject races as the Greeks. In origin it is likely that he would be a more minor and specific priest (an *aedituus* to the druid's *pontifex*) with special responsibility for the ritual at a particular centre. Etymology helps us not at all.[60]

DIVINATION

Divination can be conducted by individuals for their own convenience and that of their families, by self-appointed professionals or by publicly recognised individuals or groups.

It is the attempt to discover information or at least obtain guidance by supernatural means and those who profess to be able to do so are diviners. If divination is not a complete sham, for it is delusion to suppose that any valid divination exists, its practitioners operate according to a system of symbols and 'read' the significance indicated by those symbols in accordance with tradition. These symbol systems belong to particular restricted areas, 'languages', if you like. Diviners who judge from the behaviour of birds and in particular their flight are, strictly, *augurs*. Diviners who extract the liver from a barely sacrificed animal and read its zones practise *hepatoscopy* in Greek or *haruspicy* in Latin. In the Greek world there was a long list of languages of divination, some of which rather defeat the imagination – like divining by cheese or by a sieve. More scientific, at least in the technical knowledge the diviner must amass before making the appropriate false statements, is *astrology*. Less scientific

Figure 12.2 Divining by inspection of inner organs – 'haruspicy'

245

are German instances of divination from horses (*hipposcopy?*) or from chopped twigs (below). *Oracles* are the shrines where enquirers may pose questions of the non-existent god and receive *responses* (loosely themselves also called 'oracles').[61] The responses are generated in any divinatory manner – for instance, from the rustling of the leaves of the Oak of Zeus at Dodona. Information may also be received in dreams, particularly if one sleeps in the appropriate sacred site, the practice of incubation. Mostly, under such circumstances, the dream will deliver the information 'straight' and the indirectness requisite of divination is supplied by receiving the information or instructions in sleep-mode. But dreams may also be symbolic, as they were later for Freud, and for these purposes Greek consultants existed, *oneirokritai* or 'dream-interpreters', whose methods we may learn from instances of interpretation which we meet in ancient literature and above all in the wonderful *Oneirokritika*, a bookful of interpretations, by Artemidoros, which will tell you what it means if you dream of tortoises or cabbage.

A different mode of indirectness is *altered consciousness*: the prophet, or rather prophetess, may become possessed and utter the god's truths as a result of this condition. In reality the priestess of Apollo at Delphi practised such possession and in myth we learn of Sibyls who are possessed by Apollo and of Cassandra, the prophetess doomed never to be believed because she would not be sexually possessed by Apollo. The results might be rather incoherent or 'off-the-wall' and were transcribed, suitably modified, by (expert) male interpreters.

In Greece there was a whole industry of bogus diviners and professionals who travelled from door to door or marketplace to marketplace making a living out of divination, even the *chresmologoi* ('oracle-tellers') with their own private books of oracles, i.e. 'responses' ready for your individual circumstances. But the more interesting question is that of official adoption, of the authorisation of divination. In Greece, it seems in early times to have been routine to employ a seer (*mantis*) or bird-watcher (*oionopolos*) if you were leading an army, as frequently was done by kings, and by the magistrates or generals that replaced them. Diviners, too, might be consulted on the foundation of a colony, as they were for the Athenian colony at Thurii in southern Italy. But Greece had a Thatcherite view of divination: it was something you bought in from consultants when you needed it, there were no state seers. For the largest and most difficult questions, states consulted major oracles such as Delphi.

Rome was more organised, hierarchical and archaic. The state, in historical times the Senate, controlled divination tightly. Raving prophetesses had no place, except for the mythical Sibyl who had entrusted her Greek verses to a book which could be kept under lock and key and consulted when the Senate said so by a board of men. Approved divination came from the college of *augurs*, a state institution. They would mark out areas of the sky and watch for bird-flight; or, the portable version, they might observe the behaviour of chickens carried round in cages – do they eat lustily? The investigation of the livers of sacrificed animals was thought of as foreign and, when required, the expert *haruspices* were summoned from neighbouring Etruria (Tuscany). The Greeks learnt the skill from the Near East and the Etruscans from them, or more probably direct.[62] They certainly took it seriously, to judge by the Piacenza liver, a bronze model liver with markings very similar to Near Eastern teaching models.[63] There was also a private version of these *haruspices* whom Cato the elder in the early second century BC banned his estate-manager from consulting (*De agri cultura* 5.4). But by the end of the Republic there was already an official college of sixty *haruspices* and by the end of antiquity inspection of the liver had become a routine, formal part of pagan Roman sacrifice.

Divining seems to be particularly characteristic of eastern, underdeveloped, Europe. Tacitus stresses the interest of Germans in divining ('no-one consults auspices and lots so much', 10.1) as opposed to their relative *insouciance* about sacrifice and formal religion. They chop up sticks, mark them and throw them over a cloth. Lots in their various forms are very persistent in German paganism and lend some substance to Christian condemnation of *sortilegi* ('lot-casters').[64] They also interrogate the cries and flying patterns of birds, and in post-Roman times we find terms for bird-experts (Latin, *augurs*) such as *fogalari* ('fowler', and cf. German *Vogel*, 'bird') and *fogalwiso*.[65] They would have a line in dream-interpretation, too (Wesche 1940: 72–4). But particularly un-Roman is that they keep horses for divination and heed their whinnying. Priests are mere 'ministers of the gods', whereas the horses share in the divine knowledge (10.2)! Remarkably, in a not very different part of the world nine centuries later, we find the temples at Rethra and Arkona both keeping horses for divination, though the method is somewhat different – which foot will it step forward over the crossed swords?[66] Lithuanians, too, would divine with horses.[67] In general the ability to provide a sort of oracle was an important factor in the success of the ambitious Pomeranian Slav shrines.

Knowledge is foregrounded in some names for religious experts, particularly among the Balts and Slavs. Jan Długosz tells us of a priest[68] 'who in their language was called a/the Znincz [from the root 'know'] and who issued falsities to supplicants consulting the divinity about the future, as though he had got this from the divinity' (Jan Długosz, *LPG* 139 (also, Clemen 1936: 105)).

More universally, Simon Grunau, a Dominican monk with an excess of imagination, constructs an entire history of the Prussians involving countless priests based on the root *waid-* (Indo-European *weid-*, 'know') – an archpriest called the *kirwaido* and various *waidler, waidlotten* and in the feminine (he was writing in German) *waidlinnen*.[69] Jouet lists the functions of Baltic priests as watching over sacred fires, practising sacrifice, preserving the liturgy, and stating the law – a blend of remembering, advising and performing characteristic also of druids. But Adam (4.16) is also impressed by divination: all their houses, he says of the Balts or Slavs who live in Kurland, are 'full of divine augurs and black magic'. And they also, like textbook pagans, deduced the fortunes of battle from the blood of human victims (*LPG* 115, Jouet 1989: 154).

PRIESTS AND RITUAL: A COMMON INDO-EUROPEAN INHERITANCE?

Most of the modern languages of Europe,[70] as well as some languages to the east (Hittite in Asia Minor, Persian, Sanskrit and its successor languages in India, even Tokharian in Chinese Turkestan), are much modified forms of an ancestral language spoken maybe around 3500 BC and maybe somewhere north of the Black Sea. This evolutionary schema, which had its heyday in the age of Darwin, is greeted today in some quarters with distrust and revisionism. The history of language, however, teaches us that the replacement of our *core* vocabulary and of the grammar of one language with that of another is not lightly or rapidly undertaken – languages are not borrowed like new technological or agricultural techniques.

Language is one constituent among others that make up a culture. So, for instance, there was also an Indo-European mythology, some traces of which can similarly be identified in the descendant cultures. A fairly clear case is the myth of twin horsemen rescuing their abducted sister/wife, which is transmuted, for instance, in Greek culture into the quest of Agamemnon and Menelaos to recover the latter's wife, Helen, the foundation of the Trojan War myth.[71] Myths, however, decay faster than language (glottochronologists calculate that the core vocabulary decays at the rate of around 20 per cent per 1000 years) and there are only a few examples. Priesthood and ritual are a no less important part of a culture and it is fair to ask whether we cannot identify common features in the descendant cultures that should be traced back to Indo-European. Here we have to be guided by the vocabulary, much as though we were asking whether the Indo-Europeans had birch trees or salmon and answering yes on the basis that the descendant cultures continue the same words for these items. If we do have common words in the area of priesthood and ritual, then that is *prima facie* evidence for the Indo-European existence of the things and acts named. If we do not, then either this is one of those areas where language has evolved or discovered new words to replace old for reasons that are not always accessible to us[72] or the concept to which the word attaches did not exist or at least not in the sense we understand it.

'Priest' is a difficult case. The only candidate is the word apparently underlying the Latin *flamen* and Sanskrit *brahman*, distant but convincing relatives – could this have been an Indo-European word, something like **bhladsmen*? If so, it might just – a long shot – contain the root that gives Germanic *blōtan*, 'worship by sacrifice'.[73] The equation between *flamen* and *brahman*, however, is particularly supported by cultural detail, in particular by the taboos that restricted them:

It is *religio* (taboo) for the *flamen Dialis* to ride a horse. It is also *religio* for him to see a 'girded order', i.e. an army bearing weapons, outside the *pomerium* [the religious city limits] and for that reason it is rare for a *flamen Dialis* to be appointed consul as wars are entrusted to consuls. Also, it is never *fas* for the *Dialis* to swear [an oath]. Also, it is not *fas* for him to use a ring, except if it has a gap and is broken. One may not bring fire from the *flaminia*, i.e. home of the *flamen Dialis*, except sacred fire. A chained person, if he enters his house, must be freed and the chains removed through the *impluvium* [central, open area in the roof for admitting rainwater] on to the tiles and let down from there out on to the street. He may have no knot on his *apex* [pointed hat] nor on his belt nor anywhere. If anyone is brought for flogging but throws himself a suppliant at his feet, it is *piaculum* [an offence requiring expiatory sacrifice] for him to be flogged that day. The hair of the *Dialis* no-one but a free man may cut. Goat and uncooked meat and ivy and beans, it is not *mos* [accepted custom] for the *Dialis* to touch or to name . . . the cuttings from the nails and hair of the *Dialis* must be covered with earth beneath a *felix* [fruitful] tree. Every day is a holy day for the Dialis. It is not permissible for him to be in the open air without his *apex*.

Gellius, *Attic nights* 10.15

This is the priest of Jupiter, the *flamen Dialis*, at Rome, the most senior figure in the state after the king and therefore comparable with the German 'state priest'. Gellius is an antiquarian, writing around AD 180, but his information is from authors going back to Fabius Pictor around 200 BC for whom these taboos were already desperately archaic. Even the adjective *Dialis*, 'belonging to Jupiter', is never used except of the *flamen*. There can be no doubt that this priesthood of the major Indo-European god has preserved intact taboos from remote antiquity, as can be seen from the systematic correspondence of the particular taboos on the *Dialis* with the taboos on Indian brahmans (Puhvel 1987: 156 f.). If the taboos are ancient, so is the priesthood that bears them.

About other nations we are not so well informed, but there are some revealing cases. The Northumbrian priest Coifi might not, because of his office, 'bear arms or, besides, ride a horse'.[74] And Gaulish druids were not required to be involved with wars, though some of them in fact were.[75]

The conclusion must be that there existed as a minimum a priest, a singular 'state priest' for each self-governing unit, who was not the king but had powers comparable with the king, himself a sacred figure, and who was subject to a large and specific range of taboos. In Chapter 10 we saw that there is some reason to suppose that there was time-reckoning, at the level of months, festivals and cycles of years, among the Indo-Europeans, and, in however rudimentary a way, there must have been a system of knowledge for supporting this. Likewise, in Chapter 14 we will find a large-scale assertion of the identity of a family of villages or tribes which also requires sacral organisation. On the other hand, there is no convincing evidence for a whole druid-like class of priests and apart from this *flamen*, there is little survival of the vocabulary for 'priest'. It may well be that, with the exception of this one priest, an apparatus of priests was not an organic part of Indo-European society and that priesthood was more subject to local variation. It was only a question of who was responsible for doing the *sacra*, the Latin *sacerdos* or Greek *hiereus* (above). That is what we would expect of a culture at approximately the Germanic level.

In appearance pagan priests tend to be distinctive and even to reverse norms. Egyptian priests cut their hair short and wore white linen. But there does seem to be some tendency to long hair and white robes among European priests. The priests of the Getai/Goths wore white, and so did the druids and the priests of Gerovit among the Slavs at Havelberg (100 kilometres north-west of Berlin).[76] The priest of Svantovit at Arkona let his hair and beard grow long, in striking contrast to the close-shaven, crop-haired local people and even to the statue of the god who had been carved in their fashion.[77] Greek priests let their hair grow long and wore white, or sometimes 'purple' clothing. Roman priests and magistrates wore white clothing with purple bands.

Turning to the environment in which any priests might have worked, the sacred itself is viewed in different ways. The descendant languages like to have two words for 'sacred', denoting the powerful and the set aside.[78] Maybe Indo-European distinguished between the following in some corresponding way:[79]

- *spent*: holy, possessing power (Avestan Persian *spenta*, Lithuanian *šventas*, Old Slavonic *svętu*, as in Svantovit)

250

- *yag: holy, respected?, demarcated? (Greek *hagios*, 'holy, Sanskrit *yajati*, 'sacrifices').

The object of worship is clearly a god in a polytheist system. A god was a *deiwos, though this word itself has been replaced in Baltic, Slavonic, Iranian and Greek languages.[80] And, turning to ritual, libation is comfortably attested, in no less than three forms:[81]

- *spend: to sprinkle a libation as a guarantee (Greek *spendo*, Hittite *šipant/išpant*; also Latin *spondeo*, 'solemnly promise')
- *leib: to drip a libation (Greek *leibo*, Latin *libo*)
- *ghew: to pour a libation, apparently into a fire (Greek *kheō*, Sanskrit *hau/ho*, as in *hotri*, a sacrificial priest; Latin *fundo* and Gothic *giutan*, 'pour').

Prayer, which accompanies libation or sacrifice, may generally not have been differentiated from other forms of asking but on occasion particularly solemn and powerful speech was called for – *wegh^w: to declare solemnly, to vow (Greek *eukhomai*, 'pray/boast', Latin *voveo*, 'vow', Vedic Sanskrit *vāghat*, 'making a vow to sacrifice' or just 'sacrifice'). Oddly, there seems to be no agreed term for the action or ceremony of sacrifice, which is what our priests should be performing, unless its last trace is left in the *bhladsmen and *blōtan, though we have already seen (Chapter 9) interesting instances of worshipping a god with a victim rather than sacrificing a victim to a god, which might just preserve an inherited grammar of sacrifice.[82] The sacrificial victim, however, and the feast you derive from it are preserved. The feast is a *dap- or *daHp- (Latin *daps*, 'sacrificial meal, Old Norse *tafn*, 'sacrificial victim', Tokharian A *tāp*, 'eat'), a word borrowed in earliest times from a Semitic language (Ugaritic *dbḥ*, 'sacrifice', Hebrew *zebaḥ*, 'sacrificial animal', proto-Semitic *ḏibḥ*, 'sacrifice/sacrificial animal').[83] The victim is, at least in Latin, Celtic and German (Chapter 9), something you bring or bear to the place, a 'to-bring', which you *ob-fero*, an *ob-latum* (oblation).

THE ROLE OF WOMEN

> *Handmaiden of the Lord, your journey would not be prosperous unless the bishop were to go with you, because demons very much lie in ambush for our sex.*
> Words of St Ita, in *Life of St Ita the virgin* xxiv[84]

In some European societies women are markedly excluded from religious service. At Rome the Vestal Virgins are in effect the sole native Roman priestesses. In Anglo-Saxon England there appears to be no trace of priestesses either in the language or in contemporary sources.[85] If we start from the view that there were indeed priestesses on the continent, then this could only represent a narrowing of approved religious specialism to men in Anglo-Saxon society, leaving only the less official areas of magic and witchcraft to women. However, it is doubtful whether there are any non-prophetic sacred women in the Germanic cultures and so Anglo-Saxon culture is not particularly out of line.

Partly this is a question of male domination of positions of perceived importance in the community. But it is also a reading of women's nature.

> Everyone regards women as the prime movers in superstition [i.e. overdoing religion]. They it is who stimulate men towards more extensive cult of the gods, festivals and appeals to the gods [*potniasmoi*, a strange word denoting cries to a goddess of *O Potnia*, 'Lady' – 'Hail Marys' might be the nearest]; it is a rare thing to find a man living on his own who goes in for this.
>
> Strabo 7.3.4

This is no isolated or ancient view.[86] Indeed, Robert Lowie (1925: 205), opening a chapter on 'Women and Religion', comments: 'If we were asked whether women or men are the more religious, most of us should unhesitatingly answer in favour of women and should presumably cite their greater emotionalism as an explanation.' I would not dare express such a view today, but it does at least seem to have some cultural basis in that male-dominated societies have been prepared to acknowledge or allege some special appropriateness of women for certain religious functions.[87] At one extreme the voice of Apollo at Delphi is a priestess, though the god is male and her utterances are 'interpreted' by males, who alone may be technical, scientific specialists and consultants in divination;[88] similarly, the original inspiration of the Sibylline books which the Romans revered was a mythical raving woman, prophesying in a foreign language, Greek, but this was interpreted into sound political action by magistrates deputed by the Senate. At the other extreme is the European persecution of witches in the Middle Ages, which, regardless of whether it evidences a continuing pagan religion, demonstrates a continuing belief by males in women's special magico-religious powers, the same that make them appropriate vehicles for furious, inspired and irrational activity.

'History preserves the name of no German prophet, but plenty of prophetesses' (Grimm 1875: i.78). Women were specially associated with divination by the Germans whom the Romans encountered. In Chapter 1 we met 'grey-haired divining priestesses' among the apparently Germanic Cimbri who regularly accompanied the army. But their prime responsibility was divination by human sacrifice. These women are mirrored in a brief glimpse of women sacrificing for the army of Spartacus.[89] At the defence of Anglesey by British Celts in AD 61, they are not visibly divining but their behaviour is characterised by its passion, though it is not clear how much is an overlay from Tacitus' own imagination and ideology: 'The opposite line [of the British] stood before the shore, thick-packed with men and weapons – and with women running in-between; like the Furies, in grim costume, hair let loose they bore torches before them' (*Annals* 14.30). Elsewhere Tacitus tells of German women turning battles almost lost in favour of their menfolk through passionate exhortation (*Germania* 8). Similarly, in 58 BC Caesar was puzzled that Ariovistus, King of the Suebi, would not engage in battle until he discovered the following from prisoners:

> Among the Germans there was a custom that their *matres famil-iae* [the wives of the heads of household] declared on the basis of lots and prophecies whether battle might usefully be joined or not; and they had said that it was not fated for the Germans to win if they joined battle before the new moon.
>
> Caesar, *Gallic war* 1.50

Plutarch adds (where did he get it from?) that they divined by looking into the eddies of rivers, judging their shape, gauging their noise.[90] Just to complete the Germanic–Celtic confusion (Ariovistus spoke good Gaulish, too!),[91] we may turn to a story which Tacitus[92] tells of a German woman from the Bructeri called 'Veleda'. She was a seer of enormous influence in AD 70: 'This virgin held wide authority over the nation of the Bructeri, through the old German custom, after which they consider many women to be soothsayers and, with superstition's power for exaggeration, goddesses' (Tacitus, *Histories* 4.61). She lived isolated in a tower and no-one might communicate directly with her. But Veleda's name is evidently the feminine of a *Celtic* term meaning 'seer' (Old Irish *filid*) and she is described not inappropriately by Cüppers as 'a Sibyl of the Celtic–Germanic cultural area'.[93]

Women and divination are frequent partners. Gothic women, the *haliur-unnae* or 'Hell-runers' (where runes are still magical song and not yet a writing system), communed with the world of the dead.[94] Our standard account of the end of the Norse world, *Ragnarök*, comes from the mouth of a seeress in *Völuspá*, 'Seeress-prophecy', the prophecy (*spá*) of the seeress (*völva*, the Nordic *Veleda*?).[95] Similarly, the Irish Saint Ita is remembered for her *prophecies* and her *Life* is that of *Beata Yta prophe-tissa*.[96] She represents some continuity from pagan times, not least in the nobility of her birth (*Life* §i). Behind her lie such figures as the *bandrúi*, 'woman-druid', well established in Irish tradition.[97] This is no person for admiration by a Poseidonios: their activities are marginal and witchlike:

Figure 12.3 Veleda, the awesome prophetess of the Bructeri

cursing, raising storms, depriving men of their senses (NB), causing deceptive appearances (the so-called 'glamour'), killing a Christian king, incantation, divination, interpretation of dreams and omens.[98] Indeed, we should not be too impressed by the claim to the term 'druid': functionally, these women continue the role of the female prophetess (*banfilid* – Veleda, or *banfáthi* – 'female *vates*') but adopt a culturally more weighty name.[99]

More feebly, Slavonic women drew random lines in the ashes by the hearth, then counted them. If they were even in number, they would be successful.[100] Such superstition is the sort of thing that women are disproportionately castigated for by Burchard of Worms (Chapter 13). Writers on Lithuania would have no difficulty, either, in identifying *vetulae* ('witches') and *prophetissae*.[101] Our sources, probably like the cultures themselves, could not accredit these females as priestesses: 'prophetess' serves to disestablish them and 'witch' to vilify.

CONCLUSIONS

Women, then, are excluded from the priestly system, except in marginal and inspirational roles. But for men there are very intricate systems of priesthood in Greece, Rome, India – the classical and therefore highly literary societies. In Rome and Gaul priesthood is closely tied into upper-class control of the state; Roman and Celtic organisations, particularly the division between pontiff–druids and *augur–wateis*, come very close and may be an Italo-Celtic cultural feature.[102] Elsewhere the evidence for priesthood looks, and is, sparse. Partly this is a question of the failure of supply of evidence for non-literate cultures: even on Gaul there is little, but for the obsession with, and overinterpretation of, druids. The Germans clearly had a standing institution of a powerful priest, practically the equal of the king, a sort of druidry in one person, making a druidic oligarchy look rather advanced. In later times, as evidence increases or their society develops, they have a proliferation of terms to cover some of the functions we might look for.

Among the various terms for religious professionals, there are few recurrences between cultures, though there are some impressive overlaps in functionality (*hiereus = sacerdos = bluostari*). Perhaps the Latin *flamen* is in fact the same word as the Sanskrit *brâhman*. In addition, the Gaulish *gutuatros* has been linked, if rather desperately, with the Germanic *gudja* and the Sanskrit *hótri* (sacrificer, priest).[103] This is very slight evidence for a common Indo-European institution, but slight evidence may be all we have a right to expect. The vocabulary of political power, too, is hard to trace back to Indo-European, despite the fact that there must have been kings or chieftains (and evidently a body of elders and an assembly of adult male warriors). Latin *rex* and Gaulish *rix* constitute the only clear connection – even the Sanskrit *rajah*, an old favourite of the comparative philologists, appears to be a secondary formation of no significance for the establishment of the word at the Indo-European stage.[104] Thus the *rex* kingship is a feature of Italo-Celtic culture. Indo-European kingship or chiefdom remains a mystery at the level of vocabulary: Greek *basileus* or *wanax*, Germanic **kuningaz* and Russian *knyaz* (borrowed from the German)[105] get us nowhere. Indo-European society itself maybe had not developed large enough structures to require a 'king', a super-chief, but it had within itself the seeds of those future societies that, everywhere, would generate kings.

The singular, state-priest, model keeps recurring. If there is a king, there seems to be a principal priest alongside him. We have seen this for 'the Germans' in Tacitus, the Northumbrian English (descendants of some of Tacitus' Germans), for the *Sinistus* among the Goths and for the Baltic Slav 'flamen' at Rethra–Riedegost. The taboos on Coifi replay those on the principal *flamen* at Rome, the *flamen Dialis*, and at another point in the Roman hierarchical structure one can see another chief priest, the *Pontifex Maximus* operating alongside the *Rex Sacrorum*, the 'king for rites', evidently a substitute for religious purposes for the former king. Even the Homeric epic presents a singular seer, Calchas, alongside the principal king, Agamemnon. This reliance on a king-equivalent in the religious dimension is resurrected in, and sometimes leads directly to, the role that bishops assume among converted peoples: in welcoming Paulinus, Edwin is in effect establishing a new state priest, a Coifi-replacement. In this light it might make sense to reinterpret a famous problem in Caesar: 'One druid is senior to all these druids and has the chief authority among them' (Caesar, *Gallic war* 6.13.8). Caesar is a little, but only a little, misleading. What we should be looking for is not an archbishop druid, an archdruid of Gaul, but one who is the leading druid, with status equal to that of the king, among a given group of Gaulish tribes, comparable with those German or Swedish tribal groupings that reunited for the nine-yearly meeting of the Thing before the statue of Thor or Wodan.

Finally, a note on the word *priest* itself. This is an early German borrowing from Latin of the Greek word *presbyteros*, an 'elder' of the Christian Church. Christianity is characterised by vocabulary shifts, by a jargon that effaces paganism: *fanum* gives way to *ecclesia*, *hearg* and other Anglo-Saxon words are deliberately avoided and replaced by *tempel* or preferably *cyrice*;[106] the dead cannot be buried in graves, much less mounds, but instead must rest in a 'sleeping place', *coemeterium*.

13

CRADLE TO GRAVE

In earlier chapters we have looked more at public religion and the ritual of the community than at the private lives of individuals. On the whole, this is what we know about – what pagan authors tell us and what Christians address. But even if we are not generally, in traditional societies, to imagine individual pagans filled with private and distinctive devotion, religion and ritual do matter very much at individual level, too, and particularly at critical moments in life. So in this chapter we look at those moments and the rituals or superstitions that surround them, before turning to the grand public burial of heroes.

A compilation of importance for this chapter is the peculiar book of Burchard, Bishop of Worms, known as the *Decrees* (*Decreta*). In this volume he collected the proceedings of church councils and synods, the pronouncements of popes and bishops, and the weighty opinions of worthy fathers of the Church, so that he might perpetuate correct understanding of religion and the religious life. Two particular parts of this work are of interest. Book 10 'deals with enchanters, augurs, *divini*, lot-casters, and various illusions of the devil, with those who curse, quarrel and conspire, and with the [appropriate] penance for each' (Burchard, *Index*). But Book 19 is the more original and informative for our current purposes; this wonderful list

is entitled the Corrector and Doctor (*Medicus*) because it lists fully the corrections for the body and the medicines for the soul and teaches each and every priest, even simple ones, in what way they may assist each individual, ordained or lay, poor or rich, child, youth, old man or decrepit, healthy or ill, in the case of every age and either sex.

Burchard 19, *Argument*

This recipe usually gives our discussion a good start.

The dividing lines between folk ritual, superstition and paganism are hard to draw. What counts as paganism? If a ritual is customary but no god is invoked, is it 'pagan'? Evidently the Church thought so and evidently it seamlessly takes its place in a larger range of ritual behaviour which is indeed based on the worship of other gods than Me. It is also of human interest.

CRADLE

We may not be well informed on rituals surrounding birth in pagan cultures, but they assuredly existed. Occasionally they can be detected from the remnants of folk custom, as when a woman who has given birth is cleansed by a special church ceremony forty days after birth (de Vries 1956: i.§137). This ritual cleansing period is what one might term a 'long month', corresponding to the period required for the return of mourners to the community (see below).[1] Periods of forty days matter in Greece, too. A woman who finds herself pregnant may not go to a shrine for forty days, and the medical writers, presumably adapting popular views, reckon the period in which menstruation continues and there is substantial risk of miscarriage also as one of forty days.[2] Childbirth pollutes the Greek woman and excludes both her and those who come into contact with her from shrines, the latter generally for two or three days.[3] This high-lights the special nature of the rites of passage for birth and death, that they must deal both with the ostensible subject of the ceremony – the incorporation of the child or separation of the dead – and simultaneously with those who are polluted by the passage.[4] So it is that Euripides' Iphigeneia speaks of Artemis, the goddess she serves, 'who keeps from her altars, considering them defiled, anyone who is in contact with murder or touches a woman in childbirth or a corpse with their hands' (Euripides, *Iphigeneia among the Tauroi* 381–3). Indeed, 'in a shrine no-one may die and no-one be born' (Nilsson 1955: i.95). Offerings are made for the purification of the woman who has given birth, though of course it might also masquerade as a thank-offering to a goddess of childbirth such as Eileithyia or even to Iphigeneia herself. Gods and goddesses act as con-venient receptacles for such offerings, an object for the ritual that must in any case take place.

The child itself, before it is adopted into the family, is nothing and occasions no ceremony. In Bronze Age Crete and in Greece it may there-fore be exposed to die if not adopted, and if it in any case dies it is not cremated but simply buried.[5] If it does not seem insensitive, I observe that we have moved back the moment at which the child is recognised by determining at what point abortions may be legitimate.

In Greece the child is adopted through the ritual *Amphidromia* ('Running around') on the fifth (or possibly seventh) day, i.e. the fourth (sixth) after birth. Those who have helped with the birth now purify their hands and they, or possibly others, in either case apparently naked, run round the hearth with the child. This is, of course, a version of circumambulation being used to incorporate the child into the family by associating it with the focus (literally!) of family life.[6] Then, on the tenth day, it will be named. Finally, there is one late piece of evidence for a festival on the fortieth day to celebrate the birth.[7] The long month completes the transition.

There is some evidence for Germans instantly bathing new-born children, given a spurious medical explanation by the great medical authority Galen in the later second century AD: 'putting the baby into streaming rivers the moment it is born, while it is still warm and then, as they say the Germans do, simultaneously trying out their physical strength and hardening their bodies, by dipping them into the cold water like glowing iron' (Galen, *On looking after health* (*de sanitate tuenda*), Kühn vol. 6, p.51). This is, then, not just a Christian baptismal practice[8] and it is paralleled by the extraordinary difficulty which Bishop Michael Junge had with his fifteenth-century Prussians: 'Item, that they should not take their children who have been baptised by their parish priests[9] and rebaptise them in rivers or anywhere else, or give them other names than those that have been given at baptism, on pain of three stones of wax (?) or strict flogging' (Michael Junge, *LPG* 158). After pagan baptism, then, there is also a naming ceremony, such as the Old Norse *nafnfestr* on the tenth day, after nine nights.[10] We are evidently in the presence of Indo-European custom.

TRANSITIONS

We have taken the view elsewhere (Chapter 3) that every purification is a transition and every transition sets up the dynamics of purification. So in Greek culture offerings at the entrance to adulthood or on the point of marriage are attached to a divinity associated with the stage which is being left behind and are claimed to fend off the anger of that divinity. As a result they 'turn aside' a supernatural danger and may be described as 'apotropaic'. Hair is a typical offering, at the grave of a dead hero or heroine who never made it into adulthood, or in the case of Homer's Achilles (and doubtless real people) to a river god, the Spercheios in his case – an instrument at once of transition and of purification. Greek youths very commonly marked their entry to the adult community – for instance, at Athens to the phratry – by hair-shearing and one day of the

Apatouria festival at which such entrance was gained was therefore known as *Koureotis*, '(day) of shearing'.[11]

A German version is seen among the Chatti, where, according to Tacitus (*Germania* 31), there was an unusual custom,[12] 'that as soon as they have grown to maturity, they let their hair and beard grow and it is only when they have killed an enemy that they cast aside this facial appearance which is a matter of a vow owed to Manliness. Only when standing over blood and spoils do they uncover their brow.' This, then, is for that German tribe the entrance into male adulthood, though it is unclear whether the cut hair is laid on the altar of any divinity and somewhat unclear what divine status Manliness (Latin *Virtus*) has in this context.[13] Shearing the hair is also known as a ritual of adoption of a stranger into a Germanic family.

ILLNESS AND CRISIS

Life is uneven and contains difficulties and crises which are posed either by natural forces – for instance, illness – or by other people. The wicked actions of others are, of course, in one's own case legitimate ambition. In all these circumstances ritual comes to our assistance.

> Have you violated a tomb, yes, when you see someone being buried and during the night break open the tomb and remove his clothes? If you have, you shall do penance for two years for the regular feast days. Have you consulted magicians and introduced them into your home to find something out by their maleficent craft or to conduct an expiation or, following the custom of the pagans, *divini* who might divine for you so that you might question them, like a prophet, on future events and those who practise lots or those who expect to know the future through lots or those who are in thrall to auguries or incantations – have you invited them to your house? If you have, you shall do penance for two years for the regular feast days . . .
>
> Have you made ligatures (knots) and incantations and those various spells which wicked men – swineherds, cowherds and sometimes hunters – make, when they say diabolical songs over bread or over herbs and over certain wicked ligatures. And they either hide these in a tree or drop them where two or three roads meet, so that they may free either their animals or their dogs from disease and misfortune and ruin those of another. If you have, you shall do penance for two years for the regular feast days.
>
> Burchard 19.5.59, 60, 63 (*PL* 140.960)

The clothes of the dead have power; magicians and diviners break down the limits of mortal capacity that frustrate us; they are specialists. Working with animals always poses difficulty, but there are means of helping one's own along and 'spoiling' one's neighbour's, if you know the old ways. It is particularly frustrating when people refuse to take a sensible attitude to you; the solution is to find enchanters or (an anticipation of the witch craze)[14] *women* who can change people's attitudes, particularly when love is involved (69). This may be a matter of general irresponsibility, but it may also be a last-ditch attempt to get your marriage back on the rails.

Herbal remedies are not in themselves maleficent and may even be thought to do some good, but they need to be Christianised: 'Have you collected medicinal herbs with other incantations than with the Creed and the Lord's Prayer, i.e. chanting *Credo in Deum* (I believe in God) and *Pater Noster* (Our Father). If you have done otherwise, you shall do penance for ten days on bread and water' (Burchard 19.5.65 (*PL* 140.961)). But illness, particularly in ancient and medieval times, leads to desperation and it is no accident that the following paragraph (66) envisages our defendant has gone back to pray at the old favourites – the springs, stones, trees, crossroads. You are lighting candles, throwing in (Martin of Braga's) bread or some other offering, feasting, all because 'you sought health of body or soul there'. Sentence: three years' fasting on feast days. You might turn to almost anything to let you know whether there is hope: as you are about to enter the house of your ill friend, you might turn a stone over and look desperately for 'a worm, fly or ant – anything that moves' (102).

The superstitions recorded in various sources from Pseudo-Theodore of Tarsos[15] on to Burchard in 1012, however trivial, show something of the unshakeable foundations of popular 'knowledge'. There are no offences committed exclusively by men, other than by reasons of anatomy. But women are particularly prone to superstition, more out of powerlessness than out of any greater natural inclination to the supernatural (cf. Strabo's comments in Chapter 12); besides, they are fictionalised into targets by male writers, displacing their own guilt. There the women are, weaving and murmuring incantations as they go; a man has died and they are burning grains where he died; they need rain, so they get out a nude virgin and the henbane for her to walk down to the river with, coming back 'crab-wise' (?). What is this woman's daughter doing on the roof or in an oven? – she has been put there to recover from the flu, as effective as most modern treatments. In a scene which looks patched together from the second-century novel of Apuleius, *The golden ass*, we find they leave their husband in bed, go out through closed doors, and substitute straw or wood for his heart.[16] Now one of them is digging up a turf on which a Christian has left his footstep in order to do him wrong and another is leaving out food and three knives for vestiges of a pagan goddess-trinity. As children who die unbaptised are formidably dangerous, they drive a stake through it, useful also for mothers who have died failing to bear their child.[17]

Then there are questions of timing. If you think there is nothing like a new moon for building a house or making marriages, you get two years' fasting on feast days (Burchard 19.5.61). And you are wrong: Hesiod, writing before 700 BC, would have told you that it is the *fourth* of the month on which you should get married (*Works and Days* 800 f.).

GRAVE

Normal people

Funeral rites and especially funeral laments are particular moments of crisis where tradition is valued and emotions pour out. This is an environment in which Christians were nervous about the perpetuation of pagan practice. Irish keening, too, 'is regarded as somewhat heathenish' (Plummer), as can be seen from a text referring to 'conducting seven days of death ceremonies as is the manner of the pagans'.[18] This is where some strange Lithuanian figures fit:[19]

> They promised also that they would not have *tulissones* or *ligaschones* among them, viz. men who are utterly mendacious actors, to be brought out as priests of the pagans at the funerals of the dead – alas for their infernal torments! (?) – saying good and ill, and praising the dead for their thefts and filthy spoils and plundering and other sins and vices which they perpetrated while they lived. And shouting out as they raise their eyes to heaven, they mendaciously assert that they see before them the dead man flying through the midst of the sky on a horse, adorned with gleaming armour, carrying a (spear?)[20] in his hand and proceeding with a great company to another world.
>
> Prussian Treaty with the Teutonic Order, 7 February 1249,
> *LPG* 42

These Wagnerian shamans have an authentic ring: *tulissones* is evidently a Slavonic (Wendish) word related by Mannhardt to a Polish word *tuliczna*, 'comforter', and *ligaschones* (perhaps the Prussian term) may have specialised in 'illness' (Lithuanian *liga*).[21] The dead are powerful and it is vital for Christian churches to have graveyards in order to appropriate them, sanitise their power, supervise the rites of the living.[22] This is why,

Christian new-speak (Chapter 12) includes the word *coemeterium*, 'sleeping-place', to neutralise the dead.

What is the Burchardian funeral like?

> Have you practised wakes, i.e. have you been present at watching over the bodies of the dead where the bodies of Christians were guarded according to the rite of the pagans? Have you sung there diabolical songs and have you performed dances there which the pagans have devised through the instruction of the devil? Have you drunk there? Have your features dissolved in laughter and have you appeared almost to rejoice in your brother's death, setting aside all piety and feelings of charity? If you have, you shall do penance for thirty days on bread and water . . .
>
> Have you performed, or consented to, those empty futile customs which stupid women generally do: while the body of the dead man is still lying in the house, they run for water, and bring back silently a jar of water and, when the body of the dead man is lifted up, they pour this water under the bier [usually over the threshold to avoid the return of the dead].[23] They observe this practice, that when the corpse is being carried out of the house, it should not be raised higher than the knees, and they do this for reasons of health. If you have, or have consented, you must do penance for ten days on bread and water.
>
> Burchard 19.5.91, 96 (*PL* 140.964 f.)

Finally, the burial: if the man has been killed, they rub ointment into his hand when he is being buried (twenty days' bread and water!), evidently to heal him for the next life (97).

So we have a wake and a burial. The wake and its songs are evidently what the *Indiculus* (Chapter 8) means by 'Sacrilege over the deceased, i.e. *dadsisas.*' This Germanic word means 'songs of lament over the dead' and there is an Old English equivalent, the *līcsang* (corpse-song).[24] It is difficult to separate out the stages at which various rituals were performed but these sound pretty immediate, as though the corpse is with the mourners, not yet interred. In German folk custom a singer will even stand in for the dead person so that the corpse may participate in the song.[25] The wake itself has a dual sinister purpose, to guard the corpse from demonic danger, but also to protect the living from it.[26] It may be watched day and night till it is safely buried; or it may be watched only at night, or only on the last, most dangerous, night. Some cultures – for instance, the Jewish, Zoroastrian and Hindu – are anxious to dispose of the corpse very quickly, within twenty-four hours; but even Zoroastrians reckon that the soul lingers on for three days.[27] The ancient Athenian two days on the bier (from Day 1 to Day 3) allows the mourners to know for certain that the person is dead, to pay their 'respects', and to bury before corruption sets in. On Day 3 the corpse is buried and there is a banquet at the grave, the *perideipnon*.[28]

The *Indiculus'* 'Sacrilege at the tombs of the dead' looks like this next stage, the burial and last meal with the dead (*Totenmahl*), typically on Day 3.[29] If a meal, then a sacrifice and also in all probability further song and dance. The songs at such feasts are presumably the Old English *byrgensang* (or, more phonetically spelt, *byriensang*, 'burial-song') and in Mecklenburg as late as 1520 they were still singing, dancing and sprinkling the graves with beer.[30] German feasts are commonly held in hostelries today (the *Wirtshaus*, *HDA* 5.1084) but originally had been held at the very grave. This pattern of activity is very widespread indeed. It is well known to Indo-European nations, embracing Greek ritual and an archaic Roman rite, the *silicernium*, another feast at the grave, possibly on the occasion of burial, or possibly to terminate mourning and release the family.[31] The burial party is likewise frequent among Finno-Ugric, Semitic and Altaic peoples.[32]

Despite what is sometimes said, the counting of days starts with death, not burial.[33] The third-day ceremony *is* the burial. Further ceremonies followed both in paganism and in its Christian successor roughly a long week later and a lunar month (four weeks/thirty days) or a long month later (forty days). The period of a lunar month is needed not so much for the dead as for the living so that they may be purified from contact with the dead and reintegrated into the world of the living in the next time cycle. So mourners in historical Athens are contaminated by 'death-pollution', 'a kind of temporary participation in the condition of the dead man, who is through the decay of the corpse "foul" (*miaros*)' (Parker 1983: 64). Indeed, so foul is the pollution of death that in Greece no priest may attend a funeral![34]

Greeks had ceremonies on Days 3, 9 and 30 (modern Greeks on Days 3, 9 and 40),[35] Romans a feast on Day 9 (*cena novemdialis*) and, possibly at one time, a ceremony on Day 30.[36] In more modern times in Germany four weeks or so has been the customary period of mourning (Geiger, *HDA* 8.1139) and this is why one may enter into an inheritance only on Day 30 (Ranke 1951: ch.4). Christians, too, prescribed days for services in memory of the dead – Ps.Theodore of Tarsus on Days 1, 3, 9 and 30, Swedish thirteenth-century authorities on Days 3, 7 and 30.[37] Similarly, a Nuremberg by-law of the fourteenth century ran: 'One shall also not place candles on the graves, save on the seventh day and the thirtieth and annually' (Siebenkees, *Materialen zur Nürnberger Geschichte* 1 (1792): 205, in Ranke 1951: 300). What happened on these days was more of a problem, as Hinkmar, Archbishop of Reims, had found:

No priest, when the priests meet together on the anniversary day or 30th, 3rd or 7th day from the death of anyone, or for any reason, should presume to get drunk or pray in honour of the saints or of the soul itself [or] drink or cause others to drink or swill to another's prayers nor contribute clapping, vulgar laughing or inane stories, or presume to sing or allow people to perform tawdry games with bear and *danseuses* (*tornatrices*) in front of him nor agree to carry before him the masks of demons, *talamascae* in the vernacular.

Hinkmar, Capitulary 1.14 (1 November 852)

This is where paganism long ago denounced by Caesarius crosses over into carnival, but it is of interest to see this jollity so closely associated with funeral observances by both Hinkmar and Burchard.

It might seem a curiosity, as it did to Herodotos (4.73.1), that Scythians (who were Iranian Indo-Europeans) drove the corpse around to friends of the dead for feasts for a period of forty days. However, the physical presence of the corpse at the *Totenmahl* is quite common. So the (Finnic) Estonians in the tenth century are reported to have feasted, drunk and played with the corpse in their midst; and Danes as recently as the nineteenth century would take the great hall of a farm, place the open sarcophagus in the middle and the food and drink for the guests around the walls.[38] If the Greeks called their *Totenmahl* a *peri*deipnon, that was because it was *around* the corpse. The presupposition behind the whole idea of the *Totenmahl* is that it is a last meal shared with the dead, a last occasion on which the dead is part of the community. If Roman sarcophagi frequently show banquet scenes, the so-called 'banquet of the blest', and if feasting and drinking are thought characteristic activities of the other world, that is not just because they are prized leisure activities, but because they transfigure this last contact with the dead. One may ask what the last dance is like, too, and it appears that there is a very widespread custom of a round dance, an encircling dance around the grave, shared with the dead man but also, as it were, circumambulating him firmly into place, often both anticlockwise (the sinister mode) and clockwise.[39]

Pagan cultures observe rites of memory for particular dead people, sometimes for long periods, in the case of the Parsis annually for thirty years. Hindu mourners spend ten or eleven days ritually restricted, then perform a sort of sign-off ceremony, the first *śrāddha* ('duty' i.e. to the dead), offering milk and *penda* (rice- or barley-balls, very sweet and delicious); a similar ceremony must be performed monthly on the day of death, then annually thereafter.[40] And Ammonios, though he is generally not believed, tells us that the Greeks celebrated the Genesia, 'for dead people on the day on which each one died'.[41]

Obviously, the annual remembrance of particular dead cannot go on for ever and pagan cultures tend to rationalise by holding a general ceremony for all the dead. So, in Athens the Genesia, with its sacrifice to Earth (*Ge*) who holds the dead, seems to have been standardised as 5 Boedromion (typically in September) around 590 BC and it may have been standardised earlier by particular clans.[42] This still survives, somewhat uncomfortably, in modern Zoroastrian systems: so the Parsis have a festival called Muktad celebrated during the last five days of the year (M. Boyce, in Hinnells 1985: 182). The end of the year, particularly if it is in February, is evidently the *moment juste* for such ceremonies. About this time of year the Athenians held the Anthesteria, a complex three-day festival of Dionysos celebrating, among other things, the new wine and the cohesion of the community (through its opposite, solitary drinking); but it ended with the cry, 'Out, *Keres*! Anthesteria is over!', which seems to refer to the expulsion of the spirits of the dead. The (September) Genesia may form a systematic pair with the (February) Anthesteria; certainly, Schmidt observed that the same points in the year are devoted to the dead by Greeks in more modern times.[43] The Genesia appears to be named after 'parents' (*genetai*) and, if so, is directly equivalent to the Roman Parentalia (below).[44] Just as in Indo-European 'brother' (**bhrātēr*) had an extended meaning and denoted a member of a brotherhood, so the sense of parenthood stretches into the generality of ancestors. Sanskrit *pitrya* means 'paternal' but also 'ancestral' or 'relating *or* sacred to the Manes' (i.e. the dead) and the derivative *pitriyana* ('path of the Manes') is also used for 'winter'.[45] The corresponding Germanic feast is Yuletide – a period of twelve days ('of Christmas') from the winter solstice which, according to Bede (Chapter 10), brings in the new year, the same period within which the Roman new year falls (1 January).[46] Evidence for Yule as a pagan religious festival may be slender but it is so very suggestive that this is the period when the Wild Hunt (*Wilde Jagd*, or the 'Raging Army', *Wütende Heer*) flies through the air, a spectral army corresponding to the ancestors once worshipped in ritual.[47] Does this awareness of the dead survive in the custom of Serbian *coledari* (derived from the Latin *Kalendae*), a sort of masked Christmas-carol group who include in their visits houses where there has been a death during the year and 'intone funeral chants and bring news from the departed'? Have they taken on the character of the dead themselves?[48]

The position of the new year start is very variable in our cultures, though there are signs of trying to lock it to an equinox or a solstice (Chapter 10). What is more constant is the release of the dead and the need to worship them as the old year dies. Irish tradition has been so confused by amateur enthused writing that it is now barely possible to know what may count as a reliable fact rather than wishful thinking and inventive antiquarianism. It is, however, possible that an Old Irish year began with winter just as the Gaulish day began with night. The eve that begins the first day of winter, Samhain, is in effect Halloween, if only one could be sure that our picture of Samhain was not simply derived from Halloween. But it does appear from the literature to be a time when the mounds of the *sid* are open and their spectral inhabitants are therefore at large (another is the opposite day in the year, the eve of May Day).[49] Perhaps one may also count in certain Scottish reports of groups of young men, masked or with blackened faces, like the Serbian *coledari*, who are confidently stated to impersonate the spirits of the dead.[50]

We learn of Lithuanian practices from the researches of Paul Einhorn in the seventeenth century:

> Such heathen superstitious practice has probably come to these people of old from the Greeks [a point not to be taken seriously], who perform these rites in much the same way. They have a special and particular time appointed for them, namely from St Michael to Sts Simon and Jude, from 29 September to 28 October. In these four weeks they hold these soul-hostings (*Seelengästereyen*)[51] and feasts.
>
> Paul Einhorn, *LPG* 467

This is a very revealing point in the year, because it embraces the date for the general Lithuanian assembly and falls into the pattern of: year-end, spirits of dead, assembly of people, new beginning (Chapter 14).

The Roman Parentalia lasted nine days (like the initial nine-day period of mourning for any dead person), days known as the *dies parentales*. Located at the dead point of the year, it began on 15 February and ended on the 21st with the final placation of the dead, the Feralia. In this period modest gifts were brought to the tombs:

> A tile covered with offered garlands is enough,
>   and sprinkled grain, and a little pinch of salt,
> and bread softened in wine and a scatter of violets
>   – leave a pot with these in the middle of the street.
>
> Ovid, *Fasti* 2.537–40

The two principal means of disposing of corpses are cremation and inhumation. There are others – for instance, leaving them on platforms for birds of prey like some South American Indians, or in a stone tower (*dakhma*) like Zoroastrians in Persia and India.[52] Indeed, it is arguable that early and middle Iron Age Celts (say, 700–100 BC) in Britain and Gaul practised 'excarnation [de-fleshing] by exposure to the air', as is tentatively suggested by Hutton (1991: 196). Cremation, however, is the most commonly found means of disposal. It continued, subdued, in Britain during the period of exposures, and came back into fashion with the advancing wave of Roman and continental culture (*ibid.* 197).

Cremation became firmly associated with pagans in Christian minds.[53] In 785 Charlemagne savagely banned it among the Saxons: 'If anyone causes the body of a dead man to be consumed by flame according to the rite of the pagans and shall reduce its bones to ashes, he shall suffer capital punishment' (*Capitulare paderbrunnense* 7). In similar circumstances, compulsorily adopting Christianity, Prussians were obliged to accept the following provision:

> The neophytes . . . faithfully promised that they and their heirs in the matter of burning the dead or of burying them with their horses or men or armour or clothing or any other precious objects or in certain other matters, either, would not observe the rites of the pagans in future but would bury their dead in the Christian manner in cemeteries and not outside.
>
> Prussian Treaty with the Teutonic Order, 7 February 1249,
> *LPG* 41 (also, Jouet 1989: 159)

Cremation appears to be the mode by which corpse and property are transferred to existence in death. This is explained, or at least hypothesised, by Peter of Duisburg:

> The Prussians used to believe in the resurrection of the flesh [a Christian perspective, this], but not as they ought to have. They used to believe that if a person was noble or not, rich or poor, powerful or without power in this life, he would be the same after resurrection in his future life. This is why armour, horses, servants and maidservants, clothes, hunting dogs and birds of prey, and other things appropriate to the warrior's life, were put at the disposal of dead nobles. With non-nobles, they burnt whatever was appropriate to their station. They believed that things when burnt would rise again with them and serve them as previously.
>
> Peter of Duisburg, *LPG* 88 (Clemen 1936: 97, Jouet 1989: 160)

There remains, however, something Christian about this insistence on the afterlife and we may be at some distance from the mentality of those who practised such rites. Barber (1990: 386) stresses the way in which cremation neutralises potentially difficult spirits, 'as a sort of pre-emptive strike against the threat from the dead'. Lithuanian funerals must, however, also have had a sort of Viking grandeur: they are said (dangerously!) to have burnt their bodies in pine woods.[54] These were, after all, sacred places in which ritual may have a powerful effect without depending on theological implications.

Grand burial

The archaeological evidence for burial mounds on the one hand and the literary evidence for heroic burials on the other suggest a widespread European and indeed Indo-European manner of burial for the aristocracy. Burial mounds may even by used to locate archaeologically the original speakers of the Indo-European language(s). This method is that of Gimbutas, who has looked at the distribution of the so-called *kurgan* culture and its various phases: 'This normally involves burial in an earthen or stone chamber, the frequent presence of ochre, and in many instances the erection of a low tumulus (Russian *kurgan*). Grave goods may include weapons and animal remains, especially of sheep/goat, but also of cattle and horse' (Mallory 1989: 183). The *kurgan* itself, even if only a metre or so high, is the most visible aspect of a distinctive social and economic culture, enabling us to identify a people who moved from the steppes north and east of the Black Sea southwards, and westwards into Europe in the time range 4400–2800 bc.[55] This sort of tradition of funeral mound and associated ceremony has its place in the discussion of Hittite royal funerary rituals and comparisons have been made with Indian funerary rituals and ancestor worship.[56]

Important scenes in the epics of Homer are built on this sort of custom and give us a view of the ceremonies that surrounded the creation of such mounds. In his *Iliad* Patroklos and Hektor each receive a warrior's burial; in his *Odyssey* there is a flashback to the burial of Achilles, which had been told at greater length in the *Aethiopis* of Arktinos, now lost except for a plot summary.[57] Hektor's parents, Priam and Hekabe, and Helen lament over Hektor's corpse: the lament is a *goös*, which a lamenter 'leads' and is evidently both shared and in some way musical – it is, in effect, a *dadsisas*. For nine days they gather wood and on the tenth he is burnt on the pyre. His brothers and comrades collect his bones, put them in a golden coffer, wrapped in luxurious purple robes, place the coffer in a trench and raise his mound. They then go and feast. Patroklos must return from the dead to remind Achilles that he needs to be buried (reminding us that funerals are a device for establishing the dead where they belong, in a separate world). Achilles' extravagant grief for his fallen comrade has displaced the period of laying out and mourning.[58] The pyre finally built is an enormous one, involving an extensive felling operation, and it is held in place with retaining walls. A mighty cortège of Bronze Age chariots then takes Patroklos to the pyre and hair sheared in mourning is cast over the corpse like flowers over the hearse of Princess Diana. In a grand gesture Achilles shears his hair, for he shall never return to dedicate it at home, and places it in the dead man's hands. *Goös* follows. It is ended, and Homer stands tradition on its head: the men are sent away to prepare their (separate) dinners (23.158)! Now, in this strangely private public funeral, the sacrifices are offered and the gifts made: oxen, sheep and, gifts for Homer of increasing barbarity but perhaps genuine parts of epic and early Greek tradition, four horses, Patroklos' dogs and twelve Trojan noble prisoners of war. The pyre is lit, with some difficulty, and blazes all night. The bones are collected, the mound raised. Then, a standard feature of aristocratic burials, games are held. Achilles' own funeral, in briefer flashback, comports: bier, hair-shearing, lament by his divine mother Thetis and a performance of a *thrēnos* (sung lament) by the Muses themselves, seventeen days of tears and consignment to the pyre on the eighteenth (epically doubling the nine days of mourning?); oxen, sheep, bone-gathering and a huge mound on a promontory over-looking the Hellespont:

> Over the bones a great and splendid mound,
> was heaped by us, the mighty army of Argive spearsmen,
> on a jutting promontory over the broad Hellespont,
> so that it might be seen from afar by men at sea
> those who now are and those who shall be hereafter.
>
> Homer, *Odyssey* 24.80–4

This was a picture that Thracians might recognise, whose aristocratic funerals are described thus:

> The funerals for the rich among them are as follows. For three days they lay out the corpse and, slaughtering all sorts of victims, feast, having wept first. Then they bury them, either cremating them or in some other way covering them with earth. When they have heaped up the mound, they hold a variety of games, in which the greatest prizes are set aside for duels. These, then, are the funerals of the Thracians.
>
> Herodotos 5.8

Germanic peoples, too, had their aristocratic mounds. Among the rhetorical noble-savage infill, we can see nuggets of genuine custom:

> They are unostentatious about funerals. Only this practice they observe, that the bodies of famous men should be burnt with particular types of wood. They do not heap up the structure of the pyre with clothing and perfumes: each man gets his weapons, and some have a (their?) horse burnt with them. Turf erects their tomb; they despise the towering laborious monument [of stone] as a weight upon the dead. Laments and tears they are done with quickly, grief and sadness slowly. It is decent for women to wail, for men to remember.
>
> Tacitus, *Germania* 27

According to *Ynglinga saga* 8, Othin 'ordained that all dead men should be burnt and brought on to the pyre with their property' so that they might enjoy in Valhöll what they had buried in the earth. 'A mound was to be raised as a memorial to noblemen; and for all such persons as had achieved any distinction "bauta-stones" should be set up' (Chadwick 1899: 22). And Beowulf's corpse, too, receives notable burial: the warriors bring timber for his pyre; the body is burnt, to grieving and to a woman's ritual lament; finally, Achillean in death, over ten days his barrow is built 'to be seen far off by ocean travellers'.[59]

Great warriors get great circumambulations. No round dances and simple songs of the dead here, but warriors riding on horseback around the grave. Twelve of his men ride round Beowulf's mound singing a tribute to his deeds and achievement (3170). The same end was earned also by Attila, whose praises were sung by select horsemen:

[Attila] was honoured by his nation in death. His body was positioned in mid-plain inside a silken tent, producing an amazing and solemn sight. The choicest horsemen of the Hunnish people, as though at a stadium, rode around the place where his body was laid out and they related his deeds in funeral song in this order:

'Chief of the Huns, King Attila, born of father Mundzucus [. . .] '

After he had been wept in such laments, they celebrated a huge feast at his bier, which they call *strava*, and, mixing opposites, they merged funeral lament and joy.

Jordanes, *Getica* 49.256–8

Finally he is buried with precious metals and valuables; and those who bury him also are killed, according to Jordanes to hide the place of burial, more likely to provide its eternal guards and attendants.

Homer's Achilles does indeed ride thrice round the corpse of Patroklos with his Myrmidons (*Iliad* 23.13), but – and this is the poet's special point – without conducting his funeral, a fact of which Patroklos' ghost complains (23.69–71). In a final grotesque pastiche Achilles makes a habit of dragging the corpse of Hektor thrice round Patroklos' tomb (24.15 f.). The Argonauts know better: they bury the Doliones they have tragically slain, heap up a mound on the third day and ride round it thrice.[60] From dances around the tomb to German folk customs of funeral processions that wind thrice round the church (Chapter 7), the fundamentals remain the same: this ceremony binds the dead to the spot while paying tribute to them and leaving them well disposed to the living; it achieves closure for the burial.[61]

Figure 13.1 The funeral of Attila

Mounds to marvel at

So the landscape is altered for ever and gains a hill with a cause. This is how chiefs, royals and important persons carry their importance into the grave and on to posterity for lesser mortals to wonder at. When the fashion for burial mounds has long passed, the mounds themselves end up perceived as the powerful reminders of a lost heroic culture. Homer, Greeks *and we ourselves* are the audience for these supposed mythic events and what matters to us is not the actual yearning of real people for posthumous recognition, but our preparedness to see the greatness of past men in the landscape, to feel a humbling past in what is presently visible. A grove or a cave has one sort of eery otherness, a mound a different one – and Cicero can appeal to both when in an *appassionata* moment of a great oration he conjures up those 'Alban mounds and groves' (*For Milo* 85).

These tombs belong to the special dead and these dead may gain their own special divine status. So, at Kaliningrad, Bishop Michael Junge specified:

Item, that no Prussian man or woman shall practise any abuses or abominations in future according to the rites of the pagans once

272

they have been made Christians, particularly next to the mounds and tombs of those who are called Geten or Cappyn in their language, in drinking sessions, feastings or any other revelry.

Michael Junge, *LPG* 158 (also, Clemen 1936: 102)

In Ireland, too, they went in awe of the *fir síde*, the men of the mounds (*síd*),[62] and in Greece they sought help in adversity from past heroes. If the hero had no name, it made no difference – he might simply be 'Hero Doctor' or 'Hero General'.

Men of the past, like men now, fall into two categories: great men and us. Aristotle observed how the men of mythology called each other 'hero', reflecting antique custom, but with the necessary reservation 'Only the leaders of the ancients were heroes – the people were just men.'[63] Saxo knew this, too, as, reproducing the sentiments of Danish oral poetry, he put into the mouth of the hero Biarco Latin hexameters as powerful as any since Statius:[64]

non humile obscurumve genus, non funera plebis
Pluto rapit vilesque animas, sed fata potentum
implicat, et claris complet Phlegethonta figuris.

It is not those of humble or obscure birth, corpses of ordinary folk, that Pluto snatches nor cheap souls, but the dooms of the powerful he enmeshes, filling Phlegethon [i.e. hell] with famous figures.

Saxo 2.7.21, p.65 Holder

14

UNITY IS THE THING

In this final chapter tantalising themes at last come together: the location of the sacred site, the role of the grove, the assembly of the whole community, the awful sacrifice and the renewal of time. Together they make sense and the diverse phenomena of the book become more than the engaging miscellany of paganism.

GAUL: CENTRALITY OF THE SHRINE

Centrality of the shrine – a recurring theme. Some shrines are so shaped that they give a sense of centrality in themselves. So the Gaulish shrines with their characteristic square structure with a surround portico proclaim centrality. Similarly, the temple of Svantovit at Arkona confines the god within a square curtained area within a square temple. And then it is a puzzle of religious history that gods have such a tendency to multiple heads or faces. One explanation, which at least fits Svantovit, is that he gives a sense of facing all quarters, of facing all those sub-peoples in whose centre he is situated.[1] Unity in the god.

It is, maybe, not surprising that temples should be built on high ground and not inconvenient that they should on occasion be centrally located. But we can be more imaginative than this and Gaul will help us to be so. The Gauls, before Roman rule, developed fortified trading and political centres where the people might assemble. These are called *oppida* by the Romans and by us, though the Gauls must have called them **duna*. By the first century, tribal states (Latin, *civitates*) had developed, each with a small number of villages (Latin, *pagi*) united around an *oppidum*. At least forty-two such sites, and probably many more, were called Mediolan(i)um, 'Centre-plain' (if 'plain' catches whatever nuance **lānon* had).[2] This is a remarkable number and it must be the commonest of all Celtic placenames. The following are some of the descendants of this name in France:

- *Mediolanum*: Mâlain, Maulain, Meillant, Méolans, Meslan, Mesland, Meulan, Meulin, Meylan, Moëslains, Moislains, Molain, Moliens, Mollans, Molliens, Miélan.
- *Mediolanium*: Malange, Molagnies, Maligny, Malandry.
- **Mediolaniacum*: Malansac.

Two particularly old examples are Milan in Italy and Gournay-Moyenneville (north-east of Paris), where fourth-century BC sacred foundations mark the site where the *oppidum* will be built in later centuries. From this Brunaux (1988: 8) concludes that '*Mediolanum* must therefore be a particular, and also the oldest, form of the *oppidum*'. So sanctuaries have an important place in the developing consciousness of statehood among the Gauls and the religious focus points the way forward towards the socio-political focus represented by the *oppida* that have become practically universal in Gaul by the first century BC. That is why they are so often found in *oppida* and not infrequently *antedate* them.[3] In fact the sanctuary validates the politico-military assembly at the *oppidum*. Even in an instance where the native, and militarily too successful, *oppidum* was replaced by a new Gallo-Roman town, when Gergovia was replaced by Augustonemetum ('Augustus-sanctuary', Clermont-Ferrand), it shows by its name that a sanctuary was at the heart of the new foundation.

Brunaux has observed how Gaulish sanctuaries tend to be either at centres or at margins[4] and recently he has emphasised how a very great number – around fifty in northern France – may be seen as being on raised land dominating the surrounding area (thus clearly at the centre of the **lānon*). Often they are sufficiently high so that from one it is possible to see the next one up to seven kilometres away, and so on in a chain.[5] So the Gaulish sanctuary often serves as the focus of a working locality and the centrality which it represents assists the development of a *civitas*.[6] The situation in Britain cannot have been very different: there, too, the builders of rural temples 'often sought out high ground with a good view' (Lewis 1966: 130 f.). We are not talking here about mountaintops, or even necessarily hilltops: plateaux are sufficient for a hundred of them in France.[7] This situation seems to be paralleled in Ireland if it is right that the provincial capitals 'almost without exception . . . stood on hills, or at least on artificial mounds' and that they had sacred characteristics such as embracing burial places (Rees and Rees 1961: 166 f.).

THE GERMANIC THING

What consciousness did pre-Roman or pre-urban peoples have of their nationhood? The answer seems to be that they had a very developed sense. We see in many Indo-European nations an ideological centring of the constituent peoples of a nation on a special, sacred place. There may be a regular, periodic grand meeting to celebrate religious ceremony and to reach legal decisions and arbitrations.

The best defined of these groupings is the Thing, an institution common to all the Germanic peoples since earliest times, as can be seen from the presence of the term in various Germanic languages. The first solid evidence is two inscriptions found at Housesteads on Hadrian's Wall:

To the god Mars Thincsus, and the two Alaisiagae Beda and Fimmilena, and to the godhood (*numen*) of Augustus Germanicus, the citizens of Tuihantus have paid their vow freely and deservedly.

RIB 1593

To the god Mars, and the two Alaisiagae, and the godhood of Augustus Germanicus, the citizens of Tuihantus, of the troop of the Frisians of Ver(covicium), of Severus Alexander's, paid their vow deservedly.

RIB 1594

These inscriptions from the reign of Alexander Severus (AD 222–35) identify 'Mars', god of the Thing and the eponymous divinities of the Old West Frisian Bodthing and Fimelthing; these dedicants come from Twente (Overijssel, Netherlands).[8] The god is probably *Tiwaz, as in *Tuesday*, the god of the Thing, as in the Dutch *Dinsdag* (Chapter 10). This is the god who had a grove where the Thing met in Denmark – *Tislund*.[9] And if we turn also to the *Teutoburgiensis saltus*, where Roman soldiers were grimly sacrificed (Chapter 9), its very name, implying a word *Teuto-burgium* ('nation fortified-centre'), shows that it was not just a wood which happened to be there. In fact it was *the grove which contained the Thing-place.*[10]

There is, of course, nothing unusual about early societies structuring government through the three levels of (1) king or magistrates, (2) a council of elders and (3), what is at issue here, an assembly of the male warriors.[11] The Thing, however, is different. When it meets frequently – for instance, at the full and new moons – it obviously covers only a local range of peoples.[12] But it is an institution of more formidable significance when it occurs less often and with correspondingly greater range, uniting a variety of peoples who claim to belong to the same stock. Longer periods between meetings imply wider geographical coverage, just as the twelve-yearly Kumbha Mela in north India summons pilgrims in their millions.[13]

The variety of possible geographical ranges is well dissected in *Guta saga*:

> People used to trust in woods [groves] and hills (*hauga*, cf. *hearg*), in sanctuaries (*wi*) and in staff-precincts [containing a *Pfahlgott*, pole-shaped idol?] and in heathen gods. They performed *blot* [sacrifice] using their sons and their own daughters, and cattle with food and beer . . . The whole country held a supreme *blot* amidst (?) the people. Furthermore, each thirding held its own; and smaller Things held lesser *blotan*, with cattle, food and beer. They were called 'fellow-worshippers' (*suþnautr*) because they all worshipped together.
>
> *Guta saga*, A 44 verso (cf. also Boyer 1992: 158)

In Norway, though there might be partial Things – the þriðjungþing (one third), the Fjórðungþing (quarter), Heraðsþing (eighth) – the principal meeting was of the Alþing (all) or Þjóðþing (people's, *Teuto-*). The Icelandic Althing used to meet every summer at its regular place, Thingvellir, at the south of the island.[14]

GROVES AND ASSEMBLIES

In several Indo-European cultures a grove is the meeting place for an authoritative assembly.

Leaders of the Batavi could be invited to a feast in a 'sacred forest' (*sacrum nemus*) by Julius Civilis in AD 69 (Tacitus, *Histories* 4.14.2) where the words *nocte et laetitia* ('night and merriment') evoke something of the *Biergarten* in modern groves of chestnut trees. Yet we should not take the religious ambience too lightly, for it was also from 'woods and groves' that the Germans who joined Civilis took their 'statues of wild animals'[15] with which they processed to war. Similarly, legations from all the 100 villages (*Germania* 39.3) of the Semnones met centrally in a grove to transact business, beginning with a human sacrifice. And the remarkable cult of Nerthus was celebrated in a grove by another, rather miscellaneous, section of the Suebians – the Longobardi, Reudigni, Aviones, Anglii, Varini, Eudoses, Suarines and Nuitones – *in commune*, jointly (*Germania* 40.2, cf. Chapter 9).

Celts in Galatia (Asia Minor) also met at a *nemeton* which appears to be a grove. These Galatai were divided into three peoples – not an atypical division, as can be seen from the three tribes which constituted the Dorians and other Greek examples. Each people in turn was divided into four tetrarchies. 'The Council of the twelve tetrarchs consisted of 300 men and they met at the so-called *Drunemeton* ('Oak shrine'). The Council, then, passed judgement in cases of murder, whereas the tetrarchs and judges dealt with other cases' (Strabo 12.5.1).

There are still traces of meetings of assemblies in groves in Greece and Rome. The territory of Aigai in the northern Peloponnese owned 'the Amarion, the grove of Zeus [i.e. Zeus Amarios], where the Achaeans used to meet to deliberate about state affairs' in the third/second century BC (Strabo 8.7.5). And back in 411 the Athenian assembly was convoked at the temple of Poseidon Hippios in the grove at Kolonos, two kilometres outside Athens, to deliberate on a change of constitution.[16] Evidently, a special occasion like this called for special authority, whatever role may have been played by pragmatic concerns.

In the early, legendary, period of Roman history Livy tells us that King Tarquinius Superbus called meetings of elders, and of the armed soldiery, in the grove of the spring Ferentina at the foot of the Alban Mount.[17] And at Iguvium (Gubbio) an assembly of the state, apparently for elections, was held in the grove of Jupiter.[18]

The Romans belonged to the Latin group of Italian tribes who, according to legend, once, under the leadership of their *dictator* Manius Egerius Baebius of Tusculum, had dedicated the grove at Aricia to Diana (the famous *Nemus*), as a focus for the identity of the twenty-eight or thirty participating townships.[19] All that would seem needed is a human sacrifice and it could just be that the quirky tale of the King of the *Nemus*, the slave (i.e. captive) who is 'king' for a period but only within the grove and then slaughtered, though by the incoming 'king', has its roots in more straightforward Germanic-style barbarism.

As in Greece, Rome had resorted to groves at moments of special constitutional difficulty. The trial around 385 BC of Manlius Capitolinus, who had led a popular insurrection, was transferred to a grove. In 342 BC such an assembly granted an amnesty to the plebs who had seceded from the state in the *Lucus Petelinus* by the *Porta Flumentana* ('River Gate'). Some time between 289 and 286, during the last such secession, the authority of the *Comitia Tributa* was settled by a law, the *Lex Hortensia*, passed in the *Aesculetum* ('Oak Grove'), possibly the same grove.[20] This assembly has been argued by Palmer to be the archaic, religious and in historical times practically redundant *Comitia Curiata*, whose purpose is to give a single forum to thirty *curiae* thought of as people dwelling in distinct places: 'They also seem to have been local groupings . . . each with its own meeting-place . . . The *curiae* were probably the basis of the oldest military organization and certainly the elements of the oldest Roman assembly' (T.J. Cornell and A. Momigliano, in *OCD*3 s.v. 'curia'). The number is obviously similar to that of the participants in the Latin league, as also to the number of men's groups attending the Spartan

Karneia (27, cf. Chapter 10), numbers curiously similar to the number of days in a lunar month. Palmer has further argued, in a remarkable piece of detective work, that the site known in Rome simply as the *Comitium* ('Assembly') may in fact itself once have been a grove outside the city. Indeed, to take the auspices without which the *comitia* could not be held, a *templum* had to be marked out. A *templum* is a hallowed area, only later the building constructed in that hallowed area. To mark out a *templum*, a standard way was to identify trees as the limits of the area.[21]

Part of the evidence which Palmer (1969: 45) uses for the supposition that the Comitium was a grove is the remarkable number of 'wellheads' (*putealia*) that have been found in this area. A *puteal* is indeed 'a structure surrounding the mouth of a well (including the lid to cover it)'[22] but the same structure was used particularly to enclose a *bidental* – a place struck by lightning, expiated by the sacrifice of a sheep (archaic and poetic: *bidens*, 'two-tooth'), and marked off as a taboo (*triste*) area in which no-one may tread.[23] In the nature of things it is likely that these would mark trees. This mentality demonstrates another aspect of the power of the grove – as a focus for the lightning bolt, something we have seen earlier (Chapter 11). 'A grove', says the fourth-century AD grammarian Charisius, presumably repeating some more ancient and knowledgeable author such as Varro, 'is a place struck by lightning and covered thickly by trees.'[24] This seems somewhat garbled: a *lucus* in principle should be a clearing in a wood or forest; lightning today is a major cause of forest fires[25] and it may be that a clearing can be caused by such a fire.

There is nothing obvious about meeting in a grove. It is perfectly possible – and for a whole army maybe more convenient – to meet in the open. The Roman *Comitia Centuriata* met in the open on the Campus Martius, though even that was within a bounded space, the so-called 'sheep-pen' (*ovile*). To meet in a grove is something more than this. There may be some protection while you meet, but overwhelmingly the sense is one of religious sanction which contributes to the authority of decisions. It is notable that some instances we have seen are of constitutional change, where a grove on the one hand serves the function of distinction from other votes, as a two-thirds majority may today, and on the other acts as an 'outside', an 'elsewhere', a religiously sanctified margin, where a society may make the transition from one set of state rules to another. To obtain similar sanctification in historical times, you would have to meet in a temple – just as the Roman Senate sometimes met in the temple of Bellona.

It may be of some significance that Italian groves are often found at margins between properties (Chapter 6) – and between nations or their components, like Marklo, a placename in Saxony, meaning 'border-grove'.[26] They are a neutral and sacral place at which to meet. The *Lucus Ferentinae* is therefore appropriate for early Latin hosts to assemble. In the same way the *Lucus Feroniae*[27] for which the *Ager Capenas* was celebrated (Vergil, *Aeneid* 7.697) occupied something of a border region between Etruscans, Latins and Sabines.[28] This gave it an international dimension, reflected both in the multinational attendances alleged for its early history by Livy (1.30) and Dionysios (3.32.1) and in the almost Delphic wealth that drew Hannibal to plunder this 'temple at that time famous for its wealth: the people of Capena and others who lived near it brought the first-fruits of their harvests there and other gifts according to supply and kept it adorned with a quantity of gold and silver' (Livy 26.11.8).

One final oddity emerges from Caesar's remark that Gaulish chieftains sometimes live in the heart of woods or seek out the proximity of woods and streams (*Gallic war* 6.30). Caesar claims this is purely a question of amenity – avoiding the heat – but this is rightly challenged by Le Roux and Guyonvarc'h (1986: 230 f.), who discern in it an attempt to arrogate 'centrality' to themselves. I simply add here that these chieftains are also those who would summon an assembly of fighters which would naturally meet in a grove because of its special authority.

PERIODICITY AND LEAGUES

We have seen that the problems posed by attempting to synchronise the lunar and solar years lead to the adoption of time periods larger than a year used for intercalation (Chapter 10). One typical large-scale period is that of nine years. A clear example is the festival of Fricco (Freyr) at Uppsala, described by Adam of Bremen, designed to reintegrate the community: it is 'a common rite of all the provinces of Sweden', held 'after nine years' (4.27), though we do not know whether in the Greek inclusive sense which we would call every eight:

> For nine [successive] days feastings and that sort of sacrifice are celebrated. On each day they sacrifice one man together with other animals, in such a way that over nine days there are seventy-two animals that are sacrificed. This sacrifice happens at the spring equinox.
>
> Adam, *W Schol.* 141 (137)

Though nine years is more likely, reflected by each of the nine days of sacrifice, 'after nine years' might mean in the eighth year and each of the days of *eight* sacrifices (9 × 8 = 72) might represent the whole spread of eight years.[29] Something similar may be happening in the grand sacrifice of Nestor at the beginning of the third book of Homer's *Odyssey*:

... they [the people of Pylos] were sacrificing victims on the
 shore of the sea,
bulls all-black to the deep-dark haired earth-shaker [Poseidon].
There were nine places and 500 people sat
in each, and at each point they offered nine bulls.

Homer, *Odyssey* 3.5–8

These look like the nine constituent areas of the community uniting for
their special periodic feast (after nine years?) with their eighty-one animals for Poseidon, god of this community, very frequently of male initia-
tions and therefore of the male community, whether you call it
Männerbund or Thing.[30] 'Nine' is also the number of days that Odin
hung, a sacrifice to himself (Chapter 9), a moment certainly of renewal
of authority and of human sacrifice, a recurrent theme in this context. A
similar[31] festival was held in Denmark at Leire (8 kilometres south-west
of Roskilde) until 934:

There is a place in these parts, the capital of this kingdom, called
Lederun (Leire), in a village called Selon, where after nine years
in the month of January, after the time at which we celebrate the
Epiphany of the Lord, all gathered together and there to their
gods they sacrificed ninety-nine men and the same number of
horses, together with dogs and cocks and hawks, thinking for
certain, as I have said earlier, that these would serve the same –
the dead – and act as compensation with the same for the crimes
they have committed. How well our king [Henry I, Saxon King of
Germany] did in putting an end to their practice of so loathsome
a rite.

Thietmar 1.17 (9)

Such large-scale festivals of reintegration, sometimes with a judicial
dimension, are not restricted to Germanic culture, as we can see from
the Galatai at Drunemeton, or the Roman *comitia*. We should not leave
druids out of the picture, either:

These meet at a fixed time of the year in the territory of the
Carnutes [whence 'Chartres'; they also had an *oppidum* Cenabum
– Orléans] which is the middle region of the whole of Gaul in a
consecrated place ['*nemeton*'?]. Here everyone who has a dispute
anywhere comes and accepts their decrees and judgements.

Caesar, *Gallic war* 6.13.10

Caesar, or his source, exaggerates. This is the meeting of one Gaulish
equivalent of the Thing, that of the Carnutes *foederati*, 'federated

Carnutes' as Pliny the elder calls them (4.107), not of the whole of Gaul. A similarly inexact statement (and the two refute each other) is made by Diodoros when he claims that the Celts even now 'honour Alesia [Alise-Ste-Reine, Côte d'Or, fifty kilometres north-west of Dijon] as the hearth and mother-city of all the Celtic land'.[32] The solution is that both places are *centres for particular leagues*; the characteristic heavy emphasis on centrality may be authentically Gaulish, reflected also in the Mediolanum names (above). Leagues, then, are not to be seen as a development of historical times but a prehistoric inheritance. Periodicity, too, seems attested for Gaul: Diodoros (5.32.6) relates, presumably from Poseidonios (*FGH* 87F116), that criminals were kept back for human sacrifice at five-year intervals, the period of the Coligny Calendar when necessarily time must be renewed.[33]

Ireland is particularly associated with an ideology, for instance, of quarters and centre. Though this, too, has been the stuff of overenthusiastic writing, there can be no doubt that it represents a version of the traditions we are looking at here.[34] There were three striking *oenaige* ('gatherings'). One is at Tara, the seat of the High King (*ard rī*), a 155-metre hill in Meath, the 'middle' province of Ireland. Around Meath are arranged the four provinces of Ulster, Leinster, Munster and Connacht, leading to diagrams that look like a Gaulish temple or the ground-plan of Svantovit's temple at Arkona and which recall something of the world geography of the *Rig veda*.[35] There are traditions also of other arrangements, involving, for instance, the centring of twelve chieftains around the single king, which Rees and Rees compare not only with mythology but with the system of twelve divisions of the Icelandic Althing. Legend tells of the great 'Feast of Tara', held at Samhain, at which the four provincial kings and their peoples assembled – just as it is only with the arrival of the Five Kindreds that the Cosmic Year can be renewed in the *Rig veda* and the 'first sacrifice' repeated. Heady stuff, this, and Rees and Rees, who have put together this picture, certainly deviate towards the visionary side, but it is a tempting collection of evidence even to a writer as down to earth as Byrne (1973: 58 f.). In any case this festival appears to have taken place every seven years:[36] 'The preparation of the feast of Tara lasted 7 years and it is again at the end of 7 years that the general assembly of all the men of Ireland took place at the feast of Tara' (*Ordeals of Ireland*, in Le Roux and Guyonvarc'h 1995: 57). The feast was last held under King Diarmid in 560.[37] At the feast legal disputes were settled just as Caesar reports they were by druids of Chartres (above) and the rule of law was asserted (Byrne 1973: 31). Even the word Samhain may mean 'reunion, gathering'.[38] And just as the Scandinavians had their smaller Things, so in Ireland 'assemblies similar to those of the great centres of Meath were held at provincial capitals and at lesser centres' (Rees and Rees 1961: 168).

Tailtiu, or Teltown, is halfway between Nava/An Uaimh and Kells/
Ceanannus Mor (Meath).[39] There a second festival requiring a general
gathering of the Irish people was held annually between 15 July and 15
August. The meeting is actually focused on Lugnasad, the festival of Lug,
on 1 August, and it supposedly went back 303 years before the birth of
Christ. For its duration there was what Greeks would have called a 'sacred
truce': those travelling to the *oenach* were sacrosanct. In addition, something which is interesting in the light of Lithuanian customs (Chapter 13),
it seems to have had some character of mourning the dead because Tailtiu
was a burial site also. The great altar of Rome and Augustus was dedicated at Lyon on 1 August in 12 BC;[40] by it stood sixty statues of the tribes
of Gaul and this was to be the site where Gaulish notables were to
foregather to worship Rome and Augustus, on the day, in effect, of the
oenach, to all appearance appropriating a festival of union and identity of
the Gauls. There are similar implications in setting up a new centre called
Augustonemeton at Clermont.

A third and final *oenach*, held at Beltane (May Day), involves a different centre in Meath, namely Uisnech, where Mide the chief druid (the
eponym of Meath) is supposed to have lit the first fire – and the ceremony,
of course, involves the creation of new fire, by a 'fire-drill', not so different
from the crucial and decried use of 'need-fire' by the Germans. Sugges-
tively, at one annual ceremony of renewal at Uisnech, where the peoples
had gathered, Lug was killed. Lug is a leading candidate for identification
with the Gaulish Mercury and (Chapters 5, 7) with Wodan–Odin, who in
a peculiar way 'human-sacrifices' himself. In any event the ceremony at
Uisnech, arranged by druids, is described as an *oenach*.

Turning to Italy, the Etruscans, those non-Indo-European neighbours
of Rome, as mysterious in Italy as the Basques in Spain, reinforced their
national sense by annual ritual. The nominally *twelve* towns of Etruria
assembled for annual ceremonies at the shrine of a god Voltumna, reckoned 'the principal god of Etruria' by Varro (*De lingua latina* 46), at
Volsinii (by Lake Bolsena). The lake and the River Marta, which connects
Volsinii with Tarquinii, just like the lakes and rivers of their northern
neighbours the Celts, received offerings and there was a chief priest
relative to this whole assembly of peoples, just like the chief druid.

The relationship of Rome to the Latins was originally a question of
membership of a league, the Latin league.[41] This met at the Alban Mount
to worship Jupiter Latiaris and, as we have seen, at the grove at Aricia to
worship Diana. At the former, the *Feriae Latinae*, we are told that use was
made of *oscilla* ('danglers'), which in this instance seem to be swings but
which in many other cases are human masks hung up on trees, which one
ancient writer suggests may go back to a custom of placing heads on
poles.[42] I have never much believed in 'mitigations of an old custom of
human sacrifice', but the German comparisons in this case suggest just

that.[43] Roman traditions of 'danglers' get confused with Greek traditions of 'danglers' (*aiora*), where puppets and swings were on occasion attached to trees and one specimen of the goddess Artemis was known as Artemis *apanchomene* ('throttled/hanged') – which provoked even the cautious Nilsson to think of Odin's self-immolation.[44] The Italian custom of the *Ver sacrum* (Chapter 9) might also belong here. Massive representative sacrifice, recalling Uppsala, is approved by the community under the patronage of its chief god, whether Jupiter or maybe more likely Mars, with a view, at least on the one historical occasion we know about, to the next five-year period. Other legends connect the Sacred Spring with the formation of new nations from old, which we call colonisation.[45] On purely *a priori* grounds, if we admit that new societies were formed by splinter groups from the old (and this is not just obvious but a recurrent message of Greek mythology), then we may wonder whether there could be any other possible occasion for this redefinition of affiliations than a plenary meeting of the Thing, whatever it was called in that society (at Rome is was called the *populus Romanus Quirites*).[46]

In Greece political reintegrations might seem lacking, but there are some remnants. The originally *twelve* states of the Ionian Greeks met for the Panionia (All-Ionian festival) at Priene at the shrine of Poseidon Helikonios, the so called Panionion. They used the occasion to make political decisions, too, especially in the 490s BC in the resistance against the Persians. I suppose it is also possible that the four-yearly Greek meetings for masculine games that are oddly international – the festivals at Olympia, Nemea, Corinth and Delphi – might also go back to some earlier Thing with more than local coverage, though obviously not national or competitive with other Things at that stage. If a Thing-like organisation had been inherited, it might also explain why a tribe of Greeks as primitive as the Aetolians, a mere *ethnos* (people) still living like Germans in villages,[47] might so easily have advanced in the fourth century BC to the political organisation of a 'league'.[48] The Aetolians met twice-yearly, at the beginning and end of the campaigning season (at the beginning of summer and the beginning of winter?). The meeting took place at Thermon, where there must have been *hot* (*thermos*) springs giving rise to the cult of Apollo Thermios.[49] This was where they traditionally held an annual festival-cum-fair, an *oenach* as it were, where they kept their valuables (cf. all those Slav temples) and elected their magistrates.[50] The precise setting was evidently the shrine of Apollo, a god whose name has led to various explanations. However, one possibility, which Burkert in particular has promoted (it goes back ultimately to Plutarch), is that Apollo is the god of the *apella*, the male-warrior assembly of the Dorian and west Greeks typically held annually because a month can be named after it (Apellaios).[51] This may in the end be one reason why Apollo is so associated with the creation of new states, colonies, twenty-five of which were even called 'Apollonia'.[52] So the Aetolian picture would then be complete: Thing, Thing-place, Thing-god, periodicity and primitive statehood. The only difference is that instead of hanging bodies in trees, they hang suits of armour, taken from bodies as trophies of those bodies, in porticoes (Polybios 5.8.9).

There may be some traces in Greece of the German model of a periodic festival with human sacrifice, though in each case it is possible to explain away the sacrifice, especially as a myth designed to dramatise changes in social status. Nevertheless, in the light of the German model it may be that we should be less sceptical about 'original' human sacrifices. The cultic centre for federated Arcadians (and again I will suppose a pre-federation) was the shrine of Zeus Lykaios on Mount Lykaion – he even appears on their coins. Here men were supposed to turn into wolves for a period of nine years and it was also supposed that human sacrifice took place.[53] It would take worryingly little to transpose these details into an Uppsala-type periodic festival or Zeus into a bloodthirsty Wodan. Another Zeus was worshipped on Mount Ithome, spiritual centre of the Messenians, and there, too, their king, Aristomenes, was supposed to have sacrificed 300 prisoners of war including the Spartan king Theopompos.[54] Greeks may normally be studied within the context of civilised cultural achievement, but there is no reason why their original cult practices should have been any less revolting than those of early Germanic peoples. Finally, the Thessalians, who were notable for the early display of 'federal organisation', worshipped Zeus Laphystios, Zeus who 'gorges' like a pre-datory animal, at Alos where another human sacrifice story is told.[55]

These ceremonies specifically preserve a sense of nationhood at a higher level than that of the tribe, the highest level normally considered. But at the same time they do not embrace much more than a county or *départment* in our terms. The people meets periodically and worships a formidable god of war and/or lightning. Human sacrifice, in particular, is on the menu.

A special human sacrifice is that of a king at the end of a fixed period of office. This format, which Frazer tried to establish in *The golden bough*, would, if genuine, have the effect of superimposing a drastic reinstitution of kingship over the Thing-and-renewal ceremonies that I have been envisaging.[56] The complication is that all the tales of kings being killed are mythical and it is in the nature of myth to dramatise the issues it plays out. If kingship is to be renewed, then myth quite naturally and idiomatically depicts it as the immolation of the old king, even on occasion by himself, and the accession of a new one. In the real, non-mythic world, however, the same king resumes his reign, refreshed, just as the whole society is. Thus, my view is that the evidence adduced by Frazer is of genuine interest for periodic festivals of renewal, but where it alleges royal sacrifice it should not be taken literally. It is the period of renewal which matters and which Homer attests in the following extraordinary lines:

> And among them [the cities of Crete] is Knossos, a great city, where Minos
> at nine-year intervals [i.e. eight] used to become king,[57] he who communed with great Zeus.
>
> Homer, Odyssey 19.178 f.

A rather strange dialogue attributed to Plato explains this passage as meaning that every nine years Minos (was this the official name of the Cretan king, as Midas was of the Phrygian kings?) went to the Cave of Zeus to give an account of what he had learnt from Zeus in the previous nine-year period and to learn some more ('Plato', *Minos* 319e). What cult reality underlies Homer or this explanation is not clear, but it does lie within the field of periodic renewal.

HUMAN SACRIFICE AND BEGINNINGS

The nine-yearly celebrations of the Thing at Uppsala and Leire were marked by human sacrifice. This provides the context for a grim passage of Tacitus about the Semnones which we cited more fully earlier (Chapter 6):

> *At a fixed time the peoples of the same name and same blood* come together in deputations into a wood sanctified by the auguries of their fathers and through ancient awe: slaying a man in public, they celebrate the gruesome opening of their barbarian rite.
>
> Tacitus, Germania 39 (my emphasis)

This barbarous culture should perhaps also include a final example, from the Althing in Iceland in 999: 'The pagans took the step of sacrificing two men from each quarter (farthing) of the country and invoking the pagan gods not to let Christianity take control of the country' (*Kristni saga* 12).[58]

At Uppsala it is for Thor that the unfortunate victims were drowned in the sacred pool, then hung on trees in the grove (Thor is also the recipient of the offerings of Dudo's Norsemen, Chapter 9). This fits with the archaeological evidence for human sacrifice around AD 400 in Denmark at a place called Torsbjerg.[59] Thor is very much associated with the Thing and it is on Thursday, so it is said, that the Thing is opened (*FW* s.v. 'Thor' 1109). Clearly there is a Scandinavian area in which Thor is the god of the Thing, in contrast to the *Tiwaz of our Frisians (above).

Wodan seems more to be involved with the hanging of warriors, as we have seen, but he may be meant when Tacitus speaks of the 'Mercury to whom on certain days [Thing days?] they have the custom of sacrificing also human victims' (*Germania* 9.1).

Human sacrifice may seem a German barbarism at the Thing. But we should recall that the Gauls who met at such 'centres' as Chartres were known for human sacrifice, that such sacrifice was associated, at least by the baroque Lucan, with groves and that the priesthood that dealt with the centralising festival – the Gaulish Thing – was the druids, who were infamously associated with human sacrifice.

Prussians, too, conducted human sacrifice of captives and the Lithuanians, also Balts, seem to have conducted their human sacrifices (attested, e.g., in 1338, 1345 and 1365) in the context of annual festivals, held in groves, that asserted national identity and cohesion. These festivals are described by Jan Długosz in the later fifteenth century:

> It was an ancestral custom and ceremony of the Lithuanians while the murk of paganism possessed them to collect crops around the beginning of October and go to the woods which they thought sacred with their wives, children and family; they would then offer to their ancestral gods oxen, calves, rams and other animals over a three-day period, both as sacrificial victims and to be burnt whole. When they had made these offerings and sacrifices, in the same three-day period, taking time off for revelry, they feasted and roistered with games and dancing and fed upon their sacrifices. This was considered the most important and solemn sacrifice of all, one which no-one might miss. And bringing back a triumph or booty from enemy territory, too, on their return they constructed a woodpile and pyre, to whose construction everyone contributed some wood. They threw on top and burnt the most outstanding and notable of the captives, thinking their gods were most pleased and gratified by this sort of burnt offering.[60]
>
> Jan Długosz, *LPG* 143 f. (also, Clemen 1936: 106)

It no longer happened in the time of Długosz – King Vladislav had chopped down the groves at Vilnius.

Similarly, the Slavs of Pomerania celebrated human sacrifice at their central shrines of Rethra and Arkona. The impression is given by the writers that these shrines, like Delphi, attracted individual travellers by their fame, suggesting 'pilgrimage' as the model we should adopt (Deržavin 1948: 32). But the Redarii who ran Rethra were a major division, one of four principal peoples, of the Ljutiči and it looks very much as if Rethra was the 'central' sanctuary of the loosely federated Ljutiči.[61] As well as being the central sanctuary, it was, according to Adam (2.21), their *antiquissima urbs*, 'oldest city', and this takes us back again to the origin of the Gaulish *oppidum* in a central shrine (above) and maybe also further into mythology. As we approach the end of this book, I leave the reader with a final glimpse of these pagans:

> There grew strong in those days (*c.*1135) throughout Slavia the manifold worship of idols and the error of superstitions. For, quite apart from the groves and household gods with which the fields and towns overflowed, first and foremost were Prove god of the land of Aldeburg, Siwa goddess of the Polabi, and Radigast god of the land of the Obotrites. These had dedicated to them *flamens* [pagan priests] and offerings of sacrifice and the manifold worship of religion. Furthermore, the priest announced the ceremonies to be held for the gods according to the indication of lots. Men and wives met together with their little ones and slaughtered victims to their gods, oxen and sheep and several even [sacrificed] Christian people whose blood they proudly asserted their gods enjoyed. After the slaughter of the victim, the priest tasted some of the blood so that he might be more efficacious in grasping oracles – that demons are summoned more easily by blood is a common opinion. Once the sacrifices had been completed in accordance with usual practice, the people turned to feasting and clapping. The Slavs had this amazing erroneous practice: in their feasts and drinking bouts they circulate a bowl into which they contribute words, I would say of consecration but of execration in the name of gods, that is, a good one and a bad one, because they made out that all prosperous fortune came from the good god and all adverse from the bad one. So it is that in their language they called the bad god Devil or Zcerneboch, that is 'Black God' [Helmold translates the Slavonic correctly]. Among the manifold divinities of the Slavs the most powerful was Zvantevith, the god of the land of the Rugiani, because he was more efficacious in [oracular] responses. In comparison with him they considered the others more like demigods. As a result it was in his special honour that they were accustomed annually to sacrifice to the same a Christian person whom the lot had marked out. Indeed, all the Slav provinces used to send fixed funds to him for the sacrifices.
>
> Helmold 1.52

Human sacrifice, then, appears necessary and done for its own sake. It is not just a form of capital punishment, but slaves are bought from other communities, preferably Christian so that they are alien not only to the sacrificers but estranged from the gods to whom they will be sacrificed. In an utterly perverse way this testifies to the religious sensibilities of those who sought human victims.

THE BEGINNING OF THE WORLD

It is a great and formidable thing to create place. Not simply temporarily to occupy, for a while to be at, some point in the continuum of space, but to give it the identity and meaning that only permanent human habitation can. Roman land-surveyors set up terminus-stones over still-warm pits of sacrifice (Chapter 9). Gauls marked out their sanctuaries with copious quantities of bones, in pits or in boundary ditches. Britons, as they began buildings, dug sacrifices into pits and trenches to underlie their foundations, sacrifices which encompassed not only animals but sometimes human beings. 'What appears to have survived longest', says Vendryès (1948: 317) of the Britons, 'is the slaughter of victims offered to the gods to consecrate the foundation of a building.' He refers to a tale told of the British king Vortigern, whose *magi* (priests/magicians) advised him:

> 'Go to the ends of your kingdom and you shall find a fortified stronghold to defend yourself, since the race you have taken into your kingdom [the Saxons under Hengist] hates you and will kill you by trickery and will occupy all the land you love with your whole people after your death . . . [Vortigern proceeds to Snowdon and is then told:] 'Unless you find a baby with no father and it is killed and the castle is sprinkled with its blood, it shall never be built.'
>
> Nennius, *History of the Britons* 40

This is the last, rather weak, evidence for British foundation sacrifice: in this myth, an aetiology for a placename beneath Snowdon, the child is not after all sacrificed: it turns out to be a gifted seer, Emrys in Welsh, Ambrosius (Aurelianus) in Latin, a later ruler of Britain. Geoffrey of Monmouth (6.17) will tell us that this was none other than Merlin. But the evidence is more solid in earlier times: 'Single human beings of both sexes were found buried under the ramparts of the Iron Age forts of Maiden Castle, Hod Hill and South Cadbury' (Hutton 1991: 194).

At Tanagra (Boiotia, Greece) an ancient legend told how its founder Poimandros had killed his own son Ephippos as he leapt the ditch with which Poimandros had just marked out the new town.[62] And Rome itself could only be founded in a primal myth that encompassed the killing of one twin by another – Remus as he leapt the walls which Romulus, founder, was creating[63] – or was it the ditch crying out for its human offering?

Twins and their archetypal fratricide go back in Indo-European lore to the very beginning of time, and of the world. It is hard work reconstructing Indo-European mythology, so let us be grateful to Bruce Lincoln, who has done it:[64]

> At the beginning of time . . . there were two brothers, a priest whose name was 'Man' (*Manu*) and a king, whose name was 'Twin' (*Yemo*), who travelled together accompanied by an ox. For reasons that are not specified, they took it upon themselves to create the world, and toward that end the priest offered up his brother and the ox in what was to be the first ritual sacrifice. Dismembering their bodies, he used the various parts to create the material universe and human society as well, taking all three classes from the body of the first king who . . . combined within himself the social totality.
>
> Lincoln 1991: 7

We do not have to subscribe to every detail of Lincoln's reconstruction and we may pause at the Dumézilian tripartition of society (Chapter 12), but the fact remains that this is the myth that makes sense of the bundle of features that we have examined in this chapter. It is right, too, that the end of this book should be a myth.

The Semnones celebrated the 'beginnings of their race' (Chapter 6, and above) with a human sacrifice in their special grove, all 100 villages assembled. It takes little prompting now to realise that this is a ritual replay of their creation myth (Lincoln 1991: 13) – or to start wondering about druids. Are druids not experts on the origins of the race in 'father Dis', now king of the Underworld like the Indian *Yama*? Are they not also experts in human sacrifice at periodic intervals among federated tribes given to meeting in centres? It may be a leap of the imagination, in defiance of those sources that look blinkered at the druidic paradox of philosophy and barbarism, but this replay of the Creation is where druids belong (*ibid.* ch. 14).

Incas, as I write, are being said to have renewed time through abominable child-sacrifices on icy mountain-peaks. Our ancestors, too, apparently believed that at great intervals of time, as the moon and sun came back into harmony, the various constituent limbs of the nation must return together to their place of creation beneath the trees – inward, centripetal motion, growth displayed in reverse photography. Creation and the initialisation of time could then take place in an equal and opposite, outward, centrifugal movement. The catalyst was the human sacrifice that had begun creation in the times of myth, a paradigm for ever.

AFTERWORD

It would be false to paganism to draw general conclusions about what it is and what it must be. Like the gastronomy of Europe, it responds to local materials and local needs, and also, irrespective of any determining causes, maintains a sensuous variety, forming an essential part of the identity of a nation, a village, a household.

The difficulty with learning about European paganism has always been that the evidence for so many areas is so limited or patchy: these traditions turned very rapidly from valued inheritance to despised pre-Christian primitivism best forgotten. Conversely, in a few areas, particularly the Greek and Roman, these are huge fields, studied in detail and with ever-increasing expertise and sophistication by dedicated scholars. My aim has been to manage and reconfigure this material so that we feel the wealth, not the poverty, of our information and always to privilege evidence that is characterful. To the very last moment of writing, I have found passages which have cried 'Include me!' – and in they have gone.

The result may be miscellaneous and incomplete. But it has flavour and it develops its own internal coherence. Perhaps I have spent too long on groves, but they are very special and stand in all sorts of relationships to our pagan societies, to modern sensibilities and above all to the authors that report them. These authors are not just legal witnesses, nor do they supply bare unconditioned pieces of 'evidence': every statement has a character of its own and every author reveals so much about himself by the very fact of considering something religious or pagan. Poseidonios, simultaneously admiring and appalled by these strange Gauls at the fringes of the known world; Pliny the elder writing *Encarta* for the Roman world before he died in the eruption of Vesuvius; Caesarius on the scent of the last vestiges of paganism and with all his mighty archiepiscopal authority; Bede thanking Jesus for preserving him from a tradition which he feels impelled to record; Charlemagne first massacring Saxons then sternly legislating so that he may don the cloak of the Christian, and Roman, Emperor; Adam of Bremen recounting the struggles that underlay the establishment of the bishopric of Hamburg; Paul

Einhorn, somewhat like Bede or rather as we wish Bede had done, writing whole books on the terrible errors of the Prussians (read all about it). And all those saints confounding their pagan enemies: were the Gauls more impressed by Martin's arguments about tree-stumps and *de rigueur* miracles or by the armed guard he had with him?

Nature is variably powerful: as any motorway traveller knows, much of it is exceptionally dull. But identifiable parts are magical even for us. We have seen springs, lakes, rivers, trees, rocks, groves, meadows and caves. But this is not simple ecology and our post-industrial nature is not in the end their nature. Only gradually through seeing the actual evidence do we gain some sense of the contribution of environment to veneration.

Finally, most startling of all has been the picture which gradually comes together feature by feature, like themes in the last movement of a Bruckner symphony: these Indo-European nations had inherited a particular and fundamental festival. A nation, a tribe (call it what you will), so it emerges, is perceived as a federation united by religion. It assembles at a particular point in the year or, with advanced understanding of lunar and solar years, at intervals determined by intercalation. The nation starts again: a primal, mythic human sacrifice is actually and horrifically re-enacted in a grove to achieve the renewal of time, order and law. These were our European ancestors.

NOTES

1 APPROACHING PAGANISM

1 McNeill and Garner 1938: 3.
2 *Pisteuein eis* = believe in.
3 *Paganismus* and *paganitas* begin with such authors as Marius Victorinus, *TLL* s.vv.
4 See Chuvin 1990: 8 f.
5 Hutton discusses this issue well in a forthcoming book, siding with Chuvin.
6 Onions s.v.; Grimm 1875: i.1 n.1.
7 *Wildnisbewohner*, Winkler, in *HDA* iii.1635. My thanks to Ronald Hutton for drawing my attention to the difficulty in Gothic, even if I persist in underrating it.
8 Notably Jones and Pennick 1995: ch.1.
9 Dowden 1992a: 3 f.
10 Judaism was seriously in the business of conversion elsewhere in Europe, cf. Fletcher 1997: ch.9, 'Rival monotheisms'. Source for the Vladimir story: the *Nachal'naya letopis'* for the year 6494 (986), Cross and Sherbowitz-Wetzor, pp.96–111.
11 Note that the Bulgars were a Turkic race, or at least élite, not the Slavonic Bulgarians we know today (Fletcher 1997: 337); in the ninth century they were still pagan, worshipping a principal god Tengri (*ibid.* 339). This association of Bulgars with Islam is, however, rather curious. Had anti-Byzantine sentiment briefly assimilated them to the world of Islam, or is this an error in the perception of the chronicle?
12 Chuvin 1990: 84 f.
13 *Codex theodosianus* 16.10 and 2.8. Chuvin 1990: 38 f., 65, 71.
14 Mylonas 1961: 8.
15 Turcan 1996: 44 f.
16 Lizzi 1990: 168, but it looks more like public servants to me.
17 Fauduet 1993: 93 f.
18 *Codex theodosianus* 16.10.20. Chuvin 1990: 91 f.
19 No missionary: Fletcher 1997: 76. Moses or Elijah, see Wolfram 1988: 76.
20 Todd 1992: 164 f.
21 Ulfila's compromise Arianism: Wolfram 1988: 79, Heather 1996: 60 f.
22 Their kings had already been converted: Chuvin 1990: 129.
23 Sulpicius Severus, *Chronica* 2.51.
24 Facts about, and dates for, the conversion of these peoples are not specially controversial. In standard histories of Europe, scant attention is paid to conversions, e.g., G. Livet and R. Mousnier (eds), *Histoire générale de l'Europe*, 3

vols (Paris 1980), which deals with Scandinavia at i.344 and Czechs, Poles and Hungarians at i.345! It is better to consult books specifically on pagans and Christians, in particular the exhaustive account of Fletcher 1997 and the useful briefer account of Jones and Pennick 1995: e.g., 126–37, 168–73, 188, 190 f.

25 Unbegaun 1948: 389.

26 There are some other written remains that should be mentioned: the remains of Umbrian in Italy, in particular the Iguvine tablets (those from Gubbio) which are ritual texts (Poulteney 1959); enough Iberian inscriptions to gather that it belongs with Basque but not to learn anything substantial about religion (Villar 1996: 470–3).

27 There was a time when scholars tried to deny its all too explicit meaning, cf. von Richthoffen's discussion in *MG* and de Vries 1956: i.§285.

28 Fire made from rubbed wood, see the *Indiculus superstitionum* (Chapter 8).

29 On Iolo, real name Edward Williams, see Hutton 1991: 139–41.

30 De Vries 1961: 24 ('fast gar nichts').

31 For a clear-headed evaluation of the usefulness of the *Mabinogion* see Hutton 1991: 147 and de Vries 1961: 27.

32 Jackson 1964: 23–8 on the Ulster Cycle; Hutton 1991: 148.

33 McCone 1990: ch.1 powerfully challenges the idea that an oral tradition independent of Christianity somehow preserved Irish paganism in antiquarian aspic.

34 Unbegaun 1948: 389 f.

35 I found it convenient to cite Poseidonios from the edition of Jacoby in *FGH*, which includes the fragments of only his historical and geographical writing (with which we are exclusively concerned); the modern editions of *all* Poseidonios' fragments are Edelstein and Kidd 1989 and Theiler 1982. The numbering varies between the editions so that, e.g., fragment 17 Jacoby = 69 Kidd = 172 Theiler; modern editions have 'concordances' at the back to deal with this problem.

36 Norden 1923: 104 thinks so.

37 Reading H.L. Jones's *aedizesthai* (in the Loeb edition of Strabo, also adopted by Edelstein and Kidd 1989: fr.274 without attribution) for the unbelievable *aethizesthai* ('I found it unusual'!), where the theta has crept in from neighbouring words such as *synetheian* and *thean*.

38 He gives the impression of knowing the Toulouse region (cf. F34 on the 3000 stades from Narbonne to the Atlantic) and refers to his Massiliot host telling him about an event in Liguria (F58). He may well have got further, cf. the views cited by F. Fischer in *Germania* 75 (1997): 597 f.

39 Cimbri, as in the Welsh for Wales, *Cymru*, and requiring an initial *h-* by Grimm's Law if they are to be Germans (as in the name of the region *Himmerland*). German, e.g. Strabo 7.1.3 (presumably from Poseidonios, though Norden 1923: 74–8 argues that Poseidonios did not 'yet realise' that they were Germans).

40 Piggott 1975: 74 and, superbly illustrated, 78. Other mentions, e.g. Green 1986: 147, Duval 1976: 96 f., Filip 1961: 174.

41 Jonas, *Life of Columbanus* 53; Fletcher 1997: 96. It also appears in the Gaulish worship of Mercury-Teutates according to the scholiast on Lucan 1.445 (Chapter 11).

42 Brunaux 1996: 95 mentions gold mines in Aquitaine.

43 *FGH* 184T7, F8, F14 (Balisia/Basilia/Balcia/Baltia are variant forms). Cf. how Adam of Bremen thought Estonia was an island (Chapter 9).

44 Spain is the only one with books to its credit: Asklepiades of Myrlea (*FGH*

697), *Periegesis of the nations in Turdetania*; and Sosthenes of Knidos (*FGH* 846), *Iberika*.
45 Ironically, Jacoby thinks Strabo has copied this passage from an earlier author (*FGH* 847F1b).
46 De Vries 1961: 54.
47 'Teilweise erstaunlich gute Unterrichtung auf Gebieten der Religion und des von ihr schwer zu trennenden Rechtes', Jankuhn 1966: 425.

2 DIVIDING THE LANDSCAPE

1 Beekes 1995: 40.
2 I am, of course, largely considering the religion of sedentary populations, not mobile nomadic peoples, cf. Barnatt 1998: 92 f.
3 M. Lejeune in *BS* 93–101.
4 Wissowa 1912: 468 n.6, also citing Pliny, *Letters* 10.71.
5 As Nilsson 1955: 74 observes.
6 Burnt with the rest of the Acropolis by Xerxes in 480, but miraculously sprouting a new shoot a cubit in size the following morning, Herodotos 8.55.
7 Nilsson 1950: 488; see some reservations in Parker 1996: 19 f.
8 Brunaux 1996: 67.
9 There is a useful brief account of the acceptance, or not, of 'archaeoastronomy' in Britain in Gibson and Simpson 1998: ix f.
10 M. Jost in Alcock and Osborne 1994: 218 f., Pausanias 8.38.7.
11 J. Scheid in *BS* 15 comments on 'cette déviation étrange du raisonnement, qui fait des bois sacrés un ensemble d'arbres animés de force sacrée'.
12 M. Jost in Alcock and Osborne 1994: 219.
13 Gelling 1988: 158, 151, 257; Wilson 1992: 7, 10.
14 Gelling 1988: ch.7 deals with 'personal names in place-names'.
15 'Purity from menstrual contamination only appears as a condition for entering a temple in late sacred laws of non-Greek cults' (Parker 1983: 101 f.) On purification after sex, normal in Greece, see *ibid.* 74–9.
16 Cf. Przyluski 1950: 60, 202.
17 On statues as grown out of stones: Przyluski 1950: 64, Durand 1960: 281.
18 Przyluski 1950: 89, Durand 1960: 393.
19 Eliade 1964: §96: 'Jamais un arbre n'a été adoré *rien que* pour lui-même, mais toujours pour ce qui, à travers lui, se «révélait», pour ce qu'il impliquait et signifiait.'
20 Hamadryads are the standard model already in Grimm 1876: ii.544. Trees are the easiest case to discuss, but the same question can be asked in certain cultural contexts even of lakes and mountains, as, according to Jantzen 1988: 189 f., does *A. David-Néel, A l'Ouest barbare de la vaste Chine (Paris 1947): 66 f. in the case of west China and Tibet.
21 As at 2 Kings 23.4 (cf. N. Wyatt in *DDD* 190) or on the Naples *stamnos* (Deubner 1932: 130 and pl. 20.1).
22 Przyluski makes explicit what many writers think, hence his usefulness for Durand 1960: 281, 392.
23 *Letter to the Emperor Verus* 2.6.
24 Text and (French) translation: bibliography under 'Merovingian councils'.
25 Reinach 1908: 400 f.; de Vries 1961: 184.
26 P.R. Frese and S.J.M. Gray in *EncRel* 31 s.v. Trees.
27 The *massebah* is also found in Hittite cult: Gurney 1990: 124. There is also a very prominent role for *ḫuwaši*-stones, Goetze 1957: 168.

28 N. Wyatt in *DDD* s.v. Asherah: esp. 192 f.; J. Hastings, *A dictionary of the Bible*, vol. 1 (Edinburgh 1898): 165 s.v. 'Asherah'. There are forty references in the Old Testament, including twenty-four in Deuteronomy. Instances: 1 (3) Kings 14.15, 16.33, 2 (4) Kings 18.4, cf. Judges 6.25–30, Deuteronomy 16.21 (in all of which, revealingly, the Greek Septuagint mistranslates *asherah* as *alsos,* 'grove'). The 'tree' may clearly be artificial, e.g. Isaiah 17.8. The Jeremiah passage (p.36) is put into a general context of the worship of 'the Great Goddess' (however sweeping this concept) by Przyluski 1950: 40. For the Hittite equivalent of the *ašera,* the *ištananaš,* see Goetze 1957: 168.

29 M.C.A. Korpel in *DDD* s.v. 'stone'. Translations can obscure these references, as e.g. at Genesis 49.24 where 'stone' is rendered 'strong one' in the Revised English Bible.

30 Przyluski 1950: 65.

31 Burkert 1985: 85. Eliade 1964: §95 attributes the set stone–tree–altar to a wide variety of primitive religions and treats them as microcosmic.

32 Sourvinou-Inwood 1985: esp. 125. Kern 1899: 159 talks of the tree and altar pairing, though he overstresses the notion of the divinity actually living in the tree, something due to overwrought literary sources.

33 Artemis: Sourvinou-Inwood 1985: 128. Aulis: Pausanias 9.19.8; Birge 1994: 238.

34 Jones 1954: 15. Jones's rocks tend rather hastily to become megaliths, Ronald Hutton observes to me.

35 Byrne 1973: 27.

36 Birkhan 1997: 781.

37 Cf. Przyluski 1950: 66.

38 Jones 1954: 94 f.

3 FOCUS I: SPRING, LAKE, RIVER

1 On the various associations of water in antiquity, see Ninck 1921.

2 'Aus einem oft steinigen Boden', de Vries 1961: 116. Grimm 1875: i.483 speaks of 'das lautere, rinnende, quellende und versiegende wasser'.

3 *Divus* strictly implies a lesser god and was used in earlier times for the divinised Emperors.

4 Do ringed sacred fish underlie the story of how Polykrates recovered his ring in a fish (Herodotos, 3.40–3)?

5 Jones 1954: 108–10, Jones and Pennick 1995: 108.

6 See Dölger 1922: ii *passim.*

7 Pliny, *ibid.*; Lucian, *On the Syrian goddess* 45 (and the useful note of A.M. Harmon in the Loeb Classical Library *Lucian* vol. 4 (London 1925): 398 f.; his translation, by contrast, is diabolical). Tame fish were found 'in many places' according to Aelian, *On animals* 12.30. See also Dölger 1922: ii.177 f., van Berg 1972: 55 f., Jones 1954: 108.

8 More common even than that: for Semitic peoples, see Plummer 1910: i.cxlix, citing, among others, W. Robertson Smith, *Lectures on the religion of the Semites*, 2nd edn (Cambridge 1894): 135. For Lithuanians and Slavs, see Rowell 1994: 122.

9 Grimm 1875: i.83, Boudriot 1928: 34 f. For Spain, Blázquez 1962: 202 f. A collection of such passages is presented by Bertrand 1897: 400–3.

10 *Homilia de sacrilegiis* 3 in Boudriot 1928: 34; edition: *C.P. Caspari, *Eine Augustin fälschlich beigelegte Homilia de sacrilegiis* (Christiania 1886). Rather like the *Indiculus superstitionum*, Boudriot concludes it is put together by a

Frankish cleric in the time of Boniface on the basis of a set of excerpts from Caesarius that are no longer available to us (1928: 16). Insistence on the pagan Neptunalia, a popular Roman festival, suggests the origin of this particular material in Italy *c*. 370–420.

11 *Sermon* 13.3 on enchanters, springs, trees, diabolical amulets and so on, repeated 13.5; 14.4 on destroying *fana*, vows to trees, prayers to springs, enchanters, diabolical amulets and so on; 53.1 on vows to trees, prayers to springs, diabolical auguries, destroying *fana*, setting fire to sacred trees, toppling idols; 54.5 on vows to trees, prayers to fonts; 229.2 (W) making vows at trees and fountains, 229.4 the same plus diviners. There is a treatise on Caesarius' reports of popular religion: *R. Boese, *Superstitiones arelatenses e Caesario collectae* (Marburg 1905), though the superstitions were perhaps an inherited job-lot, rather than those of Arles.

12 See Menéndez Pidal 1952: 98–102 for much more detail, e.g. use of *lama* to mean 'water-meadow' and distribution outside Spain. The word *Lamiae* has worried commentators: Caspari 1883 considers a suggested emendation of the text to read *amnes* (a poetic word for 'rivers') but thinks it more probable that Martin has simply made a mistake; Leite de Vasconcellos 1913: iii.568 considers it either Martin's or a copyist's mistake; McKenna 1938: 95 n.76 signs up with desperate attempts to associate traditional *Lamiae* with water.

13 Pliny the elder, *Natural history* 4.115; Strabo 3.3.4.

14 *W.G. Wood-Martin, *Pagan Ireland: an archaeological sketch* (1895) 143, cited by Plummer 1910: i.cxlix n.4.

15 Jones 1954: 10, 29–49.

16 Jones in *ibid.*: 24 states that he has 'found nearly 200 examples of chapels and churches built at or near holy wells in Wales'.

17 Hope 1893: xxi f. enumerates instances of 'wells' where saints had been 'martyred, rested, or buried' and draws attention (xxii) to rag wells, particularly involving *ash* trees.

18 Part of this passage is cited by Grimm 1875: i.83 f. On Wulfstan, see Lawson 1993: 56–62.

19 *GA* iii.203 suggests sea counts too, but the sea does not really receive worship in paganism.

20 Stone Age, Much 1967: 187 f.; denunciations, Grimm 1875: i.83.

21 *MG Leges* 4.142. Liutprand was king 712–44.

22 Philippson 1929: 48 f., also Halwell, Hallikeled (Yorks, from the Danelaw), and Hollywater; Hope 1893: 76 cites the spring of a *river* Holybourne at Alton (Hants).

23 Portugal: Leite de Vasconcellos 1913: iii.570 n.2 (continuing traditions), 1905: ii.237–65 (Tongoenabiagus, pre-Roman), 266–77 (Bormanicus and others). Spain: Blázquez 1962: ch. xiv, Leite de Vasconcellos 1905: ii.238 n.3.

24 Fauduet 1993: 45 f.

25 *OCD3* 1436.

26 Servius, on Vergil, *Aeneid* 7.84, Wissowa 1912: 222.

27 Plutarch, *Numa* 13; Latte 1960: 77. The Camenae had their own sacrifice on 13 August (the Ides) during the Republic.

28 Wissowa 1912: 221, Latte 1960: 76–9.

29 Pliny 31.31 cites doctors as generally distinguishing stagnant from running water, though they run into difficulty with healthy (static) lakes and unhealthy (flowing) rivers (31.35). Pliny recommends wells (31.38) and boiling water first (31.40).

30 Laty 1996: 10–12, 40 f.; hygiene in the nineteenth century, 109–18.

31 I am therefore not inclined to put much stress on the fact that 'algunas fontes tinham realmente virtude, proveniente das qualidads medicinaes das aguas' (Leite de Vasconcellos 1905: ii.238).

32 *Microsoft® Encarta® 96 Encyclopedia* s.v. 'Wiesbaden' (© 1993–5 Microsoft Corporation. All rights reserved. ©Funk and Wagnalls Corporation. All rights reserved.)

33 A catalogue of all divinities associated with Gaulish/French springs is given by Vaillat 1932: 17–61.

34 E.g., Green 1986: 158.

35 Vendryès 1948: 279 f.

36 Holder 1904: ii.414, Ross 1967: 464.

37 Holder 1896 s.v. 'Ambrones' (and Plutarch, *Marius* 19), and cols 489–94; Menéndez Pidal 1952: 93–8; Guyonvarc'h 1959. The root was claimed for Ligurian by d'Arbois de Jubainville 1894: ii.117–24 (who saw the Ligurians as pre-Indo-European, 1889: i.365 – nowadays they are probably, in Gimbutas' terminology, 'Old European' but still in effect Indo-European), Holder 1896: i.492. But this theory was rejected by Menéndez Pidal and Guyonvarc'h. The problem, apart from distribution, is that Indo-European gh^w should in principle give g not b in Gaulish Celtic (W. Vetter, *RE* 13.1 (1926) s.v. 'Ligures', 527), though Celtic originally preserved labio-velars which is why modern Celtic is sometimes divided into p-Celtic and q-Celtic. Guyonvarc'h 1959: 170 avoids the problem by deriving the word from the root *bher(u)* 'agitate, boil', neatly, though it does not account for the *m* everywhere, for Greek *Thermo-* (coincidence?) or for the *W* in *Worms* (dissimilation?). The root, whatever it is, also leads indirectly to the name 'Bourbon'.

The Ligurians, called *Ambrones* in their own language, cannot be placed linguistically with any assurance: Villar 1996: 384–9; on Ligurians in Iberia: Leite de Vasconcellos 1905: ii.53–5.

38 De Vries 1961: 72–4, 141; Green 1986: 162

39 It is usual to suppose a Gaulish Bormo who has been identified with Apollo, but Le Roux 1959: 220 f. may well be right to argue that where 'Bormo' appears on its own it is short for 'Apollo Bormo' – 'Bormo' is, then, a title or epithet, 'of the hot springs'. Borv- forms are argued to represent an assimilation of an alien (Ligurian) Borm- to the Celtic root *berv* 'boil' by d'Arbois de Jubainville 1894: ii.120.

40 Grannus is another god identified with Apollo (whose name might even be just another variant of this Indo-European root), Le Roux 1959, De Vries 1961: 75. The Aixes: W. Vetter in *RE* 13.1 (1926) 527.

41 Leite de Vasconcellos 1905: ii.266–76, rightly emphasising that the worshippers are Celtic at 274; Blázquez 1962: 171 f.; Toutain 1917: 141.

42 MacCulloch 1911: 77.

43 'The sacred fount of regeneration', Gregory of Tours, *Histories* 8.1.

44 Nilsson 1955: 103; Parker 1983: 50 f.

45 Parker 1983: 226 f.

46 Nilsson 1955: 247.

47 Jones 1954: 116 f.

48 Burkert 1985: 175.

49 Jones 1954: 115.

50 De Vries 1956: i.§212. Evidently the circumambulation harnesses the power of the well, but it may also be 'apotropaic' or 'cathartic' (cf. Bremmer 1983: 314).

51 E.g., Tomlin 1988, Hutton 1991: 238–40, Woodward 1992: 71 f. Wells are not the only places for such *defixiones*: 140 tablets have been found apparently

from the walls of the temple of 'Mercury' at Uley (Gloucs) (cf. Tomlin 1988: 60 f.), a remarkable number for a single rural temple, as Ronald Hutton observes. On curse tablets in general, the standard work is A. Audollent, *Defixionum Tabellae* (Paris 1904; repr. Frankfurt 1967); there is a good recent account in Graf 1994: ch.v.

52 The translations are mine, but they differ very little from Tomlin's excellent work.

53 On the strange power of mirrors, see Vernant 1991: ch.7.

54 The type of dream one may see and the rites, such as fasting, that one must perform in preparation are described by Deubner 1900.

55 Hünnerkopf, in *HDA* i.1674 f. s.v. 'Brunnen'.

56 Jones 1954: 88–91.

57 Examples from *ibid.*: 35.

58 Plummer 1910: i.cxlix-clii.

59 Adamnan, *Life of Columba* 2.11, MacCulloch 1911: 181 f.; France, Vaillat 1932, Vendryès 1948: 280.

60 Jones 1954: 37 f.

61 Dowden 1992b: 53.

62 De Vries 1956: i.245–8; *Völuspá* 28, 45; Hollander 1962: 9 n.65.

63 Geiger in *HDA* i.979.

64 Tholenzi, Helmold 1.21. Sorb or even Ljutiči, Niederle 1956: 112.

65 Perhaps it was called Belenus? (cf. Chapter 5 on Mount Belenatensis)

66 Piggott 1975: 77. I think the ultimate source for this must be *J.-G. Bulliot, 'Le culte des eaux sur les plateaux éduens', *Mémoires lus à la Sorbonne*, 1868 (cited by Bertrand 1897: 193 n.9); Bertrand 1897: 211 f.; MacCulloch 1911: 181; Ross 1967: 48 f.

67 There is a nice evocation of rivers also in Max Müller 1878: 176 f.

68 G. Schmidt in *KlP* s.v. 'Flussgötter', 585.

69 On the vital force of water, see Ninck 1921: 23 f., 26–8.

70 Wissowa 1912: 219.

71 Detschew 1928.

72 Cf. Grimm 1875: i.499.

73 Nilsson 1955: i.236–40. Waser 1909, with catalogue at 2791–2814, but the rivers are variously Greek, Roman or Near Eastern and often they are only found to be divinities because they are depicted on coins.

74 They have 'explicitly human shape' in Homer, Weiss 1984: 13.

75 On this type of portrayal, there is an art-historical treatise: S. Klementa, *Gelagerte Flussgötter des Späthellenismus und der römischen Kaiserzeit* (Köln 1993).

76 Weiss 1984: 21–3 highlights the problem that Sicilian and south Italian colonies have a predilection for depicting river-gods on their coins.

77 Stengel 1920: 135, Nilsson 1955: i.238 f.

78 Latte 1960: 131 on calendar. Ennius, *Annals* 242.

79 Ennius, the father of Roman poetry, early second century BC. Leite de Vasconcellos 1905: ii.224. On the cult, see J. Le Gall, *Recherches sur le culte de Tibre* (Paris 1952).

80 Shrine: *CIL* I^2 336, Wissowa 1912: 225.

81 Cicero, *Nature of the gods* 3.52 and A.S. Pease's commentary; Latte 1960: 132.

82 Ross 1967: 46–8.

83 Vendryès 1948: 279; Ross 1967: 47; cf. Hutton 1991: 218.

84 Holder 1896: i.1273, Leite de Vasconcellos 1905: ii.244; 'goddess' and rivers Deva, d'Arbois de Jubainville 1894: ii.271.

85 Holder 1896: i.1276. The *i* in these forms has crept in from the Latin *divus*.

86 Holder 1896: i.1274 f.

87 Blázquez 1962: ch.14 'Deidades acuáticas' also lists an Aturrus, Assaecus, Frovida, Navia, Reva, Salama; possible also, Aquae Eleteses the source maybe of the Yeltes and Lupianae of another river. The Douro example is at pp.174 f.

88 Livy, *Periocha* 55; Florus, *Res in Hispania gestae* 1.33.12; Silius Italicus, *Punica* 1.235 f.; Pliny the elder, *Natural history* 4.115; Leite de Vasconcellos 1905: ii.225–33. The idea that the river produced forgetfulness (in those who do not accord it the proper observances?) may be folk reinforcement of pagan ritual, cf. Leite 233.

89 Grimm 1875: i.497. This item made its way also into *A. Réville, *Les religions des peuples non-civilisés* (Paris 1883): ii.198 and from there into Leite de Vasconcellos 1905: ii.228.

90 Nilsson 1955: i.237 n.9, Dölger 1932: 13–21.

91 *CIL* 11.4123, Dölger 1932: 13.

92 Brunaux 1988: 94 f. for the data.

93 Achilles Tatius 1.18.

94 On this point, and for examples, see Leite de Vasconcellos 1905: ii.227 f.

95 Herodotos 6.76.

96 Lucian, *Alexander, or the false prophet* 48.

97 Aristotle, *Politics* 7.17 (1336a); de Vries 1961: 116 seems to misread this passage, alleging that Aristotle attributes this practice to the Gauls (Aristotle attributes the *following* practice of sparse clothing for babies to Celts) and locates it at the River Rhine (which I think he has imagined).

98 G. Kazarow (Kacarov), *RE* 6A (1936) 476.

99 *SIG* 1024.27–29, Nilsson 1955: i.237. Other instances: Frazer 1913: iv.197 f., including bulls (Diodoros 5.4) and a Russian example of drowning a horse; Stengel 1920: 135.

100 Frazer 1913: iv.198 f.; another example is found in the sea near Baiae, Pliny the elder, *Natural history* 31.5.

4 FOCUS II: STONE AND TREE

1 Plummer 1910: i.clvii. On stones which return or move, see Reinach 1908: 411–13.

2 *E. Piette and J. Sacaze, *Bulletin de la Société d'Anthropologie* (1877): 287, cited by Bertrand 1897: 45 f. (I have translated). Aquae Onesiae: Bertrand 1897: 195. Other details of Pyrenean cults, for instance, obscene phallic rites focused on stones in the Luchon region, may be found in Alford 1937: 88–94; her plate opp. p. 92 depicts a rock surmounted by a cross as described in this passage.

3 *Ibid.* 237, in Bertrand 1897: 398 f.

4 Dowden 1989: 137–40.

5 Kervadel is a *lieu-dit* in the commune of Plobannelec, and Kernuz in the commune of Pont-l'Abbé (both, Finistère). Details in Déchelette 1924: i.434 f.

6 Reinach 1908: 401, Toutain 1917: 362 f., de Vries 1961: 186.

7 Philippson 1929: 49.

8 *Ibid.* 50.

9 See also Davidson's note on Fisher's translation, ii.26, where it is suggested that Saxo is confused and that it is a coronation stone, on which the new king stands, that is at issue. Either way, the steadfastness is what matters.

10 Cult of stones in Greece and Rome: K. Latte s.v. 'Steinkult', *RE* 3A.2295–305 esp. 2297 f. *Omphaloi* and Apollo, Latte 2301 f. Apella, see Chapter 14.

11 Burkert 1985: 85 f.

12 Moscati 1968: 66.

13 E.g., M. Gérard, 'La grotte d'Eileithyia à Amnisos', *Studi Micenei ed Egeo-Anatolici* 3 (1967): 31 f., with illustrations.

14 Toutain 1917: 362 f.

15 *CIL* 2.2403, Leite de Vasconcellos 1905: ii.266 f.; Leite de Vasconcellos 1913: iii.196 f.

16 Nilsson 1967: 210.

17 Plummer 1910: i.clvii.

18 De Vries 1956: i.§213, Le Roux and Guyonvarc'h 1986: 303 f.

19 Similar examples from France: Reinach 1908: 406 f.

20 Antiquarian in Philippson 1929: 49.

21 Rowell 1994: 122, Plummer 1910: i.clvii, Pennick 1996: 41 f.

22 For a delightful romantic paragraph on trees: Max Müller 1878: 175.

23 Gamkrelidze and Ivanov 1995: i.389.

24 *FW* s.v. 'Birth tree'.

25 Birge 1994: 235 is concerned to stress broadly political associations, though I do not think this is necessarily a large category and it misses the religious power of the tree.

26 Boetticher 1856: 50 f. *Xoana*, Nilsson 1955: 486 f. Karyai, Pausanias 8.23.6. Helen in Rhodes, Pausanias 3.19.10, Nilsson 1955: 315. Temnos, Pausanias 5.13.7. Magnesia, Nilsson 1955: 576, *FGH* 482F5. Pentheus' pine, Pausanias 2.2.6 f..

27 Livy 1.36; Dionysius of Halicarnassos, *Roman antiquities* 3.71.5; Festus 168–70 L (according to whom the fig tree was called 'Navia').

28 Attus Navius, see also Tacitus, *Annals* 13.58, and Boetticher 1856: 28–30.

29 Przyluski 1950: 81 on the *Ficus Ruminalis*, latex and Buddhism.

30 *Ivos* and so on, de Vries 1961: 187, Lambert 1994: 195; but *if* is viewed as a borrowing from Germanic in Onions 1966 s.v. 'yew'. *Eburones*, de Vries 1961: 187, MacCulloch 1911: 202; but derived from *eburo-* ('boar') by Lambert 1994: 34.

31 *CIL* 13: Beech 33, 223–25, Six Trees 129, 132, 175; Oak 1112.

32 *DIL* s.v. 'bíle'.

33 MacCulloch 1911: 201 f. See Bibliography.

34 Byrne 1973: 27.

35 *Bile Tortan*, the *bíle* of Tortu, in *Verse Dindshenchas* iv.240–7, notes iv.440–1.

36 Boyer 1992: 158.

37 *Vita sancte Samthanne* §xviii (Plummer 1910: ii.258).

38 De Vries 1956–7: i.§249, ii.§427. Pliny the elder refers to 'two oaks of Jupiter Stratios (of armies)' near Herakleia in Pontus (northern Turkey), *Natural history* 16.239.

39 It is not difficult for a Greek to confuse Celts and Germans and we have to be incisive about this clear instance (Grimm 1875: i.55 is halfway there).

40 Pausanias 8.23.4 f. On this topic generally, see Birge 1994: 234.

41 Nilsson 1955: 211.

42 Renaud 1996: 163, from *Landnámabók*.

43 Boetticher 1856: 46.

44 *Ibid.* 49. For Germany, see Charlemagne's *Admonitio generalis* (Chapter 3).

45 Boetticher 1856: 50 and figs 22, 26, 36, 56.

46 *Codex theodosianus* 16.10.12.

47 Kern 1899: 159.

48 O. de Cazanove in *BS* 112 f.

49 Revealingly, this tale is not present in the original version of Constantius' *Vita Germani Episcopi Autissiodorensis* (in *MGH ScrMer* 7 (1920): 225–83) but only in the interpolated version (in J. Bolland *et al.* (eds), *Acta sanctorum* (Antwerp, Brussels, etc. 1643–1894), under 31 July). The interpolated version was versified by Heinricus Monachus (in *PL* 124.1142–50) and this story was taken also into Jacobus de Voragine's *Aurea legenda* ('Golden Legend'): ch.107. MacCulloch 1911: 204 (slightly garbled), who also cites Maury (*v. infr.*).

50 Boyer 1992: 158, citing *Hervarar saga ok Heidreks konungs*.

51 Nilsson 1906: 235 f. talks of hanging up sacrifices in trees.

52 To this context belongs also the Greek *tropaion*, a monument commemorating where the opposing army was defeated (*trope*, 'rout'), whence our word 'trophy'.

53 Cato, in Paulus ex Festo p.81 L; Fronto, *Letter to Verus* 2.7.6 (Loeb edition ii.181); *Digest* 47.7.2; *Gaius* 4.2.

54 Livy 1.26.6, Palmer 1969: 34 f., cf. 46.

55 'Grove with the timber of years' – and oaks reaching the stars – also in Silius Italicus' portrait of the miraculous instant emergence of the ancient grove of Dodona, *Punica* 4.688–90.

56 *Annual report of the Society of Jesus* 1583, *LPG* 437 f.

5 AREA I: LAND

1 Thietmar 7.59 (44); see also Chapter 12.

2 'Samivel' quoted by Jantzen 1988: 117.

3 Jantzen 1988: 1.

4 Bachelard 1943: 18 identifies 'axiomatic metaphors' of height, rising and falling, and posits their inexplicability – rising to the classic line, 'toute valorisation, n'est-il pas verticalisation?' Similarly, Eliade 1964: §34 and Durand 1960: 138–41 citing Bachelard and authorities back to Aristotle.

5 Van der Leeuw 1948: §7; Jantzen 1988: 190 ('lien instinctif').

6 Jantzen 1988: 5.

7 *Ibid.* 10; 'le moindre colline, pour qui prend ses rêves dans la nature, est inspirée', *G. Bachelard, *Terre et rêveries de la volonté* (Paris 1948): 384 cited by Durand 1960: 142.

8 Toutain 1917: 131.

9 *Ibid.* 144: Jupiter Ladicus, Candamius, Andero, Candiedo. Mountain, Holder 1896: i s.vv. The provenance, however, of these inscriptions is uncertain, Leite de Vasconcellos 1905: ii.342.

10 Grimm 1875: i.126–8; de Vries 1956: §245.

11 Philippson 1929: 156, 158, 161 f., Wilson 1992: 11, Gelling 1988: 161. *-bury* should strictly be a *bur(g)h* (fort) not a *beorg* (hill or 'barrow'/tumulus, Gelling 1988: 132–4) but there is laxity in the evolution of these placenames, cf. Gelling 1988: 133.

12 Philippson 1929: 161. One should not get too excited about this passage: like most of this introductory part of the sermon (1–209), it draws heavily on Martin of Braga's *De correctione rusticorum* (Pope 1968: 671, Caspari 1883: cxiv–cxxii), in this case para. 7. The crossroads item runs thus in Martin: 'Then another daemon wished himself to be called Mercury . . . for whom, as a god of profit, greedy men threw stones as they passed crossroads and gave him heaps of rocks in place of sacrifice.' An earlier part of para. 7, if not on

Mercury, tells how 'The devil, or his ministers the demons cast out of heaven, . . . began . . . to seek from them [men] that they should bring sacrifices to them on high mountains and in leafy groves.' Aelfric is just about sufficient evidence for Danes doing something on mountaintops for Odin, Pope 1968: 715 f.

13 In fact there is a particular concentration of Mercury cult in the Auvergne, as also in Languedoc, Grenier 1934: vi.308.

14 Gregory of Tours, *De gloria confessorum* 5.

15 M. Jost in Alcock and Osborne 1994: 218 f.; Pausanias 8.38.7.

16 Grimm 1875: i.511 f.; Bremmer, personal communication. Grimm regards the fires for the feast of St John as the corresponding south German fire-festival, but these tend to be local bonfires rather than hilltop fires – all over Europe except (p.519) in Serbia.

17 Dowden 1989: ch.7, esp. 162–4 is three-quarters of the way to this point!

18 Marstrander 1915: 248.

19 Leite de Vasconcellos 1905: ii.202 n.2 comments that 'muitos promontorios antigos eram consagrados a divindades especiaes, ou tinham meramente o epitheto de *sagrado*', citing 'Sacrum Promunturium' in Ireland and in Corsica, a Promontory of Juno in Spain, of Mercury in Sardinia. He also observes that his own Portuguese coast is full of Christian sanctuaries.

20 Toutain 1917: 148 f.

21 Strabo 3.1.4; Ephoros, *FGH* 70F130; Toutain *ibid.*

22 Leite de Vasconcellos 1905: ii.201.

23 Cf. scholars cited by Leite de Vasconcellos 1905: ii.203.

24 Van der Leeuw 1948: §5.1 in particular warns of this danger and tries to steer us to a more authentic feel for the 'power' in natural phenomena. J. Scheid in *BS* 16 f., I fear, however, is in danger of throwing out the religious baby with the German romantic bathwater.

25 Deubner 1932: 17–19.

26 'verso la sera e'l securo del di' – the second half of this phrase rather foxes me and those I consult: 'the part free of the (heat of) day'? 'the carefree part of the day', i.e. leisuretime?

27 Grimm takes the author to be St Augustine talking about North Africa, but these sermons are put together from various sources and the one stating that 'this practice remains from paganism' is clearly, at least at this point, Caesarius. The custom could be local to Caesarius, or it could be inherited from an Italian preaching tradition (Ambrose?), something made slightly more likely by the example from sixteenth-century Naples.

28 *Microsoft® Encarta® 96 Encyclopedia.* © 1993–5 Microsoft Corporation. All rights reserved, s.v. 'Avalon'.

29 The Greek text, though the general sense is clear, does not look right here and has not been satisfactorily emended. It also has 'Samnites' for 'Namnites'.

30 Alcuin was writing this life between 785 and 797; St Willibrord lived AD 658–739; this is an event of around 700, under Pepin. The passage is used by Adam of Bremen 4.3 and Altfridus' *Vita S. Liudgeri*. Discussion: Grimm 1875: i.190–2; de Vries 1956: i.§198, and ii.§518 on the Norwegian god Forseti.

31 Pennick 1996: ch.6 and esp. 94.

32 Dowden 1989: 91; Faure 1964: e.g., 115–22.

33 Gregory of Tours, *Life of St Arredius the Abbot* 6.

34 Pennick 1996: 97 f. for brief account; Easting 1991 for medieval texts.

35 Easting 1991: lxxxiv.

36 *Tractatus* 193, 315 ff. (Easting 1991: 126, 129 ff.).

37 Croesus according to Herodotos 1.46; Philip, Aelian, *Varia historia* 3.45.

6 AREA II: GROWTH

1 Grimm 1875: i.186 f., de Vries 1956: ii.§451 f.

2 Grimm *ibid.* (Onsöe).

3 It is usual to reject the association of *lucus* with *lux* 'light' (either because clearings are light or because groves aren't, the ancient explanation, cf. Servius in Chapter 4), but at an Indo-European level, to which both clearly go back, it is impossible to separate their roots – both seem to demand a stem **lelouk.* The simplest explanation is that a **loukos* is indeed a bright spot, one clear of objects that cast shade, as, for instance, a clearing or a meadow.

4 De Vries 1956: ii.§450.

5 Philippson 1929: 139–42.

6 Deubner 1932: 47.

7 *Ibid.* 68 f.

8 Deržavin 1948: 178.

9 Jouet 1989: 130 f.

10 *FW* s.v. 'field spirit'.

11 F. Coarelli in *BS* 47.

12 Jankuhn 1966: 421; Much 1967: 185–7.

13 Meringer 1924: 118–20.

14 Serbian/Croatian *kresati* ('strike sparks'), referring to a feast of St John, i.e. summer-solstice festival, cf. Grimm 1875: i.519.

15 Jones and Pennick 1995: 182.

16 Tomlinson 1976: 28 f. tries to explain it through the wooden posts necessary to support sleeper beams to support ambitiously wide roofs that early mudbrick walls were too weak to support themselves.

17 Cf. Grimm 1876: ii.xxxviii.

18 Like that of Pelops in the Altis at Olympia (Pausanias 5.13.1). I interpret Alkinoos' precinct as an instance of Homer's proleptic attitude to hero-cult: the heroes who inhabit his poems and will be worshipped in historical times already receive honours typical of their later cult *in advance of their death* in Homer's recreation of heroic times.

19 This association is well made by F. Graf in *BS* 27.

20 The Greek word *alsos* looks as though it is somehow the same word as Gothic *alhs*, 'temple', or Old English *ealh*, 'grove/temple', Lithuanian *alka*, a 'sacred grove or hill of sacrifice' (Rowell 1994: 121), or Latvian *elks* 'idols' (cf. Philippson 1929: 185). Others have wished it to derive from a verb referring to the vigour of natural 'growth', also seen in the Latin word for 'tall', *altus*, which the trees of a grove must obviously be. Others again have tried to link it to the German *Wald* ('wood') or to Russian lyes' ('forest'). The name of the sacred grove at Olympia, Altis (as *Nemus* is of Diana's grove at Nemi), may point to the original shape of the word (**altyos, *altwos?*) but gets us little further. Could it even be that *lucus* and *alsos* are the same word? It would then be somewhat like those shifting Indo-European roots which begin *Hwl-*, cf. Gamkrelidze and Ivanov 1995: i.413 (wolf/fox – *vulpis* or *lupus?*), 177 and 495 (*wool* or *lana?*). On the material cited, see E. Boisacq, *Dictionnaire étymologique de la langue grecque* (Heidelberg 1950): 47, noting that the word apparently gives us a toponym in Linear B Greek *asee*, i.e. *alseiei*, showing it has no initial *w-* like *Wald*; P. Chantraine, *Dictionnaire étymologique de la langue grecque*, i (Paris 1968): 65; J. Pokorny, *Indogermanisches etymologisches Wörterbuch*, i (Bern 1959): 26.

21 There are poetic references to laurels and a grove at Delphi (Birge 1994: 243

n.49) and obviously there would have been trees; the site may, however, not be well suited to display of a full-scale grove.

22 For a detailed study of what a paradise was in these various cultures, including the Septuagint (Greek) Genesis, see Bremmer 1998, on whom I draw heavily here.

23 J.N. Bremmer, in *OCD*3 s.v. 'Amaltheia'.

24 A *hortus*, itself, was in origin an 'enclosure' and in fact is the same word as the Slavonic *grad/gorod* which now means 'city', as well as our 'yard'.

25 *Res gestae* 23; Suetonius, *Augustus* 43.

26 Other inscriptions, F. Coarelli in *BS* 46 f., who rightly states that '*lucus* è proprio un *quid* in qualche modo artificiale, se può essere dedicato da un magistrato'.

27 *Commenta bernensia* on Lucan, 1.452.

28 De Vries 1961: 189 thinks these are oak *trees* serving as divinities; in fact they are the statues of Lucan's scene (and the hewing derives from Lucan's Caesar).

29 *Gallic war* 6.25, a passage scarcely by Caesar himself, cf. F. Kraner, W. Dittenberger, H. Meusel (eds), *C. Iulii Caesaris commentarii de bello gallico* ii (Berlin 1920): 192–9. The sixty days appears to come from Mela 3.29.

30 *Ibid.* 6.27, also in Pliny the elder, *Natural history* 8.39 of the *achlis*, which he distinguishes from the *alcis*, and sites in the island of Scadinava (Swedish moose, then – cf. *OLD* s.v, and *Monty Python and the Holy Grail*, opening credits).

31 Mela 1.117, 3. 37; Pliny the elder, *Natural history* 4.89, 6.35. The function of the missing Greek source is to transmit and philosophically transmute Herodotos' nation of Argippaioi (4.23) into the Mela–Pliny Arimphaioi; the source must also account for the particular portrait of the Hyperboreans. We know that Poseidonios was interested in both Celts and Hyperboreans (87F103); alternatively, this type of account might just fit with Hekataios of Abdera on Hyperboreans (264F12) or even Hellanikos on Hyperboreans living on tree-fruits (4F187).

32 Also in Greek, if rarely: *nemos,* a wooded glade (whence the placename *Nemea,* the direct Greek equivalent of the Latin plural *nemora*).

33 There was a 'grove sacred to Augustus' (*Augusto lucus sacer*) at Perugia, *CIL* 11.1922 (= *ILS* 5434), and *ILS* 5433 shows the dedication of a grove at Aquilonia to Caracalla in AD 213.

34 Pliny the elder, *Natural history* 3.37.

35 *Itinerarium Antonini Augusti* 295; Pascal 1964: 115.

36 Plummer 1910: i.clv n.4. He also cites examples derived from *fid* ('wood') and *coill/caill* ('wood').

37 Palmer 1969: 26 n.135.

38 Jones 1962: 194 f.

39 *Satire* 1.5.24. Anxur is the local Volscian for Latin Tarracina (Italian Terracina) according to Pliny the elder, *Natural history* 3.59.

40 Vergil, *Aeneid* 7.800, referring, like Horace, to the grove at Tarracina-Anxur (cf. Jupiter of *Anxur* in 7.799).

41 W. Smith (ed.), *A dictionary of Greek and Roman geography* (London 1873): ii.212 s.v. 'Lucus Angitiae'.

42 Birge 1994: 233 n.8 lists these, though it is notable that one such forest is called *Aphrodision* (8.25.1) and another supplied the wood for ritual statuettes (9.3.4).

43 Latin texts of surveyors in *RF*; discussion, Dilke 1971. Silvanus, see Dolabella in *RF* i.302, Dilke 1971: 98 f. Groves between two/three properties, Dolabella *ibid.*, Julius Frontinus, *RF* i.57

44 Palmer 1969: 26 f.

45 'Nemus', Strabo 5.3.12; other ancient sources on the *Rex* and the *Nemus*: Ovid, *Fasti* 3.263–72; Suetonius, *Caligula* 35.3; Servius on Vergil, *Aeneid* 6.136; Statius, *Silvae* 3.1.55 f. Discussions: Wissowa 1912: 247–9; Altheim 1930: 145 f., 150–6; Latte 1960: 169.

46 Servius on Vergil, *Aeneid* 7.515; Latte 1960: 169 is very old fashioned, dwelling on Diana as a moon-goddess, when the whole point is the luxuriant growth of the grove, not celestial observation.

47 Strabo 5.3.12.

48 Torchlit procession, Ovid, *Fasti* 3.263–70; Statius, *Silvae* 3.1.59.

49 I cannot bring myself to believe 'the dedicator' and so read *dictator* not *dicator*.

50 Herodotos 6.75.3.

51 Plummer 1910: i.cliii.

52 *Semnos* means 'venerable' in Greek and lurks behind this description: this is not Tacitus, it is Poseidonios.

53 This is a compelling emendation of 'all the peoples of the same blood', though it makes no difference for our purposes, Lund 1988: 215 f.

54 Presumably in the Hercynian Forest (cf. Strabo 7.1.3).

55 *L.L. Hammerich ('Horrenda primordia', *Germanisch-Romanische Monatsschrift* 33 (1952): 228–33) suggested a ritual dismemberment recreating the origins of the world. Though this idea is dismissed out of hand by de Vries 1956: ii.34 n.5 ('ein ganz aus der Luft gegriffener Gedanke'!), it makes a certain amount of sense in the light of the stress on origins at the end of this passage and Lincoln 1991: 7–12. See further, Chapter 14.

56 Rowell 1994: 121, citing e.g. *Encyclopedia lituanica* I (Boston 1970): 76 s.v. '*alka*'.

57 Thomas refers back to Augustine, *City of God* 15.23 where Augustine describes *Dusii daemones* as incubi that are worshipped by the *Gauls*, a passage which is later taken up by Isidore and Hinkmar of Reims and, in Thomas's time, Vincent de Beauvais (Holder 1896: i.1387 f.; MacCulloch 1911: 355 n.3; *LPG* 48). The word apparently survived in the Breton *duz* (a type of fairy) and, less likely, our word 'dizzy' (MacCulloch, *ibid.*). It is, however, coincidentally similar to words in Lithuanian and in Slavonic languages (Lith. *dvase*, Russ. *duch*, 'spirit').

58 *Historia regum terre sancte*, in Clemen 1936: 95.

59 Rowell 1994: 121.

60 Ovid, *Fasti* 3.266.

61 Servius, on *Aeneid* 6.136. See also Boetticher 1856: ch.21.

62 Servius, on *Aeneid* 6.118 states that Juno Inferna really means Persephone and that, syncretistically, Juno is used as an umbrella to unite Persephone with Diana: Vergil 'couldn't just call her Persephone because of the groves belonging to Diana'.

63 Silius Italicus 3.286.

64 Palmer 1969: 27; e.g. Plutarch, *Gaius Gracchus* 17 (where Furrina has been identified with the Furies).

65 There were no groves there in Livy's time: Dionysios of Halikarnassos, *Roman antiquities* 2.15.4, Palmer 1969: 27.

66 Jones 1962: 193.

67 Servius on Vergil, *Georgics* 3.33.2.

68 Birge 1994: 241 for groves within city centres.

69 Varro, *Latin language* 5.43; Warde Fowler 1933: 235.

70 Jones 1962: 196 f.
71 Pliny the Elder, *Natural history* 16.235; Varro, *Lingua latina* 5.49.
72 See Palmer 1969: 26. The goddess Nemetona is found near Mainz (*CIL* 13.7253 = *ILS* 1010, dedication by a consul of AD 97) and at Alta Ripa (today's Altrip near Speyer) together with Mars (*CIL* 13.6131 = *ILS* 4586). There is also an inscription found at Bath (*ILS* 4586a, mentioned in *CIL* 13.6131) dedicated by a man from the Trier region to 'Mars Loucetius [probably *not* 'of the *lucus*'] and Nemetona'. The Slav words, eg Russian *nemets*, are generally and surely wrongly thought to originate in the word for 'dumb', i.e. unable to speak Slavonic, eg by Entwistle and Morison 1964: 27.
73 Vergil and Servius above; Pliny the Elder, *Natural history* 16.11.
74 Cf. de Vries 1956: ii. §415 *ad fin.*
75 The text gives *Coll Comair*, plainly an error for *Tomair* (Thor), not observed by Todd 1867: cxlvii n.4.
76 Tacitus, *Germania* 39.2, 40.
77 Cf. Pascal 1964: 103. The source is a series of inscriptions of rather dubious provenance, *CIL* 5.32, 34–6.
78 Birge 1994: 244 and n.50 gives examples from Pausanias.
79 Holder 1896: i.187 f., 8. MacCulloch 1911: 198. *CIR*, to which both authors refer, is *G. Brambach (ed.), *Corpus inscriptionum rhenanarum* (Elberfeld 1867).
80 Goodison 1989: 163 suggests that 'the later association of trees with prophecy reflects a survival of a Bronze Age tradition in which humans were believed to receive communication from the divine through contact with vegetation'. D. Briquel has written on 'Les voix oraculaires' in groves in *BS* 77–90.
81 Hesiod, *Shield of Herakles* 70 and scholion (= Herakleides Pontikos fr.137a Wehrli), Farnell 1907: iv.219.
82 Strabo 14.1.27. For more examples, see F. Graf, 'Bois sacrés et oracles en Asie Mineure', in *BS* 23–9.
83 The singular would not have scanned or have been so grand. A Near Eastern parallel is found at Genesis 12.6 and Judges 9.37, where there is reference to the terebinth or oak of Moreh ('the revealers/soothsayers') at the sanctuary at Shechem where Abraham built an altar. This seems to belong to a pattern of tree oracles also seen in Ugarit and Arabia; see K. Nielsen in *DDD* 1201–3 s.v. 'oak', and P.R. Frese and S.J.M. Gray s.v. 'Trees' in *EncRel* 31.
84 Alpheios very full and 'very sweet', Pausanias 5.7.1. Marshy, Pausanias 5.11.10. *Altis* and *alsos*, Pausanias 5.10.1. Oracular, Strabo 8.3.30.
85 De Vries 1961: 187.
86 Cf. MacCulloch 1911: 201, 203.
87 Nilsson 1967: i.85 f.

7 TECHNOLOGY: STATUES, SHRINES AND TEMPLES

1 Farnell 1896: i.14.
2 Repeated *verbatim* by Adam 1.8, who wrongly attributes this account to Einhard (Trillmich and Buchner 1961: 147); Rudolph, unusually, does not plagiarise this passage from Einhard (his *Vita Karoli* 7 is much sparser).
3 De Vries 1957: ii.§§351, 587. De Vries, following *G. Dumézil, *Mitra-Varuna* (Paris 1940), suggests this god may be a German cognate of the Old Irish hero Eremon and the Iranian Aryaman (Ahriman).
4 On maypoles, see Hutton 1996: 233–7 and on Irminsul specifically 234.
5 Powell 1980: 164.
6 Greek and Irish vocabulary is discussed in Grimm 1878: iii.42.

7 Nilsson 1955: 203; the Byzantine dictionary the *Souda* refers to a 'cone-like pillar'.

8 Nilsson 1955: 80–3, Vernant 1991: 153–5, 207–14.

9 Burkert 1985: 89.

10 This in principle contradicts his denial of statues to the Germans at *Germania* 9 (below) but he is evidently thinking of something more grand, skilled and Greco-Roman at that point.

11 Bestial because of the 'images of beasts' taken into battle at Tacitus, *Histories* 4.14 (Chapter 14) and because Tacitus denies anthropomorphic statues to the German (*Germania* 9.2, below).

12 I am building on Wolfram 1988: 106 and 109.

13 Philippson 1929: 186–8. Frequency, Jente 1921: 17, 10 f., respectively.

14 Jente 1921: 17–22.

15 Philippson 1929: 192, Grimm 1875: i.54.

16 Philippson 1929: 190–3.

17 Athene: J. Boardman, *Greek sculpture: the classical period* (London 1985): 110–12 and bibliography on 245. Zeus, Strabo 8.3.30, Pausanias 5.11, Brodersen 1996: ch.5 and p.121.

18 Pliny, *Natural history* 34.41, Brodersen 1996: ch.8 and pp.121 f.

19 Exodus 32.20, burning and grinding to dust.

20 Sizes, Unbegaun 1948: 416.

21 Polycephaly, *ibid.* 411, 416, 423, Christiansen 1981: ii.836.

22 Saxo 14.39.39–41, pp.577 f. Holder, Unbegaun 1948: 416.

23 Celts liked depicting sets of three mother goddesses. The depiction on an altar of *Tarvos Trigaranos,* the bull with three cranes (the bird, not 'with three heads', for which a *Greek* word is *trikaranos*) next to Esus depicted as a woodcutter has some mythic significance that is lost on us but is nothing to do with polycephaly, e.g. Duval 1976: 33 f., MacCulloch 1911: 38.

24 Cf. Brodersen 1996: 59–63 on the tourism factor, the 'Besuchungs-Attraktion'.

25 Burkert 1985. 88.

26 Publius Victor, *Descriptio urbis Romae, PL* 18.455.

27 Choudhury 1994: 78 f. A great deal more may be said about the precise significance of every aspect of the construction of the Hindu temple, see S. Kramrisch, *The Hindu temple*, 2 vols (Calcutta 1946).

28 Tonnelat 1948: 376 f.

29 Robertson 1943: 24 f., 39, 51–3. Tomlinson 1976: 28, part of an illuminating discussion of why temples turn out the shape they do.

30 Two sides of the gallery at the Puy de Dôme were walled rather than open with columns, presumably because of winds at that height, Lewis 1966: 23. Roof, *ibid.* 42.

31 You may visit a reconstructed temple of this type (depicted at Fauduet 1993: 73) at the *Archéodrome de Bourgogne* at the Aire de Beaune-Tailly near Meursault on the A6.

32 Figures, in feet, Lewis 1966: 13, 25. There is some tendency to the *cella* being two-thirds of the side of the square, *ibid.* 27.

33 Cf. de Vries 1961: 196, 1956: i.§267 f.

34 *Ibid.* 1956: i.§144, suggesting the procession was originally to mark off the site of the grave and comparing it with the introduction of a bride or a maid to her new house.

35 On circumambulation, see Bremmer 1983: 314 and the bibliography he gives in n.84.

36 Fauduet 1993: 48. Gaulish and Celtic centralising, Le Roux and Guyonvarc'h 1986: 227, and especially Rees and Rees 1961: ch.vii, 'The Centre'.

37 Round temples found in Gaul, but not Britain, Lewis 1966: 30. Round temples are clearly not on the rare Greco-Roman *tholos* model, to which, for example, the temple of Vesta at Rome belongs, *ibid.* 31 f.

38 Hekataios of Abdera, *FGH* 264A7 (= Diodoros of Sicily, 2.47); Macrobius, *Saturnalia* 1.18.11.

39 Dumézil 1954: ch.2.

40 De Vries 1956: i.§267, Renaud 1996: 161, 163.

41 Unbegaun 1948: 415, Rowell 1994: 134–7.

42 Fauduet 1993: 64 f., Lewis 1966: 32 f.

43 Renaud 1996: 160 f. suggests private or family cult.

44 De Vries 1956: i.§269, Renaud 1996: 161.

45 Saxo 14.39.7, p.566 Holder.

46 Renaud 1996: 162, 163.

47 De Vries 1956: i.§270, Renaud 1996: 162.

48 Homer *Iliad*, 17.59 f.; Porphyry, *Life of Pythagoras* 26 and the note of E. des Places, *Porphyre: Vie de Pythagore* (Paris 1982): 48 n.1; Iamblichos, *The Pythagorean Life* 63.

49 Saxo 14.39.2, p.565 Holder, Unbegaun 1948: 415, Fletcher 1997: 438–40.

50 Saxo 14.39.39, p.577 Holder.

51 Robertson 1943: 50.

52 Saxo's description is generally accepted as historical nowadays, Rowell 1994: 123 n.23.

53 Vendryès 1948: 309, Ross 1967: 62 f. There is a large bibliography on the subject, but mainly insufficiently critical. Holder 1904: ii.712, Lambert 1994: 59.

54 *Gallic war* 6.13, 6.16; de Vries 1961: 191.

55 See, e.g., Palmer 1954: 20, Beekes 1995: 165.

56 Griffith 1985: 122 reports indirectly that 'shrine' is the primary meaning of *nemet-* according to E. Felder, 'Nemavia, a Celtic temenos', in **B.S. MacAodha* (ed.), *Topothesia: Aistí in onóir T.S. O'Máille* (Galway 1982): 90–101. J.L. Brunaux in *BS* 58 supposes that *nemeton* has lost its original sense of wooded grove; on my argument, it never had this sense, though I concede that trees become gradually less essential to the Latin *lucus* (F. Coarelli in *BS* 47). Birkhan 1997: 751 treats 'shrine' as the old explanation, 'grove' as the new, and is as even-handed as possible.

57 Fortunatus, *Poems* 1.9.10; Rivet and Smith 1979: 495; d'Arbois de Jubainville 1894: ii.376.

58 E.g., by H. Meurig Evans and W.O. Thomas, *Y geiriadur mawr* (Llandybie and Aberystwyth 1958): 342 ('teml, llwyn sanctaidd'), but not by the *Geiriadur Prifysgol Cymru*, rhan xli.2604 (Cardiff 1990) 'ansicr . . . strength'.

59 On these items see *LSJ* s.v. 'nemo', Holder 1904: ii.711 f. I suppose there is some possibility that these mean, respectively, 'Holyoak' and 'Holy mountain'.

60 De Vries 1956: i.§97, *ibid.* 1961: 189. 'Les Saxons respectèrent ces lieux sacrés, leur conservèrent leur nom' (d'Arbois de Jubainville 1894: ii.377). The specialisation of meaning of *nemeton* surely rules out an ancestral IE form (even though IE **nemetón* could in principle be reconstructed – with the accent on the last syllable which would explain IE **t* > Germanic d, by Verner's law). D'Arbois de Jubainville 1889: i.334 f., 369–73 held that the Germans had undergone a period of subservience to the Celts, provoking Lane 1933: 263

into opposing excessive resort to borrowing on principle; Elston 1934: 157–9, conventionally, regards *nemeton* as an inherited word related to *nemus*.

61 Sources for these names: de Vries 1961: 189, Rivet and Smith 1979: 254 f., Johnson 1915: 330, 384, Gelling 1988: 60, 243, Ekwall 1960: 346, Mills 1991: 245. *Fana*, Rivet and Smith 1979: 363. Henges, Griffith 1985, a local study with considerable broader implications. See also, for *fanum* names, Grenier 1934: vi.301–5 and, for *templum* names, 305 f.

62 *Nemetostatio* is a correction of the *Nemetotatio* found in the *Ravenna Cosmography* (*c.* AD 700, Rivet and Smith 1979: 185); Rivet and Smith 1979: 424 f. suggest instead *Nemeto-totatio*, to be interpreted 'sacred grove of Teutatis'. I fear this corresponds more to our wishes than to the typical formation of Celtic placenames.

63 I doubt if this is evidence for a Saxon *nimid*; the *m* has in effect voiced the *t*.

64 Fichtl 1994: 153. 'Davon koseform Nemetacon', Holder 1904: ii.711.

65 Lambert 1994: 50, 85, Holder 1904: ii.712.

66 *CIL* 12.2820, Holder 1896: i.218.

67 Holder 1904: ii.712.

68 Strabo 12.5.1, Le Roux and Guyonvarc'h 1986: 227.

69 De Vries 1961: 189; a cartulary is a collection of charters kept, for example, by an abbey.

70 Gregory gives the impression that this was in the time of Valerian (ruled 253–60) and his son Gallienus (ruled, jointly at first, 253–68), which cannot be right as Chrocus was there in 306 to support Constantine in his bid for power, see Aurelius Victor, *Epitome de Caesaribus* 41.3 and Krusch 1951: 24.

71 Gregory does not use *Augustonemeton*, but tends to refer to the *Arverna urbs* or simply *Arverni* (cf. Holder 1896: i.232). Many Roman town-names in France are replaced by the name of the tribe that inhabits the town, most famously Paris from the *Parisii*, not from *Lutetia*, but also, for example, Langres from the *Lingones* not *Andematunnon*, Javols from *Gabali* not *Anderitum*, Chartres from *Carnutes* not *Autricum*; this happens around the fourth century at the same time as the rise of previous hamlets to town status, but does not happen in firmly Roman and urbanised Provence, cf. Burnand 1996: 35.

72 *CIL* 13.1.2. 4130, Krusch 1951: 25, M. Ihm, s.v. 'Arvernus', *RE* 2.1489 f.

73 From the Indo-European roots **upo* and **sta*, one who *stands beneath*, i.e. subordinate, cf. Gamkrelidze and Ivanov 1995: i.401.

74 Lewis 1966: 52–4, Fauduet 1993: 90 f.

75 Cited by de Vries 1961: 191.

76 See Chapter 5; Strabo 3.1.4, Leite de Vasconcellos 1905: ii.199 ff., Toutain 1917: 170.

77 A find from Hon is interpreted by de Vries 1956: i.§270 as a temple-treasure.

78 Jankuhn 1966: 421, Much 1967: 185.

79 Lewis 1966: 55.

80 Unbegaun 1948: 414 f.

81 Saxo 14.39.9, p.567 Holder.

82 De Vries 1956: i.377 n.1, citing J. Meier, *Untersuchungen zur deutschen Volkskunde und Rechtsgeschichte*, ii, 'Ahnengrab und Rechtsstein' (Berlin 1950): 47.

83 *MG Leges* 3.ii Index 3, p.197; dating, F. Beyerle *ibid.* p.21. De Vries 1956: i.§266.

84 Godshill, Philippson 1929: 192.

85 Lewis 1966: 55 alleges the opposite, that the Scandinavian temples ultimately derive from the Celtic temples via the southern Germans and Slavs, not an easy case to demonstrate, though it would provide a tidy genetic explanation.

86 Svantovit at Arkona also was thought 'specially effective at responses' (Helmold, 1.52, Unbegaun 1948: 412).
87 Thietmar describes this pathway as 'pretty horrible to see' (*visu nimis horribile<m>*). Special gates for those condemned to death are known in the Greek world, Bremmer 1983: 314.
88 Unbegaun 1948: 403, 410.
89 Adam 2.5, 2.15.
90 Fletcher 1997: 435–7.
91 Niederle 1956: 282, Deržavin 1948: 33, Gimbutas 1971: 153.
92 Schuchhardt 1923: Fisher-Island not suitable, 186; three towers, 189 f.; bridge, 203; *castrum Wustrow*, 204. Schuchhardt's view is accepted by Gimbutas 1971: 153; firmly rejected by Niederle 1956: 282. Site unknown, *ibid.* 115 n.9, 282, Deržavin 1948: 33.
93 Niederle 1956: 116 f., Deržavin 1948: 33.
94 Nilsson 1955: 74 cites *F.W. Deichmann, 'Frühchristliche Kirchen in antiken Heiligtümern', *Arch.Jahrb.* 54 (1939): 105 ff., according to whom temples were converted in Athens and in the west, but in the Greek east they were destroyed and exorcised.
95 Leite de Vasconcellos 1905: ii.111–46, esp. 111 and 146, Toutain 1917: 131.
96 Attwater and John 1995: 49.
97 Mercury, mountains, St Michel, Toutain 1917: 211, 334 f.
98 Some caution is advised on direct connection of St Michael with pagan divinities by Hutton 1991: 286, who stresses the spread of the cult from fifth-century Italy northwards.
99 *Codex theodosianus* 16.10: §3 (342) maintain temples for carnival events; §8 (382) open them for meetings – but generally Emperors insisted on their closure; §15 (399 for Spain and Gaul) don't destroy 'public works', that is, temples; § (399 for 'country districts') destroy them; §18 (399 for Africa) take out the idols but don't destroy the temples; §19 (407) destroy idols and altars, keep temples for public use; §25 (435) destroy '*fana*, temples and shrines'.
100 Sulpicius Severus, *Vita Martini* 9.3.
101 Jente 1921: 14, from the 'Blickling Homilies'.
102 Audoenus, *Vita S. Eligii* 2.8.
103 Goudineau and Peyre 1993: 84–8; however, they counsel caution (89) on the grounds of a break in the archaeological record between the fourth/fifth centuries and the eighth.
104 As appears from Jente 1921: 14–16.
105 Martin's preaching produced this effect among some anonymous Gaulish pagans: Sulpicius Severus, *Vita Martini* 15.4.
106 On wood and stone, cf. Capelle 1990: 86–8.
107 Boulouis 1987: 93, citing Boniface, *Letter* 33 (*MG Epp* 3, p.284), and it is revealing that Boniface had been told that these particular letters of Gregory were missing from the Record Office at Rome – like the one key book for an essay!
108 Wilson 1992: ch.3; Capelle 1990: 39 f., 84. Yeavering is also the sole example cited by G. Bonner in Gilley and Sheils 1994: 25.

8 CHRISTIAN PAGANISM

1 Exodus 32.18–19 (Vulgate).
2 Gregory the Great compares Augustine's missionary activities to the activities of Moses, *Letter* 11.36 ll. 52 ff.

3 *Sermons* 6.3, 13.4, 16.3, 19.3.

4 Boulouis 1987: 99 f. provides some useful detail on this topic. Boudriot 1928: 4.

5 Boulouis 1987: 90 f. She notes, for instance, how Augustine was chosen not for his contemporary knowledge but for his sound monastic education and knowledge of set texts.

6 *Dialogue against the Arians* 1.5, cited by Boulouis 1987: 101.

7 As so often Leite de Vasconcellos (1913: iii.573) has the balance right: yes, much imposition of standard ideas on one's *rustici*, but in Martin of Braga 'at all events, we have a few things here that are genuinely Galician'.

8 Grimm 1875: i.82 f.; Gregory of Tours, *Histories* 2.10; Rudolf of Fulda, *Translatio S. Alexandri* 3 (*MG ScrGerm* 2.676); Helmold 1.47.

9 McNeill and Gamer 1938: 419–21 offer some useful comments.

10 *Sporkelmonat*, Boretius 1883: 223 n.2, McNeill and Gamer 1938: 419 n.2; Grimm 1876: ii.658.

11 Straw, Boretius 1883: 223 n.11, citing 'Eccardus', presumably the Eckhart of Grimm (1878: iii.34) – J.G. von Eckhart, *Leges Francorum*, vol.1 (Frankfurt and Leipzig, 1720)?

12 See Maximus of Turin, *Sermon* 30 below. This is generalised pagan wash and has no basis in the observation of Germans, cf. the poverty of evidence in Stegemann, *HDA* 2.1517. McNeill and Gamer 1938: 420 n.17 refer to Hrabanus Maurus *PL* 110.78 f. for a full description, but his *Homilia* 42 only mildly amplifies Maximus.

13 Fauduet 1993: 113–17. There is a huge category of *Gliederweihungen* ('limb-dedications'), of which the Greek instances are catalogued by F.T. van Straten in Versnel 1981: 100, 105–43, with a little attention to other nations at 146–9.

14 This particular heading is interestingly illustrated by the first book of Apuleius' novel (AD *c.* 155) *The golden ass*.

15 McKenna 1938: 88–90. This invalidates the view that Martin only presented a generalised Greco-Roman pagan wash, as Chuvin 1990: 129 f.

16 Caspari 1883: 31 derives this from Burchard, *Decrees* 19.5.175 (*PL* 140.974b). Burchard does read at times as though he was drawing more elaborately on a source that Martin rushes over.

17 *Reforming the pagans* 10, cf. McKenna 1938: 96.

18 This council is thought to be a fiction (see *CC SL* 148) and its provisions merely an anthology from earlier councils. Personally, I see no difficulty with church councils plagiarising earlier councils, and oddly in this case (§23) there does not appear to be an earlier source.

19 Blázquez Martinez 1962: 202 'hasta hace poco', citing *F. López Cuevillas, *La civilización céltica en Galicia* (Santiago 1955): 417 ff. Candles at trees and fountains, Bertrand 1897: 400–3 citing the *Second Council of Arles* (above), and (what is actually) Audoenus, *Vita S. Eligii* 2.15 (*PL* 87.527–30), apparently an actual sermon of St Eligius not otherwise attested (see pp.158 f. above), and the *Admonitio generalis* §65 of Charlemagne (p.43 above).

20 Burchard, *Decrees* 19.5.66 (*PL* 140.961c).

21 On these, see McKenna 1938: 98–104.

22 Bertrand 1897: Lectures 8–9 and Annexe E, Hutton 1994: 37–9, Grimm 1875: i.513–19. Thus Vulcanalia is a generic fire-fest, just as Neptunalia is a water-fest (see Ps.-Augustine in Chapter 3). Another possibility is that Vulcan is Thor among Germanic Suebi and that some festival of Thor, or even hallowing of Thursday, is at issue.

23 *Codex theodosianus* 16.10.19. This seems to be, at least in Roman Italy, the Parentalia of 13–21 February at which families paid honour to their dead.

24 Lithuanians, Paul Eichorn, *LPG* 465.

25 On the meaning of this very difficult passage, see B. Krusch in *MG ScrMer* 4.705–8.

26 *Iocticosliottici*, 'games', *jeux*.

27 Remotely conceivable if *impurus* represents the Greek *empyros*, 'divining by fire'.

28 A reference to 'solstices' in the text here is only a gloss explaining the force of St John's feast.

29 Some saints had therefore got it wrong!

30 De Vries 1957: ii.§611.

31 Arles (524), Carpentras (527), Orange (529), Vaison (529). At the age of seventy-one, he got a good turnout of the bishops of his province for the Council of Orléans (541), though unable to go himself.

32 Text and (French) translation: bibliography under 'Merovingian Councils'.

33 See p.140. St Gall flees to King Theoderic who saves him, and later regrets having fled the opportunity of martyrdom. The event is cited by Fletcher 1997: 133.

34 This could well be *Arduinna* the goddess of the Ardennes, cf. Krusch 1951: 381.

35 *Capitulare Paderbrunnense* 21, Boudriot 1928: 34.

36 Discussed by McKenna 1938: 116, who also mentions *L. Gougaud, 'La danse dans les églises', *Revue d'histoire ecclésiastique* 15 (1914): 229–45.

37 Among the copious church fathers represented on the CETEDOC CD-ROM, the verb is used only by Caesarius, as a patois gloss on *saltare*, and in one or two derivative canons: the Council of Laodicea in Ferrandus of Carthage *CC SL* 149, p.303, and *Collection of canons* 3.60 (Title: 'THAT IN THE FEASTS OF THE SAINTS *BALLATIONES* AND TRIVIALITIES ARE A BIG SIN'!). The sole exception is Commodian *Instructiones* 1.34. The Augustine passage generally cited (cf. Brüch 1924: 124) looks like Caesarius to me; the word is a popular borrowing from the Greek *pallein* (*ibid.* 123 f.), an Americanism, as it were.

38 On New Year and dressing up as animals, see Ginzburg 1991: Part 2, ch.4 and M. Meslin, *La fête des kalendes de janvier dans l'empire romain: étude d'un rituel de Nouvel An* (Brussels 1970) [*Collection Latomus*, 115]: esp. ch.3.

39 Alcuin, *De divinis officiis* 4 (*PL* 101 col. 1177). This is the Euhemerist dismissal of gods, used by Christians such as Firmicus Maternus, *De errore profanarum religionum* and Caesarius, *Sermon* 193 ('Mercury was a wretched man . . . Venus a prostitute . . . ').

40 For more on masquerades, see Hinkmar (Chapter 13) and C. Mengis, *HDA* 8.950 f. s.v. 'Tierverkleidung'; on masks, K. Meuli, *HDA* 5.1762 f. s.v. 'Maske'.

41 Alcuin, *De divinis officiis* 4 (*PL* 101 col. 1177).

42 Other attacks on Thursday: Caesarius, *Sermon* 193.4 on not naming days after demons and not marking the day on which we start a journey; Martin of Braga, *Reforming the pagans* 9; Bede, 10.4 in McNeill and Gamer 1938: 229 (publication details, p.435 f.); Burchard of Worms, *Decreta* 19.5.92 (*PL* 140.964).

43 The eclipse of the moon had long been known as its *troubles* (*labores*), e.g. Vergil, *Georgics* 2.478; see *OLD* s.v. 'labor' (2) §6c.

44 From Liu and Fiala 1992: 102–4 the best candidates for Turin (7°41 East, 45°5 North) appear to be 17.2.379, 6.12.401 and 5.10.423. Ginzel 1899: 215 f. and Schove 1984: 68–70 list eclipses visible at Rome (and therefore Turin) in this

period as 17.12.400, 12.6.401, 6.12.401, 1.6.402, 25.11.402 and give the comet as March–May 400. Schove also dates the Claudian eclipse with some assurance. Ginzel 1899: 219–21, though considering too wide a selection of dates for Maximus through uncertainty in dating *him*, favours 17.12.400, 6.12.410 or 4.11.412.

45 The attribution of both sermons, Maximus and Caesarius, though confidently made in the respective *CC SL* editions, is speculative. They are clearly, however, by different authors and the 'Maximus' sermon is very characteristic of his crabbed and aggressive style.

46 The word is (Old Saxon) *diobolgeldae*, corresponding to the Anglo-Saxon *deofolgield* (Chapter 7); see Jente 1921: 30 and *GA* ii.52 s.v. '*deofolg[i]eld*'.

47 The kings of Essex traced their ancestry back to Woden and, in the next generation, Saxneát, Grimm 1878: iii.379, 382. He is comparable with Irmin, god of the Hermunduri and Terwing, god of the Tervingi (Chapter 7) and the eponyms specifically named by Tacitus, *Germania* 2.2.

9 PAGAN RITE

1 Versnel 1981: 1–64; but we do not know very much at all about *non*-Greco-Roman prayer.

2 Benveniste 1969: ii.216–24, Bremmer 1996a: 267 f.; Burkert 1996: 147.

3 Fauduet 1993: 129.

4 Bremmer 1996a: 268, Kurke 1989.

5 De Vries 1956: i.§287–9. *Hávamál* appears to be a Norwegian compilation, traditional by the tenth century, Hollander 1962: 14.

6 Bremmer 1996a: 279, citing *J.Z. Smith, 'The domestication of sacrifice', in R.G. Hamerton-Kelly (ed.), *Violent origins* (Stanford 1987): 202–5.

7 Bremmer 1996a: 252 and n.54 for bibliography.

8 *Eyrbyggja Saga* 4, Davidson 1993: 99, Renaud 1996: 172, Boyer 1992: 153 f., though Boyer *ibid.* and 97 n.17 observes that there is some danger that this thirteenth-century author was engaged in historical reconstruction.

9 De Vries 1956: i.§286, Onions 1966 s.v. 'bless'.

10 Helmold, 1.52 also comments that blood is good for summoning demons. It is almost as though he had this passage of Homer in mind, though surely he cannot have known Greek.

11 Detienne and Vernant 1989 is one of the most useful books on sacrifice among Greeks and to an extent others, with very useful bibliography as ch. 10. If it is true that sacrifice has been unduly singled out from other rituals, then growing interest in thinking about ritual as a whole is well reflected in Bell 1997.

12 Burkert 1996: 130 f. in this context emphasises how fundamental a word for 'to give' is in languages.

13 Grimm 1875: i.31.

14 Obviously Poseidonios, see *Commenta bernensia*, on Lucan, 1.445 in Chapter 11.

15 Lestringant 1997: 6 f. utterly rejects the view that cannibalism is *always* a myth, presented by W. Arens, *The man-eating myth: anthropology and anthropophagy* (New York 1979). But he accepts that it is exceptional, *ibid.* 8.

16 *RF* i.141 (and Dilke 1971: 98).

17 The (Italic) Umbrians seem to have sacrificed puppies, though, if that is what *katle* means in the *Iguvine tablets*, tablet IIa (Poulteney 1959: esp. 176).

18 For the Indo-European categorisation, see Gamkrelidze and Ivanov 1995: i.391 f.

19 The zoological category is identified by *ibid.* i.403 f.

20 Lincoln 1981: 65 f.

21 Puhvel 1955: 353 f., with bibliography on Indo-European horse-sacrifice. In the *Veda* as well as the Gaulish instance it is only known as a proper name.

22 Lincoln 1981: 65, citing, e.g., F.R. Schröder, 'Ein altirischer Krönungsritus und das indogermanischer Rossopfer', *Zeitschrift für Keltische Philologie* 16 (1927): 310–12.

23 Puhvel 1970: 161 and ch.15.

24 This message can be deduced from Gamkrelidze and Ivanov 1995: i.402 f.

25 Bremmer 1996a: 252 notes in addition that their bones are hard to tell apart.

26 Méniel 1992: 15 f., Brunaux 1996: 106. Méniel 1992: 16 cites Dumézil for the ideological ranking: 1. horse, 2. cow, 3. sheep, 4. pig.

27 Méniel 1992: 16, Brunaux 1996: 106.

28 Wissowa 1912: 60 f., citing Livy 22.10.2, 33.34.1, 34.44.6.

29 *Dvandvá* compounds, MacDonell 1927: 169 f. Sets and ideology, Puhvel 1970: 161 f.

30 On Greek sacrifice, see, for instance: Homer, *Odyssey* 3.430–71, *Iliad* 1.430–74, Burkert 1985: 54–60, Bremmer 1996a: 248–82, Detienne and Vernant 1989, Burkert 1983: esp. 35–48, M.H. Jameson 'Sacrifice and ritual: Greece', in M. Grant and R. Kitzinger (eds), *Civilisation of the ancient Mediterranean: Greece and Rome*, vol. 2 (New York 1988): 959–79.

31 J.L. Durand, 'Greek animals: towards a topology of edible bodies', in Detienne and Vernant 1989: ch.3.

32 All this in Nagy 1990: 145–66.

33 Benveniste 1973: 486 f.

34 Burkert 1985: 55, Benveniste 1973: 499.

35 Polomé 1987: 206, not quite his words.

36 Boyer 1992: 154, de Vries 1956: i.§311. *Dísir* is a collective for powerful female divinities, associated at the end of paganism with fertility powers: de Vries 1957: ii.§528, Renaud 1996: 149, Davidson 1993: 113.

37 Grimm 1875: i.29.

38 *Ibid.* i.30.

39 Benveniste 1973: 467, 483.

40 Hamp 1973: 318–22, Polomé 1987: 208.

41 Brunaux 1996: 114.

42 F.T. van Straten sensitively classifies the huge variety of Greek gifts in relation to the circumstances and intentions of the giver, in Versnel 1981: 80–104.

43 Fauduet 1993: 105.

44 In a thesis under way in 1994, referred to by Fichtl 1994: 39 f.

45 Poseidonios 87F273, Caesar, *Gallic war* 6.17, Strabo 4.1.13, Fichtl 1994: 41.

46 Stengel 1920: 99 f.

47 Green 1986: 143, Fauduet 1993: 117, Brunaux 1996: 77.

48 Burkert 1996: 146 writes with splendid insight on 'the ceremonial destruction of valuables'.

49 On dance in paganism, see Prümm 1954: 487–9.

50 Latte 1913: 28.

51 Parke 1977: 36.

52 De Vries 1956: i.§303.

53 Strabo 3.4.16 (3.4.15 gives Poseidonios 87F52, 3.4.17 F58a; Theiler 1982: fr.24 stops just a little short). Polybios 2.29.7 on the Battle of Telamon (225 BC) is sometimes taken to show battle-dances by Gauls (cf. Brunaux 1996: 147) but as far as I can see does not say that at all, unless strange aggressive movements by naked soldiers are automatically 'dance'.

54 The Romans deserve incalculable credit for so doing according to Pliny the elder, *Natural history* 30.4.

55 Stead and Turner 1985, Hutton 1991: 194, M. Henig in Gilley and Sheils 1994: 13.

56 I am grateful to Ronald Hutton for rescuing me on this point.

57 'Enum verstum mönnum', *Kristnisaga* 12, de Vries 1956: i.§284.

58 Quotation from Chadwick 1899: 27; marginality is the suggestion of Bremmer 1983: 303 f. *à propos* of scapegoats, though he stresses the importance of good treatment of the scapegoat 'because they realised that they could not save their own skin by sacrificing the scum of the polis' (305).

59 De Vries 1956: i.§283, *Lex Frisionum* 17.5 (*MG Leges* 3.671 with von Richthoffen's n.39), *Lex Alamannorum* 37.1 (*ibid.* 57), Canute II.3 (*GA* i.310 f.).

60 De Vries 1956: i.§284, text in Grimm 1875: i.35. The sacrifice of children is of course known from Incas and Carthaginians and there is no reason in principle why it should not have happened among Europeans; some limited evidence is presented in Grimm 1875: i.37.

61 Chadwick 1899: 7, Davidson 1993: 98; cf. also Haraldus (Haldan) who dedicates to Othin 'the souls he has cast out of their bodies by weapon' (Saxo 7.10.3, p.247 Holder).

62 Hermunduri and Varus cited by Chadwick 1899: 30 f.; de Vries 1956: i.§283.

63 As even Grimm 1875: i.36 misunderstands this, let me add that 'Scyth' just means that he is a violent barbarian (see K. Dowden in *DDD* 1485 f.) and is not meant to deny that he is a Goth.

64 Probably not the men's heads, cf. de Vries 1956: i.408 n.4; contrast Davidson 1993: 96.

65 Orosius, *History* 5.16.5 f., Chadwick 1899: 31 f.

66 Chadwick presses hard for Odin, 1899: 19 and ch.1 in general; 'God of the hanged', Boyer 1992: 98.

67 Strabo 7.3.2, 7.5.2, 7.5.12; Holder 1896: i s.vv. 'Capanna', 'Capedunon', 'dunos'. For their tribal name-type, cf. the Taurisci and maybe Ligurisci (Strabo 7.3.2).

68 *Commenta bernensia* on Lucan, 1.445, full text in Chapter 11.

69 Sidonius Apollinaris, *Letters* 8.6.15 (above).

70 In the continuation of the passage of Alcuin cited in Chapter 5.

71 Thought an invention among Roman soldiers by Zenker (see de Vries), thought more a Gaulish custom by de Vries 1956: i.§283.

72 This whole area of Strabo is out of Poseidonios, cf. *FGH* 87F45–54, esp. 49; Theiler 1982 is right to give it blanket coverage as fr.22.

73 See Chapter 1 and note also the association of Kimbroi with Kimmerioi and Galatians at Diodoros 5.32.4 (Poseidonios, *FGH* 87F116).

74 Villar 1996: 498–503.

75 'They tied up the prefect of Bernov, a man broad and fat in body, twisted his head between his legs and cut open his back with their swords, awaiting the flow of blood in their desire to divine the outcome of the war', Henry of Herford (Dominican monk, writing 1355–70), *Liber de rebus memorabilioribus*, *MG ScrPruss* 1.243 (*LPG* 115 f., Clemen 1936: 98).

76 The Eruli are supposed by Procopius to kill off relatives who become old or sick, if by a stranger's hand. Chadwick 1899: 41 n.3 (Slavs), 42 (Brunnhilde and others).

77 Grimm 1875: i.79 f., Prümm 1954: 353; the source is *Olaf Tryggvessons saga*.

78 Fletcher 1997: 45.

79 Dillon 1997 usefully draws together the Greek evidence, though it becomes

clear from xv–xvii that the term 'pilgrimage' is for him one of convenience to embrace an interesting range of Greek activities. The Greeks did not have a word for it.

80 I cannot agree with Dillon 1997: xviii–xix that an Athenian's procession to Eleusis, from centre to margin, should count as 'pilgrimage'.

81 See, e.g., J.P.C. Sumption, *Pilgrimage: an image of medieval religion* (London 1975) for 1050–1250 as the great age of pilgrimage.

82 'Toute pèlerinage médiéval est, dans une certaine mesure, une oeuvre de pénitence' (Vogel 1963: 39). He also stresses (82) that the Crusades are in principle penitential.

83 Hunt 1982; a celebrated example is the *Peregrinatio Aetheriae* ('Journey abroad of Etheria'), the journal of an Iberian or southern Gaulish woman's trip to the Holy Land (AD *c*. 400).

84 Vogel 1963: 41; Davies and Davies 1982: 30.

85 Plummer 1910: i.cxxiii n.2.

86 *Ibid.* i.cxxii n.10 cites *inter alia* Bertrand 1897: 261.

87 'The Arabs worship a god but who it is I do not know: the statue, however, I have seen and it was a square stone', Maximus of Tyre 2.8 (see Chapter 7). A.T. Welch, in Hinnells 1985: 145–9.

10 PAGAN TIME

1 Eliade 1969: ch. 2. Van der Leeuw 1948: §55 interestingly insists on the *quality* rather than the chronometry of time.

2 Gamkrelidze and Ivanov 1995: i.590 f., Onions 1966 s.v. 'moon'.

3 Dowden 1989: 82–5, 196.

4 E.g., Le Roux and Guyonvarc'h 1995: 14. Cold, Lambert 1994: 110, Thurneysen 1899: 534.

5 Usener 1903: 342 f.

6 Brown 1986: 213–15: to calculate the Muslim year, starting from the emigration (*hijrah*) of Mohammed in 622, use the formula: *hijrah* year = 1.0307 (Gregorian year − 622) + 0.46.

7 Usener 1903: 343.

8 Under the influence of Eusebius; see Bede, *De temporibus* 11, and *De ratione temporum* 44.

9 Dowden 1989: 196. MacDonell 1924 s.v. (p.245).

10 Cf. Wissowa 1912: 390 f.

11 *Ibid.* 430–2.

12 As Greeks and Romans counted inclusively, a *tri*eteric festival is one that happens every two years.

13 Plutarch, *Aetia graeca (Explanations of Greek customs)* 12.293c. The eight-year cycle for intercalation is supposed by Nilsson (1955: 645) to be of Babylonian origin, though Nilsson presents this view in the context of making the Greek months themselves a late arrival (not much before 600 BC – *ibid.* 644). This latter view is rightly rejected by Burkert 1985: 227 and it may be that the former view should also be rejected.

14 Lambert 1994: 109, R. Jackson in Brown 1986: 111.

15 Pliny the elder, *Natural history* 16.249; as this is far from unlikely, there is no need to suppose that Pliny or his source has confused years with months and is in fact referring to the two and a half-year cycle.

16 Zerubavel 1981: 111. Pietri 1984 is my main source for the week; there is an

earlier work in English: *F.H. Colson, *The week: an essay on the origin and development of the seven day cycle* (Cambridge 1926).

17 'Scarcely': Tacitus, *Histories* 5.4.5–7 already associates the Sabbath with Saturn; furthermore, Talmudic astrology appears to have associated heavenly angelic hierarchies with the week, according to Pietri 1984: 67 f. and notes.

18 Grimm 1875: i.102, orthography mostly in accordance with G. Köbler, *Wörterbuch des althochdeutschen Sprachschatzes* (Paderborn 1993).

19 The proto-Germanic form is reconstructed as **Tiwaz*. The modern German *Dienstag* for 'Tuesday' goes back to a form *Dingstag* (day of the Thing), replacing, possibly with some contamination, an earlier *Zīstag*.

20 The Goths had evidently adopted the Greek form, *sambaton* (de Vries 1957: ii.§602) – in Greek an *m* is the only way to stop the *b* being pronounced *v*, hence *sambaton* not *sabaton*.

21 Pietri 1984: 73–6. Bede, *De temporibus* 4, attributes *feria*-counting to St Silvester.

22 Trajan, Maas 1902: 157–66, 274.

23 The argument of Maas 1902: 280 that the equivalence Donar = Jupiter speaks for upper, that is, southern, Germany is fallacious: admittedly Donar elsewhere could be equated with Hercules, but the question was not 'who shall we adopt as an equivalent of Donar', but 'who shall we adopt as an equivalent of Jupiter in order to name Thursday'.

24 Chuvin 1990: 26 f.

25 *Codex theodosianus* 2.8.1 (of 321).

26 Caesarius, *Sermon* 13.5, 19.4, 52.2.

27 *Ibid.* Sermon 13.3, Martin of Braga, *Reforming the pagans* 9, McKenna 1938: 94, 118. An edict of 409 prohibited suing the Jews on the Sabbath, *Codex theodosianus* 2.8.26.

28 The standard publication is *RIG3*; there is a briefer account in Lambert 1994: ch. 9. I have found Thurneysen 1899 to be full of good sense and sound argument.

29 Indiscriminacy, see Hutton 1991: 142 f., 178; 1996: ch.40. Popularity: there are even websites, at the time of writing: (http://) technovate.org/coligny.htm *and* www.alpes-net.fr/~myrddyn/coleng.htm.

30 Hutton 1996: 410 is too sceptical: it is quite clear where the two halves of the year begin and a fair assumption that, of Samon- and Giamon-, it is Samon- that begins the year as it begins the first two and a half-year cycle, cf. Thurneysen 1899: 525 f., *RIG3*: 404 and the plates in *RIG3*. Table based on Thurneysen 1899: 525.

31 *RIG3*: pl. 15; the word *AMD* (Lambert 1994: 113) does not exist – the D is a malformed B.

32 See *RIG3*: 270 and Thurneysen 1899: 525, who tend to the opposite view.

33 Thurneysen 1899: 526.

34 *RIG3*: 296.

35 Paired months are also known in Anglo-Saxon tradition, see Grimm 1876: ii.658 and Philippson 1929: 205, citing *A. Tille, *Yule and Christmas, their place in the Germanic year* (London 1899): 148 for the view that the Germans had a sixty-day (fifty-nine, surely) double-month system until they came into contact with the Romans. There are traces also in Greek and Sanskrit tradition, Usener 1903: 342 f. Likewise, there is a strange reference in the (Umbrian) *Iguvine tables* III.2 to a festival being held at the end of a two-month, or two-monthly, period (*sume ustite sestentasiaru urnasiaru*, Poulteney 1959: 200).

36 *RIG3*: 400.

37 A solution (cited in *RIG3*: 400) has been to claim that instances which do not survive of the month-end of the one month whose month-ends are so badly preserved (Equos) were of non-standard length, 28 days like our February. But 28 days is an invalid value: only 29 and 30 can work given the length of the lunar month.

38 Dis is the rather obscure Latin lord of the dead, plainly translating a Greek statement about Plouton made by Poseidonios, cf. Graf 1991: 140 and Edelstein and Kidd 1989: fr.100.

39 Le Roux and Guyonvarc'h 1986: 260. Onions 1966 s.v. 'fortnight'; Tacitus, *Germania* 11.

40 R. Jackson in Brown 1986: 111.

41 Lambert 1994: 110.

42 Night and moon, Much 1967: 208.

43 Plutarch 293b–c: *Septerion, Herois, Charila.*

44 Wolfram 1988: 112

45 No-one knows what the word 'Yule' comes from; Grimm (1876: ii.585) tried to explain it as a variant on the inherited word 'wheel', perhaps less impossible than it looks.

46 Philippson 1929: 194, 204.

47 The Thing fundamental, Grimm 1875: i.34, de Vries 1956: i.§305, Renaud 1996: 175 f., Philippson 1929: 203–7.

48 *C. Pythian-Adams, *Local history and folklore* (1975): 21–5, cited by Hutton 1994: 294 n.2. For the three-season theory, see Usener 1903: 337, reckoning (338) that *ver*, the term for spring, had at an earlier stage denoted summer and that the year had simply been divided into two. See also Gamkrelidze and Ivanov 1995: i.750 f. for a three-part year.

49 De Vries 1956: i.§306.

50 *Ibid.* i.§305, *Heimskringla* 1.380 f. English customs, Hutton 1994: 37–9. German terms, Grimm 1875: i.513 f.

51 Grimm 1875: i.35 assumes they are pagan. Hutton 1994: 27–31 describes Tudor English rituals but actually doubts (cf. 260) whether any of these types of ritual are securely rooted in earlier pagan practice.

52 Philippson 1929: 205.

53 Parke 1977: 29 wrongly says 'before' the summer solstice.

54 Deubner 1932: 22–35. Parke 1977: ch.1.

55 Deubner 1932: 30, Pausanias 5.16.2.

56 The deduction of Nilsson 1906: 120.

57 Farnell 1907: iv.259–63, Burkert 1985: 234–6, Nilsson 1906: 118–29.

58 Usener 1903: 353, referring to Mommsen. The sums add up, but it makes nonsense of the March festivals of Mars.

59 There is little basis for the widespread supposition that he is also a god of agriculture, as Dumézil explained (1970: i.205–40).

60 Scheid 1998: 45 f. gives a comprehensive list of festivals that might be considered agricultural.

61 The name Saturnus seems to derive from the verb to sow, cf. *satus*, 'sown'. Other festivals which have been associated with the solstices (Scheid 1998: 48): the Matralia of 11 June, Wissowa 1912: 110–12; the Divalia or Angeronalia on the solstice itself, 21 December, Wissowa 1912: 241. Neither has any exceptional civic prominence.

62 Wissowa 1912: 241 f.; Ovid, *Fasti* 3.523–42 .

63 Vendryès 1948: 313. Samhain cannot come from *sam-fuin*: Le Roux and Guyonvarc'h 1995: 184.

64 Hutton 1996: 360–70, 408–11.

65 *RIG*3: 403 speaks oddly of Samon- as a *récapitulation d'été*.

66 For the meaning 'winter', see Lambert 1994: 110. Hutton 1991: 143, 178 limits the implications of the Coligny Calendar.

67 *Meitheamh, Mehefin, Mezheven*, respectively: Le Roux and Guyonvarc'h 1995: 13.

68 *RIG*3: 266–8, Thurneysen 1899: 532–5.

11 A FEW ASPECTS OF GODS

1 Unbegaun 1948: 398.

2 German names Rossitten and Ludsen, the latter marked as Ljucin on the pull-out map in Niederle 1956: opp. 420.

3 The similarity between *pop* and 'Pope' leads to a fascinating misapprehension of Peter of Duisberg (*LPG* 88, Clemen 1936: 97) that Lithuanian religion is run by a pope in an apparently non-existent place called Romow (cf. Rowell 1994: 125 f., not quite in focus on the linguistic confusion). The similarity is not wholly coincidental: the word, still used to mean parish priest, derives via Germanic from the late ecclesiastical Greek *papas*, 'bishop', like pope itself (Onions 1966 s.v. 'pope 1', 'pope 2', Gimbutas 1971: 78).

4 Except Jerome. In fact the Revised English Bible does not believe that the pagan gods existed: 'they sacrificed to demons that are no gods', 'For the gods of nations are idols every one.'

5 Cyprian, *Ad Fortunatum* (*CC SL* 3) 3 '*Quae comminatio Dei*'; Zeno, *Sermon* 1.25 (15).§5. *Codex theodosianus* 16.10.23.

6 Caspari 1883: xcvii–c collects the evidence for earlier Christian texts on *daemones*.

7 Probably Argenton-sur-Creuse (Indre), cf. Holder 1896: i.208.

8 Bettelheim 1976: 49 f. sees gods as a deduction of children (appropriately for the childhood focus of Freudians) in effect in order to supply the missing term in the equation *children are to parents as all people are to x*.

9 On the sources of this passage, see Graf 1991.

10 The first part of this passage is out of Poseidonios (Graf 1991). On wooden containers, see also Caesar, *Gallic war* 6.16.4 (Chapter 9). On Dis the underworld god, see Graf 1991: 140 and Caesar, *Gallic war* 6.18.1 (Chapter 10); I have corrected the text of the Scholiast from the impossible 'father *of* Dis' – he is father of their nation.

11 Grimm 1876–8: ii.xxxviii, iii.44 f. Usener 1903 is an extended article on threes, and other stylised sets, in Greek and Roman culture.

12 Rowell 1994: 118–20.

13 Hutton 1991: 156. Father, Caesar, *Gallic war* 6.18.1. *Taranis* is a metathesis of Donar/Thor/Thunder.

14 Curchin 1991: 157–60. There is a detailed and worthwhile attempt to bring order to Celtic gods in G.S. Olmsted, *The gods of the Celts and the Indo-Europeans* (Budapest 1994).

15 The evidence, in effect, is in Holder 1904: ii.552–72.

16 *Ibid.* ii.307–46.

17 Ross 1967: 319, de Vries 1961: 50–5.

18 Rowell 1994: 119.

19 The evidence for religion, mythology and philology can be found in: Nagy

1990: ch.7, Puhvel 1987: 226, 234 f., Jouet 1989: 107. I should also mention G. Nagy, 'Perkūnas and Perunъ', in M. Mayrhofer et al., *Antiquitates indogermanicae* (Innsbruck 1974): 113–31.

20 There are some strange Hittite parallels here – for instance, the stem *perun-* ('rock'). The storm-god *Taryu-* or *Taryuna-* and the verb *tary-* ('overpower', not so far from 'strike'?) may show a similar connection of striking and lightning; if we suppose an original initial labio-velar, they might be the real cognate words. We should perhaps be thinking also of Etrusco-Roman kings called 'Tarquinius' if lightning and the striking of fire is close to sovereignty (cf. Nagy 1990: 172 on Servius Tullius).

21 Lines from a Latvian folksong (*daiņas*) quoted in French by Jouet 1989: 109.

22 Lambert 1994: 37.

23 The Latin word has, in effect, a double *qu-* as in *quinque* (for *penkʷe*) 'five'. Deržavin 1948: 159 alleges that *grm* is the Serbian for an *oak* (in my dictionary it is a *bush*) and draws attention to a supposed Serbian god of thunder *Grom*. *Grmeti* is certainly 'to thunder' (the Russian is *gremit'*), but it is obviously onomatopoeic and the god is poorly evidenced – unknown, notably, to Niederle 1956: 280 f., 285 f.

24 Nagy 1990: 192, citing C.H. Whitman, 'Hera's anvils', *HSCP* 74 (1970)[2]: 37–42.

25 Nagy 1990: 192 n.82, Dowden 1989: 140.

26 Nagy 1990: 195–6; according to de Vries 1956: ii.§427 oaks are seldom struck by lightning.

27 Oak was considered fissile by Theophrastos, *De plantis* 5.6.1 and, e.g., Vergil, *Aeneid* 6.181. Wood is fissile because it has veins in it according to Pliny the elder, *Natural history* 16.184.

28 On lightning see Schonland 1950: 55 and Malan 1963: 151; there are few books devoted to lightning and M.A. Uman, *Lightning* (New York 1984) does not deal with oaks. This explanation of oak damage is understood by Pennick 1996: 22.

12 PRIESTS

1 I know of no comprehensive study of priesthood in modern times. It was, apparently, last done by *J. Lippert, *Allgemeine Geschichte des Priestertums* (Berlin 1883–4); a selective vision (looking at 'big' cultures: Greece, Rome, Near East, Maya, etc.) is found in E.O. James, *The nature and function of priesthood: a comparative and anthropological study* (London 1955). This chapter is, therefore, more than usually, trying to find some bearings.

2 Cf. Beard and North 1990: 4 f.

3 Deuteronomy 17.9, 21.5, Grabbe 1995: 43 and (theocracy) 65.

4 Song is apparently associated with Levites, cf. Grabbe 1995: 50, 51. It is, of course, the function of the Levites to be menial beside the priests proper, descended from Aaron, or at least that is how it developed (cf. *ibid.* 42, 52, 182). Egyptian women, *ibid.* 53.

5 *Ibid.* 53.

6 On 'false prophecy' and 'prophetic conflict' see *ibid.* 113–15.

7 Frazer 1911: *Magic art* i.245 f., 371 f., 420 f. (1905: 90 f., 127 f., 150 f.).

8 On kings and priesthood (with these passages) see Frazer 1911: *Magic art* i.44 f. (1905: 30 f.).

9 On the cultic functions of Israelite kings and the tension with the priestly record (as well as Near Eastern and Egyptian culture), see Grabbe 1995: ch.2.

10 Beard and North 1990: 2.

11 Lincoln 1981: 63.

12 Bremmer 1995. Household cult: Roman, Wissowa 1912: 156–81, (simple) Dowden 1992b: 26–30; D.G. Orr, 'Roman domestic religion: the evidence of the household shrines', *Aufstieg und Niedergang der römischen Welt*, II.16.2, pp.1557–91. Greek, associated with the worship of Zeus Herkeios, is surprisingly under-evidenced, cf. Nilsson 1955: 402–6, and barely mentioned by Burkert 1985 (255 f.). Helmold 1.52 mentions Slav household cult. Germanic, de Vries 1956: i.§135.

13 L. Weiser-Aall, in *HDA* 5.29; Onions 1966 s.v. 'goblin'.

14 L. Weiser-Aall, in *HDA* 5.30, 34, 41.

15 J.M.R. Cormack in *OCD*2 and *OCD*3 s.v. 'Thrace'; cf. Dowden forthcoming.

16 Hard-nosed, highly educated Greeks found it hard to take 'superstition' seriously – Polybius (6.56.11) took a similar view of religiosity among the Roman aristocracy. These Thracians were a religiously susceptible people, Pausanias 9.29.3.

17 McCone 1990: 136 f., Byrne 1973: 23.

18 The Macedonians, on the northern fringes of being Greek, of course retained the kingship.

19 Grabbe 1995: 54, citing *J. Renger, 'Untersuchungen zur Priestertum in der altbabylonischen Zeit', *Zeitschrift für Assyrologie* 58 (1966): 110–88, 59 (1969): 104–230 at 1966: 126. Cf. H.W.F. Saggs, *The greatness that was Babylon* (London 1962): 345. Kings originally priests, van der Leeuw 1948: §26.3.

20 This thesis, if exaggeratedly, is presented by Frazer 1911: *Magic art* i.ch.vii (with some ominously misguided thoughts on the benefits of despotism, foreshadowing the rise of Fascism and National Socialism).

21 Bremmer 1993: 155; the poem is pseudo-Hesiod, *Melampodeia*, probably not earlier than the sixth century BC.

22 Given the insensitivity of the ancients to barbarian languages, perhaps the reader will allow me a wild passing thought: are Thracian Getai a mirage? – had they been Goths all along and is there *no confusion* in the authors? If an Ostrogoth can be called Radagaisus (Chapter 9), then a German 'Thracian' can be called Vologaises.

23 *Dii* – a likely correction for the *pii* ('pious') of the manuscripts.

24 Grimm 1875: i.73 f.

25 A suggestion reported by Wesche 1940: 45.

26 Grimm 1875: i.72.

27 Jordanes, *Getica* 40; the earlier name – or perhaps the actual Gothic name – was 'Tarabostesei', those who wore the 'tyari' which Jordanes or the scribes of his manuscripts assimilate to 'tiara' (*Getica* 71). Grimm 1875: i.75.

28 J. Linderski s.v. 'haruspices' in *OCD*3, p.668. Grimm 1878: iii.39 mentions the 'three kinds of *pillei* that priests wear [in Rome]: *apex* [as worn by the *flamen Dialis*], *tutulus, galerus*' (Suetonius, fr.168).

29 Unbegaun 1948: 417.

30 Training, however, is more a characteristic of the *filid*, that Poseidonios does not know. On Poseidonios and Irish tradition, see Jackson 1964: 24–7, 39 f.

31 Bremmer 1996b: 102 says, of poets and seers, that 'both were dependent on kings, were inspired, led itinerant lives, were often represented as blind, and pretended to possess supernatural knowledge.'

32 This echoes Herodotos' (1.132) statement about the Persians that 'without a Magus [an earlier paradigm for the philosopher-priest] it is not their custom to make sacrifices'.

33 See Holder 1896: i.1270, 1320–2. There seems to be no adequate evidence for

this prefix, though Thurneysen's theory is supported by d'Arbois de Jubainville 1906: 85 and Le Roux and Guyonvarc'h 1986: 31–3, who refer also to *C.-J. Guyonvarc'h, *Le vocabulaire sacerdotal du celtique* (Rennes 1986). Other discussions: MacCulloch 1911: 293; Kendrick 1927: 16, including reference to a theory that the word is in origin Etruscan (!) and means 'skilled in sacred things'; Piggott 1975: 100 f.

34 See above p. 108 f. (with n. 52) and compare n. 35 below on *drys* and Druid.

35 *Commenta bernensia*, on Lucan, 1.450–8 also knows the oak theory, presumably from Poseidonios: 'The philosophers of the Gauls are called druids after the trees because "they inhabit remote groves" [Lucan 1.453 f.].'

Le Roux and Guyonvarc'h 1986: 32 rightly criticise those who etymologise without knowledge of a single Celtic language, but (a) there is still no adequate evidence for the 'intensive prefix' *dru-* and (b) the oak hypothesis simply implies that in the compound *dru-wid-* the root is found in the zero grade, not the e-grade (*derwo-*), cf. Lincoln 1991: 185. Greek has evidently generalised the zero grade from the genitive *druós* and from compounds like *drutómos*. Gaulish phonology is not particularly well evidenced (Lambert 1994: 42 f. discusses diphthongs), but it is possible that the second element was originally in the full grade and that *druid-* represents *dru-weid*; this would then bring the zero grade of the first element under the rules stated by Gamkrelidze and Ivanov 1995: i.192: 'Affixation of further morphemes in full grade regularly produces zero grade in all the preceding morphemes, root and affixal.' The derivation from tree/oak is accepted without argument by Gamkrelidze and Ivanov 1995: i.690 n.21.

36 See *ibid.* ii.135 s.v. '*t'er-*'.

37 Onions 1966 s.v. 'Druid', citing the Irish *derb* 'sure' and the obsolete Welsh *derw* 'true'.

38 Druids: Caesar, *Gallic war* 6.14.3, de Vries 1961: 205, citing Sanskrit material for the *guru*, too.

39 *Aeweweard*, however, has one mention only, not very Germanic: 'In Herod's days there was a very great *aeweweard* called Zachariah' (Jente 1921: 2).

40 Palmer 1969: 27; Wissowa 1912: 240.

41 Cf. Palmer 1969: 31.

42 Ausonius, *Professors of Bordeaux* 11.24.

43 The stem *dot-*, meaning 'make' (the Greek *titheinai*, Indo-European *$dh\bar{e}$*) is no longer an active part of the language in historical times.

44 Beard and North 1990: 46.

45 Burkert 1985: 95, cf. Stengel 1920: 31–78.

46 Burkert 1985: 97 f. and 386 n.31 for bibliography on the impersonation of gods in Greek and ancient Mediterranean religions.

47 *Ibid.* 95 f.; R. Garland, 'Priests and Power in Classical Athens', in Beard and North 1990: ch.3.

48 *Karawiporo* (i.e. *klawiphoros*), Beard and North 1990: 3.

49 De Vries 1957: ii.§498 associates this cult with the mention in Timaios, *FGH* 566F85 (Diodoros 4.56.4) of a cult of the 'Dioskouroi' by the 'Celts' who live alongside the Ocean (whence the 'Dioskouroi' arrived). Different manuscripts vary the name of the tribe and we have no other knowledge of them.

50 Meringer 1924: esp. 108 f., an interesting if tenuous article, associates the term with the Greek *alk-* ('power, might') and identifies in the alleged names of leaders in AD 170 of the Hasdingi (equated with the Nahanarvali) what he supposes are the actual names of the Alci, 'Raos' (cf. ON *reyrr*, 'cairn') and 'Raptos' (cf. ON *raptr*, 'pillar'). Meringer views these gods then as Dioscuri

who lead the army, rather like (p.111) our own equine mythological pair, Hengist and Horsa.

51 Much 1967: 480-2 on Lapps, and also on the name *Alci*.

52 Thietmar 7.59 (44), briefly mentioned in Chapter 5. *E. Wienecke, *Untersuchungen zur Religion der Westslawen*: 49-53. Much 1967: 480 identifies it also with the *Limios* grove in Ptolemy 2.11.13. It is not in all texts of Ptolemy and Limios itself may be a corruption, e.g. of *Alkios*, cf. H. Franke s.v. 'Limios Alsos', *RE* 13.672.

53 For German priest terms and philology see Grimm 1875: i.55 and ch.V; Jente 1921: 1-6; Philippson 1929: 180-3; de Vries 1956: i.§266, 277. Also, Boyer 1992: 153 and Renaud 1996: 162 on the *hofgoði*.

54 Grimm 1875: i.72; de Vries 1956: §399. It is hard to believe Tacitus has a particular German function-name in mind and Grimm is focusing more on the pious god-subservient mentality.

55 *Heliand* 150.24 according to Grimm 1875: i.73; dating, de Vries 1957: ii.§607.

56 Chronicle, *LPG* 75; Old Swedish, Grimm 1875: i.30. Rowell 1994: 124 attributes the mention to Peter of Duisberg, I think in error (if I am wrong, it just means that Peter has been reading OHG sources).

57 An inscription at Grenoble (*CIL* 12.2221) mentions 'Nemetiales', but unless this *nemeton* happens to be a grove (Chapter 7), they are not priestly grove-managers, but simply 'shrinespeople', *aeditui*. De Vries 1961: 122 interprets the Nemetiales, implausibly, as the plural divinities of the grove.

58 D'Arbois de Jubainville 1906: 4 similarly claims the *gutuatros* as a temple priest, though he regards this as prior to the druids.

59 De Vries 1961: 213-15; Le Roux and Guyonvarc'h 1986: 444; Holder 1896: i s.v. 'gutuatros', 1904: ii s.v. 'Moltinus'. Inscriptions *CIL* 13. 11225, 11226 (Autun), 2585 (Mâcon), 1577 (Le Puy). The distribution is narrow enough for it to be a regional term, as de Vries 1961: 214 suggests.

60 A Celtic root **gutus*, as in Old Irish *guth* ('voice', 'word'), suggests 'speaker', a possible 'Celtic priest-title' *(*Holder 1896: i s.v.). With the implausible addition that the second part is another specific root corresponding to Old Irish *athir* ('father'), Loth suggested a meaning 'prayer-father' (in de Vries 1961: 214); more likely it is a fossilised suffix to denote an agent (Le Roux and Guyonvarc'h 1986: 444). De Vries wonders whether there is not some link between *gutuatros, hotar* (Sanskrit sacrificial priest) and Gothic *gudja* and certainly Polomé 1987: 209 so connects the *gutu-* element. We could even split the word *gut-watros*: it might then include the *wates* stem, or be a garbled version of some Germanic word meaning 'god-warden'. To complete the confusion, *god* ('he who is called'?) appears to be the same word as **g(h)utos*, Le Roux and Guyonvarc'h *ibid*.

61 A person cannot be an oracle: persons may be mediums or prophets, or run an oracle.

62 R. Parker s.v. 'divination' in *OCD*3, p.488.

63 Burkert 1992: 46-51, with illustration on p.47.

64 Wesche 1940: 74-81.

65 *Ibid.* 68 and 67-72 on German augury in general.

66 Thietmar 6.24; Saxo 14.39.10, p.567 Holder; Helmold 2.108 (see Chapter 7).

67 Rowell 1994: 122 f.

68 Jouet 1989: 154. It does not help that Długosz (*LPG* 137) tells much the same story at other points in his narrative, too.

69 *LPG* 198-201; Jouet 1989: 154. Grunau was writing, and continually adding bits, 1517-29.

70 The principal exceptions are Finnish, Estonian, Hungarian and Basque.

71 I outline this at Dowden 1992a: 58–60.

72 At this point let me mention the 'euphemism' or 'taboo' move: confronted with the absence of the word for an elementary, yet powerful, concept, the scholar claims that the power of the word has made it 'taboo' and it has been replaced by one less dangerous, by a euphemism – for example, on Slavonic bears Gamkrelidze and Ivanov 1995: i.418f., Armenian leopards 426, snakes 445 f., moles 450, turtles 451, crabs 451. In all these instances some languages do not preserve what appears to be the original word and so taboo is invoked. I see no way of verifying *any* instance of the taboo explanation given a relentless (glottochronological) drive towards semantic renewal across the entire lexicon in all languages. I therefore do not believe that taboo or euphemism is a useful explanation of the difficulty in reconstructing Indo-European religious terms.

73 The suggestion of Polomé 1987: 201 f. Puhvel 1987: 156 f. reconstructs *bhlagsmen*. Benveniste 1973: 231 is more sceptical.

74 Bede, *Ecclesiastical history* 2.13, Grimm 1875: i.75.

75 Caesar, *Gallic war* 6.14.1, Le Roux and Guyonvarc'h 1986: 103–6

76 Pliny the elder, *Natural history* 16.44. Priestly dress in various cultures, Grimm 1878: iii.39 f. Gerovit = Jarovit.

77 Saxo 14.39.3 f., p.565 Holder.

78 Polomé 1987: 201 f.

79 *Ibid.* 206 f. adds further possibilities; for instance, the root of the Latin *sacer* ('sacred') seems to exist in Hittite, too.

80 Gamkrelidze and Ivanov 1995: i.210, Mallory 1989: 123.

81 Benveniste 1973: Book 6 'Religion'.

82 *Ibid.* 481–8, Bremmer 1996a: 279.

83 I am puzzled by the alleged laryngeal, '*H*', which seems to me an inconsistency in reconstruction. Gamkrelidze and Ivanov 1995: i.606 and i.772 ('That the Indo-European word is a borrowing is shown by its foreign accessive consonant sequence (see *ibid.* i.124–6) and root vowel *a*').

84 The *Vita Sancte Ite virginis* is in Plummer 1910: ii.116–30

85 Jente 1921: 4, Philippson 1929: 183.

86 It was also held by the original propagator of the myth of matriarchy, J.J. Bachofen, *Myth, religion and mother right: selected writings* (Princeton 1967) [*Bollingen Series* 84]: 85.

87 Even in so male-dominated a religion as the ancient Israelite, some women might prophesy (cf. Grabbe 1995: 115 f.). I notice also the existence of some women diviners among the Assyrians (*ibid.* 133) and the Hittites (*ibid.* 135), not to mention the Witch of Endor and her necromancy (1 Samuel 28).

88 Bremmer 1993: 153, 1996b: 98, 102.

89 Plutarch, *Crassus* 11; Grimm 1878: iii.41.

90 Plutarch, *Caesar* 19. If Plutarch's information is good, the Doubs seems the obvious river, cf. Caesar, *Gallic war* 1.38.

91 Caesar, *Gallic war* 1.47.

92 *Histories* 5.61, 65, 4.22, 24, *Germania* 8.

93 *KlP* s.v. 'Veleda'.

94 Jordanes, *Getica* 24; Wolfram 1988: 107; Wesche 1940: 47–51 with citation of glosses of the form *necromantia* = *helliruna*.

95 For other instances of Nordic and Germanic women who specialise in prophecy, see Grimm 1875–8: i.77–80, iii.41 f., Wesche 1940: 47–51. *Völva* and *Veleda*, cf. Grimm: 80.

96 *Life*, e.g. §xii, xxiv, xxxii.

97 Plummer 1910: i.clix n.4.
98 *Ibid.* i.clix–clx.
99 As argued by Kendrick 1927: 96 f.
100 Saxo 14.39.11, p.567 Holder.
101 Rowell 1994: 123 (with cfs. to Arkona and also Vikings). There is no case, however, for going back to the myths of Bachofen and proposing 'the earlier matriarchal religion of the Balts' (Rowell 1994: 124 n.28, referring to *M. Gimbutas, 'The pre-Christian religion of Lithuania', *La Cristianizzazione* 16–19).
102 De Vries 1956: i.§276, 'bei der italo-keltischen Gruppe . . . eine sehr straffe und einflussreiche priesterliche Organisation'.
103 De Vries 1961: 214f., Brunaux 1988: 62.
104 Lehmann 1993: 68, citing *H. Scharfe, 'The Vedic word for "King"', *Journal of the American Oriental Society* 105 (1985): 543–8.
105 Entwistle and Morison 1964: 26, 95.
106 Jente 1921: 14.

13 CRADLE TO GRAVE

1 See Ranke 1951: 29 for the occasions on which a forty-day period is of significance.
2 Parker 1983: 48, wrongly worrying about a 'Semitic' sound of forty days; the forty-day period is very widely distributed: Ranke 1951: 29 resumes major studies by W.H. Roscher. There is a possible reference in a Greek sacred law, though in opaque circumstances, possibly involuntary miscarriage, to a woman who has given birth being polluted for forty days, Parker 1983: 354 f.
3 *Ibid.* 50 and n.67, 352–4.
4 *Ibid.* 60–5 deals with birth, death and rites of passage and argues, in the spirit of Mary Douglas, that it is the betweenness of birth and death that creates the pollution.
5 De Vries 1956: i.§137, Nilsson 1955: i.175, 459.
6 Nilsson 1955: i.95 and n.8, 115, Parker 1983: 51. Circumambulation, see Index.
7 Censorinus, *De die natali* 11.7, Parker 1983: 52.
8 See also *Hávamál* str.158, *Rigsthula* 7; De Vries 1956: i.§137.
9 *Plebanos* (Italian *pievani*).
10 De Vries 1956: i.§138, citing *K.A. Eckhardt, *Germanenrechte* 1 (Göttingen 1953): 32 f. and *GA* i.380.
11 Nilsson 1955: i.136 f., Deubner 1932: 232–4.
12 Weiser 1927: 34–9 discusses the custom of the Chatti in the light of Van Gennep's three stages in the rite of passage. See also K. Beth, in *HDA* 8.1232 s.v. 'Übergangriten'; De Vries 1956: i.§139. On *Virtus*, see Weiser 1927: 37 f.
13 De Vries 1956: i.§282 talks as though it is and certainly Silius Italicus 4.200–2 describes a 'Gaul' vowing such hair to 'Mars'. If not, this would be one to add to Durkheim's (1915: 34) category of rites within a religious society that are wholly unconnected with a divinity.
14 Section 70 (and, more derivatively, 90) deals with women deceived by the devil, associating with a team of demons transformed into women, called 'Holda', and riding particular wild animals on certain nights. The interest of this is that Holda/Hulda is a genuine Germanic goddess of the witches, their Diana, and that this area of Burchard therefore is not restricted to universal sub-Caesarius cliché; see Grimm 1875: i.220–5 (221 n.1: Burchard was born in Hessen, a

centre for these traditions); 1876: ii.882–4 (on the witch's ride, interestingly stressing *dance* at 883); 1878: iii.87 f. (where he observes that Walfridius Strabo was the first to mention her). See further Ginzburg 1991: 89–91. Werewolves ('which popular stupidity calls a *weruwoff*') turn up at section 151 (*PL* 140.971).

15 The real Theodore was Archbishop of Canterbury 668–90; this penitential is compiled under his name.

16 These instances from McNeill and Gamer 1938: 330, 198, 289, 341, 198, 246 f., 229, 339, *Indiculus superstitionum* 30, Apuleius, *Metamorphoses* 1.8–13.

17 Burchard 19.5.175, 153, 180–1 (McNeill and Gamer 1938: 338–40); dangers of the unbaptised, etc., Geiger, in *HDA* 1.987.

18 Plummer 1910: i.cix and n.6. He also cites (ii.10 n.1) *Life of St Comgall* xix in ms. R: 'There came also his relatives and blood-relations with him and, lamenting, they performed the secular death ceremonies (*exsequiae*) – which all disturbed the brethren's peace of mind.'

19 Rowell 1994: 124 n.32 cites part of this text from V.T. Pashuto, *Obrazovanie litovskogo gosudarstva* (Moscow 1959).

20 The text says *nisum*, which makes no sense to me. What *should* a warrior carry *en route* for Valhalla?

21 *LPG* 45 f.

22 Power of the dead, e.g. Geiger, in *HDA* 1.911 f.

23 *Ibid.* in *HDA* 5.1127 f. s.v. 'Leichenzug'.

24 Grimm 1876: ii.1027 f.

25 Geiger, in *HDA* 5.1094 f.

26 *Ibid.* in *HDA* 5.1105–8 s.v. 'Leichenwache'.

27 *FW* 'burial' 173; M. Boyce, in Hinnells 1985: 180 f.

28 Kurtz and Boardman 1971: 144–7, Nilsson 1955: 179 f., *KlP* s.v. 'Totenkult', 5.897 f.

29 The day referred to in the *Indiculus* is unclear – it might, for example, be later (Geiger, in *HDA* 5.1084).

30 Old English, Grimm 1876: ii.1027 f. Mecklenburg, Geiger, in *HDA* 5.1084. For beer, cf. Lithuanian practices at trees (Chapter 4).

31 Latte 1960: 102 and n.2.

32 Ranke 1951: 353.

33 De Vries 1956: i.§145 counts from the burial, following in the wake of Geiger, in *HDA* 5.1091; the same view is taken by Schmidt 1927: 71, but note that Harpokration, s.v. '*triakas*' counts the thirtieth day *from death*.

34 Parker 1983: 53 n.80.

35 Schmidt 1927: 70 f., considering the fortieth Christian.

36 Latte 1960: 101. The Roman thirtieth is doubtful, Ranke 1951: 56 f.

37 *Ibid.* 23 f. and esp. 24 n.1.

38 *Ibid.* 57, 185, citing Wulfstan in *MG ScrPruss* 1.732 ff. Danes, *ibid.* 188.

39 *Ibid.* 297–9 with substantial bibliography.

40 S. Weightman in Hinnells 1985: 217, Ranke 1951: 63 f.

41 Ammonios, *On similar and different words*, p.36 Valckenaer, Deubner 1932: 229, Burkert 1985: 104, Parke 1977: 53 f.

42 Cf. J.N. Bremmer s.v. 'Genesia' in *EncRel*, with bibliography.

43 Schmidt 1927: 73 f., Deubner 1932: 230.

44 W. Schmidt reported by Deubner 1932: 229.

45 MacDonell 1924 s.v. '*pitrya*', '*pitriyana*'; de Vries 1956: i.§306.

46 The winter solstice is important also for Hindus and had apparently once, at least for some Hindus, constituted the new year, R. Jackson, in Brown 1986:

113. The entry of the sun into Capricorn is also one precondition for the Kumbha Mela, held every twelve years at Prayag (in 1966 15 *million* pilgrims attended), *ibid.* 115.

47 De Vries 1956: i.§306.

48 This type of masked team is found from the Balkans to the Ukraine, Ginzburg 1991: 186 f. Horsfall (in Bremmer and Horsfall 1987: 82) warns against over-hasty identification of ritual beggars with souls of the dead, but the end of the year does seem to provide the right context.

49 The obvious conclusion from the two days of the dead, if there are two, would be that we are in the presence of a system that simply does not recognise years, only half-years. That in turn, transferred to Gaul, would explain how it was possible to operate intercalation every two *and a half* years. If Gauls did not know they were living in, for example, AD 171, then they might have no reason to associate a given winter with the preceding summer rather than the following: 'belonging to the same year' would be a concept without application for them.

50 A standard, confident account is given in Rees and Rees 1961: ch.3, e.g. 84, 90, on the basis of information which is perhaps not as hard as one would wish. A sceptical review of the weakness of the evidence is given by Hutton 1996: ch.35, esp. 363–5. And in general, cf. Chapter 10.

51 Einhorn is thinking of the Greek *psychotrophia* ('soul-feeding'). The Lithua-nian is *Veļu laiks* ('dead-spirits time').

52 *FW* s.v. 'burial' 173, M. Boyce in Hinnells 1985: 180 f.

53 Cited in this context by Chadwick 1899: 41 n.1.

54 Rowell 1994: 121.

55 The theory and some of its implications are given an excellent résumé by Villar 1996: 40–52. Gimbutas's writings have been rather scattered, but see, for instance, Gimbutas 1974 for a quick guide or *The language of the Goddess* (San Francisco 1989).

56 Gurney 1990: 137–40, Nagy 1990: 85, 128 f. Even mid-fourth millennium 'Linkardstown' burials in Ireland have been claimed for the *kurgan* model (Jones-Bley 1991), though they are hard to reconcile with traditional chronol-ogy.

57 Hektor, *Iliad* 24.707–804. Patroklos, *Iliad* 23.65–225. *Odyssey* 24.35–94.

58 Homer, as often, makes good use of the motifs he does not tell: the return of Briseis at 19.282 is a vehicle for a quasi-lament, rounded off by the refusal of Achilles to eat at 19.305, itself in dialogue with the *perideipnon*, the *Totenmahl*, whose ritual consolation Achilles' grief is too extreme to accept.

59 *Beowulf* 3110–65; the quotation is from H.D. Chickering Jr (New York 1977). De Vries 1956: i.§144; Davidson 1993: 135.

60 Apollonios of Rhodes, *Argonautika* 1.1057–62. See also Statius on the burial of Archemoros, *Thebaid* 6.213–26 (anticlockwise, clockwise), Ranke 1951: e.g., 301, and the many passages cited by Pax, in *RAC* 3.143 s.v. 'Circumambulatio'.

61 Thorough treatment in Ranke 1951: 297–302. Geiger, in *HDA* 1.989 oddly views the German circumambulation as mostly for women who have died in labour (contrast Ranke 302); he also mentions the *Beowulf* example. Ranke 303–8 discusses the motivation for such circumambulation.

62 MacCulloch 1911: 63–7, though they were often, at least later, thought of as female spirits, presumably to enhance the threatening alienation of the spirit world.

63 Aristotle, *Problems* 922b, Dowden 1992a: 20 f.

64 Danish oral poetry, Saxo 2.8.1, p.67 Holder. These lines are cited by Chadwick 1899: 26.

14 UNITY IS THE THING

1 Not literally, of course he was on a promontory!
2 Forty-two enumerated by Holder 1904: ii.497–521. Falc'hun 1966: 82 f. works out the details of -ianum names producing -ange, etc. Scholars have found difficulty in assessing the degree of religious resonance in the name. Some, starting from d'Arbois de Jubainville, have associated Mediolanum very closely with Medionemeton ('Centre-shrine'); similarly, Guyonvarc'h (oddly suggesting that Mediolanum means 'Centre of Perfection') compares it with a placename Mezunemusus found in an Etruscan text, cf. Le Roux and Guyonvarc'h 1986: 227. Equally the characteristic presence of sanctuaries at centres undermines a completely prosaic explanation. Brunaux (1988: 7) strikes the balance well: 'by Mediolanum we must understand a place of assembly, certainly religious, but not only religious'. Also on this topic: *C.-J. Guyonvarc'h, 'Deux éléments de vocabulaire religieux et de géographie sacré', Celticum 1 (1962): 137–58.
3 The same picture is implied by Fichtl 1994: 52–4.
4 Brunaux 1988: 12 f.
5 Brunaux 1996: 66 f.
6 Cf. ibid. 67 f.
7 Fauduet 1993: 25.
8 H. Beck, RGA s.v. 'Ding' 443; de Vries 1957: ii.§348. We do not know what 'Alaisiagae' amounts to.
9 De Vries 1957: ii.§348.
10 I am building on Much 1967: 207.
11 R. Wenskus, RGA s.v. 'Ding' 444.
12 Ibid. 450–2.
13 See Chapter 13 n.46.
14 R. Wenskus, RGA s.v. 'Ding' 455 f., 462.
15 'Bilder der den Gottheiten geweihten, jeweils götterspezifischen Tiere', Goetz and Welwei 1995: ii.194 n.36, or should we read ferae deorum imagines, 'savage images of the gods'?
16 Thucydides 8.67, Palmer 1969: 41.
17 E.g., Livy 1.50.1, 1.52.5, Palmer 1969: 27. Contrary to the impression Palmer gives, this is not the same as the famous 'Nemus' of Diana at Aricia, cf. Stillwell 1976 s.v. 'Aricia'.
18 Iguvine tablets III.1–10 (Poulteney 1959: 157) with Palmer 1969: 32.
19 Cato, Origines Book 2, fr.28, Chassignet (fr.58, Peter), Festus p.128 L. Sometimes it is said that there were only eight towns, but that derives from Priscian, who seems to stop short at the town he is interested in (Livy 2.18.3 says there were thirty, Dionysios of Halikarnassos, Roman antiquities 5.61.3 actually names twenty-nine), cf. Chassignet 29 n.28.2. Aricia ceased to be the federal centre in 445 BC and Rome abolished the Latin League in 338 BC, in effect transferring its operations to the Diana shrine at Rome.
20 Palmer 1969: 38, 1970: 250, 271.
21 Varro, Latin language 7.8–9, cf. Palmer 1969: 44. Cf also Pliny the elder, Natural history 16.237 on the three ilices marking the site of the inauguration of the settlement of Tibur.
22 OLD s.v. 'puteal'.
23 OLD s.v. 'bidental', 'bidentalis'; Charisius, Ars grammatica 5 (p.393, Barwick).

For the '*Puteal* of Libo' in the Forum, see Festus p.448 L. Other areas, too, might be marked off – for instance, the *Lacus Curtius*, the site of the obviously mythical chasm into which M. Curtius had in 362 BC ridden and the earth had swallowed him up (Livy 7.6; Pliny the elder, *Natural history* 15.78). The *puteal* has a parallel in the rather less well-known Greek *enelysion*, a place likewise struck by lightning, dedicated to Zeus *Kataibatēs* (*Descending*), fenced off and not to be trodden (Nilsson 1955: 71).

24 Charisius, *Ars grammatica* 5 (p.393, Barwick); Palmer 1969: 45. Charisius may, however, be tendentious: from the context, his point should be a (fallacious) etymological one, e.g. that a *lucus* is called a *lucus* because it is a *locus* which has been struck by *fulmen*. It remains interesting, however, if he turns to lightning for so unsatisfactory an etymological explanation.

25 Schonland 1950: 55.

26 'Hain an der Grenze mehrerer Gaue', Much 1967: 207, 438.

27 Ferentina and Feronia do not look very different. Wissowa (1912: 286 f.) argues that Feronia (also) is a spring goddess.

28 *Ibid.* 285.

29 Scholars usually attempt to get the seventy-two up to eighty-one: for example, Adam has left out the human sacrifices, cf. de Vries 1956: i.420 n.4.

30 R. Lattimore translates 'nine settlements . . . and in each five hundred holdings', perhaps tendentiously. Poseidon and initiation, Bremmer 1987, Dowden 1989: 153. Eighty-one is also the number of Scotsmen needed to make the 'need-fire' when the old fire has been extinguished (Grimm 1875: i.506 f.).

31 So similar that Thietmar has even been thought, wrongly, to have borrowed his account from Adam, cf. de Vries 1956: i.§290.

32 Diodoros 4.19.1, assuredly Poseidonios (4.20 is drawn from him, cf. *FGH* 87F57 f.). It would follow that Poseidonios is unlikely to be the source for Caesar's statement about the Carnutes or else that he did not particularly signal the contradiction.

33 Duval sees this period as a *lustrum*, *RIG*3: 402.

34 On this Irish material see the very rich chapter of Rees and Rees 1961: ch.vii. They make the comparisons with Iceland, *Rig veda*, and the Carnutes. Further useful information in Puhvel 1987: 175 f.

35 To this may be added (Rees and Rees 1961: 162 f.) Dumézil's analysis (1954: ch.2, esp. 30–2) of *Roma quadrata* ('Rome in four squares'), an augural area on the Palatine Hill, in comparison with the rules in the *Veda* for the creation of sacred areas with sacred fires; his discussion starts from the question of why, uniquely in early Rome, Vesta's temple is *round*.

36 Le Roux and Guyonvarc'h 1995: 56–61.

37 *Ibid.* 61 n.67.

38 Vendryès 1948: 313.

39 *Verse Dindshenchas* iv.146–63, notes iv.413; 303 BC, 146 f.; 1 August, 150 f.; truce, 150–3; mourning and burials, 150–5.

40 E.g., Dowden 1992b: 60.

41 See C. Ampolo, 'Boschi sacri e culti federali: l'esempio del Lazio', in *BS* 159–67.

42 W. Ehlers in *RE* 18.1567–78 s.v. 'oscilla', esp. 1572. Festus 212 L. on a custom apparently at the *Feriae latinae*; Servius Auctus on Vergil, *Georgics* 2.389 for heads on poles.

43 The phrase is Frazer's, Dowden 1989: 35 f. The hypothesis is similarly rejected by Warde Fowler 1933: 61.

44 Nilsson 1906: 236, Pausanias 8.23.6 f.

45 See especially Strabo 5.4.12 about the Samnites.

46 Greek mythology, Dowden 1989: 62–5.

47 Thucydides 1.5–6, 3.94.

48 There is clearly more work to be done on the earlier, generally non-urban, nation-states (the *ethnē*) of the Greeks and it requires more comparative evidence than, for example, is adduced in the early chapters of J.A.O. Larsen, *Greek federal states: their institutions and history* (Oxford 1968). We need in addition new models of population movement and of 'colonisation' for the prehistoric period.

49 As in the case of Bormanicus in ch.3; on Apollo Thermios, see Farnell 1907: iv.166 f., who, however, thinks that Apollo Thermios means 'the Apollo of Aetolian Thermon' and that other instances are due to Aeolic colonisation.

50 Polybios 5.8.5, Strabo 10.3.2.

51 Burkert 1985: 144, Burkert 1975, Farnell 1907: iv.98 f.

52 Farnell 1907: iv.161 f.

53 Initiatory interpretation, but with some sense of a periodic festival, Dowden 1992b: 110–12, cf. Dowden 1989: 35, 195; *ibid.* 192 I suggested a population group of *Lykaones, which would be a suitable population for a Thing. Bonnechère 1994: 85–96, esp. 95.

54 Farnell 1896: i.42, Clement of Alexandria, *Protrepticus* 3. Bonnechère 1994: 273–5, 287 f. makes a valiant attempt to discredit the Christian Clement and identifies a possible source of confusion.

55 Herodotos 7.197. The fact that the intended victim is the eldest Athamantid, not a criminal or a captive, and the play-acting nature of the ritual suggest initiatory mock-death not genuine human sacrifice. See Bonnechère 1994: 96–102. A further possible instance is the chase at the Spartan Karneia of a runner apparently decked out for sacrifice, Burkert 1985: 234–6.

56 Frazer 1911: *Dying God*, ch.ii §3, de Vries 1956: i.§290.

57 This phrase is very difficult; it could possibly also mean 'was king for nine years at a time'.

58 From Boyer 1992: 98 and de Vries 1956: i.§284.

59 De Vries 1956: i.§284, 283.

60 'Thinking their gods were pleased by . . .' recalls Caesar's description of human sacrifice by the druids and warns us that these authors tend readily to slip into cliché. It is hard to judge whether their cliché extends to their 'facts'.

61 Ljutiči (= Veleti), four divisions, Niederle 1956: 114 f. Federated by the end of the eighth century, Deržavin 1948: 32. Mittelpunkt, central sanctuary, Deržavin 33, Gimbutas 1971: 154.

62 Dowden 1989: 59 f.

63 Livy 1.7.2.

64 Lincoln 1991: chs 1, 13.

BIBLIOGRAPHY

ABBREVIATIONS

BS   *Les bois sacrés: actes du Colloque International du Centre Jean Bérard* (Naples 1993).

CC   *Corpus christianorum* (Turnhout 1953–date):
         SL = Series latina.

CIL   *Corpus inscriptionum latinarum, consilio et auctoritate Academiae Literarum Borussicae editum* (Berlin 1863–date).

CSEL   *Corpus scriptorum ecclesiasticorum latinorum* (Vienna 1866–date).

DDD   K. van der Toorn, R. Becking and P.W. van der Horst, *Dictionary of deities and demons in the Bible* (Leiden 1995).

DIL   *Dictionary of the Irish language based mainly on Old and Middle Irish materials* (Dublin 1913–76).

EETS   *The Early English Text Society*

EncRel   M. Eliade (ed.), *The encyclopedia of religion* (New York 1987).

FC   R.J. Deferrari *et al., The fathers of the Church: a new translation* (Washington, DC, 1947–date).

FGH   F. Jacoby, *Die Fragmente der griechischen Historiker* (Berlin 1926–30, Leiden 1954–8):
         87T13 = author no. 87 (Poseidonios), *testimonium* (evidence for his life and work) no. 13;
         87F36 = author no. 87, *fragment* (see fr. below) no. 36.

fr.   *fragment*: where the text of an author does not survive, we may know something of its contents from quotations of it and references to it in other authors; each such instance is a *fragment* of the lost author and fragments are collected (and numbered) by editors (cf. '*FGH*' above).

FW   M. Leach (ed.), *Funk and Wagnalls standard dictionary of folkore, mythology and legend*, new edition (New York 1972).

GA   F. Liebermann, *Die Gesetze der Angelsachsen*, 3 vols (Halle 1903–16).

HA   *Handbuch der Altertumswissenschaft*

HDA   H. Bächtold-Stäubli (ed.), *Handwörterbuch des deutschen Aberglaubens*, 10 vols (Berlin and Leipzig 1927–42).

HSCP   Harvard Studies in Classical Philology (Cambridge, Mass.).

IG²   *Inscriptiones graecae*, 2nd edition (Berlin 1924–58).

ILS   H. Dessau, *Inscriptiones latinae selectae* (Berlin 1892–1906).

JIES   *Journal of Indo-European Studies* (Washington).

KlP   K. Ziegler and W. Sontheimer, *Der kleine Pauly: Lexikon der Antike* (Munich 1975).

LPG   W. Mannhardt (and G. Berkholz), ed. A. Bauer, *Letto-preussische Götterlehre (Latviešu-Prūsu mitoloģija)* (Riga 1936).

Mana   *Mana: Introduction à l'histoire des religions 2*, vol. 3, A. Grenier *et al.*, 'Les Religions étrusque et romaine; Les Religions des celtes, des germains et des anciens slaves' (Paris 1948).

MG   *Monumenta Germaniae historica* (Hannover 1826–date), of which there are the following series that I refer to:
             AuctAnt = *Auctores antiquissimi*;
             CapEp = *Capitula episcoporum*;
             Epp = *Epistolae*;
             Leges = *Leges nationum Germanicarum*;
             LegesII = *Legum Sectio II. Capitularia regum Francorum*;
             Schol = *in usum scholarum* (for school use);
             ScrGerm = *Scriptores rerum Germanicarum*;
             ScrMer = *Scriptores rerum Merovingiarum*;
             *ScrPruss = *Scriptores rerum Prussicarum*.

ns   new series (when a journal starts afresh with a new issue 1)

*OCD*2   N.G.L. Hammond and H.H. Scullard, *The Oxford classical dictionary*, 2nd edition (Oxford 1970).

*OCD*3   S. Hornblower and A.J. Spawforth, *The Oxford classical dictionary*, 3rd edition (Oxford 1996).

OLD   P.G.W. Glare (ed.), *Oxford Latin dictionary* (Oxford 1968–82).

PG   J.P. Migne, *Patrologiae cursus completus. Series graeco-latina*, 168 vols (Paris 1857–68).

PL   J.P. Migne, *Patrologiae cursus completus. Series latina*, 222 vols (Paris 1844–55).

PL Suppl   A. Hamman (ed.), *Patrologiae cursus completus. Series latina. Supplementum*, vol. 4 (Paris 1967).

RAC   Th. Klauser (ed.), *Reallexicon für Antike und Christentum* (Stuttgart 1950–date).

RE   W. Kroll, K. Mittelhaus and K. Ziegler (eds) *Paulys Real-Encyclopädie der klassischen Altertumswissenschaft* (Munich 1894–1980).

RF   F. Blume, K. Lachman and A. Rudorff, *Die Schriften der römischen Feldmesser*, 2 vols (Berlin 1848).

RGA   J. Hoops (ed.), *Reallexikon der germanischen Altertumskunde*, 2nd edition (Berlin and New York 1968–date).

RIB   R.G. Collingwood and R.P. Wright (eds), *The Roman inscriptions of Britain*, vol. 1, 'Inscriptions on stone' (Oxford 1965).

*RIG*3   P.-M. Duval and G. Pinault, *Recueil des inscriptions gauloises*, vol. 3, 'Les calendriers (Coligny, Villards d'Héria)' (Paris 1986) [*Gallia*, Suppl. 45].

SC   *Sources chrétiennes* (Paris 1941–date).

SIG   W. Dittenberger, *Sylloge inscriptionum graecarum*, 3rd edition (Leipzig 1915–20).

s.v. 'x'   *sub voce* (in a dictionary or encyclopaedia), under the entry 'x'.

TLL   *Thesaurus linguae latinae* (Leipzig and Stuttgart 1900–date).

PRIMARY LITERATURE: GENERAL INFORMATION AND WHERE TO FIND A TEXT AND TRANSLATION

This bibliography aims only to show where a text and/or translation of the author in question may be found; if no translation is specified, it is usually because I do not believe there is one (e.g., of the complete letters of Gregory I). The dates refer to the last item stated, whether it is the author (birth and death), his position (period of tenure) or his writing (period during which written or date of completion). An asterisk means that I have not seen this edition.

I do not have space to deal with classical Greek and Roman authors individually, but Greek and Latin texts of most authors, with facing English translations, may be found in the Loeb Classical Library (Harvard U.P.): e.g., Homer, Hesiod, Pausanias, Strabo, Tacitus. Modern translations of many may be found in the Penguin Classics and Oxford University Press World's Classics series.

Adam of Bremen, *Gesta hammaburgensis ecclesiae pontificum* (*Deeds of the bishops of the Church of Hamburg*), c. 1070–81
     Latin text: *MG Schol*, ed. B. Schmeidler (3rd edition, Leipzig 1917); *PL* 146 (1853), reprinted from *MG ScrGerm* 7 (1846); with facing German transl., Trillmich 1961.
     English transl.: Adam of Bremen, *History of the archbishops of Hamburg-Bremen*, transl. F.J. Tschan (New York 1959).
Adamnan, Abbot of Iona, 679–704, *Life of Columba*, c. 690
     Latin text: *PL* 88.725–76.
     Latin text with English transl.: (spelt Adomnán) A.O. and M.O. Anderson (London 1961).
Aelfric, Abbot of Eynsham c. 1006, *De falsis deis* (*On false gods*), 990s
     Old English text: Pope 1968: 667–724.
Alcuin, 735–804, in effect culture minister of Charlemagne
     Latin text: *PL* 101.
Altfrid, Bishop of Münster, c. 840–9, *Vita S. Liudgeri* (*Life of St Ludger*)
     Latin text: *PL* 99. 769–95; *MG ScrGerm* 2.408–19.
Audoenus (Ouen), c. 610–684, Bishop of Rouen, *Vita S.Eligii (Life of St Éloi)*, 660s
     Latin text: *PL* 87.477–592; *MG ScrMer* 4.634–742.
Bede, 673–735, monk of Jarrow
     Whole output: Latin text: *PL* 90–95.
     De ratione temporum (*On the reckoning of time*): Latin text: *PL* 90; *CC SL* 123B.
     Ecclesiastical history of the English people: Latin text with English transl.: B.

Colgrave and R.A.B. Mynors (Oxford 1969); Latin text: *PL* 95; English transl.: transl. Leo Sherley-Price, revised edition (London 1990).

Burchard, Bishop of Worms 1000–25, *Decreta* (*Decrees*, see Chapter 13), *c.* 1008–12

Latin text: *PL* 140 cols 537–1058 (Book 19 ch.5 is, however, numbered according to the edition of Schmitz, cf. McNeill and Gamer 1938: 323).

English transl., selections from Book 19 (the *Corrector*): McNeill and Gamer 1938: 321–45.

Caesarius, *c.* 470–542, archbishop of Arles, *Sermons*

Latin text: *CC SL* 103–4; *PL* 67.

English transl.: *FC* 31, 47, 66

Canute (Cnut), laws of, 1027–34

Old English and Latin texts with German translation: *GA* i.271–371.

Carloman, laws of, 742

Latin text: *MG Leges* 1; *MG LegesII* 1.

Charlemagne, laws of

Latin text: *MG Leges* 1; *MG LegesII* 1.

English transl.: King 1987, esp. ch.8.

Codex theodosianus (collection of edicts of Emperors up to the time of Theodosius, issued in 438)

English transl.: C. Pharr, *The Theodosian code and novels and the Sirmondian constitutions* (Princeton 1952).

Commenta bernensia, the marginal notes in a Berne manuscript of Lucan's epic, the *Pharsalia* (AD 65). The notes go back in part to a commentary written by a certain Vacca, maybe even as early as AD 100/120.

Latin text: Usener 1869.

Constantius, *Vita Germani episcopi autissiodorensis* (*Life of St Germain, Bishop of Auxerre*)

Latin text: *MG ScrMer* 7.225–83.

Dindshenchas (variously spelt), Old Irish rhapsodic accounts of places and placenames, earliest manuscript the Book of Leinster, *c.* 1160, texts perhaps composed *c.* 1000.

Prose: *Revue celtique* 15–16 (1894–5).

Verse: Old Irish text and English transl.: ed. E. Gwynn, 5 vols (Dublin 1903–35).

Jan Długosz ('Longinus'), Canon of Krakow, *Historia polonica (Polish history)*, *c.* 1455–80

Latin text: **Joannis Dlugossii Senioris canonici cracoviensis, opera omnia*, vols 10–14, ed. A. Przeżdziecki (Krakow 1873–8); **Annales seu cronicae incliti regni Poloniae* (*Annals or chronicles of the illustrious kingdom of Poland*), ed. V. Semkowicz-Zaremba (Warsaw 1964–date); extracts, *LPG* 137–51.

Dudo, Deacon of St Quentin, *De moribus et actis primorum Normaniae ducum (On the character and deeds of the first dukes of Normandy)*, after 1015

Latin text: *PL* 141.609–758.

Einhard, *c.* 770–840, biographer of Charlemagne

Latin text: *MG ScrGerm* 25.

English transl.: L. Thorpe, *Two lives of Charlemagne* (Harmondsworth 1967).

Paul Einhorn, Lutheran preacher, *Treatises on Lithuanian paganism*, 1631–49

German text: extracts in *LPG* 459–88.

Eligius (Éloi), *c.* 588–660, Bishop of Noyon, *Homiliae* (Sermons). For his *life* see Audoenus.
Latin text: *PL* 87.593–652.

Fortunatus, Venantius Honorius Clementianus, *c.* 540–*c.* 600, priest
Latin text: whole output: *PL* 88; poems: *MG AuctAnt* 4.1. *Life of St Rade-gund* (revised by Baudonivia): *MG ScrMer* 2.

Gregory, *c.* 538–594, Bishop of Tours 572–94
Latin text: whole output: *PL* 71; *Ecclesiastica historia Francorum* (*Histories*): *MG ScrMer* 1.1.
English transl.: *Life of the fathers*, transl. E. James (Liverpool 1985); *History of the Franks* (Harmondsworth 1974).

Gregory I ('the Great'), Pope 590–604, *Registrum epistularum* (*Letters*)
Latin text: *CC SL* 140–140a (1982); *PL* 75–9; *MG Epp* 1–2.

Gregory of Nazianzos, 329–89, Christian author based in Cappadocia (eastern Turkey/Kurdistan)
Greek text: *PG* 35–8

Heimskringla, see Snorri.

Helmold, priest of Bosau (or Bozova, near the Plönersee, between Kiel and Lübeck), *Chronica Slavorum* (*Chronicle of the Slavs*), 1167/8
Latin text: *MG ScrGerm* 21.
English transl.: F.J. Tschan, *The Chronicle of the Slavs* (New York 1935, 1966).

Hinkmar, *c.* 808–82, Bishop of Reims, *Capitulary*
Latin text: *MG CapEp* 2; *PL* 125.

Hrabanus Maurus, *c.* 780–856, Archbishop of Mainz
Latin text: *PL* 107–12.

Indiculus superstitionum et paganiarum, mid–eighth century, see Chapter 8
Latin text: *MG Leges* 1, p.19; *MG LegesII* 1, pp.222–3.
English transl.: McNeill and Gamer 1938: Appendix 1.

Irish Saints' Lives, oldest manuscripts thirteenth/fourteenth centuries, dramatic dates sixth/seventh centuries
Latin text: Plummer 1910.

Jonas, *c.* 600–*c.* 670, monk of Bobbio, *Life of Columbanus*
Latin text: *MG ScrMer* 4.61–152; *PL* 87.1011–46.

Jordanes, *De origine actibusque Getarum* (*On the origin and deeds of the Goths*, sometimes called simply *Getica*), 551
Latin text: *F. Giunta and A. Grillone, *Iordanis De origine artibusque Getarum* (Rome 1991); Th. Mommsen (ed.), *MG AuctAnt* 5.1.

Michael Junge, Bishop of Samland (region around Kaliningrad), 1425–42, *Articles to be observed by the Prussians and errors against the faith which are to be abandoned*
Latin text: extracts, *LPG* 157 f.

Knytlingasaga ('*History of the descendants of Knut*')
Old Norse text with Latin transl., extracts: *MG ScrGerm* 29.

Johann Ma(e)letius, *Letter on the sacrifices and idolatry of the ancient Prussians, Latvians and other neighbouring peoples*, 1551
Latin text: extracts, *LPG* 296 f.

336

Martin, † 579, Archbishop of Braga (Bracara, in Latin), founder of monastery at Dumium, *De correctione rusticorum* (*On reforming rustics/pagans, c.* 572–4)
Latin text: C.W. Barlow (ed.), *Martini Episcopi Bracarensis opera omnia* (New Haven 1950), reprinted in *PL Suppl* 4 (1967) 1395–1403; Caspari 1883.
English transl.: *FC* 62 (*The Iberian Fathers*, vol. 1) (1969), 71–85.

Maximus, † *c.* 415, Bishop of Turin
Latin text: *Sermons CC SL* 23 (from which I cite them); *Tractatus* iv 'contra paganos' *PL* 57 cols 781–94.

Merovingian Councils, Canons of the, 511–695
Latin text and French translation: J. Gaudemet and B. Basdevant, *Les canons des conciles mérovingiens (vi^e-viie siècles),* 2 vols (Paris 1989): [*SC* 353–4].

Merseburg, Die Totenbücher von
Facsimile: *MG Libri memoriales et necrologia* ns 2 (1983).

Nachal'naya letopis' ('*Chronicle of the beginning*' from Japheth to 1116, the so-called '*Russian primary chronicle*' or '*Chronicle of Nestor*'), 1118
English transl.: S.H. Cross and O.P. Sherbowitz-Wetzor, *The Russian primary chronicle: Laurentian text* (Cambridge, Mass., *c.* 1953).

Nennius, *Historia Britonum (History of the Britons),* 801
Latin text: F. Lot, *Nennius et l'historia Brittonum* (Paris 1934); *MG AuctAnt* 13.
English transl.: A.W. Wade-Evans (London 1978).

Ouen, see Audoenus.

Paderbrunnense, Capitulare (Capitulary of Paderborn, alias the '*Capitulary on parts of Saxony*', alias '*Charlemagne's Saxon Law*'), perhaps 785
Latin text: *MG Leges* 1, pp. 48–50; *MG Leges* 5, pp. 34–46; *MG LegesII* 1, pp. 68–70.
English transl.: McNeill and Gamer 1938: 389 f.; King 1987: 205–8.

Peter of Du(i)sburg, *Cronica terre Prussie (Chronicle of the land of Prussia),* 1326
Latin text: *MG ScrPruss* 1.1–235; extract, *LPG* 83–90.

Reginald, monk of Durham, *Libellus de admirandis Beati Cuthberti virtutibus (Booklet on the admirable virtues of St Cuthbert)*
Latin text with English summary: *Publications of the Surtees Society,* 1 (London 1835).

Rudolph of Fulda, *Translatio S. Alexandri,* 863–5, completed, starting with ch.4, by Meginhart
Latin text: *MG ScrGerm* 2, pp. 673–81.

Saxo Grammaticus, *Gesta Danorum (Deeds of the Danes),* or *Danorum regum heroumque historia (History of the Danish kings and heroes),* reaches 1185, last stages of composition 1202–8
Latin text: J. Olrik and H. Raeder (Copenhagen 1931); the standard pagination is that of *A.T. Holder (Strasbourg 1886); extracts in *MG ScrGerm* 29.
English transl. and notes: H.E. Davidson (ed.), P. Fisher (transl.), *Saxo Grammaticus: The history of the Danes: books I–IX* (Woodbridge, Suffolk, 1996, repr. in 1 vol. of 2 vol. edition 1979–80); Christiansen 1981 (Books 10–14, with barely legible facsimile of Latin text).

Saxon Law/capitulary on parts of Saxony, see *Paderbrunnense*

Severus, Sulpicius, *c.* 360–*c.* 420, *De vita Beati Martini* (On the life of St Martin)
Latin text: *CSEL* 1 (complete works); *PL* 20 cols 159–76.

Snorri, *Heimskringla*
> English transl.: *Heimskringla*, transl. S. Laing, 3 vols, revised (London 1961–4) (Everyman Library).
> Extracts, Old Norse text with Latin transl.: *MG ScrGerm* 29.

Theodosius, Theodosian, see *Codex*

Thietmar, Bishop of Merseburg 1009–18, *Chronicon (Chronicle)* or *Gesta Saxonum (Deeds of the Saxons)*, 1012–18
> Latin text: *MG ScrGerm* ns 9 (1935), ed. R. Holtzmann, 2nd edition (1955); *PL* 139.

Thomas of Cantimpré (Cambrai), 1201–*c.*1270, Flemish religious writer, *Bonum universale de apibus (The universal good of bees)*, *c.*1263
> Latin text: *(The Hague 1902); extract, *LPG* 48. *Liber de natura rerum*: H. Boese (Berlin 1973).

Ulfila, † 382, *Bible*
> Gothic text and Latin transl.: (New Testament) *PL* 18.

Venantius, see Fortunatus

Victor, Publius (*c.* AD 400?), *Descriptio urbis Romae (Description of the city of Rome)*
> Latin text: *PL* 18.437–56.

Vigilius of Thapsa, *Dialogus contra Arianos (Dialogue against the Arians)*, towards 500
> Latin text: *PL* 62.155–80.

Völuspá
> Old Norse text with commentary: R.C. Boer, *Die Edda mit historisch-kritischem Commentar*, 2 vols (Haarlem 1922).
> Text: S. Nordal (Reykjavik 1952).
> English translation: Hollander 1962; S. Nordal (Durham 1978).

Willibald, *c.* 700–86, priest, *Vita S. Bonifacii archiepiscopi (Life of the archbishop St Boniface)*
> Latin text: *MG ScrGerm* 2.331–53.

Zeno, † *c.* 380, Bishop of Verona, *Tractatus (Tractates, i.e. sermons)*
> Latin text: *CC SL* 22; with different numeration, *PL* 11.

SECONDARY LITERATURE

This bibliography lists alphabetically works referred to by author and date (e.g. Chadwick 1899) elsewhere in this book. It includes some editions of authors to help me to refer to the editor's notes.

Alcock, S.E. and Osborne, R. 1994 *Placing the gods: sanctuaries and sacred space in ancient Greece*, Oxford.

Alford, V. 1937 *Pyrenean festivals: calendar customs, music and magic, drama and dance*, London.

Altheim, F. 1930 *Griechische Götter im alten Rom*, Giessen.

Arbois de Jubainville, H. d' 1889–94 *Les premiers habitants de l'Europe d'après les écrivains de l'antiquité et les travaux des linguistes*, 2nd edition (with G. Dottin), 2 vols, Paris.

—— 1906 *Les druides et les dieux celtiques à forme d'animaux*, Paris.

Attwater, D. and John, C.R. 1995 *The Penguin dictionary of saints*, 3rd edition, London.

Bachelard, G. 1943 *L'air et les songes: essai sur l'imagination du mouvement*, Paris.

Barber, P. 1990 'Cremation', *JIES* 18: 379–88.

Barnatt, J. 1998 'Monuments in the landscape: thoughts from the peak', in Gibson and Simpson (eds), 1998: ch.8.

Beekes, R.S.P. 1995 *Comparative Indo-European linguistics: an introduction*, English transl., Amsterdam.

Bell, C. 1997 *Ritual: perspectives and dimensions*, New York and Oxford.

Bennett, C. 1994 'Hinduism', in J. Holm (ed., with J. Bowker), *Sacred place*, London: 88–114.

Benveniste, E. 1973 *Indo-European language and society*, English transl. (Miami Linguistics Series, 12), Coral Gables, Florida [French original, *Le vocabulaire des institutions indo-européennes*, Paris 1969].

Bertrand, A. 1897 *La religion des gaulois: les druides et le druidisme*, Paris.

Bettelheim, B. 1976 *The uses of enchantment: the meaning and importance of fairy tales*, London.

Birge, D. 1994 'Trees in the landscape of Pausanias' *Periegesis*', in Alcock and Osborne 1994: ch.10.

Birkhan, H. 1997 *Kelten: Versuch einer Gesamtdarstellung ihrer Kultur*, Vienna.

Blázquez Martinez, J.M. 1962 *Religiones primitivas de Hispania*, i 'Fuentes literarias y epigraficas', Rome (Biblioteca de la Escuela Española de Historia y Arqueologia en Roma, 14).

Boetticher, C. 1856 *Der Baumkultus der Hellenen, nach den gottesdienstlichen Gebräuchen und den überlieferten Bildwerken dargestellt*, Berlin.

Bonnechère, P. 1994 *Le sacrifice humain en Grèce ancienne* (*Kernos*, suppl. 3), Athens and Liège.

Boretius, A. 1883 *Capitularia regum Francorum*, t. i, Hannover (*MG LegesII* 1).

Boudriot, W. 1928 *Die altgermanische Religion in der amtlichen kirchlichen Literatur des Abendlandes vom 5. bis 11. Jahrhundert*, Bonn.

Boulouis, A. 1987 'Références pour la conversion du monde païen au viie et viiie siècles', *Revue des Etudes Augustiniennes* 33: 90–112.

Boyer, R. 1992 *Yggdrasill: La religion des anciens scandinaves*, 2nd issue, Paris.

Bremmer, J.N. 1983 'Scapegoat rituals in ancient Greece', *Harvard Studies in Classical Philology* 87: 299–320.

—— 1987 '"Effigies dei" in ancient Greece: Poseidon', in D. van der Plas (ed.), *Effigies dei: essays on the history of religions*, Leiden (*Numen*, Supplement 51).

—— 1993 'Prophets, seers, and politics in Greece, Israel, and early modern Europe', *Numen* 40: 150–83.

—— 1995 'The family and other centres of religious learning in antiquity', in J.W. Drijvers and A.A. MacDonald (eds), *Centres of learning: learning and location in pre-modern Europe and the Near East*, Leiden: 29–38.

—— 1996a 'Modi de comunicazione con il divino', in G. Settis (ed.), *I Greci: Storia cultura arte società, 1: Noi e i Greci*, Turin: 239–83.

—— 1996b 'The status and symbolic capital of the seer', in R. Hägg (ed.), *The role of religion in the early Greek polis*, Stockholm: 97–109.

—— 1998 'Paradise: from Persia, via Greece, into the *Septuagint*', in G. Luttikhuizen (ed.), *Paradise interpreted*, Leiden.

Bremmer, J.N. and Horsfall, N.M. 1987 *Roman myth and mythography*, London (*Bulletin of the Institute of Classical Studies*, suppl. 52).

Bremmer, J.N. and Roodenburg, H. (eds) 1991 *A cultural history of gesture*, Oxford.

Brodersen, K. 1996 *Die sieben Weltwunder: legendäre Kunst- und Bauwerke der Antike*, Munich.

Brown, A. 1986 *Festivals in world religions, produced by the Shap Working Party*, London.

Brüch, J. 1924 'Die wichstigsten Ausdrücken für das Tanzen in den romanischen Sprachen', *Wörter und Sachen* 9: 123–6.

Brunaux, J.L. 1988 *Celtic Gauls, gods, rites*, English transl., London.

—— 1996 *Les religions gauloises: rituels celtiques de la Gaule indépendante*, Paris.

Burke, P. 1991 'The language of gesture in early modern Italy', in Bremmer and Roodenburg (eds) 1991: 71–83.

Burkert, W. 1975 'Apellai und Apollon', *Rheinisches Museum* 118: 1–21.

—— 1983 *Homo necans: the anthropology of ancient Greek sacrificial ritual and myth*, English transl., Berkeley.

—— 1985 *Greek religion: archaic and classical*, English transl., Oxford.

—— 1992 *The orientalizing revolution: Near Eastern influence on Greek culture in the early Archaic age*, Cambridge, Mass.

—— 1996 *Creation of the sacred: tracks of biology in early religions*, Cambridge, Mass.

Burnand, Y. 1996 *Les Gallo-romains*, Paris (*Que sais-je*, 314).

Byrne, F.J. 1973 *Irish kings and high kings*, London.

Capelle, T. 1990 *Archäologie der Angelsachsen: Eigenständigkeit und kontinentale Bindung vom 5. bis 9. Jahrhundert*, Darmstadt.

Caspari, C.P. 1883 *Martin von Bracaras Schrift de Correctione Rusticorum*, Christiania (i.e. Oslo).

Chadwick, H.M. 1899 *The cult of Othin: an essay in the ancient religion of the north*, London.

Choudhury, A.R. 1994 'Hinduism', in J. Holm (ed., with J. Bowker), *Sacred place*, London: 62–87.

Christiansen, E. 1981 *Saxo Grammaticus, Danorum regum heroumque historia, Books X–XVI: the text of the first edition with translation and commentary*, 3 vols (*British Archaeological Reports*, International Series, 118).

Chuvin, P. 1990 *A chronicle of the last pagans*, English transl., Cambridge, Mass.

Clemen, C. 1936 *Fontes historiae religionum primitivarum, praeindogermanicarum, indogermanicarum minus notarum*, Bonn.

Cunliffe, B. (ed.) 1988 *The temple of Sulis Minerva at Bath*, vol.2, 'The finds from the sacred spring', Oxford (Oxford University Committee for Archaeology, monograph 16).

Curchin, L.A. 1991 *Roman Spain: conquest and assimilation*, London.

Davidson, H.R.E. 1993 *The lost beliefs of northern Europe*, London.

Davies, H. and Davies, M.-H. 1982 *Holy days and holidays: the medieval pilgrimage to Compostela*, Lewisburg and London.

Déchelette, J. 1924 *Manuel d'archéologie, préhistorique, celtique et gallo-romaine*, vol.1, Paris (continued by Grenier, q.v.).

Deržavin, N.S. 1948 *Die Slaven im Altertum: eine kulturhistorische Abhandlung*, Weimar (transl. from the Russian original of 1946).

Detienne, M. and Vernant, J.-P. (eds) 1989 *The cuisine of sacrifice among the Greeks*, Chicago.

Detschew, D. 1928 'Βεδυ als makedonischer Gott', *Glotta* 16: 280–5.

Deubner, L. 1900, *De incubatione capita quinque*, Leipzig.

—— 1932 *Attische Feste*, Berlin (2nd edition, ed. B. Doer, 1966, repr. Hildesheim 1969).

Dilke, O.A.W. 1971 *The Roman land surveyors: an introduction to the Agrimensores*, Newton Abbot.

Dillon, M. 1997 *Pilgrims and pilgrimage in ancient Greece*, London.

Dölger, F.J. 1922 *Der heilige Fisch in den antiken Religionen und in Christentum*, vol.2, Münster.

—— 1932 *Antike und Christentum: kultur- und religionsgeschichtliche Studien*, vol.3, Münster.

Dowden, K. 1989 *Death and the maiden: girls' initiation rites in Greek mythology*, London.

—— 1992a *The uses of Greek mythology*, London.

—— 1992b *Religion and the Romans*, London.

—— forthcoming 'Thracian religion' in J.N. Bremmer (ed.), *A dictionary of ancient religions*, London.

Dumézil, G. 1954 *Rituels indo-européens à Rome*, Paris (*Études et commentaires*, 19).

—— 1970 *Archaic Roman religion*, English transl., 2 vols, Chicago.

Durand, G. 1960 *Les structures anthropologiques de l'imaginaire*, Paris (9th edition, 1982).

Durkheim, E. 1915 *The elementary forms of the religious life*, English transl., London.

Duval, P.-M. 1976 *Les dieux de la Gaule*, augmented edition, Paris (repr. 1993).

Easting, R. 1991 *St Patrick's Purgatory: two versions of Owayne Miles and the Vision of William of Stranton together with the long text of the Tractatus de Purgatorio Sancti Patricii*, Oxford (*EETS* 298).

Edelstein, L. and Kidd, I.G. 1989 *Poseidonios*, i, 'The fragments', 2nd edition, Cambridge.

Ekwall, E. 1960 *The concise Oxford dictionary of English place-names*, 4th edition, Oxford.

Eliade, M. 1964 *Traité d'histoire des religions*, Paris (cited by section).

—— 1969 *Le mythe de l'éternel retour*, Paris.

Elston, C.S. 1934 *The earliest relations between Celts and Germans*, London.

Emanuel, H.D. 1967 *The Latin texts of the Welsh laws*, Cardiff.

Entwistle, W.J. and Morison, W.A. 1964 *Russian and the Slavonic languages*, 2nd edition, London.

Falc'hun, F. (with Tanguy, B.) 1966 *Les noms de lieux celtiques: vallées et plaines*, Rennes.

Farnell, L.R. 1896–1909 *The cults of the Greek states*, 5 vols, Oxford.

Fauduet, I. 1993 *Les temples de tradition celtique*, Paris.

Faure, P. 1964 *Les fonctions des caverne crétoises*, Paris.

Fichtl, S. 1994 *Les gaulois du nord de la Gaule (150–20 av. J.C.)*, Paris.

Filip, J. 1961 *Die keltische Zivilisation und ihr Erbe*, German transl., Prague.

Fletcher, R. 1997 *The conversion of Europe: from paganism to Christianity 371– 1386 AD*, London.

Frazer, J.G. 1905 *Lectures on the early history of the kingship*, London.

—— 1911–15 *The golden bough: a study in magic and religion*, 3rd edition, 12 vols, London (as the numeration of the volumes is difficult to follow, I have included brief volume titles in citations).

—— 1913 *Pausanias's description of Greece*, 6 vols, London.

Gamkrelidze, T.V. and Ivanov, V.V. 1995 *Indo-European and the Indo-Europeans: a reconstruction and historical analysis of a proto-language and a proto-culture* (*Trends in Linguistics: Studies and Monographs*, 80), English transl., 2 vols, Berlin and New York.

Gelling, M. 1988 *Signposts to the past: place-names and the history of England*, 2nd edition, London.

Gibson, A. and Simpson, D. 1998 *Prehistoric ritual and religion: essays in honour of Aubrey Burl*, Stroud, Gloucs.

Gilley, S. and Sheils, W.J. 1994, *A history of religion in Britain: practice and belief from pre-Roman times to the present*, Oxford.

Gimbutas, M. 1971 *The Slavs*, London.

—— 1974 'An archaeologist's view of PIE* in 1975', *JIES* 2: 289–307.

Ginzburg, C. 1991 *Ecstasies: deciphering the witches' sabbath*, English transl., London.

Ginzel, F.K. 1899 *Spezieller Kanon der Sonnen- und Mondfinsternisse für das Ländergebiet der klassischen Altertumswissenschaften und den Zeitraum von 900 vor Chr. bis 600 nach Chr.*, Berlin.

Goetz, H.-W. and Welwei, K.-W. 1995 *Altes Germanien: Auszüge aus den antiken Quellen über die Germanen und ihre Beziehungen zum römischen Reich: Quellen der alten Geschichte bis zum Jahre 238 n. Chr.*, 2 parts, Darmstadt [R. Buchner, F.-J. Schmale, *Ausgewählte Quellen zur deutschen Geschichte des Mittelalters*, Band Ia].

Goetze, A. 1957 *Kulturgeschichte des alten Orients*, iii.1, 'Kleinasien' (*HA* III.1, 3.3.1), Munich.

Goodison, L. 1989 *Death, women and the sun: symbolism of regeneration in early Aegean religion*, London (*Bulletin of the Institute of Classical Studies*, suppl. 53).

Goudineau, C. and Peyre, C. 1993 *Bibracte et les Éduens: à la découverte d'un peuple gaulois*, Paris and Mount Beuvray.

Grabber, L.L. 1995 *Priests, prophets, diviners, sages: a socio-historical study of religious specialists in ancient Israel*, Valley Forge, Penn.

Graf, F. 1991 'Menschenopfer in der Burgerbibliothek', *Archäologie der Schweiz* 14: 136–43.

—— 1994 *La magie dans l'antiquité gréco-romaine: idéologie et pratique*, Paris.

Green, M.J. 1986 *The gods of the Celts*, Stroud.

Grenier, A. 1934 *Manuel d'archéologie, préhistorique, celtique et gallo-romaine*, vol. 6, Paris (begun by Déchelette, q.v.).

Griffith, F.M. 1985 'A *nemeton* in Devon?', *Antiquity* 49 (226): 121–4.

Grimal, P. 1943 *Les jardins romains à la fin de la république et aux deux premiers siècles de l'empire: essai sur la naturalisme romain*, Paris.

Grimm, J. 1875–8 *Deutsche Mythologie*, 4th edition, ed. E.H. Meyer, 3 vols, Berlin (using this edition's pagination).

Gurney, O.R. 1990 *The Hittites*, revised 2nd edition, London.

Guyonvarc'h, C.J. 1959 'Le problème du Borvo gaulois: mot ligure ou celtique?', *Ogam* 11: 164–70.

Hamp, E.P. 1973 'Religion and law from Iguvium', *JIES* 1: 318–23.

Heather, P.J. 1996 *The Goths*, Oxford.

Hinells, J.R. 1985 *A handbook of living religions*, London.

Holder, A. 1896, 1904 *Alt-keltischer Sprachschatz*, Leipzig, 2 vols and 2 supplementary fascicles (1896–1913).

Hollander, L.M. 1962 *The Poetic Edda translated with explanatory notes*, 2nd edition, Austin, Texas.

Hope, R.C. 1893 *The legendary lore of the holy wells of England including rivers, lakes, fountains, and springs*, London.

Hunt, E.D. 1982 *Holy Land pilgrimage in the later Roman Empire* AD 312–450, Oxford.

Hutton, R.B. 1991 *The pagan religions of the ancient British Isles: their nature and legacy*, Oxford.

—— 1994 *The rise and fall of merry England: the ritual year 1400–1700*, Oxford.

—— 1996 *The stations of the sun: a history of the ritual year in Britain*, Oxford.

Jackson, K.H. 1964 *The oldest Irish tradition*, Cambridge.

Jankuhn, H. 1966 'Archäologische Bermerkungen zur Glaubwürdigkeit des Tacitus in der Germania', *Nachrichten der Akademie der Wissenschaften in Göttingen, Phil.-hist. Klasse* 10: 411–26.

Jantzen, R. 1988 *Montagne et symboles*, Lyon.

Jente, R. 1921 *Die mythologischen Ausdrücke im altenglischen Wortschatz*, Heidelberg (*Anglistische Forschungen*, 56).

Johnson, J. 1915 *Place names of England and Wales*, London (repr. 1994).

Jones, Francis 1954 *The holy wells of Wales*, Cardiff.

Jones, G.D.B. 1962 'Capena and the Ager Capenas', *Proceedings of the British School at Rome* 30: 116–207.

Jones, P. and Pennick, N. 1995 *A history of pagan Europe*, London.

Jones-Bley, K. 1991 'The earliest Indo-European burial tradition in pre-Celtic Ireland', *JIES* 19: 1–13.

Jouet, P. 1989 *Religion et mythologie des Baltes: une tradition indo-européenne*, Paris.

Kendrick, T.D. 1927 *The druids*, London (repr. 1994).

Kern, O. 1899 'Baumkultus', *RE* 3.155–67.

King, P.D. 1987 *Charlemagne: translated sources*, Kendal.

Krusch, B. 1951 *Gregorii Episcopi Turonensis libri historiarum X*, Hannover (*MG ScrMer* 1.1).

Kurke, L. 1989 'Pouring prayers: a formula of IE sacral poetry?', *JIES* 17: 113–25.

Kurtz, D.C. and Boardman, J. 1971 *Greek burial customs*, London.

Lambert, P.-Y. 1994 *La langue gauloise*, Paris.

Lane, E. 1971 *Corpus monumentorum religionis dei Menis*, vol.1, 'The monuments and inscriptions', Leiden (*Etudes préliminaires aux religions orientales dans l'empire romain*, 19).

Lane, G.S. 1933 'The Germanic-Celtic vocabulary', *Language* 9: 244–64.

Lang, A. 1913 *Myth, ritual and religion*, new edition, 2 vols, London (repr. 1996).

Latte, K. 1913 *De saltationibus Graecorum capita quinque*, Giessen.

—— 1960 *Römische Religionsgeschichte*, Munich (*HA* V.4).

Laty, D. 1996 *Histoire des bains*, Paris (*Que sais-je*, 3074).

Lawson, M.K. 1993 *Cnut: the Danes in England in the early eleventh century*, London.

Lehmann, W.P. 1993 *Theoretical bases of Indo-European linguistics*, London.

Leite de Vasconcellos, J. 1905, 1913 *Religiões da Lusitânia na parte que principalmente se refere a Portugal*, 3 vols, Lisbon (1897–1913).

Le Roux, F. 1959 'Introduction à une étude de l'Apollon Gaulois', *Ogam* 11: 216–26.

Le Roux, F. and Guyonvarc'h, C.-J. 1986 *Les druides*, 4th edition, Rennes.

—— 1995 *Les fêtes celtiques*, Rennes.

Lestringant, F. 1997 *Cannibals: the discovery and representation of the cannibal from Columbus to Jules Verne*, English transl., Oxford.

Lewis, M.J.T. 1966 *Temples in Roman Britain*, Cambridge.

Lincoln, B. 1981 *Priests, warriors and cattle: a study in the ecology of religions*, Berkeley, Los Angeles and London.

—— 1991 *Death, war and sacrifice: studies in ideology and practice*, Chicago.

Liu, B.-L. and Fiala, A.D. 1992 *Canon of lunar eclipses 1500 BC–AD 3000*, Richmond, Virginia.

Lizzi, R. 1990 'Ambrose's contemporaries and the Christianization of north Italy', *Journal of Roman Studies* 80: 156–73.

Lowie, R.H. 1925 *Primitive religion*, London (repr. as B.S. Turner, *The early sociology of religion*, vol. 9, London 1997).

Lund, A.A. 1988 *P. Cornelius Tacitus: Germania*, Heidelberg.

Maas, E. 1902 *Die Tagesgötter in Rom und den Provinzen aus der Kultur des Niederganges der antiken Welt*, Berlin.

MacCulloch, J.A. 1911 *The religion of the ancient Celts*, Edinburgh (repr. London 1992).

MacDonell, A.A. 1924 *A practical Sanskrit dictionary*, London (repr. Oxford 1954).

—— 1927 *A Sanskrit grammar for students*, 3rd edition, Oxford.

Malan, D.J. 1963 *Physics of lightning*, London.

Mallory, J.P. 1989 *In search of the Indo-Europeans: language, archaeology and myth*, London.

Marstrander, C.J.S. 1915 'Thór en Irlande', *Revue celtique* 36 (1915/16): 241–53 [= 'Tor i Irland', *Maag og Minne* (1915): 80–9, according to de Vries 1956: i, p.xxxi].

Maury, A. 1896 *Croyances et légendes du moyen âge*, Paris.

McCone, K. 1990 *Pagan past and Christian present in early Irish literature*, Maynooth.

McKenna, S. 1938 *Paganism and pagan survivals in Spain up to the fall of the Visigothic kingdom*, Washington, DC.

McNeill, J.T. and Gamer, H.M. 1938 *Medieval handbooks of penance: a translation of the principal* libri poenitentiales *and selections from related documents*, New York (*Records of Civilization: sources and studies*, 29).

Menéndez Pidal, R. 1952 *Toponimia prerrománica hispana*, Madrid.

Méniel, P. 1992 *Les sacrifices d'animaux chez les gaulois*, Paris.

Meringer, R. 1924 'Indogermanische Pfahlgötzen (Alche, Dioskuren, Asen)', *Wörter und Sachen* 9: 107–23.

Mills, A.D. 1991 *A dictionary of English place names*, Oxford.

Moscati, S. 1968 *The world of the Phoenicians*, English transl., London.

Much, R. 1967 *Die Germania des Tacitus*, 3rd edition, ed. H. Jankuhn and W. Lange, Heidelberg.

Müller, F.M. 1878 *Lectures on the origin and growth of religion*, London.

Mylonas, G.E. 1961 *Eleusis and the Eleusinian Mysteries*, Princeton, NJ.

Nagy, G. 1990 *Greek mythology and poetics*, Ithaca, NY, and London.

Niederle, L. 1956 Славянские древности, Moscow (Russian transl. of *Rukověť' slovanskych starožitností*, new edition, Prague 1953).

Nilsson, M.P. 1906 *Griechische Feste von religiöser Bedeutung, mit Ausschluss der attischen*, Leipzig.

—— 1950 *The Minoan–Mycenaean Religion and its survival in Greek religion*, 2nd edition, Lund.

—— 1955 *Geschichte der griechischen Religion*, 2nd edition, vol. 1, Munich (*HA* V.2.1) (3rd edition, a few notes added, 1967).

Ninck, M. 1921 *Die Bedeutung des Wassers im Kult und Leben der Alten: eine symbolgeschichtliche Untersuchung*, Leipzig (repr. Darmstadt 1960).

Norden, E. 1923 *Die germanische Urgeschichte in Tacitus Germania*, 3rd edition, Leipzig.

Onions, C.T. 1966 *The Oxford dictionary of English etymology*, Oxford.

Palmer, L.R. 1954 *The Latin language*, London.

Palmer, R.E.A. 1969 *The king and the comitium: a study of Rome's oldest public document*, Wiesbaden (*Historia*, Einzelschrift 11).

—— 1970 *The archaic community of the Romans*, Cambridge.

Parke, H.W. 1977 *Festivals of the Athenians*, London.

Parker, R.C.T. 1983 *Miasma: pollution and purification in early Greek religion*, Oxford.

—— 1996 *Athenian religion: a history*, Oxford.

Pascal, G.B. 1964 *The cults of Cisalpine Gaul*, Brussels.

Pennick, N. 1996 *Celtic sacred landscapes*, London.

Philippson, E.A. 1929 *Germanische Heidentum bei den Angelsachsen*, Leipzig.

Pietri, C. 1984 'Le temps de la semaine à Rome et dans l'Italie chrétienne (IVe–VIe s.)', in *Le temps chrétien de la fin de l'Antiquité au Moyen Age IIIe–XIIIe siècles* (Paris): 63–97.

Piggott, S. 1975 *The druids*, 2nd edition, London.

Plummer, C. 1910 *Vitae sanctorum Hiberniae*, 2 vols, Oxford (repr. 1968).

Polomé, E.C. 1987 'Der indogermanische Wortschatz auf dem Gebiete der Religion', in W. Meid (ed.), *Studien zum indogermanischen Wortschatz*, Innsbruck.

Pope, J.C. 1968 *Homilies of Aelfric: a supplementary collection*, vol.2, London (*EETS* 260).

Poulteney, J.W. 1959 *The bronze tables of Iguvium*, Baltimore and Oxford (American Philological Association, monograph, 18).

Powell, T.G.E. 1980 *The Celts*, new edition, London.

Prümm, K. 1954 *Religionsgeschichtliches Handbuch für den Raum der altchristlichen Umwelt: hellenistisch-römische Geistesströmungen und Kulte mit Beachtung des Eigenlebens der Provinzen*, Rome.

Przyluski, J. 1950 *La grande déesse: introduction à l'étude comparative des religions*, Paris.

Puhvel, J. 1955 'Vedic *áśvamedha-* and Gaulish *IIPOMIIDVOS*', *Language* 31: 353 f.

—— 1987 *Comparative mythology*, Baltimore.

—— (ed.) 1970 *Myth and law among the Indo-Europeans: studies in Indo-European comparative mythology*, Berkeley.

Rackham, O. 1970 *Trees and woodland in the British landscape*, London.

Ranke, K. 1951 *Indogermanische Totenverehrung*, vol.1, 'Der dreissigste und vierzigste Tag im Totenkult der Indogermanen', Helsinki (*FF Communications* 140).

Rees, A. and Rees, B. 1961 *Celtic heritage: ancient tradition in Ireland and Wales*, London.

Reinach, S. 1908 'Les monuments de pierre brute dans le langage et les croyances populaires', in *Cultes, mythes et religions*, vol.3, Paris, 364–433.

Renaud, J. 1996 *Les dieux des Vikings*, Rennes.

Rivet, A.L.F. and Smith, C. 1979 *The place-names of Roman Britain*, London.

Robertson, D.S. 1943 *Greek and Roman architecture*, Cambridge.

Ross, A. 1967 *Pagan Celtic Britain*, London.

Rowell, S.C. 1994 *Lithuania ascending: a pagan empire within east-central Europe, 1295–1345*, Cambridge.

Scheid, J. 1998 *La religion des Romains*, Paris.

Schmidt, B. 1927 'Totengebräuche und Gräberkultus im heutigen Griechenland', *Archiv für Religionswissenschaft* 25: 52–82.

Schmitt, J.-C. 1991 'The rationale of gestures in the west: third to thirteenth centuries', in Bremmer and Roodenburg (eds) 1991: 59–70.

Schonland, B.F.J. 1950 *The flight of thunderbolts*, Oxford.

Schove, D.J. 1984 *Chronology of eclipses and comets AD 1–1000*, Woodbridge, Suffolk.

Schuchhardt, C. 1923 'Rethra auf dem Schlossberge bei Feldberg in Mecklenburg', *Sitzungsberichte der Preussischen Akademie der Wissenschaft, Phil.-hist. Klasse*: 184–226.

Sourvinou-Inwood, C. 1985 'Altars with palm-trees, palm-trees and *parthenoi*', *Bulletin of the Institute of Classical Studies* 32: 125–46.

Stead, I. and Turner, R.C. 1985 'Lindow Man', *Antiquity* 59: 25–9 and pls iv–vii.

Stengel, P. 1920 *Die griechischen Kultusaltertümer*, 3rd edition, Munich (*HA* V.3).

Stillwell, R. (ed.) 1976 *The Princeton encyclopedia of classical sites*, Princeton, NJ.

Theiler, W. 1982 *Poseidonios: die Fragmente*, i, 'Texte', Berlin.

Thurneysen, R. 1899 'Der Kalender von Coligny', *Zeitschrift für keltische Philologie* 2: 523–44.

Todd, J.H. 1867 *Cogadh gaedhel re gallaibh: the war of the Gaedhil with the Gaill, or the invasions of Ireland by the Danes and other Norsemen*, London (Rolls series, 48).

Todd, M. 1992 *The early Germans*, Oxford.

Tomlin, R.S.O. 1988 'The curse tablets', in Cunliffe 1988: ch.4.

Tomlinson, R.A. 1976 *Greek sanctuaries*, London.

Tonnelat, E. 1948 'La religion des Germains', in *Mana* (see 'Abbreviations').

Toutain, J. 1917 *Les cultes païens dans l'empire romain*, vol. iii, 'Les cultes indigènes nationaux et locaux', Paris (repr. Rome 1967).

Trillmich, W. and Buchner, R. 1961 *Quellen des 9. und 11. Jahrhunderts zur Geschichte der Hamburgischen Kirche und des Reiches*, Berlin.

Turcan, R. 1996 *The cults of the Roman Empire*, English transl., Oxford.

Unbegaun, B.-O. 1948 'La religion des anciens Slaves', in *Mana* (see 'Abbreviations').

Usener, H. 1869 *M. Annaei Lucani commenta bernensia*, Leipzig.

—— 1903 'Dreiheit' (Fortsetzung), *Rheinisches Museum* 58: 321–62.

Vaillat, C. 1932 *Le culte des sources dans la Gaule antique*, Paris.

Van Berg, P.-L. 1972 *Corpus cultus deae Syriae*, vol.I.1, 'Répertoire des sources grecques et latines (sauf le Dea Syria)', Leiden (*Etudes préliminaires aux religions orientales dans l'empire romain*, 28).

Van der Leeuw, G. 1948 *La religion dans son essence et ses manifestations: phénoménologie de la religion*, amplified French edition, Paris (cited by section, partly to facilitate consultation in other languages).

Vendryès, J. 1948 'La religion des Celtes', in *Mana* (see 'Abbreviations').

Vernant, J.P. 1991 *Mortals and immortals: collected essays*, transl. F.I. Zeitlin, Princeton, NJ.

Versnel, H.S. (ed.) 1981 *Faith, hope and worship: aspects of religious mentality in the ancient world*, Leiden (*Studies in Greek and Roman Religion*, 2).

Villar, F. 1996 *Los Indoeuropeos y los orígenes de Europa: lenguaje e historia*, 2nd edition, Madrid.

Vogel, C. 1963 'Le pèlerinage pénitentiel', in G. Ermini (ed.) *Pellegrinaggi e culto dei santi in Europa fino alla Iᵃ crociata* (Todi 1963): 37–94.

Vries, J. de 1956, 1957 *Altgermanische Religionsgeschichte*, 2nd edition, 2 vols, Berlin (cited by section, except for footnotes).

—— 1961 *Keltische Religion*, Stuttgart.

Walcot, P. 1963 'The divinity of the Mycenaean king', *Studi micenei ed egeo-anatolici* 2 (1967): 53–62.

Warde Fowler, W. 1933 *The religious experience of the Roman people from the earliest times to the age of Augustus*, London.

Waser, O. 1909 'Flussgötter', *RE* 6.2774–815.

Weiser, L. 1927 *Altgermanische Jünglingsweihen und Männerbünde*, Bühl.

Weiss, C. 1984 *Griechische Flussgottheiten in vorhellenisticher Zeit*, Würzburg.

Wesche, H. 1940 *Der althochdeutsche Wortschatz im Gebiete des Zaubers und der Weissagung*, Halle.

Wilamowitz-Moellendorff, U. von 1931, 1932 *Der Glaube der Hellenen*, 2 vols, Berlin.

Wilson, D. 1992 *Anglo-Saxon paganism*, London.

Wissowa, G. 1912 *Religion und Kultus der Römer*, 2nd edition, Munich (*HA* V.4).

Wolfram, H. 1988 *History of the Goths*, English transl., Berkeley.

Woodward, A. 1992 *English heritage book of shrines and sacrifice*, London.

Zerubavel, E. 1981 *Hidden rhythms: schedules and calendars in social life*, Chicago.

INDEXES

INDEX LOCORUM

Passages Cited or Reported

INDEX NOMINUM I

Gods, Mythic Entities and Festivals

For rituals other than named festivals, see the Index Rerum

INDEX NOMINUM II

(Real) Persons, Peoples and Places

* indicates that there are further references to the author
in the Index Locorum

INDEX RERUM

Topics and Themes

INDEX AUCTORUM

Modern Authors